RATIONALISM IN GREEK PHILOSOPHY

quam aram sibi parare potest, qui rationis
maiestatem laedit?

RATIONALISM IN GREEK PHILOSOPHY

BY GEORGE BOAS

THE JOHNS HOPKINS PRESS, BALTIMORE

27089

This book has been brought to publication with the assistance of a grant from The Ford Foundation.

TO F. L. LUCAS

Preface

IT IS ONLY PROPER THAT before we start on our historical study of rationalism in classical antiquity, I explain what I
mean by rationalism. Roughly speaking, very roughly, there are
two sources of knowledge: perception and inference. Perception
is supposed to give us the facts, the qualities of things and the
spatiotemporal relationships between things and events. No extended discussion is needed to show that if we want to know
what the color, sound, taste, or texture of something is, we look
and see; and if we want to know where something is and when
it occurs, we also look and see. (The names of other senses can
be substituted for looking and seeing, if my statement appears to
be obscure.) But since all perception is of particular, localized,
and dated things and events, no act of perception can give one a
general law. And general laws are what is wanted in science and
philosophy. Regardless of the problem of how we reach our general laws, whether it is simply by abstraction from perception of
characteristics observed to be shared in common, or by intuition,
or otherwise, once they are established, we use them to serve as
premises for systematic study. By systematic study I mean the

sort of thing one is supposed to have in geometry, where from the premises we deduce by logical means alone certain inferences, or theorems. It makes little difference here whether the deductions are made by the substitution of equivalent terms or by syllogisms or by the procedures of relational logic, for that is a problem for specialists. But, regardless of many-valued logics, which are of the greatest theoretical importance, the logic which is used in classical geometry and in traditional science is two-valued, and the two values are truth and falsity. In short, the Law of Contradiction is the principal rule which we try to follow. There are of course other rules as well, but I think no one will deny that a rational system relies above all on consistency as its aim.

But, as Kant pointed out in different terms, if the general premises of a system are to mean anything, they must have some content, and that content eventually comes from perceptual experience. And if perceptual experience is to have any rational significance, it must be organized into classes all of whose members are similar in some respect. The child who learns to call things by common nouns has already begun to classify. His classifications are not his own, to be sure, but inherited with his language and taught him by his associates, parents, brothers and sisters, and schoolteachers in the main. There are, however, hundreds of possible ways of classifying anything, since even if we had only five senses, we would have at least five ways of grouping our experiences together, and there are, besides the five, combinations of them and combinations of the combinations. If everything we speak of could be perceived by all the five senses, there would be many hundreds of combinations and permutations as a start. But when we say that something, for instance, is a dog, we are not classifying exclusively on the basis of its sensory qualities; we have other information, furnished by zoologists, to guide us and that is only slightly sensory. For the internal anatomy of the animal and its relationship in a phylogenetic series also determine its genus and species.

Moreover, though a child might call his dog his playmate and friend, and a host of other endearing things, such names would be of little scientific interest. For the way we group things is determined by their relation to other things which are irrelevant to our feelings and our daily life. We enter a world which has already been systematized by others and our task is to locate our own personal experiences in that larger system of ideas. We have to translate something which is not an idea at all, but a thing, here and now, bathed in emotions of love and hate, fear and aspiration, associated with our past and perhaps indicative of our future, into an idea which in turn can be situated in a larger group of ideas. This is accomplished very early in life in a rudimentary way, but as life goes on, complications and refinements enter, and by the time we begin studying any one of the sciences, we wake up to the fact that things are not as they seem. The moment at which table salt becomes sodium chloride, the world takes on a new and sometimes bewildering aspect, for though you might say that it is only a question of terminology, in fact the terminology orients one in a vastly different direction from that of crude perception.

The rationalist will attempt to make his classifications in accordance with whatever scientific methods are generally accepted at the time at which he is working. These methods have all turned out to be open to question, but one cannot question an idea of which one knows nothing. That is obvious. What is important is that when a method of study is accepted as right, a body of information compiled according to the method will exist and any new information will be expected to be consistent with it. That is an essential trait of what I mean by rationalism. To take but a single example, in Aristotle we find that the elements are classified according to their being hot or cold, wet or dry. For reasons which no one knows any longer, it was established before his time that there were four elements, Earth, Water, Air, and Fire. They were the cold-dry, the cold-moist, the hot-moist, and the hot-dry.[1] It will be noted that each of the qualities can be di-

[1] For further details, see Aristotle *De generatione et corruptione* ii. 4.

rectly perceived by our senses. Moreover, each of the elements, in an impure form, can also be perceived directly. And what is more, the typical behavior of the elements, Earth always falling downward, Fire always rising upward, is verifiable by perception. And since the elements were reproduced in the human body in the four humors, and each humor when predominant determined a temperament, though this elaboration is not attributable to Aristotle so far as we know, one had a thoroughly systematic and verifiable account of an important set of facts. That is what rational science stood for in ancient Greece and what it stands for now. Involved in it, as a method, is the ability of every man to check its results to see if its truths are interpersonal. And the method is indifferent to the individual's feelings, his moral life, his religious ideas.

But a rationalistic technique is also supposed to produce results which are of the nature of fertile theorems, that is, laws from which the future can be predicted, other things being equal, and effects can be inferred from the presence of causes. This is a minimum requirement. The child is again a rudimentary rationalist when he learns that whining and wheedling will produce the results he wants from his mother, or that in order to make his tricycle move he must push against the pedals. He would be irrational if he imagined that by talking to his tricycle or slapping it he could induce it to get under way, just as he would be irrational if he did not whine and wheedle his mother once he had established the opposite causal law. This is why rationalism is always an opponent of superstition, magic, sacrifice, and prayer. The battle between rationalism and religion has always been a fierce one and, though religion may produce moral, aesthetic, political, and in general emotional satisfactions which science seems unable to produce, and may be high, deeper, more spiritual, and indeed more valuable to human life than science, that does not make it identical with science. On the contrary, when science is rational, it is bound to be an adversary of religion if the two are concerned with the same problem. It may be religious to ask people to pray for peace or rain or plentiful crops; prayer is not the rational way to get such results. I am not saying that it is not the more successful way, though as far as crops are concerned—I say nothing of peace and rainfall—scientific procedures of agronomy seem to work better. It may also be a good thing for people to have years of famine and drought and war; the rationalist is not necessarily interested in what is good or bad if what he is studying is causal relations. I can think of no scientific discovery, even in medicine, which has not been put to questionable, if not downright evil, uses. But that is irrelevant to the difference between rationalism and irrationalism or nonrationalism. To condemn painting because some painters have painted obscene paintings, or Catholicism because of Alexander Borgia, would be no more reasonable than to condemn physics because the release of nuclear energy has slaughtered 150,000 innocent Japanese or because biochemistry has been used to poison people.

This book then is a historical study of rationalism, as I have described it, in classical philosophy. It has resulted in a story of degeneration. I have not been able to discover all the causes of the change, nor have I attempted to study rationalism in all fields, for both would demand knowledge which I cannot claim to possess and years of further study which I cannot hope to have. I have simply taken on the whole four subjects: the distinction between appearance and reality, the method used to establish the distinction, the appraisal of life made by the men studied, and something about their ethical theories. I have not attempted to write another history of Greek and Roman philosophy as a whole; that has been done by many others. I have thought of philosophy, as of science, as a sheaf of problems bound together by a common name. It would therefore be futile to look in this book for the complete philosophy of anyone mentioned in it. It is not an encyclopedia or dictionary. I have, moreover, dealt only with the pagans, except in the case of Philo Judaeus whose influence on his pagan successors was too important to be omitted. In every case I have reread the texts used in the original and have interpreted them according to my own lights and not according to what some other historian has had to say on the subject. There is an element of *hybris*, I suppose, in this but if I had read everything that has been written on any one of the men treated in this study, not only would the book never have been written, which might not have been deplorable, but I should never have been able to reconcile the results of my reading. I have tried to reduce the number of footnotes to a minimum and have inserted textual references in the body of the text.

I cannot send this book to press without some words of acknowledgment to individuals and institutions who have helped me write it. First, to the American Council of Learned Societies which gave me a grant for travel and consequently for leisure; second, to the University of Pittsburgh which, in giving me the chair of Andrew Mellon Professor of Philosophy for a year, also obviated the necessity of spending most of my time in teaching; third, to the graciousness of their library staff who did their utmost to get me the books I needed. But I should also like to express my appreciation of the help which I received from my friend Harold Cherniss of the Institute for Advanced Study, as well as of that which I have received over the years from Arthur O. Lovejoy, whose historical writings have been to me a model of what such studies should be.

G. B.
Paris 1959, Pittsburgh 1961

Contents

PREFACE vii

I   THE BEGINNINGS 1

II   RATIONALISM IN ATHENS 56

III   THE RATIONALISM OF PLATO 129

IV   ARISTOTLE 188

V   THE FIRST BREAK IN THE SYSTEM 240

VI   REASON VS. REASON 312

VII   THE ACCEPTANCE OF AUTHORITY 357

VIII   THE EVIDENCE OF REVELATION 393

IX   THE FINAL CAPITULATION 435

INDEX 481

RATIONALISM IN GREEK PHILOSOPHY

CHAPTER 1

The Beginnings

WHATEVER ELSE MAY BE SAID about early Greek philosophy, it is safe to maintain that from its very origins it made a distinction between the world as it appears to man and the world as it really is. Philosophers differed about what was appearance and what reality and about how one knew which was which, but as soon as they began to write, they turned their critical faculties upon the uncontrolled experience of their fellows and said that it was not as it appeared to be. If it is true that the pre-Socratics maintained that the world was really some form of matter in various stages of condensation and rarefaction, then they were at the same time agreeing that it did not look like that. For if the kind of matter in question was one of the elements, Air or Earth or Fire or Water, no one could have said that everything appeared to be one of these. A modern chemist similarly might say that everything is a combination of some of the numerous elements in the Table of Atomic Weights which have taken the place of the ancient four, but he too would not say that water looked like a combination of two gases, one of which is highly inflammable and the other of which "aids," as the textbooks say, combustion. To confront a highly heterogeneous world and reduce it to simplicity, whether the simplicity of material substance or of law or structure, demands an intellectual technique which goes beyond the limits of uncriticized observation. Just what the technique was in the sixth century B.C. we no longer know. But that such a technique must have existed is indubitable.

To say that something which we experience is *really* something else demands a definition of "reality." In general the men who were the first Greek philosophers defined the real as the unified and the permanent. The data of uncriticized experience are a heterogeneous series of colors and sounds and other sensory percepts which come and go, some lasting longer than others but none permanent. They can be grouped in certain classes of events, named by our common nouns and adjectives, words such as "red" and "blue," or, on a more abstract plane, "color." But to classify them is already to note their similarities, and when men think that it is better to spend their time on the similarities rather than on the peculiarities, they have begun to discard certain features of the world in which they live as unimportant. It is as if they were saying that the various colors may appear and disappear, but color itself is one of the enduring qualities of the visual world. But once the tendency toward generalization has begun, it will continue until the human mind can go no farther. And before long, to continue with our example, they will reach the concept of visual experience which may be of any color whatsoever, but will at least be visual. By applying the same technique to other perceptions they will attain an idea of sensory percepts in general which have the common property of being those experiences which we apprehend by our sense organs. I am not saying that any specific early philosopher actually thought in this manner, for we do not know how they thought. But the degree of abstraction which they attained could not have been attained without some such technique.

But once a man has reached this point, he has still remained in a world which is impermanent and disunified. For, however similar all sensory percepts may be in their origin in sensation, they are still various in that some are visual, some auditory, some olfactory, and so on. This variety cannot be explained away by a word, and if you are in search of unity, you must go further. Hence, you turn to something which you imagine must give rise to this variety while itself being one in kind. If there is something, no matter what, to which the origin of all the difference in the world may be attributed and which is one kind of thing, reality in one sense of that word will have been found. But it must be something which retains its unity of substance while becoming diversified under varying conditions, and those conditions must be determined by a law of its own nature. Thus if there is some material substance which goes through a cycle of expansion and contraction as an inherent law, as eggs either develop into chickens or die, then it will be said that at last a substantial unity has been reached. But it can also be reached in another way. It might be discovered that though the differences between things are not reducible beyond a point to be determined by the method of investigation, yet all things obey a law which governs all their changes and that law is one and permanent. Just what the law is may differ according to the purposes of the scientists involved in its search. So a group of biologists might agree that organisms developed from earlier organic forms and yet disagree on how they developed. To take a simple example, some might be strict Darwinians and others orthodox Lamarckians. No one in these groups would doubt that each species had a history, but the two groups would split on how that history was to be explained. The one real item here would be the law, the structure of events and their interrelations; the appearance would be the fixed species which seem to be ultimately diversified.

I

UNFORTUNATELY we do not have enough evidence of the actual writings of the earliest Greek philosophers to know much about their intellectual procedures. Our information comes first from the introductions to Aristotle's *Metaphysics*. Aristotle lived in the fourth century B.C., a hundred years or more after the men whose views he was reporting. Moreover, he was interested in seeing how far they anticipated his own theory of causation, and the investigations of Harold Cherniss have demonstrated how far afield his interest led him from historical accuracy.[1] Then we have the quotations from their works and summaries of them made by the doxographers, who, as Diels has shown,[2] derive from Aristotle's pupil, Theophrastus. These men lived, some as late as the second and third centuries A.D. In some cases, those of Hippolytus, St. Augustine, and Eusebius, we have authorities who were only too happy to show up the opinions of their pagan predecessors either as superstition or as anticipations of Christianity. In almost all cases they give us nothing but the conclusions of the men whom they are quoting and nothing of their reasoning processes. One of the sources on which too many historians have relied is the biographical sketches of Diogenes Laertius, a man whose dates are unknown but who must have lived in the early Christian centuries. Moreover, as Richard Hope has shown,[3] the sketches all follow a set pattern which is filled out by legend, incorporated into the text with a kind of gullibility which is, to put it very mildly, suspect. Diogenes, moreover, as if he wished to show no partiality, included the conclusions of several of his predecessors, whether they were in agreement with one another or not. In the third century A.D., we have the figure

---

[1] See his *Aristotle's Criticism of Presocratic Philosophy* (Baltimore: Johns Hopkins Press, 1935).

[2] See H. Diels, *Doxographi graeci* (Berlin and Leipzig: De Gruyter, 1929), esp. the Prolegomena.

[3] *The Book of Diogenes Laertius* (New York: Columbia University Press, 1930).

of the skeptic, Sextus Empiricus, who by way of criticizing the views of the men whom he calls dogmatists quotes or summarizes their ideas, and sometimes his quotations and summaries are helpful in clarifying the philosophy of men whose works would otherwise be almost unknown. But they are for the most part men for whom he had little regard and whom he was trying to demolish. So that, until we come to Plato, fourth century B.C., we have no one whose works have come down to us entirely or in large segments. The insecurity of our sources must always be kept in mind when we read a history of early Greek philosophy, including the remarks which follow.

1. The earliest recognition of the distinction between appearance and reality that is left to us is in the fragments of Anaximander who, according to tradition, lived in Miletus on the shores of Asia Minor in the middle of the sixth century B.C. What seems to have impressed him most was the eternal process of change which was going on in the universe. This process of change looks disorderly until one penetrates below the surface of things. It requires no great concentration of attention to perceive that in some changes there is a regularity which can be formulated in words, or laws if one prefers. Such are the changes which occur in the birth, growth, and decay of living organisms, changes which later were to be called "coming-into-being" and "passing-away." Then there are also the regular changes in the positions of the heavenly bodies, beginning with the sun and the moon and after them the planets. The regular sequence of the seasons, of the tides—though the tides are not too dramatic in the Mediterranean —of eclipses of the sun and moon, were observed at a very early date. Perhaps the orderliness of the digestive process and of other physiological events may have impressed men at the beginning of their speculations. But in most such cases the end terms seem on the one hand to come into existence out of nothing and to disappear into nothing. For what similarity is there between the fertilized ovum and the baby, between the corpse and the dust into

which it decays? How can the sun which rises in the East and sets in the West be the same sun on the morrow, since no one sees it travel back to the East during the night? What happens to vegetation during the winter? The question of whence and whither must have disturbed Anaximander, for in one of his fragments he says that the process is boundless, "eternal and without age," and that the things which come into being when they disappear return to the primordial mixture from which they arose.[4] Just what this mixture consists of, we do not know, nor do we know whether Anaximander even raised the question. What apparently interested him was demonstrating, as far as possible, that universal change was somehow orderly and that it was a change of genesis and destruction. But the genesis and destruction were only apparent, since the process was endless.

What must first strike the modern reader is that, as far as our evidence goes, the philosopher never raised the question of the origin of the universe in time. By this I mean that he formulated no creation myth, nothing either like that in our Bible or like that in Hesiod's *Theogony*. There was, according to his way of thinking, no need to assume that once there was nothing and afterward the world. On the contrary, the world seems to have been eternal in his philosophy, as it later was in Aristotle's. For it is as if he thought that for something to have arisen out of nothing would have been a logical impossibility. And that may well have been the reason why he assumed an infinity of beings existing from all time. We cannot on the basis of the remaining texts assert this dogmatically. But on the other hand there would have been little reason for him to assert that the infinite mixture was everlasting if he had been able to believe in genesis out of nothing. Creation *ex nihilo* is something which we see when we are not critical; criticism alone shows us that it is impossible.

2.   When we come to Anaximenes, a younger contemporary

[4] Diels-Kranz, *Die Fragmente der Vorsokratiker* (5th ed.; Berlin: Weidmann, 1934), fr. A15, from Aristotle's *Physics* iii. 4. 203b 6. Cf. fr. A9, from Simplicius, sixth century A.D. Hereafter I shall cite Diels's numbering of the fragments in the text without mentioning the source except when of interest.

of Anaximander, we have fragments which throw more light on the process of change. To his way of thinking a mechanical process was sufficient to explain the varied appearance of things, and that process was the simple one of condensation and rarefaction. Once again, coming-into-being and passing-away do not look like rarefaction and condensation, but they really are. He gives as his example the air (Fr. A5, from Simplicius). When it is rarefied, it turns into fire; when it is condensed, it becomes wind, then clouds, and finally water. To have imagined the possibility of such a simple explanation is his achievement. He takes a process with which we are familiar in the condensation of moisture and generalizes it into a universal law. But more than that, he sets the tradition, which was later to be interrupted, of maintaining that a mechanical process was a sufficient explanation of all change. No purpose is given, so far as we know, by Anaximenes for cosmic changes. No God, no Universal Mind, is interested in them. He seems to have been satisfied with an account of the mechanism through which the changes come about. It is as if he had said, This is the way things happen, not in a helter-skelter fashion, but according to law. Unfortunately we do not know whether he went so far as to state the conditions under which rarefaction and condensation would take place, nor do we know even whether he raised the question. The two processes were presumably always taking place and in some order. The word "why" in this sort of thinking does not mean "to what end," but "according to what rule."

3. The eternal process of change became a cardinal principle of the philosophy of Heraclitus, a late-sixth-century thinker living in Ephesus. Behind or above or below the change there is no stability, nothing out of which or into which the changing objects pass. The flux is the one reality. This flux he described in a famous passage saying that this world was made by none of the gods or men, "but was, is, and ever shall be an everlasting fire, kindled according to measure and put out according to measure" (fr. B30, from Clement of Alexandria, third century A.D.). The

kindling and extinction of the cosmic fire are thus orderly and not random. To men who follow their senses the universal law is not known. But the wise man, who follows reason, will understand.

The one thing which is fixed in the universe is the law by which the flux is ordered. Once again, we do not know the details of this law; we know only that it exists, that it is universal in its application, and that it is understood only by the reason. We have fragments which hint at a cyclical change in what later were to be called the four elements, but even if such scraps are authentic, they tell us little about the conditions under which the changes occur. It is more likely that Heraclitus was not so much concerned with that problem as with the consequences entailed in the reality of the flux. For most of the remaining fragments deal with the apparent paradoxes resulting from the instability of things. If everything is in a state of change, the names which we give them become misleading, for as soon as we label something, we seem to give it a "nature" which is lasting. But if nothing endures, all such labels are a vain and childish attempt to arrest the passage of time, to grasp at fleeting shadows, to distinguish that which will not bear distinction for it is melting into the whole. If the world were smoke, says Heraclitus (fr. B7), the nose would sniff out differences in it. For the differences are our way of seeing things. To put the matter in modern language, which is anachronistic, *things* are congealed out of the flux by our sense organs; the reason will show us that there are no *things*.

With this in mind the fragments of Heraclitus which assert the coexistence of contradictory attributes in the same subject become clearer. When he says (fr. B58) that good and evil are one, he probably means that the distinction is made by man, not by nature, and that from the rational point of view there is no distinction to be made between them. They are resolved into one in the flux. So too when he says (fr. B62), "The immortals are mortal, the mortals immortal, the former living the death of the latter, the latter dying the life of the former," the distinction between gods and men, life and death, evaporates when one meditates on the nature of reality. All distinctions are human reifications, fictions with at most pragmatic value, and if one is going to be philosophic, one will see that they do not hold good of reality.[5]

We have now come a long way from the simple observation of Anaximander, that the world is an eternal process of change. For Heraclitus not only accepts this position but dwells upon its consequences for human life. We therefore have here for the first time, though such conclusions are obviously limited by the texts at our disposal, the idea that a knowledge of reality is inherently better than a knowledge confined to appearance. This is of course an assumption on the part of the philosopher. One might very well conclude that reality itself is evil and that knowledge of it is knowledge of evil. If we are to know evil, we might be called upon to shun it, not to seek it. If philosophy gives us a picture of the world in which our distinctions both of fact and of value are meaningless, then it might be argued that we ought to turn away from philosophy and follow the dictates of human nature, instincts, intuitions, and undisciplined appetites. But that conclusion has never been drawn to the best of my knowledge, not even by Schopenhauer. Occidental rationalistic philosophers have sought that which they called the real, and regardless of whether their findings negated all the aspirations of the human animal or not, they have urged us to live in harmony with it.

4. Meanwhile there was developing in Italy a group of philosophers of whom the most famous are Parmenides (perhaps early fifth century) and his pupil Zeno, who, taking sharp issue with the conclusions of Heraclitus, inferred no less paradoxical ideas about reality.

In the fragments of Parmenides we find a distinction between Truth and Opinion which was to have a long history. Aside from

[5] For a thorough analysis of the fragments of Heraclitus and a study of their relation to Greek folklore and religion, see Clémence Ramnoux, *Héraclite, ou l'Homme entre les Choses et les Mots* (Paris: Les Belles Lettres, 1959).

all other traits of Truth, it was said to be something which is reached by pure dialectic, not by observation, and if its teachings contradict common belief, tradition, observation, so much the worse for them. They are in the realm of Opinion. This clearly is an application of what later was called the Law of Excluded Middle. Now the middle is always excluded when one asserts either a proposition or its contradictory: an apple is either red or not-red; a plane figure is either a triangle or a nontriangle; a man is either alive or dead; a billiard ball is either in motion or at rest. When it is a case of simply adding the word "not" to the verb "is," the technique is simple enough. But when the negative is attached to the predicate noun or adjective, trouble ensues. For one may have several possible predicates which are other than the predicate asserted of the subject. How one knows *a priori*, that is, by logical or rational means alone, which predicates are mutually exclusive and which not, is still not clear, for logical manipulation alone will not tell one. A nontriangle may be a square, an oblong, a circle, and any number of polygons. Hence it is obvious that one cannot infer that if a plane figure is a nontriangle, it must be a square or any selected one of the other plane figures which are also nontriangles. If, however, one sticks to the general term, "nontriangle," one is safe.

It looks on the other hand as if the discovery of mutually exclusive terms, neither of which is simply the negation of the other, was based upon what we have come to call by the very vague word "experience." We may assume that a body must be either in motion or at rest, and hence on the basis of that assumption we may substitute for the sentence, "The body is not in motion," the sentence, "The body is at rest." But within the confines of pure dialectic, the second alternative must remain a mere negation. No one could learn from negating the verb "to move," that he would come up with the verbal phrase "to be at rest." That information comes from a realm beyond logic. In so far as logic is a purification of experience, it absorbs terms from experience and thus seems able to tell us what possibilities exist. This lesson has not always been learned and it certainly was not learned by the followers of Parmenides. The importance of insisting upon it here is that the dialectical method of the Eleatics, as these philosophers were called after their place of residence, has remained in western philosophy the one road to certainty down to our own times.

Parmenides utilized the method to uncover the nature of existence as a whole. The fragments do not use the term, "existence as a whole," but the argument of Parmenides would not apply to anything less than the whole of things, when that whole is thought of as a single being, the Cosmos, the Universe, Being, or Nature. Now all that can be said of such an all-inclusive being is that it exists. The negative of existence is nonexistence, nonbeing, or even nothing. With this and the Law of Excluded Middle as a start, the philosopher can argue that Being must have existed from all time, for it could not have come from nonbeing. (The Jew or Christian will ask, "Why not?") Therefore it must have come from Being, that is, from itself, which is identical with saying that it had no origin. It must, moreover, be everlasting, for it will either turn into nonbeing or remain itself. The former is impossible, for something cannot turn into nothing, and the latter is equivalent to holding that it is everlasting. Thus whatever existence is, it is without beginning or end. Second, it must be continuous, without gaps. For the gaps would either be nothing or itself. And once more we are forced by the dialectical situation to conclude that between all supposititious bits of it there are other bits of it. And this would make it continuous. Third, it must be immutable, for it could change only into itself or into something else. But there is no something else, for the Universe includes everything. And to change into oneself is to remain immutable. Finally, it must be bounded and not infinite, for if it lacked boundaries, it would not be all-inclusive. An opponent of Parmenides might reply that it must be bounded by itself or by nothing. In the former case it would be infinite in extent and in the latter unbounded. If one asks why Parmenides did not think of that, the answer is that Parmenides was probably more interested in arguing that existence as a whole lacked nothing, and since the adjective "infinite" was a privative term, meaning the lack of limits (*fines*)—and the same is true of the Greek term—to be self-bounded was to be self-enclosed or one.

Since I have interpreted this fragment somewhat freely, it might be well to quote the words of Parmenides himself, for they will not only do him more justice than a modern paraphrase can do, but also illustrate the poetic vagueness which is combined with the dialectic sharpness in the original.

One conclusion alone lies before us: that *It is*. In this direction are many signs: Being is unborn and indestructible, a whole unique in kind and motionless as well as without end. Neither was it once nor will it be, since it exists now, all in one place, one, continuous. For what origin would you seek for it? How and from what source would it take its growth? . . . I shall not let you say or think that it arose from Nonbeing. For Nonbeing cannot be either said or thought. And why should it have arisen later or sooner, had it been born of nothing? And so it must be all together as a whole or not be at all.

Nor will the force of argument lead us to say that anything but itself ever arises from Nonbeing, wherefore Justice has not loosened her fetters to permit birth and death but holds fast. And the verdict concerning these matters is as follows: It either is or is not. But surely it has been decided, as necessity demands, that the one road is unthinkable and nameless (for this is not the true road) and that the other really is and is the true road. How then could what is perish? And how could it come into being? For if it comes to be, it is not now, nor does it exist now if it is going to come into being. In this way genesis is ruled out of court and destruction unheard of.

Nor is it divisible, since it is homogeneous. Nor is one part of it stronger than another, which would prevent its being continuous, nor weaker, but all being is a plenum. The whole is continuous, for Being is in contact with Being.

Moreover it is immovable, bound in the confines of great chains, without beginning, without end, since genesis and destruction have been driven far away and true belief has rejected them. It is always the same and stays self-contained and remains steadfast in one place. For strong Necessity has it in the chains of its limits and holds it in on all sides. Wherefore the law prevents Being from being endless, for it lacks nothing. Otherwise it would lack everything.[6]

The apparent implications of this argument may be summarized as follows:

(1)   If one is to talk about the whole, of Being-as-Being, of the all-inclusive, one can say of it only that it is, or exists. For all predicates attributed to it turn out to involve negations of their "opposites." If we say, for instance, that the universe-as-a-whole —assuming that the qualification "as-a-whole" means something —was created, then we are implicitly denying that its all-in-clusiveness includes the past. If we say that it arose out of some-thing else, then we deny that all possibilities are included within it. Similarly, if we affirm that something is everywhere, then we deny that it is here rather than there. And so it goes. If then the word "reality" is to cover everything, we are driven to the con-clusion that it is no more this than that, and the one affirmation which we are reduced to is Parmenides' *It is.*

(2)   If one select any single being, a rock, a tree, a man, and discuss it in isolation from everything else, confining attention to it as if it were a universe in itself, then similar conclusions result. For internally it can undergo no change, no beginning, no end; it must remain this rock, this tree, this man. Whether it is psy-chologically possible to think of anything whatsoever in this man-ner is questionable, but philosophers ever since the time of Par-menides have thought it was. Thus every common noun was believed to name something which could change only at the price of its name becoming ambiguous. Once, for instance, you have defined a man as a rational animal, then the irrational child or the idiot is not a man. And by the application of the principle, Noth-ing can come from nothing, the being under discussion can have no origin and must be eternal. The individual man could be born, grow, and die. But his animal rationality has a different kind of

---

[6] Fr. B8. The last sentence is questionable. The Diels-Kranz translation reads: . . . *fehlte ihm aber der, so würde es des "ganz" bedürfen (?).* But the text has been emended, following Bergk.

existence. One could of course simply maintain that such beings merely pop into existence in some inexplicable manner, which would not be a rational explanation, or that we are from time to time confronted with things of certain attributes and let it go at that. But that too would be an abandonment of rationalism. For rationalism, besides everything else, demands that we explain all events as far as possible. The limits of explanation give rise to another problem and the technique of explanation a third. But we are not discussing those questions here. We are more interested for the time being in pointing out that in so far as one is using dialectical means alone, unsupplemented by observation, experience, or other supposed sources of information, the individual, whether it be a person, the universe, a specific quality, or, as was discovered much later, God, can be named but not described unless one puts it into a class of similar beings. And to the extent that it is unique, to that extent it is ineffable.

(3)   The technique by which this result is reached is in itself of importance. First, one assumes that of two logical possibilities only one may exist, not in the realm of logic but in that of fact. Man, for instance, must be either rational or irrational. There is no midway point between the two extremes, no graded series of rationality, though surely the philosophers must have observed that some men are more rational than others. This furnishes the investigator with a world of "opposites." Opposition itself, if we may trust to the etymology of the word, arises from a basic metaphor which is spatial. Literally, two things are opposite if they are located at the ends of a straight line. Let us call these two ends the Right and the Left. If something is on the Right, it cannot be on the Left at the same time, and vice versa. This would appear to be obvious. The use of this metaphor of opposition is common to most ancient philosophy and is an integral part of the dominant tradition of thinking right down to our own times. If, as in Heraclitus, all things are in a state of change, then Right is turning into Left and Left into Right and our line as a whole is no more oriented to the Right than to the Left. The

paradoxes of Heraclitus can all be interpreted as arising from reasoning of this sort. They disappear as soon as one concludes that there is no *It* to be the subject of the verb *to change*, and, unless I have seriously misread Heraclitus, that is his position. He seems to have asserted that the only permanent being in the universe is the law of change itself and that there are no substances which undergo the changes. In our own times this was the position of Bergson and Whitehead, for to the former the only permanence was the *élan vital* and to the latter, process.[7]

(4) It was also assumed that if reasoning gave one an irrefutable conclusion, one was bound to accept it, regardless of whether it was in conflict with observation. This is standard operating procedure in our day too, though we are more interested in drawing our premises from observation than our forebears were. Yet nothing could be more contrary to common sense than the belief that the earth moves round the sun. We see the sun moving from point to point between dawn and sunset. But we have reasons for assuming that the sun is stationary and the earth in motion. These reasons are based not merely on the relation between the two bodies in question, but also on their relations to the other planets. But clearly, if we had only to consider the relative positions of the earth and the sun, it would be just as reasonable to believe that the earth is fixed and the sun moving as the contrary. We could then, if we wished to push our observations further, plot the positions of the planets from the position of the fixed earth and we would get a system like that of Ptolemy. In fact, this was his method. My point in introducing this here, in spite of repeating something of what we have said before, is to indicate that no matter how rational we may wish to be, we shall have to start with certain premises which we shall take for granted. But once they are assumed and their implica-

---

[7] Though Bergson did not believe that there was any formula which would describe the action of the *élan* and Whitehead introduced what he called "eternal objects" into his system which explained the regularity of certain changes.

tions drawn out of them by logical means, we shall be forced to accept the conclusions, no matter how strange they may seem.

Some of the conclusions of the Parmenidean technique of reasoning were drawn in the fifth century by Zeno. These conclusions come down to us from Aristotle's *Physics*. Whereas Parmenides had said that the whole did not move, his disciple attempted to prove that nothing whatsoever could move.

One of the arguments is called the Puzzle of the Arrow. The argument runs that a moving object, in this case an arrow, cannot move from one place to another, since at every moment in time it is at some position in space. And to be in a position at a given moment is to be at rest. The moving object must be in different positions at different times, but there is no explaining how it gets from one position to another, since it is always somewhere at some time and that is to be at rest. Now Zeno does not deny that we see arrows flying through the air; he merely says that there is no rational account of how they do this. A second puzzle is that of the race between Achilles and the tortoise, chosen obviously as symbols of the fastest of men and the slowest of beasts. If you give the tortoise a head start of any length, Zeno argues, it will be impossible for Achilles to overtake the beast, for he must begin with reaching the point at which the tortoise started, and during that time the tortoise will have moved on a bit. This will continue as long as the race continues, for as Achilles moves ahead, so does the tortoise. If we assume that Achilles covers half the distance between him and the tortoise in each stage of the race, the series of distances will keep decreasing by, let us say one half, but it will never reach zero. Yet we see fast things overtaking slow things. The problem is, how can this be explained rationally?

We shall not enter into a discussion of Zeno's assumptions about space, the interrelations between points and instants, the composition of spatial magnitudes, but confine ourselves to one aspect only of the argument. This is, where there is a conflict between common sense, ordinary observation, and reason, it is reason which we must follow. If reason shows us that the universe is a solid immovable being, without beginning or end, then, regardless of what we see or feel, our observation must be abandoned for what we know "really" is. The test of the rational is logical consistency and the self-evidence of our premises. But the only self-evident premises are those which contain no reference to fact. It is self-evident that a human being must be blue or not-blue. But it is not self-evident that he must be blue, white, green, red, or any other specific color which can be named. It is self-evident, to take an example of Aristotle's, that you will be either alive or dead tomorrow; but it is not self-evident which you will be. But Zeno's procedure could be reversed and the testimony of the senses retained as the test of truth. Such a procedure, however, has never been consistently followed by anyone, for, if it were, we should have to abandon the use of common nouns and all other symbols of universals. And, if that were done, knowledge would be reduced to sensory apprehensions at a given moment (though we would be unable to date the moment) and these apprehensions would be ineffable. The moment we tried to express them in words, we should have to use terms which transcend the particularity of our apprehensions and consequently drop out of sight everything which individualizes them. We shall see what happened when the Sophists attempted to do this.

5.   An Italian contemporary of Parmenides, Empedocles, seems to have been influenced by Eleatic arguments, though there is no evidence worth taking seriously that he had actually studied his elder's writings. We consider his views on the two worlds here because of his dates and because of a possible logical, if not historical, connection between them and those of Parmenides. If the real is indestructible and ungenerated, then, as Parmenides had shown, there is no logical explanation of change. But one might introduce a postulate here to the effect that all change is combination and separation of substances which themselves are im-

mutable. Empedocles makes this assumption. The permanent substances he called the elements, and he appears to be the first ancient philosopher to reduce them to four and to identify them as Earth, Water, Air, and Fire, though in view of the use of the last three of them in earlier theories, it is at a minimum possible that he simply added Earth to the list to provide two couples. Be that as it may, we find the four distinguished in his fragments as the "roots of all things," and in a fragment which seems to carry on a thought of Parmenides, he says,

> There is no permanent nature of any mortal things, nor any termination by destructive death, but there is only a mixing and an exchange of what is mingled. Nature, on the contrary, is but a name given by men.[8]

The mortal things are the things which we find about us, which seem to come into being and pass away. These things are made by combinations and dissolutions of the four elements which do have permanent natures. There is no termination of their existence by destructive death, since their elemental substances remain after the compounds have been broken down. This is equivalent to saying that there is no such thing as water; there are only hydrogen and oxygen, combined in the proportion of two to one. It is clear, one might think, that when one says, "There is no such thing as . . . ," one should have a fairly definite idea of what one means by "is" or "exists." When we say that there are no such things as ghosts, we do not mean that most people do not see ghosts, that what they see are not the spirits of the dead, immaterial but yet occupying space. So when we say that there is

---

[8] Fr. B8. This difficult fragment comes from Plutarch, who introduces it with the words, "Empedocles says that there is no nature of anything, but a mixing and separation of the elements." It would seem that Plutarch here thought of "nature" as a permanent characteristic of that to which it was attributed, and he interprets the fragment as contrasting the characters which depend on mixture and separation and those which are rooted in things. There is, however, abundant room for dispute over the meaning of "nature" here as elsewhere. For some of the various interpretations of the passage, see J. Burnet, *Early Greek Philosophy* (3d ed.; London: Adam & Charles Black, 1920), p. 205, n. 4.

no such thing as water, we must mean that water is not elemental but can be analyzed. When Empedocles said that mortal things have no permanent nature, he either meant something like that or he was not quite sure about what he did mean. He too was looking for permanence and found it in the elements.

Along with them he believed in the necessity of having two opposing forces which could unite the elements and separate them from whatever mixtures they might be in. The force of union he called Love, that of separation, Strife. It seems to be assumed here that the elements of themselves would never combine, nor would they separate once they had been combined. Though we shall return to this later when we come to the question of explanation, it is important to indicate here that this would seem to be the first entrance into philosophy of the assumption that nothing would ever change *of its own accord*. "Natures" are self-maintaining.[9] It is only when a change occurs that an explanation is required and that explanation will lie in the direction of finding something outside the changing event which produces or causes the change. The distinction between active force and passive matter has a long history and remains part of the western tradition down to our own times.

Oddly enough, these two opposing forces once posited, the question arises of why the whole world does not at some time disintegrate into its elements or why at some other time it does not form a block, like the Being of Parmenides, and remain fixed as such. Empedocles provides no more reason why this does not happen other than to say that at times Love seems to have the upper hand and at other times Strife. The fragments suggest that

[9] Cf. Cicero, four hundred years later, *De finibus* iv. 7. 16: *Omnis natura vult esse conservatrix sui, ut et salva sit et in genere conservetur suo.* And he adds the astonishing words, *ad hanc rem aiunt* [the Stoics] *artes quoque requisitas quae naturam adiuvarent.* In Aristotle too, art was invoked to "complete what nature is unable to bring to a conclusion" (*Physics* 199a 15), but the word "nature" is so vague in Aristotle that one should be astonished at no use being made of its many meanings. Cf. G. Boas, "Some Assumptions of Aristotle," *Transactions of the American Philosophical Society*, n. s., XLIX, Part 6 (1959), 47 ff.

this occurred in cycles, probably on the analogy of the life cycle in animals and plants. What interests us here is that sooner or later a philosopher is driven to stop and say, "These are the facts." The facts may be a simple hypothesis which seems self-evident; they may be an analogy or metaphor in terms of which everything else is to be explained. But whatever they are, they present a limit to explanation. Beyond them there is no asking why. The cycle of change is the basic fact for Empedocles, and it is an extension of the idea of birth and death. It is perhaps superfluous to point out that a given individual does not repeat the life cycle, like the phoenix, but if the individual is the world as a whole, it must rise from its death or die forever.

6. A second attempt to meet the challenge of Parmenides was made by the atomists, a group who seem to have been headed by Leucippus, who otherwise is unknown, and his younger disciple, Democritus, a fifth-century figure. Democritus went further than Empedocles in his daring, for he simply pulverized the Being of Parmenides into atoms and made each atom an everlasting whole without mutable parts. The atoms were infinite in number and constantly moving about in the void. They differed merely in shape and position. Whatever they were made of was one, and it was the arrangements of the atoms in gross conglomerations which determined the specific natures of things. In our own times this would be analogous to saying that there is only one basic kind of matter, let us say, as Prout said in the nineteenth century, hydrogen. When hydrogen atoms are combined, they would form various substances. Whether Democritus' atoms also differed in weight is a matter of dispute which we cannot hope to settle here. But in any event they were all falling through infinite space and apparently hooking on to one another and building up macroscopic bodies. Reality then was the atoms and the void, and all the rest was appearance.

One has here a theory which is an anticipation of modern materialism. But it was not in any important sense an anticipation of Dalton. Dalton's atoms did differ in their chemical constitution, and their interactions were not determined simply by the laws of motion. We know too little about Democritus to say whether he laid down the conditions under which his atoms would combine and separate. But we do know that he was willing to assert that the observable properties of things need not pre-exist in the matter of which they were composed (fr. B9). This is important since it rejects implicitly the assumption that absolutely everything found in an effect must have pre-existed in its cause and thus denies the almost universally accepted rule of *ex nihilo nihil*. It did not deny the universality of the causal principle, however; it reinterpreted it to mean that a given cause would always produce a given effect and that no change occurred without a cause. Democritus was to use this principle in his theory of knowledge and, if the ethical fragments are authentic, in his ethics. But in dealing with this man we are talking of a philosopher who was a contemporary of Socrates, living at a time when new problems had arisen. He was not a primitive thinker at all, though this may mean nothing more than that we have more fragments to go on in his case than we have in the case of the Milesians and Heraclitus. If we discuss his views here, it is largely because he lived in the colonial areas of the Greek world rather than in Athens.

7. By the middle of the fifth century it was pretty well established that things are not what they seem. On the level of common sense this distinction arises when a man realizes that he has had an optical illusion, such as seeing the curbstones of a street or the rails of a railway converging in the distance though he knows that they do not "really" converge. Or he may have a negative afterimage, as when, after looking at an intensely red object, he turns his eyes to the white ceiling and sees the same object up there as green. He becomes aware that the world of his dreams is different from that of his waking life, that things in dreams disappear without any apparent cause, that they turn into other things, that, as in *Through the Looking Glass,* you have to run fast to stay in the same place or to eat dry biscuits to quench your thirst. Or he may notice the differences between the perceptions of dif-

ferent people, one man finding something sweet and another not-sweet, one man finding a burden heavy and another finding it light. These discrepancies, he concludes, must be resolved and harmonized. He maintains that a thing, regardless of human beings and their findings, must be either red or not-red, sweet or not-sweet, heavy or not-heavy; that the laws in accordance with which the thing behaves must be uniform and not shift from moment to moment. This is no different from the philosopher's belief that the world must be describable in constant laws. If things appear to vary among observers or here and there, or under varying conditions, the variations must be able to be correlated with a set of stable conditions. The variable characters he will call appearance, or some synonymous term, and the stable characters he will call reality. If he follows Heraclitus, he will conclude that the only stable thing in the universe is the law which says, *All is change*. If, on the contrary, he follows Parmenides, he will conclude that change is the illusion and stability the reality.

Why the ancient Greeks favored stability, unity, homogeneity, we cannot say. The earliest philosophers were living in a society which was in a state of change, indeed of revolutionary changes, and it might be surmised that their philosophy was an attempt to construct a world in which there was at least intellectual stability. But as a matter of fact the dominant tradition in the West has always been a search for stability and unity, whether of substance or structure or origin or purpose, and surely Europe has varied in the amount of social upheaval.[10] Men, moreover, as a whole have an extraordinary ability to adapt themselves to any kind of social condition, and philosophers who sought reality in stability are just as frequently found in stable societies as in unstable. But even the Marxians believe that reality lies in the dialectical movement of history which certainly is not on the level of uncriticized

[10] For an orthodox Marxian interpretation of ancient Greek philosophy, see George Thomson, *Studies in Ancient Greek Society*, Vol. II: *The First Philosophers* (London: Lawrence and Wishart, 1955).

observation. There are, finally, different kinds of philosophers living in single societies and cultures, and there is no proof that the early Greeks were more troubled by popular revolutionary movements than by the ordinary difficulty of explaining multiplicity and change. The organization of experience into a few homogeneous classes of things which follow determinable and, it is hoped, rational laws is after all the common task of the intelligence. Hence to say that the early Greek philosophers were identifying themselves with the aristocracy which was losing power and combating the democracy which was gaining power, may be true, but it is the result of conjecture rather than evidence. We know altogether too little about the lives of the early philosophers to draw any conclusions about their psychological motivation.

One thing appears clearly, however, even in the disjointed fragments which remain. That is that they all saw that there are two kinds of knowledge, one which is reliable, the other unreliable, or, to use a distinction which appears in Parmenides and was utilized by Plato, one of which was opinion and the other knowledge. What they all meant by "knowledge" was a set of logically consistent propositions. To get such a set, one had to have a subject which did not change its meaning from moment to moment, and a set of conditions in terms of which one could explain the apparent changes. Such propositions would be descriptive and universal. It would not do, for instance, to conclude that sometimes things are multiple, sometimes unified, unless one could also say, "Under conditions, C, things will be multiple; under conditions, C', things will be unified." And if one did reach that point and could describe the two sets of conditions, it would also be demanded that the conditions themselves be strictly identifiable. Roughly speaking, and very roughly, men divided into two camps on this point: one group found the conditions in the kind of knowledge which was relied upon as an index of truth, whether perception or reason; another found them in the things which formed the substance of the universe. This division is largely theoretical, for most philosophers in this early period were interested in both problems, as far as we can tell. It was only later that they began to specialize and to maintain that one's theory of knowledge would influence one's metaphysics.

II

THE FRAGMENTS which are preserved, unfortunately for the historian, give us only the conclusions of the early philosophers and tell us little or nothing of their reasons for reaching these conclusions. We know pretty well the interpretations of these reasons as given by Aristotle and Theophrastus, but these are too unreliable to use. The situation is as if we were told that Copernicus believed that the sun was stationary and the earth moved round it; that Newton believed that gravitation was universal and that as an apple fell to the earth, so the earth was falling on the sun; that Darwin believed that men descended from an apelike animal; that Planck believed that there was a universal constant connecting the frequency of a radiation with its quantum of energy; or that Faraday believed that all forms of electricity were one. How could we ever be confident that we could work out their reasons for holding such beliefs on these data?

1. In the case of Anaximander we do have a fragment which gives us some idea of his method of thinking in one case. This fragment (fr. A30) was quoted some six hundred years after the time of its supposed author. It says that according to Anaximander man was originally born from some other animal because, though all animals soon after birth find food for themselves, man alone has a protracted infancy and lives on his mother's milk. Hence had he come into the world as an infant, he would have died. We are told that this other animal was supposed by Anaximander to be some kind of fish which, after man was capable of taking care of himself, put him ashore. This, let it be said for the benefit of those who believe that Anaximander was a proto-Darwinian, has

next to nothing in common with modern evolutionary doctrines. It is based presumably (1) on the assumption that man, and perhaps by extension, all other animals, had an origin later in time than the origin of the other things, and (2) that the present conditions of his survival obtained at the time of his first appearance on earth. The demand for origins is common to all cultures; we have for that matter a creation story in the first two chapters of *Genesis*. But Anaximander's belief, such as it is, that natural law as we discover it today applied even in the early stages of the world's history, a belief that was later to be called the Uniformity of Nature, is more interesting. For it is essential to an intellectual reconstruction of the past, and though it seems reasonable enough to us, it is unusual to find it in a period when miracles and divine interventions of other sorts were also commonly accepted as credible. The philosophers were more interested in combating mythology and folklore than in being the spokesmen for the dominant economic class. Colonial Greece, like most societies, was not all of a piece, and it is as foolish to talk about the Greek Mind as it would be to talk about any other group mind. Minds are found in individuals and the individuals, when it is a question of philosophic matters, are frequently in conflict with one another. But they are also united in their search for rational descriptions of events, and that search will lead them away from improbabilities and caprice in the natural order.

2. Anaximenes, as far as one can tell, relied on analogies to construct his philosophy. According to Aëtius, who wrote not fewer than nine hundred years after Anaximenes, he said that "just as our soul, which is air, holds us together, so the *Pneuma* and air hold the cosmos together" (fr. B2). And he adds that according to Anaximenes the words *pneuma*, which was later translated into English as "spirit," and air are synonymous. Whether, as Burnet says,[11] this is "an early instance of the argument from microcosm to macrocosm," is far from certain, but what is certain is that Anaximenes did extend what he believed to be a fact

[11] *Op. cit.*, p. 75.

of human physiology to the cosmos as a whole. Plutarch (fr. B1) maintains that Anaximenes also used a human analogy in proving that rarefaction of the air made it warmer and condensation colder. For when we exhale, the air is warm, while when our mouths are closed, it is cold. If he thought of this as experimental proof, it is strange that he did not also observe that it is our breath which is warm and not the circumambient air. In any event, we cannot attribute to him any insight into what we should call the experimental method; the most we can say is that he made observations and used them as the basis for certain analogies.

3. In Heraclitus we have a more fully developed method of inquiry preserved for us. In the first place, it is clear that he was willing to accept the testimony of the senses as evidence of the flux. He estimates the eyes as better witnesses than the ears (fr. B101a);[12] again, "of whatsoever things I can see, hear, and learn, these are what I prefer" (fr. B55); and many of his paradoxes are simple perceptual observations. For instance, there is nothing mysterious in his saying that cold things become warm and warm things cold, that the moist dries and the dry becomes moist (fr. B126); these are clear statements of what goes on before one's eyes. Similarly, the relativity of perceptual qualities, expressed in such sayings as the preferences of asses for straw rather than gold (fr. B9), that swine wash in mud and barnyard fowl in the dust (fr. B37), that fish can drink sea water whereas men would die if they drank it (fr. B61), that all things are beautiful and good and right to God whereas men make a distinction between right and wrong (fr. B102). Surely such conclusions must come from ordinary perception and its implications, if one relies on ordinary perception. That qualities vary with the perceiver became one of the main proofs of skepticism in later times, and one form of skepticism was attributed to the followers of Heraclitus.

But this did not imply to his way of thinking that no knowledge was attainable. Far from it. One had to understand that there

---

[12] But see also fr. B107.

was a law according to which these variations occurred. The world of perception could give one no firm place on which to stand, and if one remained in it, one was doomed to live in the flux. That was one solution to the problem. The desire to escape from it has the rational, if not the psychological, motive embedded in the assumption that truth must be absolute, which in practice meant that a true proposition must somehow or other escape from any system of relations. Yet once a system of relations is discovered and accepted as basic, truths which are relevant to it are just as absolute as any others. That knowledge free from and independent of all conditions is unattainable does not seem to have occurred to Heraclitus: one could escape from the flux by finding the law in accordance with which all fluctuations, all changes, took place. On the cosmic scale we have a hint of such a law in the fragment which says that there is a transmutation of elements from air to fire, from earth to water, from fire back to air, and from water back to earth (fr. B31). There is also an emphasis on the identity of wisdom and a knowledge of the law "by means of which all things are steered through all" (fr. B41). There is also the famous fragment (fr. B94) in which he says that the Sun will not stray from his course; if he did, the avenging Furies would discover him and presumably whip him back to his proper place. Because of ignorance of this law, the poets and philosophers, Hesiod and Pythagoras and Xenophanes and Hecataeus, have learned nothing (fr. B40).

It is understandable that if the senses show us a world in which nothing can be said of any particular thing, because nothing remains what one apprehends it as being, reason will tell us that all things must really be one. The eyes and ears by the very mutability of their testimony show men that behind them must be something whose nature is always the same. That something is symbolized by the everliving Fire. Dark though such sayings may have been both to the ancients and to modern interpreters, they present no greater difficulty than the attempt to attribute one predicate to anything which is in process. The life of a man from conception to death confronts us with a similar problem. How can we name the nature of a man if he changes from moment to moment? One can describe his history step by step, but one can do no more when it is a question of covering his whole biography in one adjective than to say in a tautology that he is in a state of change. There is nothing easier—nor more prudent—than to attribute contrary predicates to such a process. But in doing so, we are misled by the character of our language. As we have said before, a common noun or adjective, being by its very nature universal, confers stable properties upon that which it names or qualifies, and if one believes that there is an image of the world in the language which we use to describe it, one inevitably encounters paradoxes.

In one of the fragments of Heraclitus occurs the word *logos* (fr. B1). Though we are avoiding as far as possible textual criticism in this book, it is necessary to dwell for a moment or two on this word. The fragment reads,

> Although this *logos* is everlasting,[13] men are devoid of understanding of it, both before they have heard it and when they have heard it for the first time. For although all things happen in accordance with this *logos*, they resemble people without experience of them, trying words and deeds such as those which I relate as I distinguish each thing according to its nature and indicate what manner of thing it is. But other men do not know what sort of thing they do when awake, just as they forget what sort of thing they do in sleep.

Now the primary meaning of *logos* is "word," but it came to mean reason, theory, even definition. The Stoics later were to use it as if it were the name for the voice of God, and in Philo Judaeus it was to be called the Son of God, as of course it was also called in the opening of the Gospel according to Saint John. I have used the term, universal law, because I find it hard to believe that Heraclitus, if correctly quoted by Sextus Empiricus from whom we get the fragment, would emphasize the truism

---

[13] Or "true evermore" according to Burnet, *op. cit.*, p. 133. Cf. C. Ramnoux, *op. cit.*, reference *s.v.* in *Index des thèmes*, for illustrations of the problem.

that other men before they had heard his theory were ignorant of it. But if the *logos* is the universal law which governs the flux, then whether men had heard of it or not, they might be expected to know of it by instinct, as the law of their own nature. Heraclitus may have been dark, but the historian's duty is to illuminate his authors as far as possible. I have therefore interpreted Heraclitus' *logos* as that which can be known to lie behind the flux. The flux is apparent to the senses and the *logos* is incorporated in sensory percepts. The problem which other men have not solved is the extraction of the *logos* from the heterogeneous flow of perception. For, though eyes are better witnesses to the truth than ears, "both the eyes and the ears are bad witnesses to men if they have barbarous souls" (fr. B107). Barbarous souls are souls which do not speak or do not understand one's language, and in this context one has a right to interpret that language as the language of the senses. It tells us both about the flux and about its regularity.

There is one more detail which should be indicated. Heraclitus seems to believe—"seems" since he gives us no overt statement of his belief—that if something changes, it must change into its opposite. Much of the sting of his aphorisms is based on this belief. It is obvious of course that if something changes one of its qualities, the change may be symbolized by its passing from *P* to *not-P*. But whether the particular *not-P* is an opposite in any sense of the term approaching the literal, remains a matter of observation. If, however, all change is between opposites, then the whole process of change will include both poles, and, just as he says (fr. B60) that the way up and the way down are one and the same, so he can fuse all opposites into one balanced pair and do so logically by considering them as termini of various processes. We cannot read his mind and shall not pretend to; we merely say that such an interpretation would throw some light on his obscurities. The assumption that change was always from one pole to its antithesis became a cardinal assumption of Aristotle as well.[14]

[14] See G. Boas, *op. cit.*, pp. 61 ff.

4. Parmenides and Zeno flatly reject the testimony of the senses. Distinguishing between Truth and Opinion, they maintain that the road of Truth is, as we have seen, laid out by the reason as it argues in a purely dialectical manner. The poem of Parmenides does not give grounds for rejecting perceptual evidence, and indeed Aristotle said that he believed in nothing else. On the other hand, Zeno, in so far as he survives, gives us puzzles entangled in the acceptance of such evidence and argues to the very contradictory of what it tells us. We see the arrow fly; we see Achilles overtaking the tortoise; we see that magnitudes can be increased by addition; we see that people can walk about in space. The puzzles try to show us that such experiences cannot be trusted since they will not sustain logical analysis. Reality must be rational, that is, describable in noncontradictory language. So a fifth-century Eleatic, Melissus, argues clearly that we see change, yet know that nothing changes.

His critique of perception is based on the assumption that, as he is quoted by Simplicius as saying, though we see things changing into other things, the hard becoming soft, the soft hard, "It is clear . . . that we do not see correctly, nor does it appear to be true that those things are many, for nothing would undergo a change if it were true being" (fr. B8). Though a saying of Melissus cannot commit Parmenides to anything, a reading of his remains will convince one that he reproduces his master's arguments. What must strike a modern reader as strange is that no attempt seems to have been made to explain why perception led us so far from the truth. If the explanation was given in passages now lost, the question still remains of why later writers were so uninterested in them that they did not preserve them.

5. Empedocles gives us more details of the process of knowledge. If we accept the order of his fragments as given by Diels, he rejected very early in his poem the idea that any one of the senses was any more trustworthy than any other. The goal of the intellect is clarity and clarity will be attained by the intellect through all the senses indifferently (fr. B3). One thing, and this

echoes Parmenides, is certain, that nothing can come from nothing and nothing can pass away into nothing (fr. B12). As we have
seen, that which is everlasting is the four elements. If these elements could have been destroyed, there would be no reason why
they should have survived, for whence would they have derived
the stuff which kept their quantity constant (fr. B17)? Since
everything is made of the four elements, so must men be made,
and by laying down a rule which remained an integral part of
European philosophy, Empedocles was able to conclude that there
is a kind of sympathy which attracts like to like (fr. B90). The
Fire within us sees the external Fire; by love we know Love and
by strife Strife (fr. B109).

This principle, according to Aristotle's pupil Theophrastus (*De
sensu* 1), divided the Greek epistemologists into two camps, the
likeness school and the unlikeness school. It was assimilated to the
causal principle that only similars could stand in a causal relation.
Hence it oriented the researchers when they were looking for
causes. In epistemology it resulted in the doctrine that there
must be some sort of homogeneity between subject and object so
that, for instance, a material object occupying space could not be
conceived as being known by an immaterial mind which was essentially spaceless. In Empedocles little is said by way of explanation, but since he believed also that "there are effluences of all
things which have come into being" (fr. B89), it is likely that he
also believed these effluences to enter the soul through the sense
organs, which apparently were little orifices. He gives a poetic
description of the eye (fr. B84) in which he says that it is made
of Fire, entrapped there by the various ocular membranes, and
adds that there is very little Earth in it (fr. B85). The doctrine of
effluences is found also in what remains of Democritus. Such doctrines are not unlike those of our own times which maintain that
air waves or light rays impinge upon the auditory or optic end
organs and there set up nerve currents which eventuate in sounds
and sights. The difference between the two sorts of doctrine is
that the effluences were probably little particles of the objects

themselves. But at this point we step across the frontiers of conjecture. It would be more prudent to draw back.

6. The one authentic fragment of Leucippus comes to us from Aëtius and runs, "Nothing comes into being without a cause, but all from reason along with necessity" (fr. B2). This simple and apparently innocent sentence can be and has been interpreted in a variety of ways. The Latin methodological slogan, *ex nihilo nihil*, which Lucretius attributes to Epicurus, is our usual way of putting the thought which is concealed in it. But whether we use the Latin or the Greek, the vagueness of the phrase remains.

First, there is no way of telling whether or not the things which come into being are material things or not. As the principle was used later, it was an explanatory rule applied exclusively to material things and it directed the scientist always to look for some material source of the matter which had seemed to come into being. The importance of this was that it was equivalent in use to the principle of the conservation of matter, or mass, and could be employed in criticism of attempts to show that rabbits could be pulled out of hats in which they had not previously been put, or, to take a more elegant example, that matter could be created.[15] It had a corollary to the effect that no matter could be lost, and when the two principles were used together, one drew out of them the theorem that all changes in amounts of matter were apparent and not real. Strictly speaking this did not imply that nonmaterial things could not be created and destroyed, and consequently, even as early as Democritus, sensory qualities did not have to pre-exist in their causes. As long as one could discover the causes in terms of which their appearances could be explained, all was well. The sensory qualities, however, are not the only things which did not seem to pre-exist in their causes; there was also vitality or animation. How one could explain on the principle *ex nihilo* the origin of bees in rotting beef or of eels in horse

---

[15] Recently it has been asserted by some astronomers, Hoyle for instance, that matter is created in certain parts of space.

troughs remained a problem until the disputes between Pasteur and Bastian pretty well demonstrated the Law of Biogenesis. But all such puzzles arose from interpreting the principle too literally, and sometimes it was taken to mean not that the effect must pre-exist in the cause, but that there must be sufficient and necessary conditions for the occurrence of the effect and that these conditions were determinable.

Second, then, the preposition *ex* was used merely to assert that all change has some cause which presumably must be antecedent to it. If we explain the growth of a seed into a plant on the basis of the water which it has received, the warmth of the sun, the fertilizer in the soil, we are not saying that the growing plant pre-existed in these three things. We are simply asserting that when we have them, we may expect the seed to grow and when we do not have them, we should expect no such thing. But it should not be forgotten that not very long ago biologists were seduced by the theory of preformationism, according to which the mature plant or animal was actually pre-existent in the seed or ovum and that growth was only an unfolding of what was folded up within them.

Third, the Greek word which I have expanded into the phrase "without a cause" was used by the poets to mean "idly," "fruit-lessly," and we find in Aristotle, a century later than Leucippus, the word meaning "in vain," where he says, "Nature does nothing in vain." But here we are not asked to search for an antecedent material cause for what has come into being, but a purpose which it is supposed to be achieving. This type of explanation is obviously very different from that of the materialist, for if it is used as a unique methodological principle, which it seldom is, then the words *ex nihilo* mean "to no end," "for no purpose." Whether this entails the belief that all purposes must be the purposes of some mind, we need not discuss at this point, but it is easy to see that such a conclusion would be normal.

Fourth, where Leucippus combines reason with necessity, we have no way of knowing just what he was referring to. The combination may mean that all change is rationally explicable and that once we have found the explanation, we can be sure that it will always apply. That we are not indulging in logic-chopping here is shown by Aristotle's concern with the concept of necessity and in modern times by that of David Hume. For there are both logical necessity and causal necessity, the former of which need have nothing to do with the actual course of events. It is the kind of necessity which we have in purely formal arguments whose premises need not be true in order to have a conclusion which logically follows from them.[16]

Causal necessity has been used to prove that there is a kind of compulsion in the course of events, the sort of thing which one finds in human life when a man is forced to do something against his will. We say that if a stone is dropped through the air from a height, it has to fall to the ground: there is nothing else that it can do. Two observations should be made about this conception of things: (1) that if things always do occur in predictable ways, we are likely to read necessity into them, and (2) when we ourselves acquire habits from having done things in regular ways, we feel a compulsion to do them always in such ways. The necessity of the usual or the regular or the uniform may be simply read into them as a projection from our own experience. This has some

---

[16] The standard examples of such consistent arguments would be syllogisms of the following types:
 (a) All men are triangles
   Socrates is a man
   Therefore, Socrates is a triangle.
(Here the major premise is false, the minor true, and the conclusion false, though the syllogism is formally correct.)
 (b) All triangles are mortal
   Socrates is a triangle
   Therefore, Socrates is mortal.
(In this syllogism, the two premises are false and the conclusion true, and the syllogism correct.)
 (c) All triangles are plane figures
   Socrates is a triangle
   Therefore, Socrates is a plane figure.
(Here, the major premise is true, the minor false, the conclusion false and the syllogism once more correct.)

substantiation in the common experience of surprise when things do not occur in the ways to which we have been accustomed. The trouble here probably comes from our failure to observe events carefully enough and to see the conditions under which they occur. If we included all the conditions in our descriptions of events, we should see that there is no irregularity in the way they happen. But it is also probable that if we took this seriously, by which I mean if we took absolutely all the circumstances into consideration, we should not stop until we had included the position of the planets and the temperature of the farthest star. To avoid this the scientists have elaborated what they call laboratory conditions, which restrict the amount of probable irregularity.

But these are technical matters which did not seem to bother the men who had the genius first to imagine a cosmos in which regular and general rules could be verified.

Now one of the ways to bring about a situation in which the principle that nothing comes from nothing can be exemplified is to attach the genesis of those beings which might cause trouble to a set of other beings, so simple in their nature that they would vary in a few determinable ways and by the various relations which they would sustain to one another would cause the appearance of the more troublesome things. This was the technique used by the nineteenth-century chemists who were able to explain the properties of chemical compounds on the basis of the spatial arrangements of the elemental atoms which composed them. It was also the technique of such a philosopher as John Locke, who by means of the so-called primary qualities, extension in space, shape, motion, and rest, was able to construct a material world which would conform to all the laws of physics. It would also, he thought, be capable of causing in human minds the existence of the secondary qualities of color, sound, taste, smell, and touch. These latter qualities were thus no part of the material world, did not pre-exist in it, but would come into being when the material objects stood in certain definable relations to the human organism. Just what those relations were Locke did not attempt to say. It sufficed for his purposes to demonstrate that the secondary qualities were not ingredients of the nonhuman part of nature.

In Democritus we have an analogous technique. He seems to have accepted the conclusions of Parmenides that there must be something which underwent no internal changes. But instead of finding that something in the cosmos as a whole, Being, he broke up the material world into a very large number of tiny particles of matter which he called atoms, each of which was a Parmenidean world. These atoms moved about in empty space and they differed from one another, as we have indicated above, standing in various spatial relations to one another. Whether by size he meant volume, or whether he meant weight, has been questioned, but most historians are agreed that he meant volume, that is, the amount of space which each occupied. As examples of the atomic shapes, he cited roughness and smoothness, roundness and angularity. We must think of them as very small balls and polyhedra, both regular and irregular. As they move about, they collide and some adhere to others. In this way they build up the macroscopic objects which our senses perceive.

It is these perceptible objects made of atoms which give rise to our sensations. In one of his most famous fragments we find the words, "By custom there is color, by custom sweetness, by custom taste, but in truth there are only atoms and the void" (fr. A49). This means that on the atomic level there are no sensory qualities. But to what extent he meant that these qualities were purely subjective is more questionable. For when he came to explain the origin of the qualities, he based it, as Empedocles did, on effluences from agglomerated atoms, or macroscopic objects. These effluences, at least in the case of vision, were little images of the objects seen, which moved through the air and entered the eye. But in the case of the other senses, the effluences could not be images in any literal meaning of that word, but were actual sounds, odors, tastes, and textures.[17] This is consistent with his further principle that only like can affect like.[18] Consequently, though the sensory qualities may not exist "in truth," they do exist in the external world, in the world which one might call the superatomic world. Thus he was not, strictly speaking, a forerunner of John Locke. Moreover, in the same paragraph in which Galen reports his distinction between what exists by custom and what exists in truth, we find Democritus saying that the mind gets all its evidence from sensation. Sensory knowledge is therefore a copy of the macroscopic world, but its traits cannot be attributed to the atomic world itself.

Since we can have no sensory knowledge at all unless the effluences from objects enter our bodies, contact is essential, and therefore Democritus maintains that touch is our primary sense. If he means, however, that we are aware of the contact between our eyes and color, between our ears and sound, a new complication would arise, for it does not seem plausible that we cannot see color without also being aware of the impact of its effluence on the eye. On the other hand, if we may enlarge on the fragments, we do speak of striking colors, soft sounds, and smooth tastes, and he may have observed our attribution of tactual sensations to qualities which are not tactual. But this is an inference and it is more likely that all he meant by touch in this context was contact.

It must not be thought that Democritus left the matter there. If Theophrastus is right, the sensory qualities are determined by the traits of the atoms. For instance, the sour comes from angular and bent atoms, whereas the sweet comes from atoms which are round and "not too small." He reduces all colors to four, the white, the black, the red, and the green, each of which comes from certain atomic shapes, white from the smooth, black from the rough and irregular, red from such as produce heat, and green

---

[17] But as John I. Beare points out in his *Greek Theories of Elementary Cognition* (Oxford: Clarendon Press, 1906), p. 29, n. 3, Democritus did not use the word *eidolon* or image, though later commentators, in particular Cicero, say he did.

[18] But see Theophrastus *De sensu* 49.

from "the solid and the void." This is far from clear, even to Theophrastus, but at least it permits us to say that the shapes of the atoms themselves determine what sensory qualities their compounds will assume. He seems, moreover, to have known something of color mixtures, but into that we need not go. What is of more interest is his attempt to reduce all complexity to intelligibility by the process of analysis. This appears to be based on the assumption that when a complex being is shown to be a structure of elementary parts and that when the relations between the parts are known, the complex demands no more explanation. Though in itself this does not presuppose the temporal priority of the simple, there has been a tendency on the part of philosophers to argue as if things began by being simple and moved toward complexity. Thus one can have a universe which starts out as a collection of a few kinds of elements and which gradually becomes complex, the elements forming larger groupings which are called wholes. That this is an illicit inference, if not an assumption, needs no demonstration. Moreover, if explanation is to proceed in this manner, one must be able to state the conditions under which the simples will combine. Democritus apparently did attempt to do this when he said that the atoms collided and that in their collision they became hooked together or otherwise agglomerated. Since there is no evidence that he thought the cosmos to have had a beginning in time, he was not forced to account for the beginning of the atomic motions: they had always been moving about and always would continue to do so. To ask what started their motion would be like asking a physicist what accounts for the first law of motion.

Though the reports of Democritus' epistemology which have been left to us are more copious than those of any other early Greek philosopher, none of them tells us what we should like to know above all: how did he explain our knowledge of general methodological principles? If all knowledge comes from, or is a complex of, sensory qualities, whence comes our knowledge of such a principle as that of Leucippus, Nothing comes into being

without a cause? To begin with, we cannot have sensory knowledge of the causes of our sensory qualities, since those causes,
ultimately the atoms, are infraperceptual. Democritus, if chal-
lenged on this point, would have had to admit that, unless he was
simply inventing his theory out of whole cloth, the atoms and
their diverse shapes and positions were inferred to exist in order
to explain what we actually do perceive. In the second place, the
very principles of inference, the rules in accordance with which
we make our inferences, are not themselves perceived, nor do
they correspond to any atomic shapes and positions, nor could
they by the very nature of the case. We cannot expect Democritus to have anticipated Kant and to have said that they are simply the way in which the human reason behaves when it is
arguing. But we might expect either him or his critics to have
asked the question. But though Theophrastus gives us a very
critical account of Democritus' theory of sensation, he says
nothing about any theory of what one might call the understanding. I mention this not merely because it is a lacuna in the
theory of knowledge of this most interesting figure—for it is
only too easy to see such things for oneself—but to call attention
to a curious feature of intellectual history. That is, that men could
reason well in entire unconsciousness of how they were reasoning. If ever there was a case of practice preceding theory, this is
one. This is the more curious in that a somewhat younger contemporary of Democritus, Socrates, was himself very much concerned with precisely this problem. And other contemporaries,
the early Sophists, were having a heyday with all the intricacies
of logical interrelations. Zeno, as well as Democritus—if some of
the fragments of the latter are authentic—knew how to handle
logical puzzles.[19]

The rationalism of Democritus, then, included an attempt to
show the causal relation between reality and appearance. He was
not satisfied with pointing out the gap between the two worlds
and urging his readers to seek one and turn away from the other.

[19] See the puzzle of the cone, fr. B155.

Our ideas of reality grow out of our ideas of appearance, not simply as inferences from them made on logical grounds alone but as effects of the impact of sensory experience upon our bodies. There are plenty of gaps in the theory, but that the two worlds are not causally disconnected is clear. It may be true that his predecessors also tried to fill the gap with some explanation or other, but if so, the passages in which they expounded their theories have not been preserved.

7. It is the historian's great misfortune to know next to nothing of the early stages of Pythagoreanism. The figure of the supposed founder of the movement, Pythagoras, is entirely shrouded in legend and those of his immediate successors are not much clearer. We have reason to believe, however, that by the end of the sixth century B.C. there had grown up in Magna Graecia a consuming interest in geometry among the so-called Pythagoreans, and a belief that the mathematical treatment of problems was that which would be most fruitful in philosophy. Such assertions as, "All is number," on the other hand, mean very little unless they are supported by elaborate interpretations for which the material is lacking. Moreover, whether Pythagoras first proved the Pythagorean theorem or not—and it is now known that it had been proved much earlier than his date, though perhaps not in southern Italy where the movement began—is a question for the historian of mathematics. But what is of importance for our purposes is that the long tradition of answering problems in natural science by the geometrical method started as early as the late sixth and middle fifth centuries. For here we have something more than an appeal to reason; we have a clear statement of what reasoning is.

The beauty of mathematics, whether it deals with numbers or with geometrical shapes or with order itself, is its certainty. If one can assume with propriety that axioms and postulates are self-evidently true, true to fact, then one's conclusions are also bound to be true to fact. And this is what the early mathematicians did assume. The axiom that things equal to the same thing are equal to each other did not simply mean to these men that equivalent formulas could be substituted for one another. It meant that if one material object was equal in quantity to another, and the second equal in quantity to a third, then the first and the third were equal in quantity. Unless one realizes this, one fails to see any relevance to fact in the slogans and mottoes of the early Pythagoreans. The followers of the mathematical technique were bound to turn away from mythologizing, from sensory perception and from scientific hearsay, and to work toward the elaboration of a set of theorems, linked together by logical bonds, which would do for the philosopher that which Heraclitus' *logos* and Parmenides' dialectic would do. This would constitute a rejection of the senses only in so far as they were inconsistent in their reports. But in so far as these reports could be systematized, they could be accepted. It also involved a purification of sensory testimony to the end that its terms would be univalent. Being univalent, they could be given a meaning arrived at by logical analysis and that meaning would never change. The mathematical circle would be immutable, the perceptual circle imperfect and varying from observer to observer. At most the latter could be thought of as an imperfect copy of a perfect original, an approximation to that which ought to be but never is. If all our ideas could be expressed in mathematical language, the imperfections of sensory experience would be eliminated, and such concepts as those which are found in biology (the horse, the dog, the man) or those which are found in ethics (justice, goodness, wisdom) could presumably be handled in the same way. Whatever the gross superstitions of the early Pythagoreans, they do seem to have had a glimpse of this possibility, and what they saw as a possibility was treated as a reality by the men whom they influenced.

It is also true that since geometry was the basic mathematical science of these early philosophers, and not arithmetic except to the extent that arithmetical relations could be symbolized geometrically, the spatial structure of the universe became the basis of all their thinking. This structure was fixed. There was an absolute up and down, right and left, center and circumference. A

Table of Opposites, which is given by Aristotle in his *Metaphysics* (986a 23), is assigned to the school, and we find in it not only such mathematical terms as odd and even, straight and curved, but biological terms such as male and female, physical terms such as resting and moving, and ethical terms such as good and bad. Now to fix a method of thinking is at least an important contribution to philosophy, and whether one estimate the contribution as good or bad is of little historical importance. Opposition, as we have pointed out, is essentially a spatial term, and when applied to values, sexes, ways of behaving, it becomes metaphorical. The two ends of a line are literally in opposition; goodness and badness are metaphorically so. When one identifies conflict with opposition and transfers the characteristics of one pair to the other, one is no longer speaking literally but figuratively. Much early Greek philosophy was expressed as a conflict between elements and forces. We have seen this in the interplay of opposites in Heraclitus, in the rarefaction and condensation of Anaximander, in the Love and Strife of Empedocles, and indeed the only philosopher treated so far in this study who does not make use of this figure of speech seems to be Democritus. It is in fact fair to say that an awareness of conflict overlying geometrical opposition is a constant phenomenon in Greek literature as well as in Greek science. Even in the tragedies the major figures have to make a choice, and, though we may be straying too far afield in saying this, the opposition between Greek and Barbarian, as in *The Persians*, between the law of the gods and the laws of the state, as in *Antigone*, the cult of Artemis and that of Aphrodite, as in *Hippolytus*, is a pretty good example of how the poets felt what the philosophers rationalized.

A geometrical universe is one in which time "makes no difference." It is like a stone monument which may represent everything except that which is in process of becoming. The outstanding beauties of such a world are its perfect balance, its unity of form, its stability. If the world is to be imagined under the form of such a monument, those of its traits which cannot be incorporated into it will be thought of as blemishes, ugliness, evil. In the famous Table of Opposites, one finds on one side all the things which the makers of the Table admired, the odd, the straight, the male, the immobile, and on the other side those which they depreciated, the even, the curved, the female, the moving. The odd is apparently better than the even because it has two extremes and a middle term between them which acts, so to speak, as the fulcrum upon which the ends are balanced. Most curves seem to the unsophisticated mind to be without a formula —the equations for curves are a discovery of Descartes in the seventeenth century—and the only curve which the Greeks seemed able to admire was the circle. The circle is admissible because it has a center from which all its circumferential points are equidistant; it is, moreover, complete, returning upon itself. The immobile is better than the moving, because it has a fixed position in space, and space is absolute and bounded. But why is the male better than the female? Is this because of the theory later expounded by Aristotle that woman merely furnished food for the foetus, the male furnishing the seed out of which the infant grew?[20] Or was there simply a folk belief exemplified in the treatment of women as subordinates which was expressed in the Table of Opposites? Did people generally believe in the inferiority of women, whereupon the author of the Table incorporated them on the evil side, or did he have some other reason for doing so? Here we have no evidence that I know of. In any event the Table illustrates a doctrine which has survived down to our own time, the doctrine that values are an integral part of nature, the universe, whatever is real, and so on. Once they are a part of the natural order, then their opposition must be accommodated to whatever other opposition is discovered to be in it. And that opposition is geometrical or spatial.

[20] This belief is at least as early as Aeschylus. See *Eumenides* 658 f. To kill one's mother is not so bad as to kill one's father, since the mother is not really related to her children. But this would not have appeared in that play in a speech of Apollo unless it were already a well-known idea generally held.

III

ONCE ONE HAS established a method of thought which leads to a distinction between appearance and reality, it is natural to appraise the life of one's fellows in terms of the distinction. Are one's fellows living in the world of appearance or the world of reality; are they following the reason or succumbing to the charms of sensation? Is life itself worth living? Is contemporary life better or worse than life in ancient times? Are all men doomed to misery or are some destined to be happy? If the former, what is the reason for it? If the latter, how can they achieve happiness? What is the good of civilization: are savages and perhaps even the beasts better off than civilized man? If so, what is there in human life which explains the failure of civilization to attain the good life? These are only a few questions which the rationalistic philosopher is accustomed to raise. In general the early Greeks maintained that if only men would follow the reason, they would be happy, not in the sense that they would be living a life of maximum pleasure, but in the sense that they would be morally better.

1.   That the Greeks as a whole were not the careless pagans which they have sometimes been depicted as being is well known. In an essay which has become a classic, on the pessimism of the Greek, Butcher destroyed once and for all any notion that people may have had to the effect that the Greeks were less melancholy than other people.[21] In Homer (*Iliad* vi. 12–19) we read how Axylus, the son of Teuthranus, who lived in a house by the roadside and entertained all who came by, was slain by Diomedes, but not one of his friends came forward at the moment of his death to meet the enemy and save him. Nestor (*Iliad* i. 260–8), an old man at the time of the Trojan War, could remember with regret the superiors of the warriors who were about him, superior in strength and courage at least. Pindar too (*Pyth.* iii) laments the disappearance of those days when "that rugged monster," Chiron,

[21] S. H. Butcher, "The Melancholy of the Greeks," in *Some Aspects of the Greek Genius* (London: Macmillan and Co., 1891), pp. 130 ff.

was alive. In the Golden Age, says Hesiod (*Work and Days* 109 ff.), men "lived like gods with hearts free from sorrow and remote from toil and grief. . . . And all good things were theirs. For the fruitful earth spontaneously bore them abundant fruit without stint. And they lived in ease and peace upon their lands with many good things, rich in flocks and beloved of the blessed gods." And again, in a poem of which we have only a fragment, "They ate their meals in common and sat together, both the immortal gods and men."[22] But it is perhaps quite needless to extend this list.

Such sentiments are a mixture of a longing for the past and a definite commitment to the thesis that primitive life is better than civilized life. Such a thesis has been called "primitivism" by Lovejoy and has two forms, chronological and cultural. The former maintains that man's first appearance on earth exhibited his best traits and the time in which he lived was the happiest period in history; the latter that the acquisitions of culture are bad. Both forms of primitivism may again be divided ideologically, though the divisions were not always clear-cut in the literary remains of the authors who espoused the ideas. One has first the kind of primitivism which Lovejoy called soft and then that which he called hard. The description of the Golden Race in Hesiod, a race which lived in ease, was typically soft; whereas in Aratus, the first men lived without war, foreign trade, or the eating of flesh and approached something like a hard condition. But whether the primitivist is chronological or cultural, hard or soft, he believes in a fall of man from his original condition, analogous to the fall of man in Scripture.

The Scriptural fall was presumably caused by man's disobedience to the commands of God. Just what was symbolized by the eating of the fruit of the Tree of Knowledge is a matter of dispute and we are fortunately not engaged here in Biblical exegesis. But

[22] Fr. 22 (216), ed. Rzach (Leipzig, 1902). For a longer account of the Golden Age and of related legends and ideas, see A. O. Lovejoy and G. Boas, *Primitivism and Related Ideas in Antiquity* (Baltimore: Johns Hopkins Press, 1935).

among the Greeks there were various accounts of the loss of primeval felicity. In Hesiod's classic account of man's degeneration, no reason is given for the fall nor is human degeneration uninterrupted. The Iron Race, which is our own, is the worst of all five races, physically and morally. Its life is one of toil and war, both internal and external. Zeus will destroy its members "when they reach the point of being born with graying temples." Force will take the place of justice and evil passions the place of good. No one cause accounts for the disappearance of the successive races; no cause at all is assigned to the disappearance of the Golden Race; the Silver disappears because of overweening pride and impiety; the Bronze through internecine war; the Heroes through external war; the Iron will disappear by exhaustion and perhaps from evil-doing. That there were early beliefs, however, that the one cause of the fall was moral, is seen in such a passage as that referred to above from Theognis (1135 ff.), in which Hope alone is left to man, Good Faith, Moderation, and the Graces having fled the earth, "and no one dreads the deathless gods, and the race of pious men is past and justice and piety are no longer known." In Empedocles (fr. B128) the cause of degeneration is the entrance of Strife into the historical cycle; when Love was supreme, all was well. The fall apparently to his mind was not attributable to any wickedness on the part of our primordial ancestors, but rather to the inevitable cycle of history. Similarly in the myth of the dethroning of Cronus by his son, Zeus, and the identification of the Age of Cronus with the Golden Age, no reason is given for Zeus's action and, what is more surprising, in view of the character of Cronus, none is given for thinking of his reign as one of earthly happiness.

Such accounts of human history, with the exception of Empedocles', are obviously vague and philosophically trivial. But they do at least indicate that the early Greeks were hardly satisfied with life as they lived it. Whether they believed that the Fates were intrinsically misanthropic or that the gods were jealous, as in the story of Prometheus, or merely that there was more evil in the world than good and no explanation could be given for it, there was a prevailing atmosphere of melancholy which could be breathed by those who were not congenitally blind to evil. The same depreciation of humanity is found in the early philosophers. The very fact that most of us are content to follow the way of opinion, the vagaries of the senses, is enough to make a philosopher who is a rationalist look down with disdain on his fellow mortals. The existence of a set of taboos, as drawn up by the early Pythagoreans, is some evidence, if slight, that they were uneasy when following the ordinary life of men and felt they must protect themselves from those evils which might lurk in the eating of certain foods or in the performance of certain acts. Such an attitude need not be based upon a rational critique of life, but if one has already accepted a rationalistic technique and applies it to common practices, then it is likely that one will reject a good part of life as senseless.

2. The existence of Greek tragedy is another indication that the life of man may contain an element of defeat which cannot be avoided. This element is not always the same by any means; we have no single explanation to offer of what makes a drama a tragedy. But there is no extant tragedy which does not present the life of its protagonists as doomed to disaster from the start. Sometimes, as in *The Persians*, the disaster is attributable to too great self-confidence, the kind of self-confidence which induces a great king to attempt the conquest of a smaller but more upright people and to link together two continents which the gods had separated by water (*Persae* 739 ff.). Sometimes, as in the Oedipus trilogy, it comes from a man's unwittingly committing a crime which he could not avoid. Sometimes, as in *Antigone*, it emerges from a conflict between two equally legitimate claims, the claim of Heaven and that of Earth. And sometimes, as in *Hippolytus*, it comes from an exaggerated worship of one divinity to the exclusion of a rival divinity. But whatever the precise cause of the tragedy may be, its effects were unavoidable. In *Prometheus Bound*, which to be sure is only one play out of a group of

three, the hero is punished for having been man's benefactor; but here his crime is to have thwarted the will of Zeus. In *Agamemnon* the hero is murdered by his wife for having sacrificed her daughter, but she herself is murdered in the *Choephoroe* for having slaughtered her husband. Even in *Antigone*, of which we usually think of the girl as the main character, Creon too is punished and neither the proponent of the law of the gods nor the proponent of the law of the state is rewarded. Thus it seems wrong to say, as is so often said, that Fate is the preponderant force.

One might with more justice say that the tragic poets were all convinced that every act had inevitable consequences and that any decision would entail effects which were unavoidable. In some tragedies the main characters are aware of this and say so. Thus Prometheus in *Prometheus Bound*, though he rebels against the cruelty of Zeus to man, nevertheless knows that his benefactions were bound to lead to catastrophe, and in his very moving opening speech he makes this clear (101 ff.). In short, this world was to the early dramatists a rational world, as it was to the early philosophers. By this I mean simply that it was theoretically possible to know how events were linked together and, if one did know this, one would see that there was no escaping the consequences of one's decisions. The outstanding exception to this generalization is the *Eumenides*, which ends with a debate between the Furies and Apollo, a debate which is won by Apollo. This victory could not be foreseen by the people involved in the drama. But this victory is not irrational; it is not the result of a miracle which by its very nature upsets the laws of reason. It is the triumph of the reign of Zeus over that of Cronus, though it is not put in those words by Aeschylus.

It is also notable that the Greek tragedy was not a conflict of individual characters, of heroes against villains. There are no Iagos, no Edmunds, no King Claudiuses, as far as I have been able to discover, in the Greek tragedies.[23] The villain is man's fate. This does not mean that the tragic poets did not recognize

---

[23] But note that there are more lost than extant tragedies.

the existence of wicked people. On the contrary, the most horrible crimes are committed. But it is made clear that such crimes, as in the Oedipus trilogy, are committed unwittingly, or, as in the *Oresteia,* as just punishment for the evil done by others. But it is possible, if not certain, that the poets were thinking that punishment was to be given by the gods, not by men. To take the law into one's own hands seems to have been the most prominent crime. And yet each man has a will of his own which guides him. It is only when man's will is consonant with the will of the gods that he will live out his life in peace. But sometimes the will of the gods is concealed or known only through ambiguous oracles. Man does not always know what they have in store for him. Consequently he acts according to his personal insight and therefore often meets a tragic doom. What is important for our purposes here is not that men run headlong into disaster in ignorance of why. For the historian of philosophy it is more important to observe that there existed a feeling that concealed laws governed the behavior of man as they did that of everything else, or, to use one of the favorite clichés of the school, that man was a part of Nature. If he could reach a knowledge of those laws, he might be able to better his condition in life. But in general he neither wishes to nor is prepared to. The philosophers were the few who tried to instruct the many in the rationality of nature.

3. Man therefore is envisioned as groping in the dark and sometimes as content to do so. The tirades of some of the early philosophers make this clear. Xenophanes pours out his scorn on the athletes, the swift runners, the winners of the pentathlon, the boxers, the wrestlers, all of whom Pindar was to celebrate a century later. "Better," he says (fr. B2), "is our wisdom than the strength of men and horses."[24] He has nothing but contempt for those of his fellows who have taken their ideas from Homer and Hesiod, who have "attributed to the gods all sorts of things such

[24] According to Burnet, *op. cit.,* p. 117, n. 2, "art" would be a better translation than "wisdom."

as are shameful and disgraceful among men, stealing and adultery and deceit" (fr. B11). For, he goes on to say, men believe the gods to be like them, to be begotten, to wear clothes, to speak with voices, and have bodily frames (fr. B14). And, he adds in his best-known fragments (frs. B15, 16), "If oxen and horses and lions could paint with their hands and make things as men do, the horses would give their gods the form of horses, the oxen would make them like oxen. . . . The Ethiopians make their gods snub-nosed and black and the Thracians blue-eyed and fair-haired." These absurdities are attributable to man's ignorance, for "The gods did not teach men all things at the beginning, but in time men find out what is better by seeking" (fr. B18). It is this search for truth which will raise men out of their state of ignorance; the burden is put upon them. And presumably the search is to be guided by reason. Yet Xenophanes is no dogmatist, for the skeptic Sextus Empiricus reports him as saying, "No man has been born nor will one ever exist who knows for certain about the gods and what things I speak of, for even if he should happen to speak the perfect truth, he himself does not know it to be so" (fr. B34). Yet he himself seems sure that he has discovered at least one perfect truth, namely that there is but one god, unlike mortals in every way, and governing without toil all by his mind alone (frs. B23, 25).

Heraclitus is even more scornful of his fellow men than Xenophanes is. "The crowd," he says (fr. B17), "give no thought to what they experience, nor do they learn if they are taught, but think that they do." He even puts Homer, Hesiod, Pythagoras, and Xenophanes into the same class of ignoramuses, saying that "much learning does not develop intelligence" (fr. B40); otherwise these four polymaths might have been wise. For "Wisdom is but one thing: to understand the thought by which all things are governed [or steered] through all things" (fr. B41). This wisdom apparently belongs to God alone, for to him (fr. B102), "all things are fair and good and just, whereas men think some things unjust and some just." It may be that this fragment, which comes to us from Porphyry (third century A.D.), is a simple statement of his faith that *sub specie aeternitatis* there is neither good nor evil. The odd thing is that he does not say that to God there is no good or evil, but that the distinction between good and evil exists on the human plane alone. It is worth pointing this out, since according to his general metaphysics, in so far as we can reconstruct it, good and evil ought to coalesce and be one, in which case to God there would be neither one nor the other. Here one can only raise a question: is he accepting the Greek commonplace that according to Nature everything is good and that man will find his goodness in "following Nature"? Just what following Nature would consist in is not clear; would it be accepting sensory evidence or knowing the cosmic law? In any event he insists in some passages on turning away not merely from this man's opinion or that man's, but from human opinion as a whole. "The human way has no wisdom," he says (fr. B78), "but the divine has."[25] But again he gives us no clue in the surviving fragments to just what the divine way would be.

Elsewhere (fr. B104) we find him castigating men who put their trust in the poets and the mob, "not knowing that many are evil, few good." As for his immediate fellow citizens, the Ephesians, they "from their youth upward" ought to be strung up and made to leave the city to adolescents, "for they have exiled Hermodorus, the most useful man among them, saying, Let there be no most useful man among us, or else let him go elsewhere and live among others" (fr. B121). Hermodorus, according to tradition, went to Rome after his expulsion from Ephesus and is said to have taken part in drawing up the Twelve Tables.[26] If this tradition is founded on fact, Heraclitus' contempt for the Ephesians may be based on their reluctance to accept a codified set of laws, such as seem to have been drawn up in many ancient cities during the seventh and sixth centuries. These laws acted to freeze

[25] Cf. frs. B79 and 83.
[26] For the evidence, see Burnet, *op. cit.*, pp. 131, n. 1, and 141, n. 1.

custom and we are told that the ancient world during this period was overthrowing the ruling power of the aristocracies and instituting something resembling popular government. It is probable that Heraclitus was a supporter of the old regime. To him (fr. B44) the people ought to fight for its laws as for its city walls. One surmises that the law to his mind was like the Law which steers the stars in their courses, the Furies which would pursue the Sun if it stepped out of its orbit.

In Empedocles we find a similar melancholy over man's fate, but it is expressed with none of the contempt expressed by Heraclitus. As we have said, the cosmos is going through a series of cycles in which Love and Strife have supremacy alternatively. In the reign of Love, the Golden Age, there was no war, no internal conflict, and even blood sacrifice was unknown (fr. B128). As in many other accounts of primitive times, men lived at peace with the beasts (fr. B130). But since Strife inevitably takes over the rule of the cosmos from Love, man is doomed to live in a period of bloodshed and even of human sacrifice (fr. B137). The one hope which a man living in an evil period of the cycle may have is the hope of rebirth in a happier time and in a happier form. There is one fragment (fr. B146), for instance, which comes to us from Clement of Alexandria (second century A.D.), which says that the souls of the wise will become gods. These wise men are presumably the prophets, composers of hymns, healers, and chiefs who will be welcomed to live among the gods. One may guess that such men arise because of the waning of Strife; at any rate they do appear as man's benefactors, somewhat like the culture heroes, and are a prefiguration of what life might be under the rule of Love. One might hazard the further guess that if Empedocles were asked for his appraisal of human life, he would reply that it would depend on what part of the cycle we were living in. But since it was customary for men who believed in the existence of a Golden Age also to believe that it was either in the remote past or that it would come into being in the equally remote future, Empedocles would have believed that his contemporaries were living in the Iron Age, as Hesiod did before him.

One would expect men who had definite ideas about the value of life to have written books on good and evil, or those corrective essays on human behavior which are written to reform the human race. We have, however, no fragments from any book on ethics written before the fifth century. Among the philosophers whom we have been considering, it is oddly enough Democritus, the atomist and materialist, whose ethical fragments survive. Odd, since after all, if only atoms and void are real, why should one worry about values?

Democritus, like most materialists, identifies goodness with pleasure and evil with pain (fr. B188). But unfortunately men seem to find their pleasures in passing things rather than in lasting (fr. B189). How then is one to discover what is of lasting pleasantness? The answer is, through the use of the reason (*logos*) which dwells within one's soul (fr. B187). Just how the reason operates is not clear, but there is some evidence that it accumulated experiences which would show it how some pleasures or goods are followed by pains or evils. It is not, if this evidence is worth anything, a purely *a priori* matter. According to Stobaeus, Democritus (fr. A167) called the state of mind which would characterize the happy man by a variety of names: happiness, cheerfulness, well-being, harmony, balance (symmetry), and peace of mind (*ataraxia*), terms which are also found in the writings of the Epicureans. Whether he actually used these particular terms or not, he apparently was interested in achieving a kind of inner calm which would result from a man's reflections, seeking pleasures without giving a thought to their consequences. If he believed that such advice was needed, it is obvious that he also thought most men to be heedless in the way they lived. He seems on better authority to have maintained that they are also burdened with superstitious fears, such as the fear of death (frs. B199, 206). Lacking understanding they wish to prolong life even if it is lived without pleasure (fr. B201). Such sentences are too short to be more than suggestions of his type of criticism, but in any event it is clear that he thought he had a way of improving man's lot and that he felt it needed improvement. This desire for an untroubled mind grew more and more common in the philosophic literature of antiquity, though, as it is hoped we shall see, the power of reason to satisfy the desire weakened and religious faith took its place. How deeply the philosophers felt the pressure of political revolution and social change, how poignantly they felt those sorrows which invasions and military defeats bring with them, we can only surmise. But it is indubitable that in their writings they all agreed that the solution for man's ills was to be found not in social organization against evil but in self-reliance. Their hatred of *The Many* is symptomatic of their individualism. A single man could find salvation for himself without the help of a church, a school, or any other institution. This, we hope, will become clearer when we come to discuss the ethical writings of the Epicureans and Stoics. Life then is to be appraised in accordance with the amount of harmless pleasure which it affords, according to Democritus. Harmless pleasure is pleasure which does not beget pain. And when it is found, man will have acquired peace of mind, an unruffled spirit, and final happiness.

It is clear then that the early philosophers, among whom we have intentionally included Democritus, had no lofty idea of the general run of their fellows. They believed, moreover, that the sole corrective to the evils of life was within the individual, not in the hands of fate, the gods, or of society. It has been pointed out by others that the Greeks as a whole were extreme individualists, having no organized religion, no church, but a collection of deities each of whom had his own cult. The advantage of this was the greater freedom of conscience which it encouraged in the individual; the disadvantage that it permitted the mob, acting in the name of tradition, to persecute the philosopher. Similarly in political affairs there seems to have been no noticeable loyalty to the city. The accounts of political leaders who did not hesitate to turn their coats, when it was to their profit to do so, are astonishing.[27] In intellectual matters the philosophers also differed on doctrinal theses, but on the whole they at least agreed that reason, in the sense of straightforward logical investigation, without the help of intuition, allegory, "the heart," revelation, or any other nonrational or suprarational insight, would show them the way to truth. Once one understood the difference between appearance and reality, one could adjust one's way of life to reality. And that would be the answer to the most urgent problems.

[27] The list of such men would include Hippias, the son of Pisistratus, who was to have been *Gauleiter* of Athens under the Persians, if they had won in 490; Alcibiades, whose shifts of allegiance are notorious; Themistocles, who prepared himself by a year's study for service under the son of Xerxes; Iphicrates, who served Thrace against Athens; and perhaps Antiphon and Theramenes, though opinions differ about their characters.

CHAPTER II

Rationalism
in Athens

THE PHILOSOPHERS WHOM WE have discussed so far are all associated with the periphery of the ancient world, the Pythagoreans in southern Italy, Anaximenes and Anaximander in Miletus, Heraclitus in Ephesus, and Democritus in Thrace. Yet there seems to be no peculiarly colonial character in their philosophies, nothing which would make them any different from other men's theories. One sees no striking influence of Oriental thought on those who wrote in Asia Minor, nothing especially primitive in the ideas of those who lived near the early Italians or Scythians. If we have grouped them together, it is partly because they are chronologically earlier than the men of whom we treat in this chapter, though that would not apply either to Zeno the Eleatic or to Democritus, and partly because it is traditional to do so. The notion that for some reason or other they were particularly interested in cosmological problems, such as the origin of things, is not borne out by the fragments which remain of their works, for these show quite as much interest in biology, and, in the case of

Parmenides and the Pythagoreans, in dialectical technique. The traditional interpretation of them as cosmologists derives from the first chapters of Aristotle's *Metaphysics*, but that was written to see to what extent his predecessors had made use of his four causes in their writings. And he found that for the most part they were interested only in his material cause. In fact, it is largely because of the fragmentary character of their literary remains that they are seen as precursors of the Athenian philosophers, rather than as their rivals. If we had their books in their entirety, it is likely that, in spite of the use to which Aristotle put them, we should see that they showed the same interest in noncosmological questions as their successors.

The fifth and early fourth centuries are usually and justifiably thought of as the period of Athenian cultural supremacy. It is the period which opens with those glorious years known as the Periclean Age (roughly 460–430 B.C.) and closes with the death of Aristotle (322 B.C.) and the decay of his school, the Lyceum. But this must not be taken to mean that something utterly new and unprecedented began at a given date and that it ended abruptly at another. On the contrary, we can see the same problems which are found in the early philosophers reappearing in the Athenians and the same problems which Aristotle investigated being elaborated in even greater detail after his death. We simply have more texts to go on from this period and consequently more information about what the philosophers thought and why they thought it, as well as more insight into the intellectual conflicts which stimulated philosophical reflection at this time. We have, moreover, more nonphilosophical writings, in which philosophical ideas are either reflected, combated, or reported, than in earlier periods. We know more about the political history of the time, more about cultural developments, more about the fine arts, and more about the personalities whose influence on philosophy may have been decisive. Yet in spite of this we do not know with any impressive degree of certainty why this age should have contained so many men of genius.

Throughout European history there have been similar periods which are named after powerful individuals, usually rulers. We have the Augustan Age in Rome, the Age of Charlemagne in northern Europe, the Age of Lorenzo de' Medici in Florence, the Age of Elizabeth I in England, the Age of Louis XIV in France. All these ages have in common a concentration of the arts and sciences either about a court or in a city or its surroundings. The personal influence of a ruler such as Pericles or Augustus or Charlemagne, his interest in enriching his capital, his desire to protect men of outstanding ability, his willingness to spend money for the attainment of such purposes, must not be discounted, however fashionable the purely economic interpretation of history may be. The wealth of the Spanish rulers after the conquest of South America did little if anything comparable to Periclean Athens or Augustan Rome in the Iberian peninsula, nor has the unprecedented wealth of modern North America produced in the United States an Aeschylus, a Sophocles, or even a Euripides. Without riches, it is unlikely that Pericles could have beautified Athens, but riches have not sufficed elsewhere to produce a Phidias. What has to be explained, moreover, is not the appearance in a given locality of a great architect, a great poet, a great philosopher, or a great statesman. On the contrary, the problem is to explain the appearance of a group of such men all working at the same time and in the same city. But that would seem to be, as far as Athens is concerned, a unique event and the unique is precisely the inexplicable or, if one prefer, the accidental.

The Periclean Age lasted for thirty years. It was followed by continued war and the political overthrow of Athenian independence. Pericles died in 429, two years after the outbreak of the Peloponnesian War, which ended a generation later (404 B.C.) in the utter ruination of the city. But in the middle of the fourth century (338 B.C.) she was conquered by Macedonia and from then on declined in military and political strength. But that did not prevent the rise of men like Plato and Aristotle, to say nothing of the great orators, the writers of the New Comedy, Zeno the

Stoic and Chrysippus at the end of the fourth century along with Epicurus a bit later.[1] In sculpture we have the names, if not the works, of Paeonius, Myron, Polyclitus, and of course Phidias, while in the fourth century we have that of Praxiteles. The works of these men are no longer stylish and current taste prefers more "primitive" art. But nevertheless, during the Italian Renaissance and in the so-called Neoclassic Period, they were the inspiration—through Roman copies and modern casts—of artists who were by no means contemptible. But we are not interested in appraising such artists; we are simply saying that their existence and their influence are enough to prove that cultural life in Athens, and indeed elsewhere in Greece, did not die out with military defeat and economic decline.

I

1. The earliest in date of the philosophers living in Athens is Anaxagoras who came there from Clazomenae. Most of the fragments which remain deal with cosmological and epistemological questions, but there appears dimly in them a notion that behind the veil of sensory perception lies a truth which most men do not apprehend. That truth is that regardless of perceived changes, there is no mutability in the real world. "The Greeks," he says (fr. B17), "are wrong in thinking that there is coming-into-being and destruction. For nothing comes into being, nor is it destroyed, but from the things which are there is both mixture and separation." Here he agrees with Empedocles. "Therefore they would rightly call coming-into-being mixture and destruction separation." It is because of the weakness of our senses that we do not see the truth (fr. B21). Now what would we see if we did see it? We should see that all qualities are always present in everything,

---

[1] So in our own times, to take but one example, France throughout most of the nineteenth century has been the victim of wars, revolutions, financial disasters, and political turmoil, and yet has produced writers, painters, sculptors, and architects of genius.

but in such tiny amounts that they are imperceptible to us now. Yet the fact that we cannot perceive them does not entail the belief that they do not exist: our organs of perception are simply too weak to apprehend them. Their existence, then, is inferred from the principle which had been used by other philosophers, namely, that it is irrational to believe in the spontaneous appearance of anything. In the beginning, says Anaxagoras (fr. B1), "all things were together, unlimited both in multitude and in smallness. For smallness too was unlimited [infinitesimal?]. And since all things were together, nothing was discernible because of its small size."[2] As we have said, behind this argument there seems to lie the principle *ex nihilo nihil*, since Anaxagoras is emphatic in denying the possibility of genesis and destruction. His critique then is once more a critique of sensory experience.

But, like most of his contemporaries, he is also interested in the problem of how things got to be the way they are. In other words he not only makes an epistemological analysis of the world but also assumes the historical point of view. Epistemologically the world is split between what our gross senses perceive and what the reason knows to be the case. Our sense organs are too obtuse to grasp the mixture of qualities which is present in everything. So today a painter might point out that if we looked through a magnifying glass at his canvas, we should see little grains of yellow and of blue pigment in the areas which appear green to the naked eye. He could then say, if it served his purpose, that the area of the canvas is "really" covered with yellow and blue grains, but that it appears to be green. This might include, as one sees, an explanation of why the area in question appears to be green, an explanation based on the laws of perceptual psychology. Similarly one might say that the world which we experience is really molecules or atoms or whatever is believed to be inside the atoms, and presumably descriptions could be elaborated of how and why it does

[2] The problem remains of how Anaxagoras would have measured "size." Would it have been by volume or by weight? Or is he thinking of sensory qualities?

not appear to be so. But no such statement would be historical in the sense that it would give us a chronological account of how things once were subatomic particles whirling about in empty space, of how they came together to form atoms at a later date, of how then the atoms formed molecules which finally cohered to build up macroscopic objects. Such an account would be logically independent of the epistemological analysis, in that, though it assumes the chronological priority of the elemental particles, one could also assume their chronological postcriority. For we have no revelation that the analytically simple is first in time.

But to Anaxagoras an account of reality had to include an explanation of the origin of things as we find them. Since there is no such thing as genesis and destruction, he was driven to concluding that all qualities were mixed up together at the beginning of the world. The process of cosmic history is the separating out of the mixture of the various things which we perceive. "But before these things were separated from one another, when all things were together, not even color was visible, for the mixture of all things prevented it, both the mixture of the moist and the dry and that of the hot and the cold, and of the light and the dark, and of the great quantity of earth that was in it and of the mass of unlimited things resembling one another in no way. For none of the other things"—that is presumably the other qualities—"resembles any other. And since these things are so, we must believe that all things are inherent in the whole" (fr. B4). How then did the separation take place?

Here Anaxagoras, like Empedocles, assumes that nothing would change "of its own accord." But whereas Empedocles introduced the two agents of Love and Strife to do the attracting and repelling, Anaxagoras assumes the existence of only one agent, which he called *Nous* or Mind. Now *Nous* is both unlimited and self-ruled, "and is mixed with nothing, but is alone by itself and in itself" (fr. B12). It has none of the seeds of things in it but is the power which brings order into them. Though he uses physicalistic terms to describe it, calling it the lightest and purest of all things, he also attributes to it mental powers. He speaks of it as having "all knowledge of everything," and "the greatest strength." Moreover, "it rules over all things whatsoever that are animate, both greater and smaller. And *Nous* ruled over the revolution of the whole, so that it revolved in the beginning." The revolution began on a small scale and then spread in wider and wider areas, until now the heavenly bodies are moved around in it. It is because of this revolution, started by *Nous*, that the elemental qualities were separated. Hence the agent of change is something mental in its nature and change is separation and, presumably, recombination. The introduction of physicalistic terms in the description of *Nous* is no stranger than the Stoics' use of a material substance, the *Pneuma*, or Spirit, as their active force. The *Pneuma* was a material being and yet it behaved as something divine.

The introduction of a mental agent, completely distinct from all other things which are inert, incapable of initiating any change, was seen by the ancients themselves as something novel in philosophy. Plato makes Socrates (*Phaedrus* 270a) recall the influence of this thesis upon Pericles and he has him say (*Phaedo* 97b, c), "Having once heard someone read from a book, so it was said, by Anaxagoras," in which it was maintained that *Nous* is the orderer as well as the cause of all things, he was very pleased and interpreted the word "cause" to mean the purpose of all change. If he was to show him that the earth was either flat or round, he would also show him why this was good, and he would demand no other kind of causality. But (98b) he failed to do this and his *Nous* was no better than any other kind of cause. Aristotle also, in a famous passage in his *Metaphysics* (984b 15), says that when a man, whom he identifies as Anaxagoras, said that mind (*Nous*) was present in all things as the cause of the cosmos and of its order, he seemed like a sober man in contrast with the babblers who were his predecessors. But Aristotle too, like the Platonic Socrates, was disappointed in him, for to his way of thinking a causal explanation should include purpose. Anaxagoras' *Nous* then, though mental, was not teleological. It was apparently sufficient for it to be an orderer. Its work seems to have been entirely mechanical and what was separated out of the primordial mixture, in spite of being spoken of in qualitative terms, was moved about in space. The mind then could move material things as the human mind moves our muscles. That the one predominant cause of things is distinguished from the inert grosser things is the start of a dualistic theory which was to grow to much larger proportions in later times. For before it was completely elaborated, mind became the universal agent; it became immaterial, spiritual, acting either in accordance with something to be called the reason or as it saw fit. It had purposes analogous to human purposes. Its patient became the material world, inert, utterly inefficacious. There were thus in later times two occupants of the philosopher's universe, Mind and Matter, God and Creation, Soul and Body, according to his predilections. And the former of each of these couples became Reality, the latter Appearance, though there remained no way of experiencing Reality except through its Appearances. But when the difficulties inherent in this point of view became pressing, men then tried to define a being which would never appear and yet remain purely active.

2. It is no longer possible to discover why Anaxagoras picked out the Mind as the one active being in the cosmos, but it is possible that men's attention had been directed toward mental activity by the simple experience of having to make great decisions in the face of external dangers, such as the Persian War. At such a time and after such battles as that of Marathon in which an army of ten thousand men defeated one of fifty thousand, it would have been as difficult to imagine that men's deeds were all determined by external material forces as it would have been after the Napoleonic Wars.[3] The human will could not be thought of as ineffectual except by some elaborate metaphysical theory which no one at that time had drawn up. Not even as late as Aristotle was any

[3] Cf. the remarks of the Abbé Bautain as quoted in G. Boas, *French Philosophies of the Romantic Period* (Baltimore: Johns Hopkins Press, 1925), p. 33.

sharp distinction made between the will and the reason, any distinction such as was to be made for religious purposes by the early Christians. The basic distinction was rather that between the reason and the passions, and in the word "passion" was the connotation of "being acted upon" in contrast to "acting." It was assumed as a matter of course that unless a person was constrained by force, he was free to make whatever decisions he wished to make. He could make bad decisions to be sure, but they too were his own and not the result of unknown outside influences acting upon him.

The break between appearance and reality which we have seen in Anaxagoras was paralleled in human affairs by that between nature and custom. Other historians[4] have pointed out how the development of an urban civilization demanded closer attention to psychology and consequently to the procedures of thinking. It has been said that the rise of courts of law in which all citizens might be called upon to act as both judge and jury, to defend themselves, to argue and plead and debate, was enough to arouse the desire for skill in both the logic of persuasion and that of conviction. There is doubtless some justice in this explanation. But the dialectical skill of Parmenides is certainly as great as that of any Athenian and he lived in a minor settlement in southern Italy. The puzzles of his disciple, Zeno, have not yet been satisfactorily solved,[5] and if we work over them today, it is not because of any need to win suits in court or to defend ourselves against charges of felony. The most we can say is that during the Periclean Age we have evidence of more interest in forensic technique than we have for any earlier period.

There is no need for me to hold back the information that the men who are said to have done most in this field are the Sophists

---

[4] See especially E. Zeller, *History of Greek Philosophy*, trans. by S. F. Alleyne (London: Longmans, 1881), Vol. II, p. 394; and G. Grote, *History of Greece* (London: John Murray, 1888), chap. 67.

[5] One of the latest and most interesting solutions is that of Adolf Grünbaum, "Modern Science and Refutation of the Paradoxes of Zeno," *The Scientific Monthly*, LXXXI, No. 5 (November, 1955), 234.

and Socrates. For our immediate purposes we can say that for the Sophists truth, goodness, and beauty were determined by custom, not by nature. The reverse was true for Socrates. Just what was meant by the two opposing terms requires further analysis.

When the colonial philosophers spoke of Nature, they seem to have meant something equivalent to the cosmos, the universal order of things. They also seem to have assumed that there was one consistent body of laws covering the behavior of everything both animate and inanimate. Their epistemology drew upon the data of investigations into such laws. One of the great differences, if we may trust Theophrastus, in the epistemological theories of the Greeks was their assumption of how sensory objects influenced the sense organs, some maintaining that each organ was affected by qualities similar to something in the organ, others that each was affected by something dissimilar. This conclusion is, as all such conclusions must be in view of the fragmentary nature of the evidence, a bit shaky. They may indeed have made psychological investigations which have been lost, since what is preserved is what interested the people who quoted them. But when we come to the Athenian philosophers, the question was bound to arise of how the supposed universal laws of Nature could cover human behavior and at the same time permit the variations, of which everyone is aware, in what human beings do and want and esteem. Laws, in the sense of customs and traditions, vary to a great extent, whereas Law, in the sense of natural law, ought to be uniform. If then all behavior of the human race obeys natural law, there should be no such variations. The conflict between Nature and Custom then was one which would be observed directly when a people came into contact with people of different cultures. That there was such conflict had already been noted by Herodotus. But, with the exception of the Egyptians, that historian and traveler seemed to have no feeling that the customs of non-Greeks or Barbarians were worthy of more than noting as ethnological curiosities. The situation was similar to that which prevailed among aestheticians up to recent times. The arts of Savages, and indeed even of the Chinese and Japanese, were not thought of as genuine works of art; an ethnologist might describe them, but an art critic would have nothing to do with them.[6] For that matter it is only lately that ethnologists have dropped the distinction between civilized and uncivilized peoples. The most that writers would concede to the latter was that they were primitive, that is, the seed of our own civilization, baby cultures of which we were the mature fruit. In German such people were called *Naturvölker*, natural people, as if they were controlled by laws resident in the cosmic order, something akin to the animals, who had no civilization added to what Nature had bestowed on them. The distinction between a natural and a civilized people thus seems to rest upon the assumption that Custom was added to Nature. And when a philosopher had a high esteem for Nature, he was likely to depreciate Custom.

Custom in that sense became the logical equivalent of appearance; Nature the equivalent of reality. Like reality it had to be uniform and immutable. To discover it one had to penetrate the screen of local diversities and mutabilities. In an anonymous manuscript which apparently dates from the end of the fifth century, usually referred to as the *Dissoi Logoi* (or *Dialexeis*), we find a list of the contrary opinions held by various peoples concerning good and evil, beauty and ugliness, right and wrong, truth and falsity, the difference between sanity and insanity, wisdom and ignorance, and on the awarding of offices by lot.[7] This, along with an extract from a treatise on correct behavior preserved by Iamblichus (fourth century A.D.), the author of which is referred to as Anonymus Iamblichi, and which is dated as of the middle of the fifth century, is the source of arguments which tend to prove that human values are determined by Custom.

The *Dissoi Logoi* is a perfect example of the kind of conflicting opinions which must be reconciled if moral and other standards

---

[6] This was also true even of "primitive" Italian painting as late as the opening of the Jarves Collection at Yale, for which an apologia was found in its historical interest.

[7] For the Greek text, see Diels-Kranz, Vol. II, pp. 405 ff.

are to be demonstrated as based on Nature; it is merely one of those bits of moral advice which we find in more copious form in such writers as Maximus of Tyre (second century A.D.). A quotation from the *Dissoi Logoi* will serve to illustrate the source of the problem.

Double opinions are held in Greece by those who philosophize concerning good and evil. For one man says that the good is one thing and evil another; but another says they are the same, which to one man is good and to another evil. And to a given man a thing may at one time be good and at another time evil.

This obviously does not mean that there is no distinction to be made between good and evil, but rather that the value given a thing is determined by the occasion on which the value is assigned and on the person who assigns it. For the quotation continues by saying that food and drink and sexual intercourse are bad to a sick man but good to a healthy man who needs them. Oddly enough, here the value is determined by the effect of the things in question upon the individual, so that the author of the passage seems to be maintaining that apart from the individual's appraisal, the things themselves may have some value. But, though the distinction is not made in so many words, it is clear that two kinds of value are being discussed: the value the thing has as a pleasant or unpleasant experience, and the value which it has as an instrument for the attainment of some end, in this particular case, health. The confusion between the two kinds of value appears throughout. Thus food, drink, and sexual intercourse may be bad for the incontinent but good for the person who makes money out of them. Shipwrecks are bad for the shipmaster, but good for the shipbuilder. For iron to rust is good for the smith but bad for other men. After pointing out the relativity of these values to individuals and groups, the author proceeds to point out the logical difficulties involved in identifying good and evil. If a man is asked whether it is good to beget many children and replies that it is, then, if good and evil are identical, it is also bad to beget many children. Such apparent paradoxes arise from forgetting what seemed to be the initial premise, namely, that values are assigned by the individual with regard to the situation in which he finds himself. But a reading of the *Double Words* will convince the most sympathetic critic that it is far from being a careful analysis of the question. Its burden is simply that good and evil are determined by human beings, not by Nature.

Now "nature" is one of the most ambiguous words in Greek literature. In Homer, where the word occurs once (*Odyssey* x. 303), it refers to the character or quality of a thing. But at least as early as Sophocles, it refers to the permanent or innate quality, as contrasted with the transitory. For instance, in *Philoctetes* (902) we find the clause, "When a man forsakes his own nature and does unseemly deeds." Again in *Ajax* (472), when the mad hero is accused of cowardice, he tries to show that the accusation is false, and cries, "Some deed must yet be sought to show my aged father that his son is not in his real nature a coward." The use of "nature" as the name for reality as contrasted with appearance is shown in the titles which the doxographers gave to the works of the early philosophers: "About Nature." In Plato's *Laws* (891c) we find Plato saying that when the early philosophers made fire and water and earth and air the primary elements, they called them the nature of things. It was this sense of the word which was contrasted with custom or law. But here again, what is characteristic of custom is its variability, and the real, it was assumed, could not be variable. Hence if good and evil were determined by Nature, they would be immutable and obviously not subject to tribal whims or traditions. The Sophists, as far as is known, were inclined to accept custom as the basis for good and evil; the anti-Sophists, Nature.[8]

3. The earliest and most serious of the Sophists was Protagoras and, though we have but one quotation from his works, "Man is the measure of all things," we have reason to believe that a long

[8] For a detailed account of Nature as norm, see Lovejoy and Boas, *Primitivism in Antiquity*, chap. 3 and Appendix. The index to that volume, *s.v.*, will provide references to specific passages in which the normative meaning of the term is used.

speech of his given in Plato's dialogue, *Protagoras* (320c–323a), represents some of his ideas. We shall first discuss the various meanings of "Man is the measure."

This quotation is first given by Plato, as follows (*Theaetetus* 151e): "The measure of all things is man, of things that are, that they are, of those that are not, that they are not."[9] This may mean (1) that existence and nonexistence are determined by human nature as a whole, that there is no escaping the human equation or what Bacon was to call the Idols of the Tribe, that to penetrate to the character of Nature as if human nature did not exist is impossible, and that consequently all truth is human truth. But it may also mean (2) that each individual man determines his own individual truth and that there is no resolving the differences in opinion. In other words, human nature is as impossible to describe as Nature itself. There is no such thing as general laws true of all human beings, but each man's experience is a self-contained universe in which he is enclosed. It may furthermore mean (3) that the measure in question is not man's total experience, but his perceptions. Since perceptions vary with each individual, according to his age, state of health, sensory acuity, and the like, there will be no bridge between man and man and no possibility of criticizing the opinions of anyone. The reason for interpreting Protagoras in this way rests upon the belief that he accepted a kind of Heraclitean theory according to which the objects of perception are always in a state of flux and that therefore our perceptions of them are similarly unstable. He may indeed have believed this, though it would be singularly self-contradictory for a man both to argue that individual perceptions were alone true and to maintain anything whatsoever of the extraperceptual world. Philosophers have, to be sure, been guilty of inconsistencies, but this one would be so flagrant that a man of any critical skill would have avoided it.

It seems more reasonable to conclude that the import of the

---

[9] This is quoted again in the same words by Sextus Empiricus, *Adv. math.* i. 60.

statement is the denial of the distinction between appearance and reality. What had been called appearance, Protagoras seems to be maintaining, is the only reality which we have. It is therefore useless to search for another reality behind the appearances. If this is what he was driving at, it is understandable that he also is quoted by Eusebius (fr. A4) as saying that he did not know whether or not the gods existed, not that they did not exist. And in Diogenes Laertius (ix. 51) he is said to have added that the obscurity of the question and the shortness of life prevented his knowing. If Diogenes is quoting him exactly and if Protagoras was serious, he was apparently saying that if a question was clear, it could be answered. But for a question put by one man to another to be clear entails the belief that meanings are interpersonal. In which case at least some knowledge is common to several individuals. This is fortified by the acknowledged fact that Protagoras was a teacher.

We are a bit more fortunate in our knowledge of a contemporary of Protagoras, Gorgias of Leontini, though what remains of him is also fragmentary. There is first the account given in Pseudo-Aristotle's *De Melisso, Xenophane, Gorgia*, and a long argument preserved by Sextus Empiricus in his *Adversus mathematicos* (vii. 65 ff., fr. B3). The quotation from Sextus is taken from a book by Gorgias called *About Nonbeing or Nature*, a significant title. The two accounts are fairly consistent, but since Pseudo-Aristotle is probably the earlier writer, we shall follow him here. The argument runs in summary (a) that nothing exists, (b) that if anything existed, it could not be apprehended, (c) that if it could be apprehended, it could not be put into words and communicated to others. The nonexistence of anything is proved as follows. He first collected the opinions of others, as in the *Dissoi Logoi*, which showed both belief in Being as many and in Being as one, in Being as having never been produced and in Being as having been produced. He then maintains that if anything exists, it must be either one or many, without beginning or with beginning. But for anything not to be, is for it to be Nonbeing, and that amounts to asserting the paradox that what is not, is. But Nonbeing is Nonbeing and Being is Being; therefore both exist. But since there must be a basic contrast between Nonbeing and Being, if Nonbeing is, then Being must not be. Hence nothing could exist unless both Nonbeing and Being were identical, Q.E.D. In Sextus the argument is slightly different. He puts it as follows: If anything existed, it would be either the existent or the nonexistent, or both. The nonexistent cannot exist, for if it did, then it would be both existent and nonexistent, and that is absurd. Moreover, if it did exist, the existent would not exist, for that would make nonexistence an attribute of existence, which is again absurd.

Now if anything is, it must have always been or have come into being. If it has always been, then it is limitless (infinite), but the limitless cannot exist anywhere. For if it were somewhere, it would be in something different from itself and that something would limit it. But nothing can limit the limitless. Therefore it has not always existed. But neither can it have come into being. For nothing could come into being either out of Being or out of Nonbeing. It could not come into being, for that would constitute a change in Being—into Becoming?—nor could it come into being out of Nonbeing, for then Nonbeing would cease to be inexistent. And nothing can come into being out of nothing. Hence since everything must either have been forever or come into being at some time and both are impossible, nothing can be.

Before moving on to the impossibility of knowledge, it may be worth while to examine this argument. First, it will be observed that this is exactly the same type of dialectic as that used by Zeno in his proof against the existence of motion. For in both cases it is assumed that whatever is being discussed must belong to one of two classes which exhaust the universe. If it belongs to one, it cannot belong to the other. Second, the Law of Contradiction is applied as if it were an existential description. Now so far as existence is concerned, a thing cannot move and be at rest at the same time and in the same respect. But obviously a thing can now move and now be at rest. There is similarly no reason why something cannot now exist and then cease to exist. But if the term "the existent" is equated with everything which ever has been, is now, and ever will be, then it is removed from time and becomes the name for something to which the Law of Contradiction is irrelevant in so far as that law contains any reference to dates and respects. But though we use the same word "is" both to mean the copula which attributes a predicate to a subject and also to mean existence, Gorgias fuses the two meanings and slips from one to the other as suits his purpose. Third, it will be noticed that when Gorgias argues about the impossibility of both the existent and the nonexistent existing, he is not denying that some things now exist and then cease to exist, but that all things lumped together into a whole which he calls the existent, do not also not exist. For if it were a matter of individuals or groups less than the whole, there would be no reason why some things such as "chariots racing on the sea" (Ps-Aristotle, 980a) to which we might add chimeras and mermaids should not exist, while other things, such as men, trees, and mountains should and do exist. But Gorgias has to have one all-inclusive subject for his sentences. Fourth, though the whole argument is *a priori* and purely dialectical, he does resort to experience when he says, according to Sextus, that if the existent exists, it must be either a quantity or a continuum or a magnitude or a body. Regardless of the exact meaning of these terms, which is far from clear, how does Gorgias know that they exhaust the possibilities? The color red is none of them, a dream is none of them, and a law is none of them. And each is one thing in some reasonable sense of the word "one." Sextus tells us neither on what grounds Gorgias thought the four to be exhaustive of the possibilities nor even if there could be any doubt about it. Moreover, Gorgias says that each of the four, according to Sextus, can be divided, and he uses this as an argument against their unity. But why should not a unit be divided? Presumably because, like

Aristotle later, he maintained that *One* is not a number but that of which numbers are composed,[10] and that it is atomic.

Since his two remaining theses are presented more clearly in Sextus than in Pseudo-Aristotle, we shall follow the former in presenting them. The second thesis then is that if anything existed, it could not be thought. He reasons first to the conclusion that some things that are thought, such as flying men and chariots running over the sea, do not exist, thus making a sharp distinction between thought and existence. This turns the whole debate into an *a posteriori* argument, for unless one already knew that men did not fly, one could not conclude that all things which are thought need not exist. Without such previous knowledge, one might argue that the limits of thought and existence were coincidental. But if they were coincidental, then that which is not thought would not exist and what does not exist would not be thought. But again we know that some nonexistent things, such as Scylla and the Chimera, are thought to exist. Gorgias is slipping here for he is no longer using purely logical arguments. Indeed he continues to slip and we find him saying, "Just as the things seen are called visible because of the fact that they are seen . . . and we do not reject visible things because they are not heard . . . (for each object ought to be judged by its own special sense and not by another), so also the things thought will exist, even if they should not be viewed by the sight nor heard by hearing, because they are perceived by their own proper criterion. If then a man thinks that a chariot is running over the sea, even if he does not see it, he ought to believe that there exists a chariot running over the sea. But this is absurd . . . " (*Adv. Math.* vii. 81 f., fr. B3). Why is it absurd? Presumably because one knows and knows truly that chariots do not run over water. But this does not follow from the argument. It is knowledge acquired previously to the dialectical web. And similarly, if "each object ought to be judged by its own special sense," then whatever "sense" judges that chariots do

[10] See *Metaphysics* 1016b 18, and Ross's commentary on 1021a 12 and 1052b 23. For the meanings of "one" in Aristotle, see *Metaphysics* ix.

run over the sea should be the test of the truth of that judgment.

What then has Gorgias succeeded in doing? Like Zeno he has shown the inadequacy of formal reasoning to demonstrating factual or existential judgments. Just as Zeno did not maintain that we do not see arrows flying, but merely that we cannot prove the possibility of motion, so Gorgias does not deny that we think of chariots running over water or of other impossibilities. The problem is how we know that they can or cannot exist as such.

His third thesis, that even if things can be apprehended or thought, our apprehension or thought cannot be communicated, is perhaps more cogent. For he points out that if all objects are grasped by special senses, vision, audition, and so on, and if our communications are made through speech, all that we communicate are words and not our sensory perceptions. Our words, moreover, are the names for the various sensory objects but are not identical with them. When spoken they are sounds. But these sounds are not the visible or other sensory things which they name. And, if one may add a point to Gorgias' demonstration, the names are universals, the things perceived particulars. Hence we do not pass on to others the sensory impressions which we receive from the external world. Each man, so to speak, lives in a self-enclosed world of his impressions and ideas, as Hume would have called it, and there is no way of breaking out of it. This version of the cognitive situation persisted in Occidental philosophy down to our own times, and we find the empiricists of both Great Britain and the United States busy with finding ways of escape, sometimes by arguing that what we perceive are universals and not particulars (essences), sometimes by what Santayana called animal faith, sometimes by maintaining, as Locke did, that some of our impressions resemble qualities of objects, sometimes by maintaining that our ideas are effects produced in us by ideas in the mind of God, to cite but a few of the proposed solutions.

Gorgias thus seems to flatten out the world into a world of perceptions which are the individual possessions of individual perceivers. That there is anything behind the perceptions which might be called Nature, cannot be proved. The question, however, will be bound to arise of why, if there is nothing in the world but our personal experiences, the problem of there being something "behind" them should ever arise. It does arise nevertheless and arises from common sense, from that stock of beliefs which we inherit from our elders and with which we grow up. Such beliefs may turn out to be unjustified, but if so, they should not raise any problems other than that of why we retain or reject them. And that is a psychological problem with relevance only to our states of mind. The problem, for instance, of why some people still believe that the world is flat is not a physical but a psychological question. That it looks flat to people who do not travel for long distances can be explained by the geographer, but if someone still believes it to be flat after its real shape has been demonstrated, the geographer can shrug his shoulders and leave the field to the psychiatrist. But in the case of Gorgias, it is doubtful whether the common-sense beliefs about existence and communication can be explained if the views held by him are accepted. The best that such a philosopher can do is to attribute such beliefs to error and leave the origin of the error untouched.

If we call a view of this sort phenomenalistic, then we can say that it never became an integral part of the classical tradition in philosophy. Its role became that of a sharp critic of other people's ideas. The skepticism which was inherent in it developed well into Christian times and was of use to Christian apologists. It is interesting to note that Eusebius preserved the views of Protagorus about the gods in his *Praeparatio evangelica* to show that even some of the pagans were skeptical about polytheism. Moreover, even Plato felt the necessity of refuting the opinions of the Sophists as a group, sometimes contemptuously but sometimes, as when he deals with Protagoras and Prodicus, with respect. But it is precisely because their ideas were plausible that they required refutation, for philosophy progresses by debate. For our purposes they constitute the first serious attack on rationalism, and it was made by the rationalistic technique itself.

4. Just what Socrates stood for is no clearer than what the Sophists stood for. They, moreover, wrote copiously and bequeathed next to nothing to posterity; he wrote nothing and bequeathed more than any other one man except his pupil Plato and Plato's pupil, Aristotle.[11] There are three primary sources for our knowledge of this extraordinary man, Aristophanes, Xenophon, and Plato. And unfortunately their testimonies differ in important respects. To Aristophanes he was a mischievous and pretentious scientist, teaching for money and willing to take on pupils who would learn to argue in order to win suits, regardless of the merits of their cause. His main caricature of Socrates appears in the *Clouds* where, it is clear, Socrates is guilty of denying the traditional gods of Athens, just as he was accused of doing at his trial. In the middle of the play Honest and Dishonest Reasoning engage in debate, as in a morality play. Honest Reasoning is a spokesman for the Good Old Times when boys walked down to their music master's soberly in a column, behaved with modesty, and spoke in low whispers, whereas Dishonest Reasoning points out that such a life is hardly worth living. Dishonest Reasoning becomes the spokesman for Socrates.[12] The debate is one between cunning logical tricks, "making the worse appear the better reason," playing on double meanings, holding out seductive pleas-

[11] It is interesting to note that in the Parian Chronicle (264–263 B.C.) his death seemed an important enough event to be recorded along with the return of the Ten Thousand as the two outstanding events of the year. See Marcus N. Tod, *A Selection of Greek Historical Inscriptions* (Oxford: Clarendon Press, 1948), Vol. II, p. 308.

[12] The debate begins at l. 889. In view of the discrepancy between the Aristophanic and the Xenophontic-Platonic picture of Socrates, the German philologist, Karl Joel, in his *Der echte und der Xenophontische Sokrates* (Berlin: Gaertner, 1893–1901), maintained that the Socrates of the *Clouds* is not a historical portrait of the man but a synthesis of him and Antisthenes. But it should be recalled that in Plato's *Symposium* (221b) we find Alcibiades quoting l. 362 from the *Clouds* as at least an accurate picture of Socrates' appearance. Moreover, in the *Frogs* (1491–9) we have another picture of Socrates which agrees with that of the *Clouds*. But is there anything unusual in finding a single man portrayed in diverse and conflicting ways by various writers? Americans have only to recall the various literary portraits of F. D. Roosevelt which have not ceased to appear or the harshly opposing interpretations of John Dewey.

ures as *argumenta ad hominem* on the one hand, and straightforward, honest common sense on the other. But it is also the battle between ancient simplicity and modern luxury, Spartan hardness and modern Athenian effeminacy. It is Socrates who leads youth into debauchery and incontinence, though the picture of him and his disciples in the *Phrontisterion* is one of squalor. In short, one might find in the *Clouds*, if that were all one had to go on, full justification of the charges brought against him in his trial, even of the charge of atheism. When Strepsiades swears by the gods, Socrates asks, "What sort of gods do you swear by?" and he adds that the gods are not current coin with his school (247 f.). And when he comes to invoke his own gods, he says (264 ff.),

> O Lord and Master, immeasurable Air, who holdest the earth
>   from on high,
> And thou, Radiant Aether, and ye august Clouds, hurlers of
>   thunderbolts,
> Arise, appear, O goddesses, from on high to the philosopher.

And when Strepsiades (367) asks him if Zeus is not a god, he replies, "What Zeus? Don't talk nonsense. There is no Zeus." And, finally, he asks Strepsiades whether he will disavow all other deities if admitted to his school except "these three, Chaos and the Clouds and the Tongue" (423).[13]

The picture of Socrates in Xenophon's *Memorabilia* is drawn to show that not only did Socrates not corrupt men, but he elevated them and improved them by his example and teaching. He is depicted mainly as a teacher of ethics, though full attention is paid to his method of teaching, his purgation of his pupils' minds, and his irony. The emphasis laid on his ethical teachings leads one to suspect that popular opinions supported Aristophanes, for it is safe to say that the People are more sensitive to examinations of traditional morals than to almost anything else. To them right is right and wrong is wrong and there need be no arguing about

---

[13] Socrates was also ridiculed in another comedy which appeared at the same time as the *Clouds*, the *Connus* of Amipsias. See W. J. M. Starkie in his translation of the *Clouds* (London: Macmillan and Co., 1911), p. xxix.

them. As for his atheism, Xenophon tries to refute that charge by laying stress on his piety and his dislike of cosmological speculation (*Mem.* i. 1. 11). Where Aristophanes got the idea that Socrates was an atheist, by which he meant a doubter of the old gods, I do not know. But if Socrates had read the book of Anaxagoras and if Aristophanes knew that he had read it, that might have sufficed to arouse the suspicion.

The Platonic Socrates is not discordant with the Xenophontic, but the difficulty in the dialogues is to tell who is Socrates and who is Plato. One thing is fairly certain: that in the *Apology* there would have been no reason for its author to put ideas into the mouth of his hero which were different from those which he held, though the words might be quite different. *Crito* and *Phaedo* also probably do not distort the Socratic position, since in them too an attempt is made to report what actually took place before the execution. The former tells of Crito's plan for his master to evade execution and Socrates' refusal to violate the law which has condemned him; the latter is an account of the last hours before he drank the hemlock. Plato says that he himself was ill and could not be present, but he gives a long list of those who were present, as if to point out that there were witnesses to what he reports. If then one restricts oneself to these three dialogues, one is in all likelihood not misrepresenting the thought and character of this man.

In the *Apology* (18b) Socrates recognizes the charges which were made against him by gossips, names unknown, and one comic writer (Aristophanes) that "there was a certain Socrates, a philosopher, who both meditated on heavenly things and tried to uproot all subterranean things as well as to make the worse reason the better." Such people believe that cosmologists are atheists. "These accusers are numerous and have been making their accusation for some time" (18c). The charges are then read: "Socrates is guilty and wastes his time seeking the things which are below the earth and in the heavens and making the worse appear the better reason, and teaching others to do likewise"

(19b). To the charge of being a cosmologist, he replies by a flat denial, asking who has ever heard him even discuss such a matter. It is also false (19d, e) that he has ever taught for money. He would be glad to be able to teach anything worth paying for, but he has not that gift (20c). What then does he know? He then relates the story of Chaerephon's asking the oracle of Delphi who was wiser than Socrates. The oracle replied that no one was wiser. After due search and reflection, he concluded that whereas others knew nothing but thought that they knew something, he alone knew nothing and knew that he knew nothing (21d). It was the search leading to this discovery which won him so many enemies. "This same search I still carry on as I go about, and in accordance with the god, I question anyone among the citizens and strangers who I think is wise. And when he does not appear to be so, coming to the aid of the god, I demonstrate that he is not wise" (23b.)

This habit of questioning people who have pretensions to wisdom has been taken up by the young men of leisure who have frequented his society, and when they have shown up in their turn the men whom they have questioned, it is not they but their teacher who has been held at fault. This leads to the second point: he is accused of corrupting the youth, of not believing in the gods of the city, and of substituting new gods in their place. He answers this charge by pointing out that he believes in the existence of *daimones* who are the children of gods, and hence, unless he believed in gods, he could scarcely believe in their children (27d). But there is one divinity in whom he believes and who is the cause of Meletus' accusation. "Within me is this thing which began in my childhood; a certain voice arose, which, when it spoke, always turned me away from what I was about to do, but never impelled me onward" (31d). It was this voice which now turned him away from pleading for mercy, from bringing his wife and children into court as suppliants, from conducting himself as one who thought that justice should be administered by emotions rather than by reason. This voice he believed to be divine. And after sentence of death was passed upon him, he turned to his friends and said (40b, c), "An amazing thing has happened to me. For the warning voice which has usually spoken to me at all times in the past has even restrained me in minor matters if I was about to do something wrong. But now there has come upon me, as you yourselves see, what would be thought of as the most extreme of evils. Yet neither as I left my house this morning was there any restraining sign from the god nor when I came up here to the courtroom nor when I was speaking did it hold me back from what I was about to say. And yet in other talks and in many places it has held me back right in the middle of what I was saying. But today at no time during this affair has it opposed me in anything I did or said. What then shall I assume is the cause of this? I shall tell you. In all probability what has happened to me is a good thing and the truth is that we are wrong to assume that it is bad to die. A great proof of this has been given to me. For it is not possible that the customary sign would not have stood in my way if I was about to do something which was not good."

Death, he continues, must be either a long sleep or a passage from this world to another inhabited by all the dead. Both are good, not evil. If one is to pass into a world where the spirits of the poets and warriors and of those who died an unjust death can still be seen and talked to, no greater pleasure could accrue to him. He could even continue his examination of those who think they know and know nothing. Thus his judges have really done him a great favor, though unintentionally, and that is why the voice has not spoken. He can only request that when his children grow up, they too be questioned, as he has questioned other people's children, if they show any sign of putting wealth or anything else above virtue.

In this speech of Socrates there is little which indicates a systematic theory of two worlds, it is true, but nevertheless behind it is the firm belief that this world, whatever it may be called, is of lesser importance than another, the world governed by eternal principles of right and wrong. These principles are given by God or by the gods—it matters very little to what special deities they are attributed—and are delivered through what we should call the voice of conscience. They are principles which do not vary from man to man nor presumably from tribe to tribe. The laws of a government which is unjust need not be obeyed, and earlier in his defense he pointed out how at one time he had refused to carry out the unjust orders of the Thirty (32c). The standards of good conduct then are not determined by Custom but by Nature; they are grounded in the order of the cosmos itself, and the problem becomes that of explaining how this is so. It was this problem which occupied his greatest disciple. But, as he is also represented as arguing in *Crito*, there are governmental laws which one should never disobey.

Crito gives us Socrates in prison awaiting his execution. His friend, Crito, a man of wealth, comes to visit him in order to persuade him to escape. Socrates refuses and his reasons form the philosophical basis for a reconstruction of one side of his position. His principal thesis is that he will not act until he has been persuaded by an argument which will stand up after close examination (*Crito* 46b). But reason is something that does not change from moment to moment nor because new events have taken place in the life of the examiner. The univalence of certain ideas is permanent, regardless of the number of people who deny them. Some are good, some bad, and even if the majority sustain the bad, that does not make them good. This would appear to be an out-and-out rejection of what seemed to the Sophists to be the consequences of the *Double Words*. One implication of this point of view is that there is some way of knowing which ideas are good and which bad. And this can be achieved without consulting common opinion. One has only to consult men of sagacity. "Hence," he says (48a), "we need give no heed to what the majority say to us, but rather must we listen to him who understands justice and injustice, which is one and the same as truth." If the truth, which is identical with the good, the beautiful, and the just (48b), tells us that I can leave the prison without the permission of the Athenians, then well and good, I shall do so. But if it turns out to be wrong to bribe the jailer and escape, then I must stay here and accept the punishment which has been meted out to me.

With this as an introduction, Socrates then argues that it is never right to do wrong voluntarily and that evil does not become good because of the circumstances surrounding its commission. Therefore one should never oppose wrong with wrong, if it is never right to do wrong (49c). But among the things which are wrong is that which is forbidden by the Law. The Law is the judgment of the city, and once the Law is violated, wrong has been done to the city.[14] Marriage, the education of children, the security of life, all are entrusted to the Law, and to do violence to it is to do violence to the very foundations of decent living. The city is more to be honored than one's father and mother and all one's ancestors; it is more august, more holy, and held in greater respect among the gods and among men of reason, and must be revered and given way to and appeased when angry more than a father is. One must either persuade the city or do what it commands, and suffer if it orders one to suffer something and do this quietly. And if it strikes or if it bind one, or if it leads one into war where one may be wounded or killed, one must follow, and righteousness will prevail. One must not yield or retreat or leave one's post, but both in battle and in the courtroom and everywhere else one must do what the city and one's Fatherland orders or else persuade it where justice lies. But one must never do violence to that which is sacred, either to one's mother or father or much less to that which is better than they, one's Fatherland (51a–c). If a man is not to agree to this, let him leave Athens and go where he will. But as for Socrates, he recognizes that he has given evidence that he loves his country, for he has never been willing to leave it, "except once when he went to the Isthmus." It

---

[14] The commands of the Thirty were not the Law of the city but of usurpers.

is thus all the more proper that he submit to the city's orders. If now he remains to be executed, he will have been executed unjustly to be sure, but he will at least have been a good citizen, will not have returned evil for evil (53c). "These things, my dear friend Crito, know it well, I seem to hear as the Corybantes seem to hear the sound of flutes, and in me the music of these words resounds and drowns out all else. But know that, as far as I now can tell, if you say anything against this, you will speak in vain. . . . Go then, Crito, and let us act thus, since the god is guiding us this way" (54d).

In this speech the Law is above all time and place and is the voice of the city, which is something more than the citizens. Its expression in the verdict of the courts may be wrong, but to obey it is a divine command. If we assume that Plato has given us here the thoughts of Socrates, as we have assumed, then he is in opposition to the Sophists on the point of believing in an eternal order of right and beauty and goodness.[15] It is that order which is to be contrasted with the temporal order in which goodness, beauty, and truth may vary from man to man and from place to place. It is an order which in Plato was to become the world of ideas and later the Intelligible World as opposed to the Sensible World. In Socrates it is apparently known by some form of intuition which he speaks of in *Crito* as the indications of the god, his *Daimon*.

But Socrates' belief in such an order is shown not merely in his opinions as recorded in the *Apology* and *Crito*; it is also entailed in his method of criticism. To begin with, the notion of the teacher as a midwife (*Theaetetus* 149) seems to symbolize the theory that every man possesses knowledge in an embryonic manner and that learning is largely the development of this possession. Then the discovery of the truth through dialectic seems to be based on the theory that all questions can be tested by the test of self-consistency. A point of view which is self-contradictory is

---

[15] I shall try to use the word "eternal" in this book to mean "timeless," not "everlasting."

self-condemned and one which does not give way under this test is self-substantiated. Unfortunately we have learned that consistent ideas are not necessarily true to fact and have had to make a distinction between logical coherence and factual truth, though if one's premises are true to fact, so will their implications be. In this matter Socrates appears to belong to the tradition established by Parmenides and his followers, according to which, as we have seen, an apparent truth must yield to dialectical criticism. Since the truth must be one and eternal, it can make no difference what people think about it. Error must be a factor of human psychology, not of the world outside the mind. And if one cannot find things in the objective world of daily experience which correspond to the truth, that does not prove that the truth is weakened. The truth in all cases becomes the standard by which we judge the validity of our opinions, not a generalized description of these opinions or of their subject matter. And since the word itself must be univalent, then it makes little difference whether the subject under discussion is the material world or the values which we find in it. Hence there is no separation between judgments of value and judgments of fact. Both must be tested in the same way. Just as the opinions of thousands of men cannot invalidate the truths of mathematics, so they cannot invalidate the truths of aesthetics and ethics. It is on this issue that Socrates joins battle with the Sophists.

One word more. If we make a clean-cut division between eternal and historical judgments, then there will always remain the question of how we reach the former. Since the development of the non-Euclidean geometries, it has become customary to maintain that all postulates are arbitrary or conventional. Yet the fact remains that the theorems do apply to—or control, if one prefers that word—certain events in the historical world of time. On the other hand, if mathematical propositions—or sentences— are derived from historical propositions, by abstraction or generalization, we have to face the corresponding problem of how they emerge from the temporal into the eternal world. No one denies that our knowledge on the whole is about the temporal world nor that the terms of mathematical discourse have their origin in empirical situations. But no one can deny on the other hand that we have eternal knowledge, that is, knowledge of formal logic and of mathematics, and that sometimes it does not apply to what I can only call ordinary experience. The intuitive powers which Socrates believes us to possess and which in moral questions are symbolized in his *Daimon* may be called by us by some other name. But regardless of our nomenclature the problem to which they were an attempted solution remains as much a problem for us as for Socrates.

Oddly enough a Sophist such as Gorgias is a more orthodox rationalist than Socrates. By limiting his discussion to the most general terms, such as Being and Nonbeing, the One and the Many, the Immutable and the Mutable, he was able to remain in the realm of pure dialectic. His results were nihilistic when they were turned into existential judgments and it is true that he played upon the ambiguities of such a word as "to be." But Socrates did not play with such terms and criticized rather the more concrete opinions of his interlocutors, opinions about the correct definition of moral qualities, such as courage, friendship, and virtue. Here he was trying to find the eternal in the temporal and the only mark of the eternal which he knew was the consistency of the definitions. It is doubtful whether a comic writer would have become indignant over the examination of metaphysical opinions, but when it came down to the examination of traditional beliefs about the virtues, trouble was bound to ensue. No one has ever been investigated by Congress for having said that space is curved or that the velocity of light is the maximum velocity measurable. But when someone is suspected of having questioned the advisability of saluting the flag or of keeping secret the technique of making atomic bombs, the situation has been very different.

II

1. We have no very clear idea of how Anaxagoras reached his conclusions, for the remaining fragments are too scanty to give us the requisite information. But we can see from at least two of his fragments that he clung to the axiom that nothing can come from nothing. If, as he says (fr. B17), it is wrong to speak about coming-into-being and passing-into-nonbeing, it is probably because, as he also says (fr. B10), hair could not come from not-hair or flesh from not-flesh. The result of such reasoning was that all things had to be present in the beginning and that all change could be nothing but separation and combination (fr. B17). This was obviously the denial of creation.

But he apparently also assumed that in all change there must be an agent and a patient: things could not change of their own accord. But since change was separation and combination and it was not the four elements which separated and combined, or the atoms, but bits of the macroscopic objects, there must be tiny pieces of everything in everything and also there must be no limit in size in the inherent particles or seeds. What principle of limitation there was to the kinds of change which might occur, he does not state, and if everything is in everything, one might well conclude that anything could be separated out of anything.[16] In brief, if the seeds of hair are in everything, then, given the proper conditions, to which the fragments pay no attention, hair might just as well sprout out of rocks as out of heads. The axiom that things could be divided *ad infinitum* may have come from the principle that any extended bit of matter could be divided and there seemed to be no way of setting a limit to the possible divisions. Since no change could occur without an agent, he provided one in his *Nous,* and the reason why *Nous* had to be the purest of things (fr. B12) and contain no part of anything else is not only be-

---

[16] Aristotle was firm in rejecting such an idea, for he saw that only certain changes could occur and that change was not random (*De gen. et corr.* 333b 5).

cause it must be active and thus incapable of being acted upon, but also because there must be no danger of its being diminished by losing any of its contents. "It would not have the same power over anything as it has remaining by itself" (fr. B12). There is no indication that Anaxagoras saw the possibility of the patient's reacting upon the agent. Quite the contrary, having posited one active and one passive being, the former must be incapable of being acted upon and the latter incapable of acting. As this tradition developed, the patient became matter and the agent mind. And later, when the God of the Bible became the one absolute and universal agent, creating and controlling everything, He too was never acted upon.[17]

Yet there is also a puzzling fragment in which Anaxagoras is quoted as saying that "things in the cosmos are not cut off from one another by a hatchet, neither the hot from the cold nor the cold from the hot" (fr. B8). This may be simply a reassertion of his principle of the ubiquity of all the qualities or, in view of the particular qualities which he picks, it may be a recognition that the elementary qualities form a scale in which "things" blend into one another. If this is the correct interpretation, it would seem as if activity and passivity were matters of degree, in which case the most active being would not be separate from the things it acts upon and the *Nous* free from all mixture. If the *Nous* is simply at one end of the cosmic scale and the primordial mixture at the other, it might be the most active of all beings and still not necessarily cut off from the others. The most likely interpretation of his concept is that the *Nous* is peculiar in its separateness and that its action upon the cosmic mixture is that of an efficient cause, much like the Love and Strife of Empedocles. In that case its action would be directed to something utterly foreign to its own nature. This is the more probable in that Theophrastus (*De sensu* 27) lists him as one of the few philosophers who hold that perception occurs between opposites rather than between similars. On the other hand, both Plato (*Phaedo* 97c) and Aristotle (*Meta-*

---

[17] This made the efficacy of prayer a problem.

physics 985a 18) criticize him for the little use which he made of the *Nous* once he had posited its existence.

2. The method of the Sophists, with the exception of Gorgias, seems to have few implications of a metaphysical kind. Yet to make man the measure of all things, of the things that are and of the things that are not, is to make him in some way the determinant of existence. If this is interpreted strictly, man determines his own existence as well as that of everything else. But that interpretation would perhaps be unfair. For before a man can have beliefs or make judgments, he must obviously exist. If we interpret the quotation in individualistic terms, then reality would have to be whatever each man thinks it is. If we interpret it as simply emphasis upon the human equation, then reality would be whatever the human mind as a whole believes it to be. The contribution of the Idols of the Tribe is surely not to be underestimated. As Bacon saw, the use of teleological explanation is a projection into the material world of behavior which is originally human. We find no unequivocal purposes in anything but human beings. By extension we may discover them also in animal behavior. But in that field which tradition called the meteorological, the discovery of purpose is based on pretty thin analogies. And since the only way we have of explaining any change whatsoever is through human knowledge, unless we believe that scientists are granted revelations, then we are forced to admit that knowledge may include factors which animal knowledge would not have. We rely, for instance, as the ancients realized, on our eyes for most of our knowledge. We even use words derived from vision as substitutes for cognition itself. The notions that knowledge is a reflection of an external world rather than a testing of it, that it is contemplation rather than manipulation, that our ideas are faint or bright copies of things, are all based on the metaphor of sight. If this is taken seriously, one has the right to be skeptical of our ability to know the world as it "really" is, that is, as it is when we are not looking at it. This does not imply that we have no knowledge whatsoever, but simply that our knowledge is human

knowledge and not some sort of superhuman apprehension of things-as-they-are.

In fact, even the most extreme use of the human equation in describing cognition would not make knowledge unreliable. For after all we are human beings and would be utterly lost in a completely nonhuman world. All that one has to do to accommodate this kind of humanism to science is to recognize the contributions of humanity to knowledge and to include them as some of the conditions relative to which one's judgments are true.

The method of Gorgias clearly determines what metaphysics he has. For by asserting the sharp opposition between two contraries, the denial of one becomes the assertion of the other, since it is assumed that the sum of the contraries is exhaustive of all possibilities. This is obvious in a purely logical universe. But when one is talking of the existent universe, one has first to examine the possibilities in an empirical manner. If, for instance, one observes that there are mammals, one can validly argue that all things, not merely animals, are either mammals or nonmammals. But this gives one little information about what nonmammals are. One does not even know whether some of the traits of mammals are not also found in nonmammals, as we know indeed they are. Such traits would be vision, reproduction, and so on. To continue by the method of dichotomy, a complete survey of the universe would demand a foreknowledge of just what characteristics are essential in the Aristotelian sense of that word. And though in certain areas, mathematics above all, this can be done by definition, in most it is supposed to be based upon an actual inventory of real things, not concepts. Now if one looks at the contraries which Gorgias is reported to have dealt with, one finds first existence and nonexistence, multiplicity and unity, coming-into-being and having-always-existed, motion and stability. If we assume that he has made out a good case for his thesis that there is no more reason to believe in existence than in nonexistence, and so on with the other couples, still we might argue that a possible being would be visible or tangible or located in space or in time. It is true that

Gorgias might have anticipated the modern distinction between Subsistence and Existence, according to which we say that mermaids subsist but do not exist, or that what we see in dreams does not exist but subsists. But in an argument of this sort one already knows that the word Being is used to cover all possibilities and actualities as well, all real and unreal things, and one introduces a criterion of existence such as Being-in-time-or-in-space. But to do this requires at least a grain of empirical knowledge. This was of course precisely what Gorgias was trying to avoid. As with Zeno, so with Gorgias: the dialectical method can be profitably used only in the field of purely formal science but has no applicability to experience unless its premises are true of experience.

We could for instance argue that the platypus does not exist, regardless of what explorers and naturalists tell us about it. First, one would say that an animal must be either a mammal, a bird, or a fish. (This is clearly inaccurate, but no worse than the premises of most *a priori* arguments and is, moreover, just the sort of premise that the dialectician would use.) Second, no mammal lays eggs. But the platypus lays eggs. Therefore, it must be either a bird or a fish. But birds do not have mammary glands. The platypus does have them. Therefore it cannot be a bird and must be a fish. But fishes do not breathe in the air. And the platypus is a terrestrial animal which does breathe in the air, though it also swims like the otter and the beaver. Therefore it is not a fish. But since it must be either a mammal or a bird or a fish and is none of them, it does not exist.[18] The moral of this is that our divisions and classifications do not fit the world of nature.

What is peculiarly interesting in Gorgias' argument is that he did not argue about *Becoming* as the fundamental category. In Hegel's *Logic*, for instance, Becoming is the union or synthesis of Being and Nonbeing. But if we take it for granted that our common nouns name things which are already completed, as Aristotle

---

[18] It is worth recording that the eleventh edition of the *Britannica*, art. "Monotremata," says, "In the strict sense of the term monotremes are not ... mammals."

might have put it, then things in process of becoming something are not yet that thing, but nevertheless will be. But to accept this, Gorgias would probably have had to do what Plato reports the Heracliteans to have done (*Theaetetus* 179d), to have identified sensation and knowledge. This might have given him Becoming as fundamental, but it would have ruined the equivalence of words and things. Moreover, it would have been hard, if possible, to discover the exact "opposite" of Becoming if all things are in a state of change. For what contrary could there be to a universal predicate? Finally, those Sophists who like Cratylus "spoke in the Heraclitean manner" (Aristotle, *Metaphysics* 1010a 11) maintained that all speech was wrong and that one could only move one's finger—presumably at what one perceived. The reason for this is that since everything is in a state of change, all judgments become false as soon as they are uttered, nothing remaining constant long enough to be named or described. The lawfulness of the Flux apparently did not impress such people.

3. The method of Socrates was essentially critical, though he is said by Aristotle (*Metaphysics* 1078b 28) to have discovered inductive arguments and universal definitions. These were held to concern the "starting point and origin of understanding" (περὶ ἀρχὴν ἐπιστήμης). Inductive arguments, as far as the evidence goes, were arguments based on a survey of all the examples relevant to the concept which was to be defined, and in Socrates' case, these concepts were ethical. Universal definitions would then be common properties, and the common properties, being inherent in a number of things, would have characteristics which were peculiar to them and never found in particulars. These characteristics would include the ability to appear in several places and at several times without changing, in that they would resemble those mathematical beings such as circles and triangles, which might be here and there, big and small, and yet remain the same in their essential nature. We do not know how aware Socrates was of what was entailed in his method of inquiry, but we do know that when he questioned his interlocutors about "courage" or "friend-

ship" or any other of the moral qualities in which he was interested, he always pointed out that he was looking for a general definition of the concept itself and not for particular instances of it. But a general concept might mean at least two things: (a) the general concepts held by various people and limited in their reference to beliefs and opinion, and (b) general concepts which refer to particular instances regardless of whether anyone is aware of them or not. It seems to have been the latter meaning which was that of Socrates. Thus he would have said that an act could be just or brave or good whether anyone thought it to be so or not. So a shape could be circular or square or triangular whether anyone knew the definition of circularity or squareness or triangularity or not.

It is obviously impossible to tell whether a man who holds to the inductive method first assumes that there are general concepts of this nature which will be discovered by an inductive survey or whether his inductive survey leads him to the discovery of general traits which then arouse in his mind the idea that the general traits form a world of their own which is timeless and spaceless. For either might be true. If we believe that common nouns are univalent, then whenever we use one, we are likely to maintain that it refers to something beyond its specific instances. For we might say, "Why should this thing be called a horse if it does not have characteristics which are exactly the same as those of other things which we call horses?" This would be an argument drawn from linguistic usage and still be taken seriously. It is to be found in aesthetic discussion about the essence of tragedy or comedy or the beautiful or the ugly or of any of the other terms found in such conversations. We have more history behind us than Socrates had, much of which stems from Socrates himself, and we can see that certain of such terms have been used in a variety of senses. We have no revelation to tell us that when Shakespeare entitled a play *The Tragedy of Hamlet*, he was thinking of Aristotle's *Poetics*. On the other hand, now that we have read Aristotle and dozens of other authors on the essence of the tragic, we approach the matter with the information offered by them in the back of our minds. And so we look for evidence of what they say when we read *Hamlet*. There is also the possibility that there is a feeling for the tragic rooted in human nature and reappearing from time to mind in history. Socrates of course had no such burden to carry. But he was aware of debates about morals, or arguments in court about rights and wrongs, of criticism of himself in such plays as the *Clouds*, and unless each man was simply expressing his opinions as he might express his emotions, he could conclude that they must be talking about something real, not merely uttering lyric cries.

Thus his critical method and a theory of Ideas in the Platonic sense were intimately intertwined, for unless there actually were such ideas, the critical method employed was futile. And if there were no such ideas, all arguments were no more than exercises in sadism.

Along with his critical method was what he called his midwifery. How much of this is Plato and how much Socrates, I do not pretend to know. But since most historians are agreed that he believed in his *Daimon*, it is probable that he also believed in our possession of the ideas from birth. Disregarding metaphors and myths, it is clear that if a teacher questions a pupil by the dialectical method, he assumes that the pupil knows the answer but is not aware of it. Paradoxical as the contrast between knowledge and awareness may be, it is common enough in our daily experience to be taken seriously. We know frequently enough that we like or dislike certain things without being able to tell anyone why we like or dislike them, and also without being aware of what there is in them which we like or dislike. If I prefer Mozart to Tchaikovsky, I may be aware of the fact, but I am not necessarily aware of the general characteristics of what I will call the likable and the dislikable. Similarly, if I am disgusted with cowardly or pretentious or hypocritical acts, I need not be able to give a definition of what cowardice or pretentiousness or hypocrisy is. Yet if I want to be rational about it—and that is far from being compulsory—I ought to be able to discover such definitions. Otherwise I shall feel that I am acting from impulse or passion or prejudice or servile obedience to a tradition or to something equally distasteful to a rationalist. Now it is quite possible that the *Daimon* of Socrates was simply the accumulated habits of moral judgment which he had absorbed from his total education, at home, on the battlefield, in the agora. The compulsive force of the habitual is not something superficial but becomes an integral part of our character. There are some things which a man of a given social class, religious training, and general education just will not do. He is revolted by the very thought of doing them. They may be simply the subject of food taboos or they may be the taboos of the Decalogue. Whatever their cause or origin, the man in question will strive to give reasons for his compulsions and, as soon as he enters upon that path, he must be able to present a clear and distinct idea of what he is objecting to. He is seldom, if ever, aware of the history of his distaste, to give it an earthly name. He will say, for instance, that his conscience forbids him to do certain things, or that he could not live with himself if he did them, or that they violate his deepest convictions. The maieutic of Socrates was the bringing to full consciousness of those repulsions and attractions, approbations and disapprobations. They in their turn become the innate ideas of Descartes and the English Platonists, in that one possessed them from birth but not in full consciousness of them.

The *Dissoi Logoi* and the Sophistic arguments about the relativity of standards, together possibly with the stories of varying customs told by Herodotus, could all, as we have suggested above, make men worry about their own and their country's standards. Were the laws of Athens simply the Athenian way of disciplining the citizens or were they grounded in Nature? Socrates took the latter alternative as his point of view, but instead of being dogmatic about it, tried to justify it critically. The justification would work if the men whom he interrogated did possess an inchoate knowledge of Nature's standards, but if they did not, the maieutic would not work. No historical record exists of one of his conversations. We have simply the semifictional accounts of Plato and Xenophon. But even if the actual words, or the targets of those reported conversations, are imaginary, the method is the same. Socrates does assume that his pupils already possess, but unconsciously, the ideas which he is examining, and the interrogation is to bring them into the light of day. This point of view was elaborated in greater detail in Plato's *Meno*.

The German historian, Wilhelm Windelband, has pointed out that the Socratic philosophy was "the philosophy of the dialogue."[19] A dialogue does not merely record the opinions of two people; it may also be based on the premise that at least two points of view are reasonable. It has often been noted, moreover, that the so-called early dialogues of Plato do not come to any conclusions but are "dialogues of search."[20] There is, nevertheless, one conclusion in all the early dialogues, the clarification of certain ideas by the rejection of those whose implications cannot resist criticism. To have discovered the weakness of one's own position is a conclusion. And the man who leads one to it is usually an un-

[19] W. Windelband, *A History of Philosophy*, trans. by James H. Tufts (11th ed.; New York: The Macmillan Co., 1901), p. 96.

[20] The first classification of the dialogues of which we have any record was made by Aristophanes of Byzantium (third and second centuries B.C.). This arrangement divided them into trilogies, like those of the ancient tragedies. Thrasyllus (first century B.C.), whose arrangement has been preserved, arranged them in groups of four and divided them into dialogues of investigation or search and those of exposition. For these arrangements, see George Grote, *Plato, and the Other Companions of Sokrates* (London: John Murray, 1885), Vol. I, pp. 292 ff. Albinus (second century A.D.) in his classification calls *Euthyphro, Meno, Ion*, and *Charmides* experimental, dialogues which test ideas. In Sextus Empiricus we find that one name for skepticism is the philosophy of search (zetetic). See *Pyrrh. hyp.* i. 3. Albinus did not think that the dialogues fell into classes that had nothing in common. On the contrary he believed that the Platonic philosophy forms a system. After pointing to the classifications of Thrasyllus and Dercylides, he says, "We say that there is no one and determinate beginning of the Platonic philosophy, for, being perfect, it resembles the perfect form of the circle. Just as there is no one and determinate beginning of a circle, so there is none of his philosophy." See his frs. 6 and 7 in Mullach, *Fragmenta Graecorum Philosophorum* (Paris: Firmin-Didot, n.d.), Vol. III, p. 24. For recent discussions of this and related matters, see Harold Cherniss, "Plato (1950–1957)," *Lustrum*, IV (1959), 8 ff.

pleasant fellow whom one would like to silence. When he also shows the weakness of commonly accepted opinions through his method, he becomes an enemy of society and, since society has as its basic principle its own self-preservation, he will be punished. The retention of the past gives stability to any society and, as Socrates himself says in *Crito*, one must make every sacrifice for the security of the state. But in so far as the state is a set of ideals, those ideals must be cherished and can be changed only very slowly. But the Athens of Socrates' maturity was in a condition of dramatic flux. Solon at the end of the sixth century had already reorganized the constitution. He was immediately followed by the despotism of Pisistratus and his sons, Hippias and Hipparchus, and though their rule may have been accompanied by economic success and political power for the city, the Age of the Despots was terminated by a revolution, and a democratic regime was instituted by Clisthenes just before the beginning of the fifth century. The first thirty years of that century, the period just before the birth of Socrates, were given over to the extension of Athenian power, the Persian Wars, and the foundation of what we would call today the Athenian Empire. In his youth and early manhood he lived through the Periclean Age. But that came to an end when he was forty. He saw the plague and the Peloponnesian War. He also saw the reign of the Thirty Tyrants. He had engaged in military service at the front. He saw the overthrow of the Thirty and the rebirth of the democracy. Surely no Athenian could have been more aware than he of the vicissitudes of cities. Is it not understandable that the men who were responsible for the preservation of the *status quo* should have seen in him and in the early Sophists, in anyone who was influential in weakening the citizens' faith in the old ways and ideas, an enemy? What they did not realize, and what none of their successors have realized, is that by killing a man one does not kill his ideas.

A further remark may not be out of place here. The fifth century was also the great age of tragedy. Greek tragedy is not a drama of heroes and villains; it is a drama of ideas, of laws, of customs, of choices, of divine decrees and human resistance to them. They are personal dramas only to us who are not Greeks and have no religious attachment to the stories they tell. That is why characters like Oedipus and Antigone and Prometheus can be turned into symbols for types of character. The Promethean drama can be interpreted as an allegory, just as the tragedy of Antigone can, and when we speak of the universality of the tragic themes, it makes sense precisely because the characters stand for something beyond their own personal problems. There is a legend that Plato as a young man was a dramatic poet. His dialogues have been seen as comedies in which ideas take the place of people. The Greek plays, even those of comic writers, do not simply tell a story; they also give us the battle of points of view. One of the earliest remaining examples of this is the debate between Apollo and the Furies in the *Eumenides,* to which we have already referred above. When the Chorus accuses Orestes of matricide, Apollo replies that he, the god, had ordered him to avenge his father's death. When the Furies point out that it is their function to pursue murderers, he answers that Clytemnestra too was a murderer. If, says Apollo (213 ff.), to slay one's husband is not to slay one's kin, how about the profanation of the marriage bed which dishonors Zeus, Hera, and Aphrodite? Finally Athena is called in to adjudicate the case and, after further arguments on the relative gravity of killing one's husband and killing one's mother, including a bit of biological theory, she delivers the following interesting verdict (737–44).

> The task is mine, to give the final judgment.
> My vote shall I cast for Orestes,
> For no mother have I nor did one give me birth,
> And I commend the male in all things save in marriage
> With all my heart; I am the fruit of my father.
> So I shall not prefer the fate of a woman
> Who killed her husband, lord of her home.
> Let then Orestes win, even if the votes are equal.

The votes are equal, leaving the issue on abstract grounds just about what it was before. And the grace of Athena is responsible for the decision.[21]

This sort of thing is common to the plays. In *Agamemnon* (1500–66) there is a debate between Clytemnestra and the Chorus of Elders on the justice of her crime; in *Seven against Thebes* (1105–end) we find Antigone arguing with the Herald about the necessity of burying her brother; and in the opening of Sophocles' *Antigone* we have a similar argument between Antigone and her sister, Ismene. In *Ajax* (1047–1160) is the argument between Menelaus and Teucer over the disposal of Ajax's corpse, and in *Electra* that between Electra and the Chorus (122–315) on the rights and wrongs of avenging her father's murder. But even in Aristophanes we have a mock trial, that of Euripides in the *Thesmophorians*, and in the *Frogs* the contest between Aeschylus and Euripides for the throne of tragedy. The Greek public must have both liked and have been accustomed to long debates. Is it farfetched to say that the Socratic method was a transfer to the philosophic stage of the technique of the poets? Just as Oedipus had to be brought to an awakening of what he had done unwittingly, so the pupils of Socrates are brought to an awareness of what they unwittingly know.

III

1. It was in the field of the appraisal of life that the Sophists came into their own. Their very interest in debate and speech-making is sufficient evidence that when they were serious they thought life in need of improvement. When they were not serious, they had a kind of disdain for it. In the Pseudo-Platonic *Axiochus* (369b), the date of which is sometime before the first

---

[21] There is of course much more to the play than this, for it is clear that the basic dispute is over the rights of the Old Gods and the Young, the old order against the new. For a fuller discussion of this, see Headlam and Thomson, *The Oresteia of Aeschylus* (Cambridge: Cambridge University Press, 1938), pp. 49 ff.

century B.C.,[22] Prodicus is mentioned by Socrates as having said in his presence that death was of no concern to either the living or the dead—the kind of disdain for one of the great sources of worry which is typical of those who refuse to take over the major troubles of their fellow men. This has little value as a "fragment," but probably does show the sort of attitude which Prodicus might have assumed. His speech called *The Choice of Heracles*, preserved by Xenophon (*Mem.* ii. 1. 21 ff.), is, as Xenophon admits, not an exact reproduction of the Sophist's words, but does give us, as far as we know, an idea of what Prodicus thought. This speech, which had an extraordinary fortune in the history both of philosophy and of painting as well,[23] is a simple allegory of the strong man choosing the path of Virtue rather than that of Vice. Vice offers all sorts of attractive pleasures, Virtue a life of toil. When Heracles asks Vice her name, she replies (ii. 1. 26), "My friends call me Happiness, but those who hate me childishly call me Vice." To this Virtue says (ii. 1. 28), "Of things which are good and fair the gods have given none to men without toil and care. But if you wish the gods to smile on you, you must serve the gods; and if you wish the devotion of friends, you must show kindness to your friends; and if you desire to be honored by some city, you must render service to that city; and if you aspire to be admired by all Greece for your excellence, you must try to do well by Greece; and if you wish earth to bear bounteous crops for you, you must take good care of the earth; and if you think that you may grow rich on your flocks, you must cherish your flocks; and should you long to win in battle and wish to be able to free your friends and subdue your enemies, you must learn the arts of warfare both in theory and in practice. If you wish to be powerful in body, you must accustom the body to obey the will and exercise it with toil and sweat." This road, answers Vice, is difficult to travel, whereas her own is easy and broad. But, need-

[22] It is marked as spurious as early as the catalogue of Thrasyllus. See Diogenes Laertius, iii. 57.

[23] See E. Panofsky, *Hercules am Scheidewege, und andere antike Bildstoffe in der neueren Kunst* (Leipzig: Teubner, 1910).

less to say, Heracles chooses Virtue. His Twelve Labors became emblems of the toilsome life of Virtue and in time he himself became the patron god of the Stoic Sages, though Xenophon actually does not conclude the speech with the choice.[24]

That some of the Sophists, or at any rate men who have been counted among the Sophists, had no very high opinion of human beings is illustrated by a fragment from Critias.[25] Critias was of course a man who had no reason to love his fellows, nor had they much to love him, but it is clear from this passage that he believed law to be necessary in order to keep the beast in man subdued, a task which is aided by religion. Whether his misanthropy was a rationalization of his political behavior or not, there is no saying.

There was a time when the life of man was unordered and bestial, at the mercy of force, when there was neither reward for the good nor even punishment for the wicked. And then men seem to me to have made punitive laws that justice might be lord alike for all and insolence be mastered, and that if any man should do wrong, he might be punished. And then, when the laws prevented them from doing open misdeeds by violence, they did wrong in secret; and thereupon, I think, some clever and wise man first discovered the fear of gods for mortals, so that evil men might be afraid, should they do or say or think anything in secret. He therefore introduced the divine as a spirit vigorous with imperishable life, hearing and seeing with his mind, and of great wisdom, and attending to these things and having a divine nature, hearing all that is said among men and able to see all that is done on earth. . . .

Both law and religion then are inventions to control the human race, which without them would be guilty of both overt and occult crimes. There is no thought in such a passage that man's conscience might suffice to keep him on the path of virtue. Critias' admiration for the Spartans, attested by his work on the Spartan

---

[24] For the relation of this speech to "hard primitivism," see *Primitivism in Antiquity*, pp. 113 ff.

[25] Fr. B25, ll. 1–21 (Diels-Kranz). For a discussion of this passage, which comes from Sextus Empiricus, in the context of antiprimitivism, see *Primitivism in Antiquity*, pp. 211 ff.

Constitution and the fragments which extol the rigor of their way of life, was probably not unconnected with his contempt for men who were not disciplined by the sort of law a tyrant would try to enforce.[26] Stobaeus quotes three lines from an unnamed drama of his which might have been written by La Rochefoucauld: "Whoever goes about doing favors in all ways for his friends, will replace a present pleasure with future enmity" (fr. B27). Or again, "Dangerous is it when a man unthinking seems to think" (fr. B28). Though we can no longer tell what character in the plays said such things and in what situations they were said, they are preserved as if they represented the opinions of their author. But, it is true, if only the speeches of Iago were left of Othello, and the other plays of Shakespeare were entirely lost, our opinion of Shakespeare's ethics would be vastly different from what it is now. Be that as it may, we have one fragment of Critias which resembles certain lines of Sophocles: "Nothing is certain except that once we are born, we shall die, and that while living, we meet with nothing but misery" (fr. B49).

Of Thrasymachus all that remains relevant to our present context is a fragment from a speech on Athenian politics (fr. B1), in which he argues that the Athenians ought to return to the ways of their fathers, for the miseries which they have undergone during the wars are the work neither of the gods nor of chance, but of the government. "For he is either insensible or very strong who will allow those so wishing to sin, and who will take upon himself the blame for the plots and evils of others."[27] Presumably, but this is only conjecture, men have a standard of justice, erected in ancient times, which is good forever, regardless of changes of situation and the problems which they might provoke. Their weak-

---

[26] Critias was Plato's uncle and is shown in a better light by his nephew than by others. One wonders, but must not do more than wonder, whether Plato's admiration for Sparta was not influenced by the views of Critias.

[27] Mario Untersteiner in his *The Sophists*, trans. by Kathleen Freeman (New York: Philosophical Library, 1954), p. 326, following Th. Hirzel, *Themis, Dike und Verwandtes* (Leipzig, 1907), p. 372, says that the plea to return to the ways of our fathers "was always the battle-cry when party struggles broke out." If so, the idea had no special significance.

ness is to have departed from this standard. In the first book of Plato's *Republic*, however, we have a portrait of Thrasymachus which differs essentially from any such traditionalistic spirit. There justice is defined by the Sophist as the rule of the stronger; his will makes law. Such a Nietzschean point of view would indicate no great admiration for the general run of mankind. It would appear to arise from the "realistic" observation that society is a mass of conflicting wills into which order must be brought. That order is introduced by the strong man, or by the stronger political party. There is then no ideal justice which can be defined without regard to historical considerations. Justice can presumably shift its meaning from time to time, and what might be just under tyrants would not be just under the rule of the Demos. But the only reason why the Demos would be just is that they have the power to enforce their will. A similar sentiment is expressed by Callicles in Plato's *Gorgias* (482c).

2. Ironically enough, it is Socrates, persecuted by his fellow Athenians, who seems to have a higher opinion of human nature. Like Condorcet, who wrote his sketch of human progress while under sentence of death imposed by the latest and most progressed of nations, Socrates delivered himself of his speech on the supremacy of the Law while awaiting execution. Though Plato is a bitter critic of the society in which he lived, Socrates seems to have maintained a calm acceptance of things as they were, reforming through example rather than through preaching alone. His method of examination was, to be sure, an attempt at reform, and one does not reform if satisfied with things as they are.

This apparent paradox takes on a new color when one realizes that for Socrates there stood on one side eternal man and on the other historical man. The former, an ideal, was by its very nature incapable of change and was also inherently good. The latter, being in time, did change and was an imperfect exemplification of man's eternal essence. Men as historical beings could be in error and be guilty of crimes. It was they who were in need of correction. But since they all carried within them a nucleus of the ideal, one could not despise them, though gentle ridicule might be in order. Socrates did indeed believe that the men about him were for the most part ignorant. They might behave courageously, temperately, justly; but they did not know what their behavior really meant. They were "creatures moving about in worlds not realized." They might therefore be pitied, as children are pitied, or animals, but not punished. One had merely to awaken them to full consciousness of their real nature in order to perfect them. And this awakening would come with rational insight and examination. Part of his irony lay in the disparity between the two natures, in man's ability to have what Plato called true opinion without an awareness of what truth consisted in.

The emphasis upon knowledge, knowledge based upon reason, is characteristic of the Socratic tradition, whether it appears in Plato, Aristotle, or the minor Socratics. It might look as if the man who acted bravely without being aware of the nature of ideal courage was no different from the man who acted bravely in full consciousness of what he was doing. The two acts are outwardly identical. But it is precisely the insistence upon considering human behavior from the internal point of view which sets the rationalistic philosophers apart from their opponents. The difference appears in such anti-intellectualistic proverbs as, The poet is born, not made. To a Plato the rhapsode who sings under the impetus of inspiration is not so important as the poet who knows what he is up to, if there be any such. As the rationalistic tradition loses force in the Hellenistic period and disappears under the influence of Christianity, submission to divine guidance, not only in matters of artistry, but also in matters of belief, the feeling of human impotence in almost all affairs except that of stubbornly willing to accept the will of God—these take the place of reason. But if one took it for granted that man was essentially a rational animal, one was forced to reject the irrational faculties of the soul as anything more than evidences of our animal nature. The notion that they might also partake of superhuman nature was flatly rejected, if even considered.

It was also impossible for Socrates to take such an attitude as that of Thrasymachus. One could not derive any standard of goodness from observation, for all that observation could give one was a picture of historical man. Standards must be found in the realm of eternity if they were to be binding on all men in common. And one advanced toward eternity through dialectic. Socrates himself seems never to have reached his goal, for he is never shown us as formulating any definition of his ideals. He admitted his ignorance, as we have seen, but he also knew why he was ignorant and what he must do to be wise. No definition could be more than nominal if it contained inner contradictions. Hence one could examine all proposed definitions and see whether they would withstand questioning. When Socrates insisted that he must remain in prison and drink the hemlock lest he violate the Law, he was arguing in effect that if he took advantage of offers to escape, he would be setting up a law for himself and that this would be an admission on his part that the Laws did not have universal applicability.

It cannot have escaped one's notice that if this interpretation of Socratic method is correct, then it is in conflict with Aristotle's statement (*Metaphysics* 1078b 29) that Socrates was primarily interested in inductive arguments and (1086b 3) that he did not separate his definitions from particulars. For if he did find the essences of things in the things and never separate from them, the Laws which he found would have been the laws of Athens at the time of his trial plus the laws of all other countries. There would have been inconsistencies in such a collection, as the Sophists had pointed out. If he had said that a man ought to obey the laws of his own country, regardless of their relationship to the laws of other countries, then the universal character of Law as such would have evaporated. Moreover, he must have known that even the laws of Athens had changed, for such knowledge must have been common enough to provide material for Aristotle's *Athenian Constitutions*. Which laws should he obey? If it was those of his own period, then why were they superior to those of any earlier period? This question was not discussed by him in *Crito* and we can only guess at what answer he would have given to it. Our guess is that he was thinking of Law as something above historical statutes, for once he would have admitted the relativity of law to historical incident, his whole dialectical method would have collapsed and he would have been in the same position as that of the Sophists.

There is then in Socrates a fundamental respect for the dignity of human nature, not, to repeat, of individual human beings who may be good or evil, but of humanity in the transcendent sense of that term. In both Plato and Aristotle this distinction between the perfect ideal and the imperfect temporal beings was retained. It was what gave their philosophies that air of detachment from terrestrial concerns which made them both so useful to the early Christian philosophers. They could reason to reforms in a purely deductive fashion. We have no evidence that Socrates ever went so far as they did. He indicated the way, but did not travel it. There was, moreover, in his life as a whole the source of many philosophies. He is represented as a man who was able to withstand pain and hardship by controlling his senses through reason; but he was also represented as one able to enjoy the pleasures of eating and drinking with convivial companions. If he spoke of his ignorance, he also practiced logical criticism. Though he was accused of denying the gods, he firmly believed in the presence of a god within. It is impossible to construct any single set of consistent theorems which would adequately expound all that he stood for; at any rate no one has been able to do so to date. It was his personality to which men turned for their inspiration, not to any set of dogmas which he preached. He lives on in the writings of his followers, not in any books of his own. And that is perhaps why he has remained as the outstanding master of a variety of men rather than as the head of a single school.

3. The most fervent contemners of the human race were the Cynics. Of this group the most famous are Antisthenes and Diogenes of Sinope. Though there are certain differences between these

two men which make one hesitate to group them in the same "school," nevertheless we shall follow tradition and do so.

Antisthenes is mentioned by Plato only once. He is recorded as one of those who were present at the execution of Socrates (*Phaedo* 59b), but no record is made of any comments of his or of any of his acts. Aristotle refers to him at least five times, but three of his references are to his epistemological or logical views. There is one reference to him in the *Politics* (1284a 11) mentioning his use of the fable of the Lion and the Hare. The Hare in this fable demands equal rights for all. The Lion is supposed to have replied, "Where are your teeth and claws?" If this story is a fair account of his attitude toward egalitarian democracy, it would put him in a class with Thrasymachus of the *Republic*. And a man who identifies justice with the will of the stronger can safely be called one who has a fairly low opinion of the human race. A simile of his with a comparable tendency is cited in Aristotle's *Rhetoric* (1407a 9). Here he compared the lean Cephisodotus to frankincense, "because it was his consumption which gave one pleasure." But a fuller description of the philosopher is found in Xenophon, though it is simply a speech put into his mouth at a banquet (*Symposium* iv. 34–43) and of course invented by Xenophon. But we may assume that it represents faithfully enough the speaker's views.

The speech might be called a eulogy of poverty. With a paradoxical opening, such as seems to have been characteristic of the Socratics, to the effect that the speaker, who has little or no money, yet thinks himself rich, Antisthenes then pronounces the dictum that men do not have riches or poverty in their material possessions but in their souls. Material wealth does not assuage the hunger for money: some rich men will go to any length to increase their fortunes still further; others are content with what they have. He has nothing but pity for those who are in the grip of the *amor habendi*, for it is a kind of disease. He himself needs no money, for he never eats beyond the point of satisfying his hunger or drinks except to quench his thirst. His clothing is simple, but adequate to keep him warm. When stimulated by lust, he satisfies it on any woman whom he happens upon and she is grateful since no other man would be likely to take her. But his greatest satisfaction in his poverty is that if his possessions were taken away from him, he would find it easy to replace them. When one lives simply, pleasures come easily, for it is the need for food that creates one's pleasure in eating, not its cost or luxuriousness. Finally, he is really rich who can spend what he has liberally, and both he and his master, Socrates, have that kind of wealth.[28]

The use of the reason in an argument of this sort follows a pattern which was going to predominate in literary paradoxes and set speeches. One first asks oneself, as it were, what is the reason for eating, drinking, wearing clothes, copulating, talking, working, or for any of the other customary acts of men. One next defines the act as a means to an end, omitting all traits which do not serve that end: one eats to keep alive; one drinks to quench one's thirst; one wears clothes to protect one from the weather, and so on. The third step is to look at the same acts as generally practiced and, it goes without saying, one finds that they are often performed for ends which are not resident in and sometimes obstructive to the purposes for which one has decided that they exist. Reason then tells one that such ends are bad. Only one purpose must be assigned to each act. If that purpose is pleasure, nothing else but the pleasure which it procures for a man need be considered. If it is the preservation of life, that alone is to be sought. The outcome of this practice of reasoning was sometimes more paradoxical than might have been expected. When taken over by some of the early Stoics, it led to its own refutation. Thus Sextus Empiricus notes that sometimes Reason was used to defend what was both "contrary to Nature" and "contrary to

---

[28] In the *Memorabilia* (i. 6) there is given a conversation between Socrates and Antiphon, the Sophist, in which Socrates is represented as a believer in the Simple Life much in the manner of Antisthenes. If this conversation is based on Socrates' real views, there is some justification for making him one of the sources of this type of Cynicism.

custom" (Greek), as when Chrysippus in his book on the State endorses the "unnatural" practices of pederasty, incest, and cannibalism.[29]

But the main *topos* of the Cynic was the pursuit of autarky, self-dependence, freedom from external needs, personal sovereignty. This in different ways appears as well in Plato, in the Epicureans, in the Stoics, and even in the Skeptics. The wise man was he who could dispense with goods, who was independent not only of material possessions, but also of society as an organized system of laws and regulations. To be free in the case of the Cynics often meant to "follow Nature," though they seemed to differ somewhat in their ideas of where Nature was to be found. The speech of Antisthenes, which we have briefly summarized, does not emphasize Nature as the norm of correct living. It is rather praise of the simple life on the ground that superfluities are shackles on freedom. If the end of life is freedom, and if superfluities reduce one's freedom, then Reason tells one to do away with them. There is little here of the contempt for mankind which is to be found in the anecdotes told about Diogenes. In fact, when Antisthenes condemns Alcibiades, his condemnation ran counter to the preaching attributed to Diogenes. If Alcibiades followed the Persians in committing incest, Diogenes would have said that he did no more than the beasts do and their acts are the criteria of the natural.[30] If an act is natural, what is wrong with it? But to Antisthenes, the question is not one of being natural or unnatural, but of becoming a slave to a passion. Clement of Alexandria reports him as saying that if he could catch Aphrodite, he would shoot her, for she corrupts good and decent women; love is nature's evil, a disease (fr. 35). Yet he is also said to have believed that the Sage should marry in order to have children, begetting them on the handsomest women (fr. 58). Such conflicts of opinion are to be expected when one has to rely almost exclusively on anecdotes for the reconstruction of a man's

---

[29] *Outlines of Pyrrhonism* iii. 246 f.
[30] Mullach, *op cit.*, Vol. II, p. 275, fr. 9. I shall use Mullach's numbering.

thought. We should run into more if we discussed all the various apothegms reported to be by him in Diogenes Laertius. But none of them exhibit those revolting ideas which made Diogenes of Sinope famous. We may safely say of him that he stood for simplicity but not for asceticism, was cautious of becoming entangled in civic affairs,[31] and thought that autarky was the highest good. All three of these opinions cast a shadow on the way most human beings live and Antisthenes must have looked down with a certain ostentation on the general run of mankind. Though his own words are probably no longer to be read, his very desire to deny the commonly held values is enough to establish him as a severe critic of his fellows. Most of the so-called fragments derive ultimately from Xenophon's *Symposium* and indeed his remarks in that work suffice to found a legend. But there is even less to go on in the case of the more famous Diogenese of Sinope.[32]

Since Diogenes was only about thirteen years old when Socrates was executed, he does not figure in any of the Platonic dialogues. He is mentioned once by Aristotle, in the *Rhetoric* (1411a 24), as calling the taverns the mess halls of Attica. Demetrius, the author of the rhetorical treatise *On Style*, gives us two anecdotes about him, one showing his sense of the absurd and the other his sarcasm, both being used by the author to illustrate the idea that "every form of Cynic speech seems at once like a dog fawning and biting."[33] Most of the anecdotal data are cast in that mold which still today is called cynical. Though it is precarious to systematize them, certain general ideas emerge from them all. There is first of all an extreme cultural primitivism, based on the ideal

[31] See esp. fr. 89, which may of course be spurious.

[32] The contrast between Antisthenes and Diogenes is strongly emphasized in a book by the late Farrand Sayre, *Diogenes of Sinope* (Baltimore: privately printed, 1938). This study, based on a doctoral dissertation, though the work of a "gentleman scholar" is worth reading with care and its thesis is well documented.

[33] *De elocutione* v. 260–61. W. Rhys Roberts in his introduction to this work in the Loeb Classical Library dates Demetrius at the end of the first century A.D., rather than 300 B.C., the traditional date given to Demetrius of Phalerum to whom the treatise is usually attributed. Most of our information about Diogenes comes from Diogenes Laertius.

of self-sufficiency. He is reported by Epictetus (*Discourses* iii. 24. 67 f.) to have said, "Since Antisthenes set me free, I have not been a slave. . . . He taught me what things are mine [or my concern] and what are not. Possessions, kindred, family, friends, fame, familiar places, my occupation, these are all alien to me." The use of appearances alone is a person's concern. In this realm a man is absolutely free and self-sufficient. In order to make use of appearance as he pleased, he avoided everything which was costly or which involved trouble or much labor.[34] Stobaeus in one place (*Floril.* ciii. 20) quotes him, an out-and-out hedonist, as saying, "Happiness consists solely in this—that a man truly enjoy himself and never be grieved, in whatever place or circumstances he may be." But in another place (ix. 49) this is qualified by the insistence on the "right use" of a man's sense organs: "He who uses them rightly gets pleasure from seeing and hearing, from food and sex; while for him who uses them wrongly, dangers arise from those things which are most valuable and necessary." How right and wrong use are distinguished is not explained, but one can guess that some experience is required in order that no pleasure may be sought which would infringe on a man's autarky. If this guess is correct, then the hedonism of Diogenes, in spite of the anecdotes of his shamelessness, the purport of which is that neither incest nor cannibalism were against nature, is far from being the whole of his philosophy.[35] There are also stories that he took the beasts as exemplary, as if they were more natural than man. What the beasts could do without, man could do without. For that reason he lived in the shelter of his famous wine jar, ate raw food, wore the simplest of clothes—which later evolved into the well-known Cynic cloak—withdrew from all

---

[34] Dio Chrysostom *Orat.* vi. 30–34.

[35] On the cultural primitivism of Diogenese, see *Primitivism in Antiquity*, pp. 135 ff. His shamelessness became legendary. For instance he is reported to have "performed the work of Demeter and of Aphrodite," including masturbation, in public. But when shamelessness becomes a legend, the historian becomes wary. For the persistence of the legend in our own times, see Bayle's *Dictionary*, art. Diogène.

public affairs, and in short became the stock symbol of the self-sufficient individualist.

The importance of all this for a history of philosophic ideas is the definition of the natural as an ethical norm. There is probably no ancient philosopher whose works have survived either in their original form or in secondhand reports who did not use that adjective as a term of praise and who did not criticize human behavior on the basis of its naturalness or unnaturalness. But as we have said, what they meant by this term varied widely. One might imagine that the nature of anything was revealed in the general characters of the class to which it belonged. But to discover that class involved one in a circular definition, for before one knew, one was adding the adverb "naturally" to the clause "to which it belonged." It demands no great amount of meditation to see that a thing may belong to a great variety of classes, as determined by the traits which it shares in common with other things. Man has been defined as a rational animal, an animal which laughs, a featherless biped, a social animal, a being with a sense of sin and of estrangement from God, and so on, and all of these definitions, with the exception of "a social animal," would be useful in given contexts. But to derive standards of behavior from definitions, though common practice, is a dubious enterprise, for if the definition is real and not nominal, then every member of the class defined ought to be covered by it. If then man is really a rational animal, to take but one and not the least famous of these definitions, all men ought to be found to be rational. And the problem of making them rational ought not to arise. One does not ask a person to be what he is.

But reformers have to have something to reform and in general their task, if they use the technique which we are discussing, is to devise means of making men live up to the definition which has been framed of their nature. In short, it is soon discovered that some men are unnatural. Now the definitions of "natural" which were most in use were roughly as follows. Natural man was the chronologically primitive man, in Greek legend man of the Golden

Age or of the Age of Cronus. This in Hebrew legend was man
before the Fall of Adam. The Pagan Fall was attributed to a variety of acts: uncontrolled degeneration, the institution of private
property and the desire for possessions, the love of luxury, the
emergence of injustice, the appetite for animal food; in fact, there
was scarcely any characteristic of civilized life which was not used
as the source of man's unnaturalness. Yet no one satisfactorily explained why any of these evils should have entered the scene to
corrupt human life. In spite of the Fall, there were, it was assumed, always some remnants of the state of nature to be discovered. Either reason or instinct or intuition could light upon
them, though in each case these faculties found different traces of
man's original nature. Reason, for instance, might lead to asceticism or the simple life; instinct might lead one to copy the animals; intuition might lead one to love, as in Tibullus (*Elegies* ii. 3),
or, in our own times, to the supposed innocence of childhood. In
Diogenes the animal was the natural, if we may trust the anecdotes. Hence to live according to nature was to live according to
animal ways of living. But what animal was the most natural?[36]

It is interesting to see that it was Diogenes, not Antisthenes,
who became the typical Cynic. And it is from his way of living
that our own word, "cynical," got its connotation of contemptuous, scornful of human motivation, and sneering. The later Cynics
are described in Lucian's *Cynicus*[37] as bearded, unshorn, shirt-
less, half-naked, barefoot, worn out by hardships, homeless, and
dirty. They lived on as pagan mendicants, and the German scholar,
Helm, maintains that "Cynicism disappeared with the disappearance of paganism, after monachism had taken over into itself
in part the characteristic features of the Cynic life."[38] The monks

[36] For a thorough analysis of the various meanings of "nature" and its
derivatives, we refer once again to A. O. Lovejoy's Appendix to *Primitivism
in Antiquity*.

[37] I follow tradition in calling it Lucian's, though most modern classicists
think it spurious. See *Primitivism in Antiquity*, p. 136.

[38] See his art. *Kynismus* in Pauly-Wissowa, *Real-Encyclopädie der clas-
sischen Altertumswissenschaft* (Stuttgart: J. B. Metzler, 1925), Vol. XII,
pp. 3–23.

of course were not motivated by the same considerations as the Cynics, but outwardly they were indistinguishable from them, being stimulated by an equally powerful *contemptus mundi*. And in spite of the disgusting stories told about Diogenes, his stamina was admired by many writers, among the Stoics by Epictetus and among the Neoplatonists by Julian the Apostate.

IV

In general it may be said that Greek ethical teaching split on the question of how to make man what he *really* is. The Sophists seem to have believed that men, like everything else, had no common nature, or at least none which was relevant to ethics. Socrates and the Socratics, on the contrary, maintained that man's eternal nature as distinguished from his historical nature could be discovered in a world of ideals and that it served as a standard by means of which one could correct the behavior of individual men. The aim of the Socratics was to bring eternal man down into history and the self-sufficiency (autarky) which they sought was in effect the liberation of eternal man from temporal entanglements. Yet both groups turned out, with the possible exception of Prodicus, to be individualists of an extreme type, the Sophists in utilizing society for their own ends, the Socratics in their inevitable withdrawal from society.

1. If the *Dissoi Logoi* are to be taken seriously as evidence that moral standards have no roots "in nature," but are created by men for their own ends, then it is folly to move any farther in the direction of social obligation than the extent to which it will bring one peace, or keep one out of trouble. If one is living in a society which demands military service, then one does one's military service because it is easier to conform than not to conform. If a society demands certain religious performances, such as celebrating the nation's birthday or putting a pinch of incense on the altar of the Emperor's genius, one does so rather than make one-

self a nuisance to others. But none of this means that one believes in the inherent rightness of such behavior, and if one could evade military service or the prescribed religious rites without danger, one would do so. No one can be a martyr to an ideal if he does not believe in the existence of ideals. And if what are called ideals are simply the prejudices of one's fellow men, there is no reason why one should give them more than lip service.

There is, however, one aim which can be attained without reasoning to its justification, pleasure. It is probably true that animals and children seek agreeable experiences and avoid painful ones. And since the most fantastic acts and occupations can become pleasurable, even those which are antibiological, it becomes impossible to argue that a man does anything without a hedonistic motive. Self-sacrifice, suicide, hard work, asceticism, and all the acts of saints and martyrs can be described as giving pleasure to the man who performs them. It may not be the pleasure of the majority, but that is of no account. It may be the pleasure that comes from the approbation of those whose approbation one seeks. It may be the pleasure that comes from self-approbation. But in both cases the hedonist will call it pleasure. What ought to be done is what one does. And if all men seek some sort of pleasure, then that is what they ought to seek. That this leads to moral anarchy is indubitable, if one is thinking of the theoretical structure of an ethics. Theoretically there is no reason to maintain that all men will seek the same goals, even if one use a very abstract term like pleasure to name what all men seek. Actually it may turn out that there is at least a high probability that all men's goals will be identical. For instance, it may be true that all men seek sexual satisfaction above everything else and that if they cannot get it in the normal way, will find it in abnormal ways. We have been told in recent years that the very denial of sexual satisfaction on the part of some individuals may be a disguised form of it. In any event, all that we have here is a statistical generalization of fact and there is no sense in telling men that they ought to do what they do anyway. When a Sophist such as

Thrasymachus in the first book of the *Republic* argues that justice is the satisfaction of the will of the stronger, he is making a descriptive statement and the only rule which he can give to his fellows is that of not being misled by the ideas of men who would like to substitute the fulfillment of their desires for that of someone else. *The Prince* is an excellent handbook for the disciples of Thrasymachus, for it sets down the recipes by which a strong man can induce others to accept his rule. But the thesis that all men seek to impose their will on others is not deduced from any axiomatic premise, but like the universality of the hedonistic motive, is an empirical generalization.

The *Dissoi Logoi*, as we have seen above, were opinions both of individuals and of societies. If the Sophists wondered about the cause of such a variety of opinions, we have no evidence of it. It would have been possible to ask why an individual wanted the things he wanted, whether there was something in a man's soul and body which drove him to one kind of behavior rather than to another. When it was a question of national opinions, the Athenians preferring one thing, the Spartans another, the same question might have been put. Why, for instance, did a military state put such emphasis on comradeship and so little on family life? One might even go farther and ask why Sparta became a military state. Plato in the *Republic* gives reasons why all possessions should be in the hands of the Philosopher-Kings, why children should be educated by the state, why wives should be given to men as the rulers saw fit. These reasons are of course part of a purely theoretical structure, but nevertheless analogous reasons might have been looked for in real societies. We have, for instance, some idea of why the Pharaohs and the Kings of Persia married their sisters; the reasons may not have been good ones, but they make the rule intelligible. We also can see that in a regime which permits private property, theft should be punished, and we also can see that in a hierarchical society the wickedness of homicide should be weighed against the rank of the person killed. Such investigations would seem to us, I imagine, a natural step to be taken as soon as one has become committed to any sort of cultural relativism. But we have no evidence that the Sophists took it.

The only document which we have on which to construct a Protagorean ethics would be Plato's dialogue, *Protagoras*. But here we learn simply that the Sophist believed that virtue can be taught, as if it were an art. We find him protesting against the view, suggested by Socrates, that goodness is identical with pleasure, as well as making no use of his epistemological relativism. His introduction of the myth of Prometheus accentuates his belief that man without the arts would be at the mercy of the elements, but precisely how the art of becoming virtuous would be taught is nowhere explained. We are thus left with nothing but conjecture to help us reconstruct the ethical views of the greatest of the Sophists.

2. There is both a hedonistic and an ascetic element in the behavior of Socrates himself. He is pictured by both Plato and Xenophon as enjoying the pleasures of the table and of companionship; but he is also depicted as able to withstand the rigors of war, as being satisfied with very little in the way of bodily comfort, and acting as a mild Cynic. Pleasure masters him as little as pain. Evil and good are not determined by human preferences but by a superhuman order. Temperance, courage, friendship, like truth and beauty, are ideals which do not vary but are fixed in the realm of eternity. In his opinion it would be, for instance, senseless to criticize a man for cowardice if there were no such thing as cowardice-in-itself, regardless of people's opinions about it. If you can argue about a virtue, it is because there is something real to argue about. We may not know for certain just what it is, but that amounts to no more than being unable to frame a good definition of it. Socratic ignorance is limited to the area of the definition. But such ignorance does not prevent our recognizing a virtuous act when we come across one. A person may recognize a dog or a horse without being able to formulate a good definition of caninity or equinity. Yet somehow we must possess an idea,

however nebulous and obscure, of the things which we can recognize, and it is our duty as rational animals to clarify the obscurity of our intuitive ideas.

Let us assert once more then that for Socrates ethical ideals are a part of the natural order and are not created by men. If this thesis is developed, the distinction between Greek and Barbarian as essential collapses, for what is wrong for a Greek is wrong for all men and the local laws are irrelevant to the issue. We are again faced with the problem of why in that case Socrates should have been so insistent on obeying the laws of Athens. Why should such a law not have been simply the opinion of *The Many* and as wrong as any other opinion? At the risk of reading too much into Socrates' stand, we can see that statutes could be thought of as the closest approximation to the right that men can attain; like beauty and virtue, the right is never perfectly incorporated. Or, to suggest another interpretation, that man alone is free who can discipline himself into doing something which is difficult. To evade the law is cowardice and Socrates has never been thought of as a coward. A third possibility was indicated by his defense when he said that he had not much longer to live anyway and that death is nothing to be feared. Yet there is a curious inconsistency in his attitude. He reminded his hearers that when he and four others were ordered by the Thirty to go to Salamis and bring back Leon so that he might be put to death, his four companions obeyed the order, "But I, I took myself home" (*Apology* 32d). "At that time it was not by words but by deeds that I showed that I cared little about death . . . but to do nothing unjust, nothing impious, that was my whole concern." Could it not have been said that the orders of the Thirty were just as much the Law as the orders of the court which tried him?

The difference between the two kinds of government is not brought out by Plato as the reason for Socrates' disobeying the commands of the one and refusing to disobey the commands of the other, though both commands were unjust. That difference is one which we have advanced for ourselves. But in Plato it was the promptings of the *Daimon* which determined his acts. In neither case did the *Daimon* check him in his decision and for that reason alone he felt free to act as he did. This being so, the right was revealed by intuition; he knew what was right by being told what was wrong. Generalizing, one can say that man goes about his business until the moment comes when his conscience tells him to refrain from acting. There was precedent for this in the decision of Antigone to bury her brother's body. She too had to choose between obeying the law of the gods or that of the state. And she too had to suffer death. There was therefore in Greek tradition an adumbration of the idea that right and wrong were fixed by supernatural law and that even a government could be in the wrong. To disobey its commands, even if unjust, was to suffer death but death was preferable to impiety. To this idea the Sophists had no reply. For if the right is determined by the opinion of society in general or by national tradition, then the question is bound to arise of why some individuals who are after all brought up within that tradition and subject to the same influences as everyone else within it yet are recalcitrant to its commands. Strictly speaking, one comes to the conclusion that both the state and the conscientious objector are right. There is merely a conflict between their opinions and there is no harmonizing the conflict. One could not even say that the state should allow the objector to go free since his conception of right and wrong is his own, and therefore as well substantiated as that of the state. There should be no outcome except a tragic one to such an impasse, for if the objector goes free, the state—like Creon in *Antigone*—suffers, and if he is punished, *he* suffers.

But behind all this is an idea which it is likely that Socrates held about natural law, and that is that it is always teleological. In the Xenophontic *Memorabilia* (i. 4) is a long argument which is in the nature of a cosmological proof of the existence of God. Furthermore, in Plato's *Phaedo*, which has been cited above, we find Socrates saying that the trouble with the *Nous* of Anaxagoras was that it did not work purposively; it did not explain why one kind of world was better than another. Neither of these references proves that Socrates actually had ever advanced the cosmological proof or that he thought even physical events to happen for a purpose. But they are not complete misrepresentations of his views and we may assume that they represent the general tendency of his thinking. If then natural law is teleological, to Socrates' mind this would imply that natural purposes are good. He certainly did not believe that God was evil. To conform to God's laws—or to those of Nature—would be to act in accordance with divine purposes. The harmony between moral ideals and natural law would be complete and the virtuous man would act in consonance with "what ought to be" or, in Plato's words, with what "really is real." The man whose life is "in accordance with Nature" might well be the man who could both be incapable of putting the divine law into words and at the same time have an intuition of it. Also, since it was a single universal law, it would be binding on all men. We are obviously expanding here the thought of Socrates, but it is unlikely that we are stretching it to the breaking point.

3. We have no evidence whatsoever of the theoretical framework of Cynic ethics. We simply know how the Cynic lived and the aims for which he strove. We know that these aims were bound up with the ideal of autarky and that the attainment of self-sufficiency was brought about by the renunciation of everything which a man could give up and still live. The self-sufficiency of Socrates could be inferred from his awareness of his dependence upon the Laws, however paradoxical that might seem. It was an awareness that he had to create for himself by self-examination. He had to liberate himself from common opinion, even when common opinion was true. The Cynic, as far as anyone knows, had no such thesis to defend. He gave no reason for his desire for freedom; he simply laid it down as an axiom that a man ought to be free. The repulsion which he had to slavery was largely rhetorical or, if one wishes, it was something which seemed self-evident to a Greek. If one were asked if slavery to others, to

society at large, to one's bodily desires, to material possessions, to public opinions, was good or evil, it was expected that one would immediately answer that it was evil without further debate. But that was playing upon the emotional connotations of the word "slavery." For if it was true that it was man's nature to live in society, as Aristotle was to say, and that meant also to have certain possessions, to satisfy certain bodily desires such as those for a wife and children, or to maintain a decent reputation among one's fellows, then it would be folly to name that kind of life by a pejorative word. The renunciation of the normal values of mankind is a noble end if there is some reason for it other than the emotional charge of a word. The monk, for instance, was vicariously expiating either the sins of mankind or his own, was praying to God for the salvation of his brothers, was worshiping God twenty-four hours a day. He could justify what he was doing by his theological system. But the Cynic who simply said that one must renounce the world to attain self-sufficiency and who gave no reason why self-sufficiency should be any nobler than the mutual dependence of social beings, was fundamentally capricious. When Cynics are represented by later writers as saying that the very contempt for pleasure is most pleasurable, that "those who have by discipline become habituated to its opposite find a greater pleasure in their scorn of pleasure than in the pleasure themselves,"[39] they are probably correctly pictured. For there is indeed a great pleasure in having one's own way, regardless of the obstacles which exist in the road to having it. And however anarchistic the Cynic was, he would not have thought of that as a serious objection. Social life with all the obligations to others which it entailed was an evil. The begging friars of the Middle Ages may have thought so too, but it goes without saying that one can beg only from others.

4. That the Sophists must have been interested in logic is obvious. But it is also obvious, at least from their arguments, that they

---

[39] Diogenes Laertius, vi. 71. See *Primitivism in Antiquity*, chap. 4, for further discussion of this side of Cynicism.

saw the difficulties of applying logic to a world in flux. If man is the measure of things that are and of things that are not, and if the truth is a picture of what is and falsity of what is not, then clearly man is the measure of truth and falsity. Among the *Dissoi Logoi* are examples relating to this (Diels-Kranz, Vol. II, pp. 405 ff.). They deal with the application of words to things. If a man is accused of a crime, for instance, and tells his story in denial of it, then his story is true if he did not commit the crime and false if he did. This seems to the author to prove that, since the facts are not before the court, the story is both true and false. Silly as this sounds, it points to a difficulty in determining the truth of a statement referring to the past, if we define the truth as a verbal expression of "that which is." But the criterion of truth is not the truth. Judging from the other examples given, the truth must, in order to be different from the false, be the expression of something which does not change, something which is beyond the flux. But if something is over and done with, it has been part of the flux. How then can one discover the truth about it?

The word "is" in a purely formal statement has no tenses. Mathematical formulas are timeless. But there seems to have been a preconceived idea in the minds of some of the Sophists that the verb is not merely grammatically in the present but refers also to something existing in the present. If the two meanings are not distinguished, then it is impossible to predicate anything of changing things, of past and future things, as well as to make generalizations. Yet we do make generalizations and we also assert judgments of the past and future. It is clear that the date of making an assertion is not necessarily the date of that about which the assertion is made. When Gorgias says that nothing exists, he may simply be saying that all things are changing. When he says that if anything exists, it cannot be known, he may again simply be saying that knowledge is always later in time than that which is known. There are undeniably genuine epistemological problems involved in this, but the answer to none of them is that nothing can be known, unless one has already so defined knowledge that it must always have the unchanging and the present as its object. But not only does the word "is" have two meanings in these arguments; so does the verb "to know." First it means the direct apprehension of a perceptual datum; second, knowledge about what is perceived or inferred or reported. The distinction has been recognized in modern times and given the following pairs of names, immediate and mediated knowledge, knowledge-of and knowledge-about, acquaintance and description, *kennen* and *wissen* (or *connaître* and *savoir*, i.e., *cognoscere* and *scire*). The two experiences are ostensibly different and the conditions of their occurrence are different. As early as Aristotle it was recognized that the direct apprehension of a sensory quality was not knowledge in the same sense as beliefs were knowledge. To see red, hear B-flat, smell a smoky smell, taste bitter, are not the same as to know that an apple is red, that the piano is capable of striking B-flat, that something is on fire, or that gall is bitter. One may be the origin of the other, the evidence for the other, the cause of the other, but origins, evidence, and causes are not identical with that of which they are the origins, evidence, and causes.

There is still another complication involved in logic as it was conceived by the Sophists. If falsity is the assertion of that which is not, this would seem to entail the belief in the existence of Nonbeing, a manifest contradiction in terms. Yet if there is a one-to-one correspondence between ideas, judgments, thoughts, and their objects, there must be an object corresponding to each idea, judgment, or thought. But there cannot be anything in what we have come to call the external world corresponding to that which is not. But if any ideas are to be false, there must be something which is their object. In our own day this puzzle was handled by the invention of a world of "subsistence" inhabited by illusions, falsities, impossibilities, fictions, dreams, and so on.[40] This was an effort to avoid ideas which corresponded to nothing, which

---

[40] The most eminent proponent of this thesis in the United States was the late W. P. Montague. See his *The Ways of Knowing* (London and New York: Allen and Unwin, and The Macmillan Co., 1925).

traditionally were called purely subjective. But the ancients had no fear of the mind, whereas the most influential Anglo-American philosophers have at least from the time of Hobbes treated its existence as a problem rather than a fact. The more basic question for the Sophists was involved in a notion that fused logic with ontology. And though the puzzles which they elaborated because of this fusion were often absurd and their arguments purely verbal, yet by using them and tormenting their fellows with them, they may have been responsible for Aristotle's clarification of the technique of reasoning. Aristotle did not make the distinction between logic and ontology, and his theory of truth presents as many problems as the sophistries of his adversaries, but at any rate he showed why they were sophistries and that was a step in the right direction.

It may be well at this point to indicate two other meanings of the verb "to be." Sometimes, as in parts of Aristotle's *Metaphysics*, in Neoplatonism, and some contemporary forms of theology, it means that predicate which can be attributed to everything whatsoever. Everything, whatever else it is, at least *is*, they say. This kind of Being is not supposed to be identical with existence, though sometimes it is talked about in the same language. Sometimes, as in Plato, we find the verb qualified by the adverb "really." That which is really or that which is really real *is* in a different sense from that which simply is or exists. Sometimes the verb means "equals" or "is identical with," as when we say that "two plus two is four," or, "George Washington was the first President of the United States." As in definitions, so here, the predicate may be substituted for the subject and vice versa. Aristotle in his *Metaphysics* (iv. 7) has left us the first extant set of distinctions between the various meanings of this word, and some years ago George Santayana published an article doing the same.[41] The distinctions made in that essay reappear in his *Realms of Being*.

[41] G. Santayana, "Some Meanings of the Word 'Is'" (*Journal of Philosophy*, 1924), now reprinted in his *Obiter Scripta* (New York: Charles Scribner's Sons, 1936), p. 189. Seven meanings are distinguished.

Now the Sophists played upon these ambiguities, either perversely or sincerely, and though the effect of their disputations was demoralizing to some, they were performing a useful function in awakening other thinkers to the need for clarity of definition.

In the nihilistic arguments of Gorgias one finds still another logical device to which attention must be invited. That is the device of which we have frequently spoken in this book of dividing the world into two sets of beings, such that nothing can belong to both at the same time. These sets were called opposites or contradictories. In the most abstract symbolism they are *A* and *not-A*. But here too a further distinction has to be made, and Aristotle made it, between contradictories and contraries. A thing cannot both be and not-be red at the same time and in the same respect, but it can be red and round and round is not-red. A sentence cannot be both true and false. If now I say that the apple is red, I cannot also say that it is not red. The trouble arises because we have to distinguish between negating the predicate or negating the copula "is." We can say without contradiction that the apple is both red and not-red if we mean that it is both red and round, but we cannot say that the apple both is and is-not red. These very simple examples do not seem very important, but they do illustrate the need of keeping a cool head when talking about logical matters. How does one know when of two couples of predicates one set is a set of contradictories and the other a set of contraries? How does one know that red and green (or some other color) are contradictories but that red and round are contraries? There are obviously two ways of knowing this: (1) through "experience": we see apples that are both round and red; (2) by formal definitions: we define a genus, such as color and divide it into species, red, green, blue, and so on, and then lay down the rule that nothing can belong to two species of the same genus at the same time and in the same respect. Whether we could use the second of these methods without previously having learned from experience that there are various species of color seems to us very doubtful. But those who believe in the absolutely nonempirical nature of logic and mathematics would not agree. The general trend of ancient logic was in the direction of finding nonempirical ways of splitting up classes into subclasses. One method which had a great vogue was that of dichotomy, splitting a class by negating the characteristics which were common to all the members of one of its included classes, e.g., colored and noncolored things, material and immaterial things, existent and nonexistent things. To say that something must be either *A* or *not-A* is of course valid, but to say that it is not-A does not tell us much about what it is, unless we have previous knowledge to the effect that not-A names only one predicate. But how do we know this? We can say that a thing must be or not be; but not-being may include becoming, having-been, and about-to-be, all of which are not-being. One might imagine that common sense would tell us, but one of the tasks of philosophy is to criticize common sense. Common sense tells us that people at the antipodes must be standing on their heads, that the sun rises and moves round the earth, that the stars are points of light stuck in the sky, and that the earth is flat. It also tells us all the contradictions of proverbial philosophy. Hence even if common sense happens to tell us the truth, one has to test it and find out on what foundations it is based, for otherwise we are accepting its conclusions as dogma. And dogma is the antithesis of philosophy.

5. One or two of the logical opinions of the Sophists appear in what is left of Antisthenes. Aristotle tells us in the *Topics* (104b 21) that he said that contradiction was impossible. His reason is given in the *Metaphysics* (1024b 32) as the impossibility of describing anything except " by its own *logos*," which may mean by its definition, so that truly there could be no predication. It follows from this, says Aristotle, that both contradiction and error would be impossible. Yet he admits later (1043b 24) that there was some justification for the opinion of Antisthenes "and other such uneducated people" that the essence of a thing cannot be defined, since the essence is simple and the definition is complex.

Essences, Antisthenes seems to have said, can be clarified only by similes, as when we say that silver is like tin.

One cannot reconstruct the logical ideas of Antisthenes from these few scraps. But nevertheless one can see why he held the strange conclusions which he appears to have drawn. If a definition gives us the essence of something, it is simply a long-drawn-out description of what a thing is. The peculiar quality of a thing is a single whole which is apprehended either by perception or imagination or intuition. We all know the quality of redness without necessarily being able to define it, and if we only know the definition of this quality, that it is, let us say, the color which one sees when light rays of a length approximating 0.000759 mm. are reflected from it, we still have no idea of what it looks like. Other definitions are of course possible: it is the color at the end of the visible spectrum opposite the violet; it is the complementary of green; it is the color of blood; but these are all defective. This would be the case were we trying to communicate an idea of any quality: the verbal formula may explain the origin of the quality, its position in a scale, its similarity or dissimilarity to other qualities; but none of these devices does what we want.

But Antisthenes was not limiting his objections to defining sensory qualities. If to be a man or a tree or a house has some "nature" which we can grasp as a unit, and if we can grasp it before knowing anything about it, if in other words we can be acquainted with things without being able to define them, then Antisthenes would have something to say on his side of the debate. We have suggested above that his supposed master, Socrates, did believe that certain moral ideas can be apprehended without our being able to define them. And we all know that in aesthetic matters we can be deeply moved by the quality of a musical composition or a painting and be incapable at the same time of making our feelings articulate. No verbal description of *Hamlet* or Giotto's *Annunciation* in the Scrovegni Chapel in Padua or Mozart's *Requiem* is a substitute for the direct experience of them. This is a commonplace. But if it is valid, all the predicates in the world will stop short of communicating the essence of anything. I confess that I am unable to see why this should make contradiction impossible, though it might make error impossible. But any epistemology based on immediate knowledge makes error within the area defined by immediacy impossible. No one can be mistaken about what he sees or feels, though he may be mistaken in his identification of it, as Aristotle himself admitted in the case of sensory data, in his explanation of why it occurs, in his assertions that it belongs to a physical or imaginary object. Many of our experiences are of this nature, in that "they must be seen to be appreciated." Maybe Cratylus who thought it was the course of wisdom to say nothing and only to point to things was not so stupid as he seems.[42] For if all true knowledge is direct apprehension and if direct apprehension is inarticulate, then predication at best will be only partly true and one man's experience is as valid as another's.

This would also permit the similes that Antisthenes seemed to permit. For if a man has never seen the color of, let us say, an exotic flower, one can compare it to the color of a flower which he has seen and in this way give him some idea of what it is like. Silver actually is like tin in color, though it differs from tin in more ways than it resembles it. If someone asks today what silver is, he is told that it is an element with the atomic weight of 107.88 and the atomic number 47, that it is a white, rather soft metal with the specific gravity of 10.5 and the melting point of 960.5 degrees centigrade. This works very well for an amateur chemist, but the man who asks the question would be better satisfied in all probability if he were shown a piece of silver.[43]

The denial of error in Antisthenes is not a denial of truth, though dialectically one might argue that if all statements are true, then none are true, for truth is supposed to single out certain char-

---

[42] See Aristotle *Metaphysics* 1010a 12.

[43] It will be observed that the description given in the text, with the exception of its mention of color and softness, is derived from operations which are performed upon the metal and not from sensory perceptions in the raw.

acteristics and by implication exclude all others. But if he is confining his conclusions to direct apprehensions, then he could reserve error, as Aristotle himself did, to descriptions, or what Aristotle called synthetic assertions. But since we do not know what restrictions he made, we had best not extend our discussion of his logic.

6. The Sophists by using rational techniques began the overthrow of rationalism. And they did this at the very time that two of the greatest rationalists in the history of philosophy were developing their work. It did not take very long for the suspicion to arise that all reasoning was futile and that a general skepticism was the only intelligent attitude for a man to take. More skeptical than Antisthenes was Pyrrho of Elis, whose life ran on into the first quarter of the third century. Less is known about this philosopher than about most of the others who have been discussed in this chapter, and yet his name has been given to a school of thought which exists even today. The earliest source of our information is the famous *Silloi* and the *Imagines* of his pupil and admirer, Timon of Phlius, but what we learn from him is very meager. Sextus Empiricus in his *Outlines of Pyrrhonism* and Diogenes Laertius furnish more information, but the former is probably attributing more to him than is reasonable and the latter, as usual, is largely relating anecdotes. We can at least say that Pyrrho urged his disciples to suspend judgment since nothing could be known for certain, but what reasons he gave for this are obscure. Later we shall find Skeptics who explain the ground for their skepticism and we shall discuss these grounds at the appropriate place. But it is important to note the existence of this skeptical trend as it first appeared, even if we can do no more than note it. We now turn to the major defender of rationalism, Plato.

CHAPTER III

The Rationalism of Plato

THOUGH WE ARE CONCERNED in this book with individual philosophers only in so far as they modified the rationalistic tradition, there are certain individuals whose influence has been so great that they must be treated in separate chapters. One reason for this is that their contributions to philosophy are numerous, and if they were dealt with along with their neighbors in time, chapters would become unduly extended. Another is that their extant works are very copious even when a few exist only in truncated form. A third is possibly a corollary of the second, for when an author leaves a great many works to posterity and must, because of the nature of things, write them one after another, and therefore during a long lifetime, he exhibits certain peculiarities of style and certain inconsistencies which are the concomitants of a long life: a man of eighty does not usually express himself in the same way, hold to the same interests, believe in the same things, as a man of twenty. And if the philosopher in question for one reason or another is read by many people, even when most of them are disciples, there will arise a variety of interpretations of his thought. What was *the* philosophy of Plato, Aristotle, Plotinus, Saint Augustine, assuming that each one of them had one philosophy, is difficult to answer, since, unless one is unusually presumptuous, one has to admit that one's interpretation may be erroneous and is usually at best only plausible.

In Plato's case we meet with a philosopher who has suffered from idolatry as well as from downright dislike. Both the ancients and the early Christians looked to him as the source of their doctrines, as if their consistency with his dialogues would give added proof to their theories. This is the more curious among the early Fathers with their theory of a *praeparatio evangelica*, a notion revived in our own time by Father F. C. Copleston,[1] for one might think that the Source of all light would produce His revelations without the help of heathen thinkers. The revelation to Abraham seems to have been preceded by no teaching from the Sumerian or Egyptian sages, and there is nothing, as far as I know, in the Prophets which any Biblical scholar asserts to have been prepared by Philistine, Persian, or Indian literature. It is true that in Saint Paul there are two references to Greek writers, but Paul was far from using them as authority for beliefs which he had been taught through revelation. We are fortunately not burdened with the task of untangling the pagan sources of Christian doctrine; our mention of the *praeparatio evangelica* is made only because one version of Platonism has been colored by those who hold to it. One of the dialogues, *Timaeus*, has been so Christianized by its readers that it is next to impossible to read it as something written three hundred and fifty years or so before the birth of Christ. In fact there is nothing in Plato's works or in his life which has not been a matter of debate. Fact and legend have been confused; the chronological order of his works has been so jumbled that there is only one book whose position in the series is generally agreed upon, the *Laws*, and even that has been held to be spurious.

[1] *History of Philosophy* (London: Oates and Washbourne, 1947), Vol. I.

We need not go into the question of his biography unless we think that the dialogues are inexplicable otherwise.[2] And since the inconsistencies in his works are of minor importance, I shall omit any discussion of them. Also, since we are not concerned with the development of his thought, I need not go into the chronological order of his works. Finally, since there is enough material to meet our needs in the works mentioned by his most eminent pupil, Aristotle, and accepted by the great majority of scholars as genuine, we shall consider them as authentic and base our argument upon them.

I

The doctrine of the two worlds appears in Plato in a new form. Reality is no longer that which constitutes the substance of the physical world, a kind of matter which is diversified according to the conditions under which it appears, nor yet a law which governs the flux of things. It is not even the persistence of the flux. It is not the Pythagorean numbers, whatever those numbers may have been, though in *Timaeus* the world is best understood *more geometrico*. It seems to be rather that which classes of things have in common, even when it is not found incorporated in things themselves. These common properties appear to be the start of his conception of the Ideas. And it is also probable that Plato derived the conception of the Ideas from his master, Socrates, whom he so frequently represents as trying to induce his pupils

[2] I have already done so in "Fact and Legend in the Biography of Plato," *Philosophical Review*, LVII (1948), 439 ff., without convincing anyone who did not agree with that article's conclusions before reading it. Plato himself is made to say that none of the works attributed to him are genuine in *Epistle* 2. 314c, which makes the search for Platonism easy for those who believe in the authenticity of the *Letters*. Nor shall we discuss the problem of secret or esoteric doctrines or Plato's lectures. For the former, see G. Boas, "Ancient Testimony to Secret Doctrines," *Philosophical Review*, LXII (1953), 79 ff.; for the latter, see Harold Cherniss, *The Riddle of the Early Academy* (Berkeley and Los Angeles: University of California Press, 1945).

to give him a definition of a class of things, or, if one prefer, of an abstract noun. This appears with special clarity in one of his less entertaining dialogues, *Hippias Major*. Here Plato, as if replying to Xenophon's *Symposium* (ii and v) where Socrates identifies the beautiful with the fitting,[3] gives us the Sophist Hippias struggling to see the need for general ideas, as he gives only examples of beauty to Socrates. Gold is beautiful (289e); riches, health, and a fine funeral are beautiful, says Hippias (291d), but he never reaches the point of clarifying the idea of beauty itself. But the same technique of trying to get a person to attain to a vision of common characteristics is found in many of the dialogues which have been called dialogues of search. In *Charmides* the goal is the idea of temperance or good behavior, in *Lysis* of friendship, in *Laches* of courage, in *Theaetetus* of knowledge, in the *Symposium* of love. In all of these dialogues the pupils, as one might call them, seem able to produce examples of the idea whose definition is being sought, but unable to frame the definition itself. Definitions can be given only of classes, not of individuals, and Plato seems to have been the first philosopher to recognize the ineffable nature of particulars. Particulars can be seen, felt, observed, but they are logical surds. For every time we know something, as distinguished from observing it, every time we put that knowledge into words, we are forced to use common nouns which of course are general terms. If then gold and fine funerals are beautiful and the word "beautiful" means the same thing wherever it is used, then all beautiful things must have something in common which we can define when we know it.

Yet nowhere that I know of does Plato say that the common characteristics are observable. Nowhere does he have Socrates make comparisons between things and ask what common perceptual properties they have. What he is looking for is some reason why two things should be given the same name and that reason is not a generalization from sensory experience at all. Socrates' pupils, when they are not so obtuse as Hippias, offer definitions

[3] Cf. *Memorabilia* iii. 8 and iv. 6.

of the idea under consideration, and Socrates' search is in the direction of seeing whether the definition can be made self-consistent. If, for instance, Plato was trying to define circularity, he would not be satisfied with examples of circles such as wheels, shields, coins, but would insist on a verbal statement which would be approximately true of the examples but which would not be abstracted from them. In the jargon of today's philosophies, for Plato essence is prior to existence, and its priority is in the field of cognition. The distinction between knowledge and observation is ultimate.

The common properties are not differentiated from their particulars merely by the generality. They are also differentiated from them by their timelessness. Whereas all beautiful things may be wiped out in the course of time, beauty itself, he believes, is something which remains stable and immutable. There seems to be, moreover, no special reason why any idea should ever be exemplified, though in *Timaeus* he says that eventually all possibilities must be realized. The history of mathematics shows how certain ideas can be deduced from what used to be called self-evident premises and are now called postulates, ideas which are not only not exemplified, but probably never could be. We are all brought up to believe that no perfect circle will ever be drawn on paper, nor really parallel lines. We may refine our drawings as we will, we are told, but there will always be a margin between the perfection of the mathematical ideal and the crudity of our exemplifications. Since the rise of Christianity, the thesis has been extended to moral matters. No man will ever be perfectly good this side of Paradise, and in fact it was only through the Incarnation of God in man that goodness of such perfection was ever seen on earth. And if no premises are self-evident, then the truth of no system of theorems can ever be any greater than the truth of the postulates, and consistency has to take the place of truth-to-fact. Ideas then are not dated. They have no situation in history. They are eternal. In fact, in the *Republic* where a definition of justice is sought and found, Plato makes it clear that no such idea has ever been in existence and that it probably never will be. Nor does it make much difference. If in naming the Ideas he used a noun which is etymologically related to the verb *to know*, it is because they represent what can be known, thus sharply setting them apart from what can be experienced in the world of history.

But in Greek the verb *to know* and the verb *to see* are closely related, as if to know something was to see it. We preserve this metaphor in English when we say that we see what is meant when we understand something. What is "seen" is the meaning of the idea in question. Presumably what Plato is looking for is something which could be seen in this way and which would preserve its self-identity wherever it might be found. The analogy to the beings of mathematics is again clear. For whether circularity is found in a wheel or in the orbits of the planets, it is always a circle as described by geometry, and the mathematical definition gives us a test by means of which we can tell whether we have a circle before us or something else. The self-identity of the Ideas depends on their immutability and the only things which could be immutable are those to which time is irrelevant.

An idea in this sense of the word is similar to an ideal. Since particular things in the world of history, of time, of change, of growth and decay, are never what they ought to be, never what their definitions say they really are, there must be some standard by means of which we determine both what things really are and how far they realize their natures. If we know what a frog, a dog, or a man really is, and we see that a given frog, dog, or man falls short of what the definition states, then we also see that particulars are never quite what they should be. And we soon understand that there must be certain ideals which we use to determine the nature of things and the degree of perfection which the things in question exhibit. That is, a given man may approach closer to the ideal of humanity than another. But as soon as we say that, we have assumed that we know what ideal humanity is, and when we use that ideal to judge the perfection of given human beings, men of the past as well as of the present, men of other civilizations as well as of our own, we have admitted that the ideal is not changed by local or chronological circumstances. Here a paradox enters our philosophy and one may well raise the question of how the ideal both can be the common properties of a group of things and yet not be manifested in any of them.

Now Plato, as is well known, usually presents his theories through the character of Socrates, and Socrates is said by Aristotle to have introduced into philosophy "definition by induction." This is supposed to mean that he first assembled a collection of similar things and then drew out of them by inspection that which they had in common. The paradox arises from the obvious fact that he must have known which things were similar when he began to assemble them and that consequently his search for their similarity was unnecessary. But the paradox is attenuated, if not resolved, by our common procedure of classifying things in accordance with some superficial similarity which can be easily perceived but which turns out to be only superficial. In the history of science we find many examples of this. The theory of the four elements is a case in point. We do not know why all material substances were grouped into earth, water, air, and fire, but we do know that when the classification was made, each of the elements had a single character which determined the behavior of the compounds into which it entered. Earth, for instance, always moved to the center of the world below water, and if anything which contained earth was moved upward by force, it would drop back to its normal position. To have imagined that diverse things could nevertheless have common properties also involved believing that such properties need not be sensory qualities, colors, shapes, sounds, and the like. It also involved assuming that if we could predict how anything would behave under definable circumstances, it was because of the presence of such properties, either overt or concealed. If we say that a good man will always be courageous or temperate, then we can abstract courage and temperance from the men who possess it and examine those traits independently of the conditions under which they appear. The scientist may say that a falling body *ought to fall* with an acceleration of about 32 feet per second, and he means that "other things being equal" it will so fall. Furthermore, he knows what other things have to be equal. But the use of "ought" suggests that if the thing in question does not behave as it ought to, then something is wrong. What is wrong may not be perversity or sinfulness; it may be simply something or other which prevents the thing from behaving the way the scientist says it ought to behave. As every freshman knows, a body falling through the air or water does not behave as the Law of Falling Bodies says it should behave. And he can make allowances for what he will call perhaps the resistance of the medium.

This would seem to presuppose that there is an order of things according to which classifications may be made such that all things of the same class will behave in the same way or be characterized by the same traits. That order is not the order of things observed outside of laboratories. It also presupposes that when that order is established, there are things in it which do what they ought to do and are what they ought to be. Now when we call them "things," it looks as if they ought to be like the particular things in the world of space and time. And indeed some followers of Plato did talk about them as if they were such beings. But their very perfection, their timelessness, their lack of particularity, their capacity of being used as standards, differentiate them from particulars. Our vocabulary, and to a greater extent that of Plato, makes it impossible to speak of them other than in terms derived from "experience." Metaphors and similes, myths, have to be elaborated in order to handle them intellectually, and the simple literal-minded person is bound either to misunderstand their nature or to conclude that Plato was as simple and literal-minded as he himself is. Thus when Plato speaks of everything seeking the good, it looks as if there were one good thing which all things sought and, since the adjective "good" is usually found in the context of morals, it begins to look as if Plato's universe was a universe of moral goodness. But when it is seen that the good is the perfection of each kind of thing, that is, its nature as purified of all the accidents of space and time, the problem of the good is transformed into the metaphysical problem of generic natures.

It cannot be denied, however unfortunate it may seem to enthusiastic Platonists, that the good is always the character of the class, not of the individual. If one can discover the nature of humanity, it will be that which all human beings share in common when the accidents of history are eliminated, but it will also be an eternal standard which all human beings should try to exemplify. This is not an ethics of "to your own self be true." It is on the contrary an ethics of universal ends. Plato in the *Republic* recognizes that individuals differ profoundly in their ability to attain those ends and maintains that two types of man, those who are dominated by their appetites and those who are dominated by irascibility, never will be really human. They are incomplete human beings. But he is not so pessimistic as to believe that no human beings are endowed with the capacity to be really human and merely insists that circumstances must be so ordered that they be permitted to be so. But similarly with all generic traits: members of the various classes fall short to different degrees of attaining their real natures. A dog with three legs, a calf with two heads, a mathematical proof which is either inelegant or fallacious, are also monstrous deviations from what they ought to be. The dog and the calf will be defined in part as quadrupeds which are monocephalous, and their monstrous character is recognized as monstrous only because we know that they ought to have four legs and one head. We can know what caninity and bovinity are; we can state their definitions clearly and precisely. If we could not do this, we should not be able to distinguish one kind of thing from another, though we could distinguish their existential plurality. But the very fact that we can frame and accept generic definitions, as we are used to doing in mathematics, permits us also to detect imperfections. One of the troubles with this technique is that the history of thought has shown us how the principles of classification have changed and how in consequence of this, the ideas—or ideals—of Plato have been abandoned or seriously modified. But this is a small trouble, for we still use classifications made in a manner similar to that of Plato, based on the assumption that the world is orderly and that the things in it fall into classes the traits of which we use as standards.

At a later time—especially in Philo Judaeus—a term was coined for the perfect order of the world, for those beings which are the standards of all things. This term is the "Intelligible World." It is contrasted with the "Sensible World." It would be anachronistic to use these terms in expounding Plato's own philosophy, for there is no evidence in the dialogues that he attributed to the ideas any character which would help organize them into a world at all. Each dialogue which is relevant to the problem attempts to discover the nature of some one idea; no dialogue establishes any interrelation between the various ideas. This is something which one would do well to remember, for in later thinkers it became customary to assert that the ideas formed a sort of hierarchy with the Idea of the Good at the apex and all the other ideas stemming from it, sometimes in order of generality. Plato does say that the idea of the good is preeminent, but that is simply because each idea is the good for the members of the class which it controls. But that is in no way saying, as some geometers might in their ignorance say, that since all geometric figures are in space, they can be deduced from the idea of space, or that because one can arrange such figures in order of the number of their sides, the triangle, the quadrangle, the pentagon, the hexagon, and so on, they come into existence in that order in the world of spatial beings. One does not generate—or define—a quadrangle by adding a side to a triangle and, strictly speaking, one can define a quadrangle without any reference to triangles and indeed in ignorance of their existence. Logically one might imagine that if there are three-, four-, five-sided figures, there ought also to be one- and two-sided figures from which the polygons "flow." There is then in Plato no evidence of a logical relationship between his various ideas; they all have certain common characters: eternality, unity, difference from one another, immutability, and of course the possibility of being incorporated. In fact, in *Timaeus* (29d, e), which is the source of most of the fantasies drawn from Plato, he maintains that all possibilities must be realized, a statement which, as Lovejoy has shown,[4] gave rise to "the Principle of Plenitude." This principle was not developed by Plato himself into its consequences, one of which was the *scala naturae*. On the contrary, in general Plato seemed to think of his ideas as related to one another in a network, not in a hierarchy.

This seems to be pretty well illustrated in such a dialogue as the *Lysis*. One might say that this dialogue attempts to define "friendship." No satisfactory definition is found, though Lysis himself is both good and handsome and a friend. A series of tentative definitions is presented by the boy to Socrates. They run about as follows.

(1) Friendship is that which is shown in a mother's relation to her children.

(2) It is based on one's recognition of the usefulness of others. But since one man may find another useful, and thus of two men, *A* may be a friend to *B*, while *B* is not a friend to *A*, in the case of two friends one may not be a friend.

(3) Friendship is the attraction of similars. But then two bad men may be friends, and apparently Socrates and his pupil think that friendship ought to obtain only between good men.

(4) Hence perhaps good men are friends. But the good is the self-sufficient, a mark of goodness which we have already noted and which will recur in ancient philosophies, and the self-sufficient desire nothing, love nothing, and hence have no friends.

(5) Can it be then that friendship exists only between contraries and that we love that which is different from us? But this is absurd, for though a bad man might be friendly to a good man, a good man could not possibly be friendly to a bad one. It remains

---

[4] See his *The Great Chain of Being* (Cambridge: Harvard University Press, 1936).

then that there might be some things which are neutral, neither good nor bad.

(6) In that case, friendship would be either the relation between the good man and the indifferent or between the good man and the good. The indifferent—or the mean—might love the good in order to replace the evil from which it suffers, so that we come to another tentative conclusion:

(7) Friendship is the love of the mean, or indifferent, or for the good caused by the presence of evil. This arouses, however, new doubts. In all friendship there must be an object. One cannot just be a friend in a vacuum. What is there in the objects of friendship which is common to them all? If one cannot love someone for the sake of the good, since the good has no need of love, and since the good would not exist if there were no evil, only the mean and the desire for the good would remain. Evil cannot be the source of friendship, for nothing good can come from evil. But it seems strange that only men in a middle position between good and evil could be friends. For we find men of different degrees of perfection being friends of each other. The concluding possibility is:

(8) That you love a person who is somehow like you "in nature" (*Lysis* 221), a phrase which has been translated "congenial." If "congenial" means being of the same genus, sharing the same nature, then it will do. But it is unsatisfactory since all men share the same nature and yet all men are not friends. The outcome seems absurd to Socrates and the dialogue terminates.

It is obvious that the definitions grow out of difficulties, logical or existential, with their predecessors. They are not made in order of generality, nor are they discovered by observing friends and drawing off from them their observably common characters. The speakers are made to understand what is required of a satisfactory definition of "friendship" and simply to test each one proposed by its logical consequences.

The *philia* or friendship which is discussed in this dialogue is love and in the *Symposium* Plato was to examine the matter more closely. Love is not pederasty, for which Plato has nothing but contempt. It is a warm and very affectionate friendship which makes one man want the company of another, a desire which may have its roots in sexuality, but if so, the roots are well concealed. Lysis himself is an example of a friend and yet is incapable of defining his own nature. It is this incapacity which is at the heart of the drama. It is one which appears in regard to other traits in *Charmides*, in *Laches*, and in *Theaetetus*, and it illustrates a point which Plato frequently makes, that one may be the incarnation of an idea without knowing what it is. This is very important for an understanding of his theory of knowledge and throws some light on a remark of Socrates in the *Apology* to the effect that an unexamined life is not worth living. An examined life is one in which all our motives are brought into the light of day, clarified by rational analysis, and made to resist criticism. But for our immediate purposes it is enough to point out that though the Intelligible World is the archetype of the Sensible World, it is not observed through our sensations. This of course is just common sense. We observe thousands of things daily without knowing what they are.

There is another peculiarity of this point of view which should not be passed over. That is Plato's belief that the nature of things is whatever it is independently of our knowledge of it. He is far from being a subjectivist in his metaphysics. We discover natures; we do not produce them either by our powers of observation or by our methods of inquiry. When he speaks of the love between beings which are alike in nature, it is the words "in nature" which are important. Regardless of the maddening ambiguities of that term, in Plato it names something which is certainly objective. He would be willing to say that what we call the nature of something might be determined by our special interests, as the nature of water for a cook or a sailor or a fireman would be different from what it would be for a chemist. But he would insist that, aside from all such considerations, water has a nature because of which the cook, sailor, fireman, or chemist can use the substance to satisfy his special interests. It is this nature which is to be identified with the idea and which Plato's pupil, Aristotle, was to call its essence.

II

Along with the theory of the two realms runs a dichotomy in the realm of knowledge, one part of which is directed toward the particulars or sensible things, the other toward the ideas. As in Heraclitus, the Eleatics, and probably the Pythagoreans, one type of cognition leads us into reality, the other into the world of appearance. The former alone is called knowledge by Plato, the latter being called opinion. This terminology indicates that he does not entirely reject sensory contact with the world, but that while it may accidentally give us the truth, it cannot be relied upon to do so. It gives us fleeting impressions of things as they change. These fleeting impressions may be called true, if one wishes, but they are momentarily true and true only of whatever passes by at the moment of perception. If beyond the flux there is a stable order, then clearly, though we might get a glimpse of it by chance, we could not by the very nature of things get more than a glimpse. How then are we to reach the truth?

Whatever else the truth is, it must be self-identical through time. Its object therefore must be also self-identical and the only self-identical objects are the ideas. For since the ideas cannot change, knowledge about them when once acquired will be unchanging too. The instrument which we possess for acquiring such knowledge is called the reason. If now we select a group of things, all of which belong to a single class, and wish to know them, not simply to look at them, we must purge them of every characteristic which is peculiar to them as individuals, for such characteristics vary from observer to observer and are impermanent. Such traits as size, sensory qualities, pleasantness and unpleasantness, will have to go. Two wheels may differ in size; one may be white and the other black; one may seem ugly to one man and beautiful to another. Yet they are both an approximation to something, circularity, whose real nature is not apprehended by the eye but discovered after all particularity is removed from them. For the visual circularity of the two wheels is not the circularity which the geometer is talking about. If it were, then circles too small to be seen and the circular orbits of the planets, which cannot be seen at all, would not be circular. The visual circle may suggest the geometric notion of a real circle, but the real circle is defined in terms which cannot be seen. If we define a circle as a class of points on a plane all of which are equidistant from another point called the center, we have not made use of a single concept which applies to observation. For no one can see a point or a plane. One cannot attain to a knowledge of circularity by abstraction alone, for how can one abstract from something a trait which the thing does not possess? One could never, for instance, get the idea of man as a rational animal by abstracting the common properties of a group of imbeciles or the idea of an apple by abstracting the common properties of bananas.

Moreover, there is another objection to what has been called the empirical method. It is granted that one cannot imagine anything which one has not experienced either as a whole or in part. But when one collects a large group of things, one finds that they have several traits in common which no one thinks of adding to their real nature. Dogs, for instance, are of all sizes and shapes and of a great variety of colors. But no one would define *caninity* on the basis of the size, shape, or color of the animal. The differences in size which run from that of a Chihuahua to that of a Briard or Saint Bernard, the differences in shape between a spaniel and a greyhound, the difference in color between a German shepherd and a Labrador retriever, do not prevent us from lumping them all together as dogs. A German shepherd resembles a wolf much more than he resembles a cocker spaniel, but in spite of their phylogenetic relationship, we do not classify the wolf with the German shepherd and we do classify the German shepherd with the cocker. How do we know what traits are essential and what are not? Or, to put the question in another way, how do we know what specimens to collect when we are trying to assemble a group of objects with a view to defining their real nature?

This question is taken up in *Meno*. The concept of the idea in this dialogue is perhaps clearer than it is in any other.[5] It is identified with the real nature of a thing (72b, οὐσία), with the pattern (72c, e, εἶδος), and is said to be pervasive of the things which it informs (74a, διὰ πάντων ἔστιν; 75a, ἐπὶ πᾶσι ταὐτόν). Ostensibly this dialogue is trying to answer the question of whether goodness can be taught, but it soon becomes evident that this question is involved with the larger one of how anything can be learned. We know that we do learn things and that the things which we learn may be eternal truths. Though the dialogue is too well known to require exposition here, it should be pointed out that first of all Socrates insists that one cannot say whether virtue can be taught or not until one knows what virtue is (70a–71d), that when it is pointed out that there are several kinds of virtue, Socrates insists again that all kinds must have an essential unity (71e–73c), and that the example of a good definition which Socrates gives (75b–76c) is one which overlooks the particular characteristics of the thing to be defined, for the general. We can have knowledge of the general. We do have it. How do we get it? The answer is that we have it "in our minds" before we begin our investigation and that all the investigation does is to clarify what we already know in an obscure fashion.

This is made clear in the famous myth of recollection. We come into the world, according to the myth, with a stock of ideas, to be made famous in the seventeenth century as innate ideas. These ideas are not consciously held by babies, but on certain occasions they are brought into the light of consciousness and then we know them clearly. The story of the slave boy who is made to solve a geometric theorem by the adroit questioning of Socrates

---

[5] Cf. A. E. Taylor, *Plato: The Man and His Work* (New York: Dial Press, 1927).

illustrates this process of learning. And apparently what it proves is that, given a teacher who already knows the answers, anyone can be made conscious of the knowledge which he already possesses in obscure form. I see no reason to believe that Plato was saying that any ignoramus would be a successful teacher, though he does believe in self-education. All the talk about the Socratic method, about Socrates' being only a midwife who brings to birth embryonic ideas, comes down to the simple fact that he possesses the correct method for clarifying obscure ideas. The theory of innate ideas has been ridiculed and there is plenty in it which is indeed ridiculous. But the fact remains that the appropriate rubrics under which the objects of knowledge are to be classified, the appropriate questions which we are to answer when we begin our investigations, are logically prior to the investigations themselves. Returning to our example of the dog, should someone ask, "What is a dog?" it is clear that one could answer by pointing to a dog. And that is indeed the technique utilized by the young men whom Socrates is presented to us as instructing. But the underlying question is, "What is this animal an example of?" And how is one to know that one has reached a satisfactory conclusion unless one already has accepted certain criteria of satisfaction?

The criteria which Plato uses are all involved in logical consistency. Now consistency can obtain only between assertions, sentences, not between sensory qualities or things or events. That is, there is no inconsistency between red and green, good and evil, war and peace. Inconsistency, as everyone knows and should remember, arises when the same predicate is both asserted and denied of the same subject in the same sentence. If then there can be consistency and inconsistency in the realm of Plato's ideas, the ideas must be declarative in nature; they must assert something. Hence the attribution of the fallacy of "the third man" is unjust. This fallacy, elaborated by Aristotle,[6] is the argument that between the individual human being and the idea of humanity there must be a third something which is common to the two of them.

---

[6] See *Metaphysics* 990b 17 and 1059b.

Once this is asserted, it is clear that one is caught in an infinite regress, since between the third man and both the individual and the idea of humanity there must be a fourth which they all share. Plato is partly responsible for this, since he spoke of the particulars as "participating" in the ideas. But if an idea is simply something which is true of all the members of a class, and if it is something which may be true or false, the idea must say something; it cannot be like a sensory quality pervasive of a number of individuals, like the color red. The Pythagorean theorem is true of all right-angled triangles, but there need be nothing common to the theorem and the triangles which resides between them.

The examination which Socrates gives his pupils then is an investigation into the consistency of their beliefs. It is concerned exclusively with that, not with the origin of their beliefs, nor with their feelings about them, their utility socially or economically, nor with any other feature which might ally them to history. But since consistency is not and cannot be found in a collection of individual things and events, there is no need to posit a community of qualities between the subject matter of a proposition and the proposition itself. The proposition that a given apple is red is not itself red, and the idea of redness is not red either. The fallacy of the third man would be serious if the idea of humanity, however it may be symbolized, had to possess the same properties as the men who "participate" in it. But to insist on that would be like insisting that the stars in the United States flag which stand for the states should have the same shape as the states for which they stand or that the states be star-shaped.

The ideas have been subjected to four interpretations. They have been thought of as Eleatic norms, as general principles, as scientific laws, and as common properties. They are indeed used by Plato in all four senses. The Idea of Justice in the *Republic* is a norm, a standard of what the just man or the just state should be. But it is to be observed that Plato gives us here a concrete illustration of his idea of justice, as in *Lysis* he gives us a concrete idea of friendship, or in *Charmides* a concrete picture of "temperance." Almost every dialogue in fact is an example of something, even when, as in *Parmenides* or the *Sophist*, he is illustrating a method of thinking. This would seem to give one some reason for believing that Plato is not merely interested in abstractions, but wishes also to show his readers the abstraction embedded in concrete form or, using words technically, the idea incorporated. But the ideas are also general principles, since what they say is applicable to a group of things, not merely to one thing. And the dialectical method used to reach them is applicable only to groups. Plato undoubtedly thinks that knowledge of universal applicability is more worth while than the apprehension of individuals. The ideas in the third place may be interpreted as scientific laws, which was Natorp's interpretation, insofar as such laws are regulative, general, and eternal. Inductive science, in the sense of drawing out of a group of supposedly similar things that which they have in common, rests upon certain presuppositions which are methodological, such as Mill's canons or, to take another pair of examples, the principle of the uniformity of nature or the indispensability of mechanical models. Had Plato been criticizing such methods of investigation, he would have directed his criticisms toward the presuppositions, for in many of the dialogues he is more interested in the bases of belief than in its assertions.

Of one thing we can be sure: that Plato assumed the ideas, whatever else they might be, to be internally consistent. If someone holds to an idea which is self-contradictory or which contradicts another idea known to be true, then that idea has to be abandoned. But how does one discover an idea to be self-contradictory? We can waive the matter of round squares or senile adolescents which are contradictions in terms. It is more profitable to confine ourselves to a concrete example from Plato himself. In the *Sophist* we find the role of the teacher taken by a stranger from Elea. He is a disciple of Parmenides and presumably the method of his interrogation is one which he has learned from that philosopher. After a bit of satirical play, the Stranger begins to discuss the meaning of Being and Nonbeing. The Sophists' habit of confusing two of the meanings of "to be"—"to exist" and "to have the attribute of"—leads to logical tangles from which the beginner in philosophy finds it almost impossible to extricate himself, so that he will assert both that Being is not and that Nonbeing is. The Stranger leads his young pupil to assert that truth is the assertion that what is exists and that falsehood is the assertion that what is not exists. "But Parmenides the Great, my boy, while we were still children and right up to the end of his life protested against this, saying on every occasion both in prose and in verse, 'Never whatsoever maintain,' he said, 'that Nonbeing is, but do thou direct thy thoughts away from such a path'" (*Sophist* 237a). But even to say that Nonbeing is not is to say something about it and, if we are going to say something about anything, we ought to know what it is that we are talking about. But obviously we cannot know anything about that which is the polar antithesis of every subject matter. For if we say, "Nonbeing is unthinkable" (241a), we seem to be saying that it is, "seem" in the eyes of the Sophist, for we are playing on the ambiguity of the word "is." And if we say it is anything else, we commit the same apparent error. But then it turns out that if we say anything about Being, we shall get caught in a similar trap, for the word "Being" can mean nothing unless it is contrasted with "Nonbeing."

It becomes evident, as one reads through such a dialogue, that Plato's technique consists first in distinguishing between the meanings of single words by assuming that for each word there must correspond a single thing if the word is the subject of a sentence. He also assumes quite properly that predicates are of such a nature that some are what the Scholastics were to call compossible and some noncompossible. One can therefore fall into self-contradiction by attributing two or more noncompossible predicates to a single subject. This is the case of round squares, four-sided triangles, liquid solids, hereditary sterility, and the like. When one says that a given square is round, one does not employ a negative, and yet one is involved in self-contradiction. How does one know what attributes are compossible and what not? Plato, as far as I know, seemed to believe that the human mind would know such things if left to itself in childhood. He does not say this in so many words, though in *Meno* this is suggested, and the praise of Socrates as an intellectual midwife would seem to mean that the human mind contains as its innate possession the power of distinguishing between viable and unviable ideas, a power which can be brought to fruition by proper teaching. Again, his criticism of the pre-Socratics (*Sophist* 242d–43b) seems to appeal to common sense. Yet he does not emphasize this belief in the *Sophist*; it operates as a guide to the argument. For the Stranger constantly asks his pupil whether he sees the difference between two ideas, or their identity, and never asks him to defend his vision. Thus, when the teacher identifies Nonbeing with Difference, for it turns out that to say that something is not red or round is simply to say that it is other than red or round, Theaetetus, the pupil, *sees* this; and when the question of compossibles comes up, he also *sees* that some ideas can be attributed to the same subject and others not. He assents to certain propositions not because he has been shown that they are logically consistent with other propositions to which he has already assented, but because they appear to be self-evident.

It is of course inevitable that certain propositions will have to be accepted as the case, that they will have to act as premises to any argument, and that such premises must be acquired or brought to the light of consciousness through what can only be called by some name such as insight, intuition, common sense, or faith. Aristotle overtly stated that the fundamental notions employed in thinking were grasped by the intellect spontaneously; Plato feels the situation to be about the same. "About the same," since the myth of recollection makes a difference. But what is it after all that we know through intuition? It is the categories: sameness and difference, motion (change) and rest, and being. But it is also agreed that these are universally applicable and that a given subject may be self-identical and different from other things, change in some respects and not in others, and in all respects be. This is what Plato (*Sophist* 251d) calls the mingling and partici- pation of attributes; not that all attributes mingle and participate in one another, but that some do and some do not. It is this which destroys any attempt at a monistic metaphysics in his opinion, whether it be a metaphysics of the flux (252a), of those who say that all is one and immutable, or finally of those who insist that all things fall into separate and unrelated classes. It then becomes the task of philosophy, accomplished through dialectic, to dis- cover which classes intermingle and which do not. Dialectic makes distinctions according to kinds, and the dialectician perceives clearly one idea permeating many, each one lying off by itself, and many others gathered together into one, and finally many which are entirely separated from all others (253e). This mingling of ideas is illustrated by the difference between Being and Motion and Rest: Being mingling with all ideas, Motion and Rest only with some.

Plato's method is clarified in *Theaetetus*, for that dialogue has as its object the definition of "knowledge." The young Theaetetus himself, who resembles Socrates physically (143e) and has an aptitude for philosophy (144a, b), is made to propose several definitions: that knowledge is perception (151e), that it is true opinion (187c), that it is true opinion corrected by, or perhaps accompanied by, reason (201d). The first of these definitions is attributed to Protagoras by Plato and is demolished by showing that every perceiver would be right in everything he might say, since no percept can be shown to be common to two people. Hence each perceiver would live in a world of his own from which he could never escape, and if knowledge is interpersonal, then perception cannot be knowledge. At the risk of being tedious, I should now like to examine for a moment the Socratic method in more detail.

First, Socrates proposes a clarification of the doctrine (152a): "Whatever each thing appears to be to me, such it is to me, and what it appears to be to you, such it is to you. And you and I are man." It should be observed that the text says "man" and not "men," so that Protagoras, the epistemological individualist, is made to ascribe a common quality or universal to the various perceivers. And Theaetetus grants that this is a correct interpretation of the slogan, Man is the measure of all things. If this is deliberate on the part of Plato, and we have no reason to believe that it is not deliberate, then the founder of the theory has already committed himself to an idea which by his own theory could not be justified. For if each individual has his own body of knowledge which cannot be shared by others, then our common nouns or universals would have no ground for existing. In the second place Theaetetus is induced to grant that, whatever else knowledge means, it means something which is true. But this leads to the conclusion that if an object seems cold to one man and warm to another, it is truly both cold and warm. Here we run into the difficulty of relative statements, a difficulty of which the English Platonists of the seventeenth century were to make much capital. There is of course no inconsistency in saying that something is both hot and cold so long as the two statements are completed by adding the perceiver or the respects to whom and in which they appear both hot and cold. But Plato wants a situation in which something can be asserted which will be true for all perceivers. He then proceeds to make Socrates expound the metaphysics which lies behind this epistemology, the metaphysics of the flux, whose proponents are Heraclitus and Empedocles as well as Protagoras. According to his presentation of this doctrine, the things which we perceive come and go, as in Hume, and not only do no two men have the same perceptions, but no single man ever has the same perception twice, since he is never the same from moment to moment (154a). Here Plato is supporting his dialetical argument with historical considerations, by which I mean simply that it would not follow that because all things are as they seem, each man is different from every other man, that no man remains the same from moment to moment, or that whatever world may exist as a world of possible objects of knowledge is always in a state of change. The argument therefore turns out to be no simple testing of an epistemological hypothesis, but an attack on a definite school of metaphysicians. In other words, Plato is trying to demolish the doctrine of the historical Protagoras, and just as in such a dialogue as *Charmides* he was dealing with the incorporation of an idea as well as with the idea itself, so here he is dealing with an actual case of a doctrine and not merely with a hypothetical case. Having reached this point, the next step is in the direction of purifying the idea of its historical dress and setting it forth in logical nakedness.

The first problem is that of escaping from the relativism of an individualistic epistemology into a world of absolutes. And to show how impossible this escape has become, Socrates first (157e) points to dreams and diseases and insanity which cause sensory illusions. Are we to admit that these illusions, which of course do not seem to be illusory to those who suffer from them, are knowledge? Are we to admit (158c) that there is no legitimate distinction to be made between the dreamworld and the world of waking life? Theaetetus naturally will not admit this, though, if he had been a real Protagorean he might have asked on what grounds we make the distinction. But he is not a real Protagorean and agrees that it is desirable to find a set of absolutes. He must then first answer the question of why human perception is any more reliable than animal perception (161c). Second, why should anyone study with a teacher if each man has possession of the truth (161d)? Third, does not the examination of other people's beliefs as well as of one's own become absurd? It is apparently granted by the Sophist that animal perceptions are false, not because we are human and must base our knowledge pragmatically on human perceptions, but because the dog-faced baboon or the tadpole simply cannot have true knowledge. It is also assumed that teaching and argument do produce desirable results. These are assumptions which would be made by almost anyone, though probably not for Plato's reasons, but again a convinced relativist might not grant them. Nor is Socrates represented as being satisfied with the acquiescence of his young pupil, for though it is probable, he says, that all men are not equal in wisdom or wiser than the beasts, that has not been proved. And what is wanted is proof.

Hence the analysis has to be begun all over again. Do we actually say that we know what we perceive? Do we say that we know a foreign language when we hear its sounds or see its letters? We know the sounds and the forms, says Theaetetus (163c), but we do not know their meaning. This is accepted by Socrates. But then a new difficulty presents itself. How about memory (163e)? Memory is not perception, and yet if we know a color when we see it and we are not seeing it when we remember it, then we do not know it when we remember it. But this again is absurd. If it is not absurd, then what we know, we know only at the moment when we are knowing it. The central interest of this conclusion, as far as Plato's method is involved, is the light it throws on philosophic method in general. Is Plato simply arguing about how we should use words or is there an object of study, in this case knowledge, regardless of its name, which we can study as a zoologist would study a frog or a chemist an organic compound? If we are simply talking about the meaning of words, we are engaged in a kind of lexicography. And the correct meaning becomes the most usual meaning and at most we can discuss historical semantics. In the second case we are tangled up again in the problem of *Meno* and at best can say only that we have a dim idea of what we are talking about and that the purpose of philosophy is to dispel the clouds. We know in advance what criteria we shall use to determine the satisfactoriness of a philosophic doctrine: we shall want it to be self-consistent. But we are also faced with the difficulty of choosing our premises, and here Plato, for all his contempt for the Many, seems to go back to something like common sense once more. He is well aware of the fact that if knowledge is to be true it must be true for anyone who understands it. He is also aware of the fact that we must accept remembered knowledge as real knowledge and does not question the value of teaching and self-examination. But Socrates' insistence on his midwifery must imply the belief that each of us, or, if we bear the *Republic* in mind, each of us who is rational, has within him the seeds of knowledge which the dialectical process can bring to germination. However metaphorical the statement of this, however the facts may be explained, the philosopher may legitimately be asked to say what he is taking for granted and what he will consider to be the proper test of philosophic truth. The distinction made by Theaetetus, for instance, between the meaning of a language and its perceived sounds, would probably be made by everyone, but the question remains of why, on what grounds, we accept it. Again, when it is flatly admitted that memory is not perception, are we to find some way, as Hobbes did, to turn percepts into memory images, or are we to deny that perception is knowledge?

Theaetetus ends with a confession that the theories of knowledge which have been proposed in it are "wind eggs and not worth rearing." Is a dialogue of this sort to be thought of simply as a satirical drama of ideas? Plato himself gives us the answer. "If after this," he has Socrates say to Theaetetus (210b, c), "you should undertake to give birth to other doctrines, and if you should give birth to them, you will turn out to be pregnant with better thoughts because of our present investigation. And should you be sterile, still you will be less rough with your associates and kinder, wisely not thinking that you know what you do not know. For such alone is my art able to do and nothing more, nor do I know any of the things which the others know, great and wonderful men who are now living and have lived in the past." In short, leading a pupil to examine a doctrine which he has himself proposed, inducing him to realize its inconsistencies, may not show him what doctrines are true, but it may at least show him which are false. The progress of knowledge has been accomplished, according to K. R. Popper,[7] one of Plato's severest critics,

---

[7] See his very interesting article, "Three Views concerning Human Knowledge," in *Contemporary British Philosophy* (London: Allen and Unwin, 1956).

by the refutation of regnant theories. This is precisely what the Platonic method consists in.

Moreover the presentation of philosophy in dialogue form is in itself of philosophic interest. When an author such as Berkeley or Hume writes dialogues to expound his own ideas, the dialogue form is unnecessary. Plato's *Laws* would be a good example of such a dialogue. But where a man is discussing the conflict of ideas, none of which need be his own,[8] then it is possible to illuminate the sources of the conflict, the assumptions upon which the two or more sides of the argument are based, and to move from history into logic. The points of view then become logical possibilities, hypotheses, so to speak, which one is testing, and it must be admitted that as far as Plato is concerned he sometimes succeeds, as in *Protagoras,* in doing this with sympathy. He seems to believe that ideas have a life of their own and we must all have had the impression, on our first reading of Plato, that ideas which turn out to be purely tentative and destined for refutation are those with which he is himself in agreement. There is no one formula of which I am aware which gives a satisfactory compendious account of all the dialogues, and I can see no reason to doubt the wisdom of the old editors who classified them as didactic, practical, expository, obstetric, controversial, and so on. Such divisions overlap and the labels are far from clear. Yet the recognition that Plato attempted to do various things in his writings and not just one thing is sound. It is not too difficult to realize that in a dialogue like *Timaeus* the author is not arguing but expounding, whereas in *Charmides* he leaves it up to the reader to draw his own conclusions. But two things may be said about most of the dialogues. (1) Where a definition is sought, it is a definition of an abstract idea, an essence, and it is not to be found in a recital of examples. (2) Where no conclusion is reached, a sharp distinction is made between our ability to recognize concrete examples of the idea whose definition we are seeking, and our ability to formulate

---

[8] E.g., J. Loewenberg in his *Dialogues from Delphi* (Berkeley: University of California Press, 1949).

the idea in words. This would seem to be essential, and one of the main problems of the Platonic epistemology would seem to be how we can have "true opinion," how we can see, how we can recognize, for example, a moral quality and yet not be able to "know" it. From this point of view *Meno* would be central to his thought.

Now in *Meno* Plato has recourse to a myth to explain his theory. But a myth, it will be said, is not an explanation. To speak of the soul as a charioteer trying to guide two horses of opposing character, as in *Phaedrus*, to speak of the cosmic order as a great geometric system deduced by a divine mind, as in *Timaeus*, to speak of the objects of human cognition as shadows cast on the wall of a cave from eternal archetypes, as in the *Republic*, is obviously to set forth an *as-if*. It is analogous to the scientific practice of citing examples in the form of experiments; none of the experiments proposed in Newton's *Principia* need be performed, for the theorems ought to suffice. We need no experiments in mathematics to prove or explain our conclusions. It would be absurd after adding two and two, then to take two books, lay them on a table, add two more books to them, and then add the total. Yet we demand precisely that sort of thing in arguments which demonstrate unfamiliar conclusions. It was known that the world was round and not flat in Alexandrine times—in fact, it was known to Aristotle—and all that Magellan's journey could possibly do was to corroborate the theory. Logically, adding books, apples, pebbles, and other objects together would never prove an arithmetical theorem; at most it would apply only to those experiments from which it was induced. Why then do we need illustrations, even if the only available illustrations are fictions?

The situation, if we are not misreading Plato, is the congruence of experience and reason. To know something is to see it in its proper place in an orderly system. But experience comes to us in a random order and knowledge always begins with classification, though the classification may amount to nothing more than assigning common nouns to the things we encounter. But classifications may be bad, in the sense that they may be superficial though true. For instance, the classification of material things in gases, liquids, and solids is true but it does not suffice for chemistry. Hence once the traditional classifications are made, we proceed to divide the classes into smaller subclasses. But on what principle of division? [9] What good would it do a chemist to discover that gases can be divided into those which are colorless and those which are colored? Only the good of not identifying a colored gas with a colorless gas. Sooner or later we come to the point where we realize that classifications are made on the basis of what we want to do with the things classified. To identify hydrogen with helium because both are colorless and then to use them indiscriminately might lead to disaster. I do not mean that we classify for practical ends, such as filling balloons indiscriminately with hydrogen or helium and then finding that the former burns, unless we include intellectual satisfaction under the rubric "practical." We seem to have a hunger for some design or form or order or pattern—the name is immaterial—in accordance with which we can organize our experience. If the earliest recorded orders are cast in the form of creation myths, that may be because making and producing are the most familiar activities of men living in a nonindustrial society. And if teleological explanations are the usual type, that may be because men usually think that they act to attain ends. We obviously cannot do anything about the cosmic order in the restricted sense of practical action. But if we can see in it a duplicate of the orders of production and purposiveness, then we are at home in it intellectually. It is simply an enlarged picture of human life. A God to whom we may pray, who can grant our prayers, can reward and punish us, can be a father, is a God with whom we can sympathize since He acts as a perfected human being.[10]

[9] See *Statesman* 262.

[10] Cf. *Theaetetus* 176c. On the use of myths in Plato, see L. Edelstein, "The Function of the Myth in Plato's Philosophy," *Journal of the History of Ideas*, X (1949), 463. For a bibliography of articles recently published on this subject, see Cherniss, *Lustrum*, IV (1959), 240.

The myth then will be introduced when one reaches a point of such ultimacy that nothing in experience will illuminate it. If we ask what is the beginning of all things or the end, there is clearly no experience on which we can found our answer. I do not say that such questions are inevitable—indeed to Aristotle the world was without beginning or end—but if they are raised, then one is forced into mythography. If again we make a distinction between body and soul, and assume that only material things can perish, since perishing is disintegration and not annihilation, then we can logically infer that the soul is immortal. But when we go on to ask what happens to the soul when released from the body, we once more must resort to myth, since obviously we have no empirical evidence of an afterlife. It may be retorted that such questions need not be raised and in fact some people have not raised them. But the fact remains that others have asked them and Plato was one of that number. His myths cannot be proved by empirical evidence, but they can be more or less plausible, depending on how closely they reflect rational deductions and the common events of human history. To translate them into literal language would be folly, for what they say cannot be either refuted or demonstrated. They are not true or they would not be myths. Yet they can serve as a standard for the truth of lesser ideas. They give us a concrete picture of what is neither concrete nor a picture. Our ability to do without them is measured by our ability to restrain our curiosity.

There is of course something paradoxical in Plato's satisfying our desire for illustrations. We live in a world of concrete particular experiences, of things and events colored by emotion and sensory quality. Of this world we can have only opinion, as we have said above, since knowledge is bound to demand universals. We therefore strip them of their emotional and sensory vestments, classify them, and establish relations between them and the classes to which they belong. Having done this, we turn about and try to make them concrete again. And we do this in mythography. We are thus able to bring them back, as it were, to the level of experience without restoring them to the disorder and obscurity of experience. The knowledge which we acquire through them is in this way analogous to empirical knowledge in its concreteness and yet is not simply opinion. I have found no passage in Plato which says that myths are absolutely true or that they have a higher kind of truth than rational knowledge. He may have believed that they were a substitute for the kind of knowledge which we would have if our minds were capable of apprehending it. We know the ideas by contemplation; we *see* their truth. So we can see the truth of a myth because of its vividness and its concreteness. But myth in Plato is only a substitute for reason. I mention this simply because his later disciples were to make much of the allegorical wisdom supposedly contained not only in their master's myths but also in those related, for instance, by Homer and Hesiod, for whom Plato himself had little admiration as philosophers.

III

Any philosopher who publishes his works does so presumably because he believes his ideas to be of some importance for the education of his fellows. In Plato's case this belief is dominant. Living in a time which he felt to be degenerate, having seen his beloved master put to death for the crime of teaching self-knowledge, surrounded by Sophists, he expressed his contempt not only for the society in which he lived but also for the "unexamined life" with vigor and persistence. If *Menexenus* is genuine, it is a bitter parody of the kind of false patriotic oration which did not die out in the fourth century B.C. Put into the mouth of Aspasia, the mistress of Pericles, it extols the Athenians for all the virtues and condemns the other Greeks for pretty nearly all the vices. The first speech in *Phaedrus* is a parody of Lysias whose rhetorical elegance seems to have been sickening to Plato. His attacks on the Sophists are too well known to need any illustration here. But his attack on those who patronize the Sophists is even more savage. "Are you," says Socrates to Adimantus in the *Republic* (vi. 492a, b), "like the crowd, going to maintain that youth is corrupted by the Sophists and that there are some Sophists who do their corrupting, if it is worth speaking of, in private, but are not they who say such things themselves the greatest Sophists and do they not carry out their educational program to perfection and form whomever they wish, both young and old and men and women? ... When the people are all seated together in assemblies or courtrooms or theaters or encampments or some other common meeting place in gangs, they denounce with loud noises some of the things which are said and done and they shout the praises of others, exaggerating in both cases, and they bellow like bulls and clap their hands, upon which the rocks and the place in which they are gathered re-echo twofold the noise, both the noise of denunciation and that of praise. Well, then, in such a case, how do you think that the young man's heart, as they say, is stirred?" No private education will withstand such an attack and youth will believe that what the public applauds and denounces is worthy of applause and denunciation. If anything turns out right in such a state of society, the man who attributes it to the will of God will be speaking the truth (vi. 493a). The private Sophists simply teach what the crowd holds dear and "they call this wisdom" (493a). But such wisdom is simply knowledge of the sounds made by a great strong beast on such and such occasions and what must be said to pacify or enrage it (493b). A wise man of this type would call those things fair and foul or good and evil or just and unjust which pleased or displeased, respectively, the great beast and would identify the necessary with the good without understanding the differences in their natures. The program of such people is to give the public what it wants, nor are they able to furnish more than a ridiculous proof that the public wants the really good (493d). This being so, it is folly to think that the crowd can learn philosophy. For that would rest on the belief that they could also believe that something is a universal, rather than a host of particulars (493d). They can see instances of beauty, of goodness, of justice, but can entertain no idea of beauty in itself, of goodness in itself, of justice in itself.

Plato's contempt for the crowd goes hand in hand with his dispraise of life itself as it was lived in Athens. Earlier in the *Republic* (vi. 486a) he had asked whether a man who had been busied with great things and the contemplation of all time and all existence would think human life worth much. And Socrates himself at his trial is portrayed as thinking that death is a small price to pay if teaching the truth is to be denied him (*Apology* 29). There is, moreover, in every man a many-headed beast (*Republic* ix. 588c) which is concealed beneath his skin. Life is a battle between the two natures and the task of the man who would attain a life of virtue is to tame the beast within. But this is not easy, for the beast is swayed by "images and phantasms both by day and by night" (*Timaeus* 71a) and can be controlled only by force "since it has no share in reason or intelligence" (71d).[11] That the soul has both rational and irrational faculties which are at war with each other is an essential part of Plato's teachings and he sees little, if any, chance of ensuring a victory for the rational part. For not only is the realm of reason separated from that of perception, and is neither in space nor in time, but it is clear from the *Republic* (435e) that some men are born bestial and that only a few have the potency of reason within them. The former must be curbed by the latter and they would be so curbed in a perfect state. But Plato is under no illusions about the possibility of bringing the perfect state into existence down here on earth. Perfection is found in mathematics and logic, not in space and time, though it is necessary to know what it would be like if we are even to approach its realization down here. For life is pictured by him as either a continuous struggle to understand what ought to be, as contrasted with what is, or as a renunciation of the struggle and submission to our appetites. The sensual man as well as the irasci-

---

[11] Cf. *Charmides* 155 d, e, and *Phaedrus* 230a and 246a.

ble man are characters established at birth, and since they have no instinct to be other than what they are, life is a depressing spectacle to the philosopher.

It should be pointed out in passing that Plato's descriptions of the various types of human nature started a tradition in psychology which is usually thought of as beginning with the *Characters* of Theophrastus. In discussing the various forms of state in the *Republic*, he says (viii. 544d) that there are as many species of man as there are of states. To the best kind of state there corresponds "the truly good and just man," and to the inferior forms there correspond the contentious man and the lover of fame and honors, to say nothing of the tyrannical man. To take but one example, the timocratic man (viii. 549a) is self-willed and "rather uncultivated," fond of music and of listening to talk, though not himself rhetorical, savage to his slaves, "not looking down on them as a properly educated man would do" (549a), humble before the free, always ready to listen to the rulers, loving high position and honors. He does not claim a right to rule because of his power of speaking or anything of that sort, but because of his military skill, his athletic prowess, and his ability in the hunting field. As he grows older, he becomes fonder of money, and does not see the folly of his life since he lacks reason, "united to true culture."[12] In such a manner Plato describes the types of character which correspond to the kinds of state. These men are not supposed to exhaust the kinds of human beings who may exist but are simply monarchy, aristocracy, timocracy, oligarchy, democracy, and tyranny reduced to human proportions.[13] But as the tradition developed through Theophrastus, it came to be believed that every man had a permanent character, imprinted on his soul at birth, and in such an influential writer as Horace we discover that permanence of character must be observed by the

---

[12] λόγου μουσικῇ κεκραμένου (*Republic* viii. 549b). In other words, he is not a bloodless rationalizer, but also shares in what the Muses can bestow (art, history, and astronomy), in short, a well-rounded human being, balanced, harmonious, never given to extremes. But no translation is adequate.

[13] Cf. *Phaedrus* 271d.

poet—or in modern terms, the novelist—as a rule.[14] Permanence of character in Plato, however, is not a literary rule but gives rise to political problems. For if some characters are inherently bad, some way must be devised to control them, and that way is set forth in detail in both the *Republic* and the *Laws*. For once it is assumed that the state exists for the sake of the good, all citizens must be so organized that they will co-operate in its realization. Since evil men will not do so willingly, they must be forced to.

All this, we must repeat once more, exists in the sphere of eternity. Plato nowhere says that such clear-cut divisions are to be found empirically. One must imagine what would be the case if the totality of things were arranged in logically distinct classes. Otherwise it is impossible to reason at all. Logical classes to his way of thinking are homogeneous, whereas groups which are found in experience are mixed. Logical classes, however, are timeless and whatever may be truly said of them is eternally true. The basic model of reason for Plato was geometry and each class of thing in the empirical world is thought of as if it were a geometric figure about which certain statements can be made by the reasoning process unaided by observation. He realizes fully (*Republic* vi. 510d–511b) that we cannot reach a clear intuition of first principles and that we have to utilize hypotheses as if they were first principles, but he also maintains that, once having laid them down, we should proceed from inference to inference "never utilizing sensory percepts" (511c). This is analogous to the use made of intellectual models in contemporary science: bodies moving in free space, the economic man, man in a state of nature, perfectly elastic bodies and ideal gases. He was quite aware of what he was doing. As he says in the *Republic* (x. 611e), before beginning the concluding myth, we must consider the soul as if it were "raised out of the depths of this sea in which it is now sunk, and were cleansed and scraped free of the rocks and barnacles which, because it now feeds on earth, cling to it in wild pro-

---

[14] Cf. the stock characters in the *commedia dell' arte*, in the comedies of Molière, and in the repertory companies of the nineteenth century.

fusion of earthy and stony accretion by reason of these feastings that are accounted happy. And then one might see whether in its real nature it is manifold or single in its simplicity, or what is the truth about it and how."[15] Scraping away the rocks and barnacles leaves the nature of the soul, or of anything else which may be under examination, intact and open to the scrutiny of reason. When one has grasped his method of reasoning, one also understands why it is beside the point to criticize him for failing to reach results which could be reached only by another method.

Since he is interested in discovering the nature of the ideal, it would be useless for him to describe the world of existence, for that world he believes to fall short of the ideal. So no geometer would reason from the drawings made by compass and ruler. Hence when he wishes to point out the defects of men, he turns to history; when he wishes to indicate the road to improvement, he turns to eternity. For, as he said toward the end of his life in the *Laws* (803b), "Though human affairs are not worthy of great seriousness, yet we must treat them seriously." And since he can find no worthy exemplar of the good life, he introduces a myth and gives in more or less fanciful terms a description of the earliest ancestors of the Athenians, men who lived nine thousand years previously.[16] The society of that time, we are told, was divided into classes according to the functions performed by each, priests, artisans, shepherds, hunters, and farmers, and finally the soldiers. Emphasis is placed upon the separateness of each class; none mixed with the others. Thus they reproduced the distinctness of the ideas which also are cut off from one another. Thanks to their patroness, Athena, these men surpassed all others in Virtue (*Timaeus* 24d). This story, repeated a bit more sketchily

---

[15] Shorey's translation in the Loeb Classical Library.

[16] "Earliest," that is, within the period under discussion. Plato maintains (*Timaeus* 22c) that "there have been many and various kinds of destructions of men and there will be more, the greatest by fire and water, and lesser ones by a thousand other agencies." This was to be repeated in the *Laws* (iii. 677a), "There have been many destructions of men by cataclysms and diseases and many other agencies, after which a small remnant of the race of men was left."

in *Critias* (109b ff.), adds the detail that the military class, which lived somewhat as the Guardians lived in the *Republic*, had no private property, no gold or silver, and lived abstemiously, between luxury and want.

It is a society similar to this which Socrates describes in the second book of the *Republic* (369b ff.). The origin of all states lies in the individual's inability to survive in isolation from his fellows. Food, housing, and clothing are the first of our needs and these demand specialization of labor. Since, moreover, most societies are far from being self-sufficient, imports will be needed (370e). And within the city itself there will have to be men to sell the producers' goods to the consumers (371c). The men in such a city will lead a relatively simple life, but one which does not rise above that of the animals (372d). It is a healthy state but not a state which could serve as a model for one seeking the nature of justice and injustice (372e). For this distinction arises only in a fevered society in which there are luxury, private property, and the need to defend oneself from the attacks of the envious. Step by step Plato approaches the condition of what one supposes to be his conception of Athens, in which the untrained are attempting to perform tasks for which they are not suited, and in which unnecessary desires are creating unnecessary evils. To remedy this situation a class of men should be instituted to govern (374e). These men are the Guardians. They are clearly Plato's ideal of human nature.

The Guardians are perceptive, brave, and high-spirited (375a, b) but also gentle. In short, they must be lovers of wisdom (philosophers). It requires no great knowledge of the dialogues to see how this fits in with the myth of the charioteer and his two horses in *Phaedrus* (246b ff.). The charioteer is the rational man; the good horse is modest, temperate, and "a lover of true doctrine" (253d); the evil horse is ugly, insolent, and proud. The good horse is obedient to rational command; the evil horse obeys only the cracking of the whip. Man thus is presented as torn between two impulses, the impulse to listen to reason, the impulse to listen only to appetite. Plato's appraisal of human life depends upon the role which reason plays in it. And since reason is the contemplation of the ideas, all bodily instincts which might distract one from the realm of ideas to that of perception are to be discouraged. This is not so much asceticism for its own sake as self-discipline for the sake of true knowledge. And since the city is constructed on the model of the man, there must be in the city something to correspond to the reason in the man.[17] And as Plato develops his model city, he introduces these analogous classes of men, the artisans who cater to the appetites and the warriors who nobly defend the city from its enemies. The former are to be chosen from men with inborn appetitiveness and the latter from those who are irascible—or spirited—by nature. Fundamentally Plato's criticism of his own state is that men perform functions for which they are not naturally fitted and that no instrument is provided for remedying the situation. Indeed that criticism runs through many of the dialogues. In the *Apology* (20a) Socrates points out that whereas men hire adequately trained horsemen to school their horses, the best they can do is to employ Sophists to train their sons. In *Laches* (194d) Nicias is made to say to Socrates, "Frequently have I heard you say that each of us is good in those things in which he is wise, but wherein he is ignorant, therein is he evil." Consequently the courageous man is "he who knows what is to be feared or encountered both in war and in all other things" (*Laches* 195a). Almost in the opening of *Protagoras* (311b) we find Socrates insisting that only a physician can instruct one in medicine, only a sculptor can teach sculpture, and

---

[17] In *Phaedrus* (248d, e) is a list of characters in order of decreasing goodness: (1) the philosopher or lover of beauty, (2) a legitimate king or warrior ruler, (3) the politician or businessman or financier, (4) the gymnast or someone who cares for the upkeep of the body, (5) the prophet or mystagogue, (6) the poet or other "imitative artist," (7) the craftsman or farmer, (8) the Sophist or demagogue, (9) the tyrant. This ranking of souls clearly introduces as its principle of appraisal the amount of contemplative reason required for each kind of life, the amount of attention which is given to the body and its demands, and the legitimacy of the calling. It is in no sense of the word a purely logical ranking, but rather an expression of Plato's admiration and contempt for actual occupations.

only a Sophist sophistry, a sentiment echoed in *Meno* (90b). The one-to-one correspondence between ideas and knowledge is an essential axiom of Platonism.

But since knowledge is the apprehension of the ideas, it follows that education must be a technique of purging the soul of whatever obstructs, such apprehension. Dialectic is the technique in question. If everyone were able to employ dialectic profitably, then society and the life we live in it would be in no need of improvement. But Plato's insistence on the special skill which the lover of wisdom possesses, suffices in itself to show that he did not believe in the ubiquity of rationality. And when this is added to his explicit arguments concerning the ineradicable differences in human beings, the conclusion is inevitable. Plato's criticism of his society is to be attacked, if at all, at this point. There is little sense in attacking him for having fascistic leanings, totalitarian doctrines, communistic programs, all of which can be found in him. The vulnerable point is his theory of human nature.

That moral education—and in some respects all education is moral—consists in learning how to control our desires and our manner of satisfying them, is usually admitted. Differences of opinion arise when the methods of control are being discussed. The classical tradition maintained that one's will could be made submissive to one's reason and that normally one did a thing because one believed it to be good. So in art one was supposed to have an idea of what one wanted to achieve and then went ahead and tried to achieve it. The notion that one used the reason to justify one's desires is relatively modern. One finds the most outspoken expression of this thesis in Spinoza. "We neither strive for, wish, seek, nor desire anything because we judge that it is good," he says (*Ethics* iii. 9, schol.), "but on the contrary, we judge something to be good because we strive for it, wish it, seek it, and desire it."[18] But as early as the thirteenth century Duns Scotus

[18] *Constat itaque ex his omnibus* [i.e., from what had been previously said] *nihil nos conari, velle, appetere, neque cupere, quia id bonum esse judicamus, sed contra nos propterea, aliquid bonum esse, judicare, quia id conamur, volumus, appetimus, atque cupimus.* Cf. iii. 39, schol.

maintained that God did not make the world because it was good, but that it was good because God made it. Similarly Machiavelli laid it down as an axiom that the Prince created good and bad by fiat, following apparently the definition of the law in the Justinian Code, *Ius est id quod principi placet.*[19] In any event, if we recognize the difference between reason and will, and feel the conflict which arises between them in our own lives when we are impelled to do something which we "know" to be wrong, then we can understand a theory of human nature which makes the distinction fundamental and also assigns primacy to one or the other. In Plato, as in Aristotle, only the rational could be taught; the irrational could be disciplined only through practice. Thus one can teach mathematics, but not liking or disliking. The latter are drilled into one by example, by imitation, by rewards and punishments, and by other similar exercises. When a geometric theorem is demonstrated and one has understood its premises, one cannot but accept its conclusion. But when, for instance, a literary critic writes an essay in praise of a poem, one may reach the end and say to oneself, "But I still don't like it." Similarly one may listen to a sermon on faith or hope or charity or all three combined and agree that the arguments invoked are sound and nevertheless not find one's faith strengthened, one's hope increased, or one's charity broadened. If this were not so, the race after twenty centuries of such preaching would be well-nigh perfect.

Herein are the reasons, I think, why Plato could maintain that no man could do wrong willingly. For whatever a man does is done for the sake of what he believes at the time he does it to be good. However we may define the good, if it is to be binding on groups of people, it must be something about which we may be wrong. If one cannot be mistaken about its nature, then there is

---

[19] The historical affiliation between this sentence and Machiavelli is obscure, but the thought is identical. Shocking though it has appeared to many political philosophers, the sentiment is not very different from that contained in the holier slogan, *Vox populi, vox Dei,* which Machiavelli, like Alcuin (*Epistle* 127) thought absurd. Both the *princeps* and the *populus* are sovereign.

no sense whatsoever in urging others to be good. For any sentence about the good would be as true as any other. But if the sentence, "This is good," can be true or false, and if it does not simply mean, "This is what I want to do on this particular occasion, regardless of what I may have done in the past on similar occasions and of what I may do tomorrow and of what others may have done or may do in the future," then the good must be the name of something whose nature is not determined by the likes and dislikes of any person. What it names must be similar in status to what have been called objective facts. Moreover, if it is objectively true that the earth is an oblate sphere, then two men may be right about the weight of a given bit of matter and give two different weights, for what the thing weighs will vary in accordance with the latitude and altitude at which it is weighed. But in this case we know the system of relations in which the weight is determined. If the good, again, has factual existence, then the number of people who accept certain sentences about it is no indication of the truth or falsity of those sentences. If it was wrong to execute Socrates, it was wrong regardless of how many Athenians thought it was right. In short, I am trying to say that in Plato's opinion values were facts. Presumably he also believed that if the reason were properly trained by the dialectical method, those men who had the good fortune to be rational would understand the nature of the good. But the understanding in question would be like a kind of revelation, the revelation of innate knowledge. Plato's low opinion of his fellow citizens rests on his observation of their reluctance to clarify their minds. If virtue is to be taught, he says in *Meno* (89d), there must be teachers of it, and even the most virtuous of the Athenians, Themistocles, Aristides, Pericles, and their like had sons who never attained the moral stature of their sires. Yet this cannot be attributable to their fathers' indifference to virtue.[20]

---

[20] Note that at this point in the dialogue Anytus, the accuser of Socrates, is brought in to defend the thesis that all one needs to attain virtue is the will to follow the customs of our elders. See esp. 93a.

It will be remembered that in the *Republic* (372e) the distinction between justice and injustice was said to arise only in fevered societies. So in *Meno* (99e) virtue is said to be neither innate nor acquired, but something "given us by the will of the gods without our knowing it."[21] We may have true opinion about virtue, but none of us can claim to know its nature in the sense of having looked upon it face to face. This is not far from Saint Augustine's idea of grace and election.

IV

Contempt for the Many became an integral part of classical rationalism. The Many were incapable of wisdom and hence it was folly to attempt to impart wisdom to them. It was not long before philosophers withdrew from all social contacts and obligations and the legend developed that both Plato and Aristotle had secret doctrines which they would not reveal in public. The evidence on which this legend rests is so shaky that there is no reason to discuss it.[22] But clearly, if people are divided into those who are capable of learning and those who are incapable, then there is no point in trying to teach the unteachable. If virtue cannot be taught, then schools of virtue are absurd and men who pretend to teach it are charlatans.

That virtue cannot be taught is the thesis of *Meno*, but the argument there rests upon the empirical observation that so far no teachers of virtue have appeared. It is not that virtue is not one of the ideas and that its nature cannot be apprehended. The Greek for *virtue* means also *excellence* and the virtue of a human being is the excellence of his humanity. But an excellent human being is one who has knowledge and, when that is grasped, the identity of virtue and knowledge is perhaps better understood.

---

[21] οὔτε φύσει, οὔτε διδακτόν, ἀλλὰ θείᾳ μοίρᾳ παραγιγνομένη ἄνευ νοῦ.

[22] But see, if it is desired, G. Boas, "Ancient Testimony to Secret Doctrines," *loc. cit.*

It is safe to say that for Plato the end of man is the realization of his essential nature, necessitated by the accidents of our terrestrial life.

One is always on slippery ground when one is interpreting one of the Platonic myths, but I see no reason to doubt that Plato believed in the ultimate dualism of soul and body. Though some of his myths are playful, I find it hard to believe that either that of *Phaedrus* or that of *Phaedo* is anything but serious. In the latter we find that the lover of wisdom cares nothing for the body, either for its adornment or its pleasures, but turns himself toward the soul (*Phaedo* 64e). For the body is a hindrance to knowledge and not even the senses of sight and hearing, on which we most rely, have any truth in them (65b). The soul, however, when it liberates itself from the sense organs and bodily pleasures, may attain real knowledge. It will then be capable of knowing absolute or ideal justice, beauty, and goodness (65d). None of these things can be seen with the eyes. And so with all essences (*ousiai*). Since this sort of knowledge cannot be acquired while we are associated with the body, it can be gained only when we are free of it, that is, after death. During life we may approach knowledge by avoiding any commitments to the body except those which are absolutely necessary. The asceticism preached here is purification undergone for the sake of apprehending the truth. This wisdom is true virtue, the excellence of a soul realizing its own nature.

From this it follows that the moral life is the life of self-criticism. And that is why the reason must assume authority over both the appetites and the irascible faculty. But unless the rules of criticism and the data upon which those rules operate are fixed, the reason will be as fluctuating as our sensory perceptions. By the simple procedure of arguing that if an aggregate has a common name, it must have a common property, Plato was able to conceive of a set of stable beings, obviously his Ideas, which could serve as the objects of rational insight, and the rules do not seem to have troubled him. This may have been because they seemed self-evident. He uses them in his arguments, as we all must, but their origin does not appear to have been discussed by him.[23] The reason then is not simply the capacity of a man for drawing inferences from premises; it is also his power of seeing somehow or other the ideas. Just how he sees them, Plato does not tell us. It was a problem which he bequeathed to his successors.

To use one of his examples (*Phaedo* 74a), we have an idea of "equality." When we say that two perceptible things are equal, where do we see the equality? If we have two pieces of wood and say that they are equal, we know that in some respects they are not equal and that in others they are. They may be equal in weight and not in length. Therefore it cannot be the mere perception of the two pieces of wood which gives us the idea of equality, since we perceive the length as well as the weight.[24] We must consequently bring to the perceptual experience an idea by means of which we test the objects before us. In other words, we first have an idea of equality and for some reason or other we wish to discover in what respect the two pieces of wood are equal. We do not simply glare at them and wait for an idea of equality— or some other idea—to pop out of them and enter our minds. Since such an idea cannot have come from the perceptual world, it must have been projected into the perceptual world by us. And furthermore, we must have had this and other ideas in our minds when we were born (*Phaedo* 75c). But since the soul is immortal, incapable of being either created or destroyed, these "absolute ideas" are its everlasting possession. Such knowledge grows dim at birth and is recollected on certain perceptual occasions. The pre-existence of the soul is necessitated by the possibility of true knowledge. But how about its postexistence?

Plato introduces at this point (78b) an axiom which continued

---

[23] This matter will be taken up below (Section V).

[24] The late John Burnet, in his *Platonism* (Berkeley: University of California Press, 1928), pp. 41 ff., says that the word "idea" primarily means "form" or "figure," that the theory of ideas was "a Socratic development of Pythagoreanism" which was later rejected by Plato, and that the word ought to be dropped in favor of "forms." But "form" is no less visual in meaning than "idea" and if the word denotes something which can be true or false, the visual meaning is lost anyway.

to be accepted by later thinkers, the axiom that only compounds could be destroyed. A simple thing, having by definition no parts, could not be broken up and dispersed. But first (78d), equality in itself, beauty in itself, being in itself, can suffer no change, since they are all of a piece and have no parts. Material beings, men or horses or clothes, which are characterized as equal and beautiful and existent, do change and are never the same from moment to moment. This sort of thing is apprehended by the senses, the former by the reason. This returns us to the two worlds, the world of the perceptible and that of the imperceptible. The body obviously belongs to the former world, the soul to the latter. The soul makes use of the body in its investigations and staggers about like a drunkard in the realm of change; when, however, it "investigates things by itself," it withdraws into the realm of the pure and the eternal and the immortal and remains there in communion with the ideas. "And this condition of the soul is called wisdom (*phronesis*)" (79d). The soul then in its own nature is most like "the divine and immortal and intelligible and uniform and indissoluble and never changing" (80b), whereas the body has just the opposite traits. The body therefore can be disintegrated at death; but the soul returns to the realm of ideas. Unfortunately, as Plato develops this thought, he admits that some souls have been contaminated by their bodily associations, though how a being described as always the same could be contaminated or otherwise modified is left obscure. But when Plato indulges in mythography, he forgets the niceties of logic, and here he makes Socrates expound a doctrine of reincarnation in accordance with which the future history of souls depends on their terrestrial behavior, each being reincarnated in bodies suitable to their morals, the bodies of asses, wolves, hawks, and the like. In order to escape such a fate, the wise man will follow the teachings of philosophy (82d ff.) and thus will free his soul from the chains of bodily enslavement. The strongest of such chains are pleasure and pain (83c). They can be shaken off by leading an orderly and courageous life, withstanding—as Socrates did—the temptations both to indulge in pleasure and to flee from pain. The proper adornments of the soul are temperance and justice and courage and freedom and truth (115a). And each of these upon examination turns out to be a form of liberation from the body.

Yet again we must repeat that Plato did not preach extreme asceticism. He represents Socrates as temperate but not abstemious. As Eryximachus says of him in the *Symposium* (176c), Socrates can drink or not drink and be unchanged. And indeed that dialogue, in praise of love, is a demonstration of how a pleasure which in one of its forms is debasing can become ennobling. In its primary stages, as shown in the speech of Phaedrus, the love of man for man, or of wife for husband, it incites one to deeds of bravery and self-denial, exemplified by the action of Achilles in avenging the death of Patroclus or by that of Alcestis in offering to die for her husband. The presence of the beloved deters one from doing shameful deeds, for one wants to appear noble in his presence. This is then taken up by Pausanias, who distinguishes between the Heavenly and the Vulgar Aphrodites. All the gods must be praised of course, but the Vulgar Aphrodite is indiscriminate in her workings, leading men to love for the enjoyment of the body rather than for that of the soul and caring nothing for the good or evil of what is accomplished. The Heavenly Aphrodite inspires the love of boys only, not that of women, for boys are "more robust by nature and have more intelligence" (181c). Nor is such love awakened until a boy begins to show signs of intelligence. Its purpose is virtuous. It is, moreover, says Eryximachus (186), a universal force, expressed not only among human beings but in all things that exist. This speaker makes love the force which combines things into greater wholes and reduces antagonisms. It appears in music and medicine, producing harmony and health. But unfortunately it is often replaced by the vulgar goddess. The two Aphrodites seem to turn into the Love and Strife of Empedocles, the orderly one bringing fertility and health into being, the disorderly destruction and evil.

But the love in which Plato is more deeply interested is the attraction which the ideas exercise on the soul. The various speakers in the *Symposium*, as is well known, deliver themselves of a set of customary praises of love, but when Socrates takes the floor, it is to speak of that mysterious power which is exercised over the human mind by the desire for knowledge. Socrates is careful to point out that Love is neither a god nor a mortal, but rather one of those intermediate beings, a *daimon*. It will be recalled that Socrates himself at the opening of the *Symposium* is being stopped short in meditation on his way to the banquet (174d), as he was often prevented from taking action when the action might be evil. This force too was daimonic. In fact, one might compare the *daimones* to the guardian angels of Christian mythology. In any event Love is a *daimon*. He is described as one might describe Socrates himself—poor, barefooted, sleeping on the ground, "always a companion of want" (203d), and at the same time laying schemes to entrap the beautiful and the good, brave, thirsty for truth, philosophizing, standing halfway between wisdom and ignorance. What Love desires is what he lacks, the beautiful. There are, to be sure, other forms of love (205b), and they have been described in the speeches which preceded that of Socrates, but in general Love is love of the good. And also it is love of immortality, since one wants to preserve the good forever. Lovers may attempt to achieve immortality through their children (208e) or they may do the same through producing prudence and virtue in general and producing them in communion with young and beautiful souls fit to conceive them. "Everyone would prefer to beget such children rather than human children" (209c).

There follows the famous program by which a man of philosophic mind may perfect himself. First, he will associate with people beautiful in body, but will soon learn that bodily beauty wherever found is one and the same and will become a lover of all bodily beauty and dissociate himself from the love of one only (210b). He will next rise to seeing that beauty of soul is more to be honored than beauty of body and through his love will strive to make those who possess it better. This will lead him on to the beauty of the ideal, as shown in laws and wisdom. And "he who has been educated up to this point in love, as he sees step by step the things that are truly beautiful, when he approaches the end of his erotic adventure will see something wonderfully beautiful in its nature, that very thing . . . for the sake of which all previous toil was undertaken, something which first is everlasting, neither coming into being nor perishing, neither increasing nor decreasing; second, it is not beautiful in part and ugly in part, nor beautiful now and ugly then, nor beautiful in one respect and ugly in another, nor here beautiful and there ugly, so as to be beautiful to this man and ugly to that" (210e–211a). It is not visible or corporeal; it is not a particular, but a universal and "exists by itself, always being unique, and all beautiful things partake of it in such a way that, though they are all coming into being and passing away, it in no respect is either great or less, nor is it ever acted upon by anything" (211b). The contemplation of "absolute beauty" is purely intellectual and presumably imageless. And one who has achieved this vision has become immortal (212a). One can easily see from the speech of Alcibiades which follows that Plato had Socrates in mind as the exemplar of the true lover.

The emphasis upon temperance and courage is perhaps derivative from traditional Greek ethics, but at the same time it is clear that both keep the body in subjection to the soul. One is urged to be temperate in one's courage and courageous in one's temperance: Socrates can drink as deeply as the next man and never get drunk (214a); he can be tempted sexually and not yield (219c); in war he has withstood all hardships (220a); he has no love of money (219e). And when Alcibiades comes close to the end of his speech, he gives us a picture of Socrates standing in a brown study in the cold all night long, like the man who is enjoying the vision of absolute beauty. In short, the *summum bonum* in Plato's opinion is knowledge of the truth and the restraints upon action are simply instruments for its attainment.

In the *Republic* (iv. 427e ff.) is a list of the virtues which make a state just. Heading them is wisdom, possessed only by a few

(428e), the rulers, who, it will be recalled, are specially marked by the gift of reason. Then comes bravery, the outstanding virtue of the soldiers, which is the preservation of true and lawful belief about what is to be feared and what not (430b). The third is temperance which, unlike wisdom and courage, does not belong pre-eminently to any single class, but is found in the association between governors and governed, for temperance is self-control, the control of the lower self by the higher, and the artisans obviously are the lower self of the state (432a). When there is temperance in the state and the governors are wise and the military brave, then each class will be doing that for which it is best fitted by nature, and justice, the fourth virtue, will prevail. This scheme of virtues in the state is paralleled in the individual (435b). Corresponding to the three classes of the state are reason, irascibility, and appetite in the individual (436a). But since the appetites are not self-disciplining (439b), there must be something in the soul to control them and this something is obviously the reason. The irascible faculty too, though closer to the reason, needs control. The just individual, like the just state, is governed by the reason. He is the man in whom each faculty performs its proper function and never interferes with its fellow faculties. And the virtue or excellence of each faculty will be named as it was named in the state—wisdom, bravery, temperance.

Plato's emphasis on the rightness of each man's doing what he is naturally fitted to do is in harmony with his theory of ideas. The idea as archetype and the idea as class character unite in the idea as a standard. That the class character is a standard which the members of the class ought to exemplify is an assumption which became an integral part of the rationalistic tradition. The reasonableness of the assumption may be questioned, as may that of all assumptions, but nevertheless its influence has been such that one is forced to ask why it has been so persuasive. It is clear that once a concept has been defined, any candidate for subsumption under it must conform to its strictures. If we have decided to use the word "triangle" to name plane figures bounded by three straight lines, then no figure with more than three sides can claim to be a triangle. Similarly if we define justice as the harmony of the three psychic faculties, then clearly a disharmonious soul cannot be just. But so far nothing has been said to make one think that it is better to be a triangle than to fail to be one, or to be just than to be unjust. The claim to belong to a given class is made by the classifier, not by that which is being classified. But Plato, and indeed most philosophers, takes it for granted that every individual being does make a claim to belong to some class or other, and presumably, if that is so, then it *ought* to be as perfect an example of its class as possible. It ought to indeed if it wishes to make things easier for a classifying mind, but there is no reason to believe that things are constituted to that end. The history of scientific classification illustrates the conventionality of our genera. It is the human being who classifies and not the Goddess Nature. But since we inherit our common nouns and other classifiers with our mother tongue, it is normal to believe that they name groups of things which are not merely similar but identical. When we spot deviations from the statistical mode, we give them a bad name, such as "abnormal" or even "unnatural." Thus we fall in line behind Plato, whether we know it or not.

This technique has been the necessary, if not the sufficient, condition of science, for no science can move forward at all until it has discovered the similarities which are concealed by differences. The ancients grouped all material substances under the headings of the four elements and thereby were able to erect an intellectual model of a relatively simple universe to take the place of the helter-skelter diversities of sensory perception. The nineteenth century replaced this classification, which by Aristotle's time was seen to be based on the spatial position of the elements in the cosmos when all was according to Nature, by one based on atomic weights. But in scientific cases the interests of the investigators are paramount: the scientist need not think of the happiness or unhappiness of his subject matter. In ethical—as in aesthetic—situations, we may classify human beings and the types of human behavior as we will for purposes of understanding them, but the moment we try to make them conform to our class concepts, we move out of the sphere of understanding into that of control. If one of Plato's artisans wants to be a soldier, it is the duty of the rulers to see that he remains an artisan, and if one of his soldiers should show less irascibility than normal, then he should be either reduced to the rank of artisan or encouraged to be more high-spirited. But since Plato has assumed that types of personality are fixed, such a problem would never arise to plague him. He, like the Baconian scientist, has made a preliminary submission to Nature and he is controlling her by obeying her. If Nature has decreed that we fall into certain classes, then we must see to it that her dictates are followed. The fundamental question then becomes that of how different two things must be to become essentially different. For the point must come somewhere at which we correct our classifications and our language as well.

There was, however, in all probability something more than pure intellectual interest which induced men to identify descriptive and normative concepts and to make the class concepts standards of goodness and beauty as well as of truth. The Athenian lived in a small city-state in which descent from a common ancestor gave all citizens a mythological family tie. As one reads classical Greek literature, one sees how the distinction between Greek and Barbarian, Athenian and Spartan and Theban, in short how purity of blood was a dominating idea. To be a member of the clan was to share kinship with the other members of the clan, in the sense that there was an actual identity of substance throughout the clan. This is very different, as far as its emotional overtones go, from the feeling of a subject for his king. One is not lower in the social hierarchy than anyone else in the group and neither poverty nor riches can influence one's status. But to belong to the clan is to live up to certain ideals, in the case of Socrates to the Laws, ideals which by their very nature cannot enforce themselves but which exact obedience through consent. Plato, as we have seen, knew that sometimes noble fathers had ignoble sons, but nevertheless he also seems to have seen that it was the duty of children to live up to the nobility of their fathers. As a matter of common sense this is understandable, but as a matter of logic it is absurd. Since Plato was a bitter critic of his fellow countrymen, he tried to put the whole argument on a different foundation, for once he could induce people to admit that certain acts were just, brave, temperate, in other words right, it was no longer a question of holding up exemplars before them as anything more than illustrations of good conduct. If the clan of Jones is essentially a military clan, and if I am a Jones, then I cannot escape my destiny by trying to be a philosopher. The military spirit is inherent in me from birth; it is partly that which makes me a Jones. With such an attitude put into one by long tradition, it is easy to see why one should believe in the inherence of common traits throughout a class of beings of any sort, and also why one should believe that these traits were also ideals which the members of the class should make every effort to attain. The whole argument is metaphorical and rests on mythical bases. But that does not make it the less persuasive. It is interesting incidentally to see how in the Indian epics, for instance, in the *Ramayana*, the rank of the characters, their divine descent, plays a pre-eminent role, whereas in the *Iliad*, though Odysseus may rail against Thersites and the Rule of the Many, no hero claims more privileges than any other because of his lineage. It is true that all the main figures are kings and princes, so that there is social equality among them. But at the same time little is made of this.

If one bases one's idea of Plato's ethics on the *Republic* and the *Laws*, one will see little pleasure in the life which he thinks is the best. Yet it would be false to turn him into a long-faced Puritan. For the whole pursuit of knowledge is shown to be one of the most pleasurable of activities. Plato, it is true, does not use the hedonistic test of its goodness, but he does insist that to indulge in argument, to converse with intelligent men, to discover the truth, are the most agreeable ways of spending one's life. Indeed he seems to take the point of view of one who would maintain that any type of activity may be either pleasant or unpleasant, that pleasure and displeasure cannot be found in separation from the acts to which they pertain. The pleasures of the body are bad, but they are not bad because they are pleasant; their evil comes from their attachment to the body. The pleasures of the soul are good, but again, not because they are pleasures but because they are psychic.[25] This appears very clearly in that puzzling dialogue, *Protagoras* (351b ff.), when Socrates points out that when people object to overindulgence in food and drink and love-making, it is because these things bring in their train diseases and want, and not because they are painful. Similarly some painful things, such as gymnastic training, military service, medical treatment, are good. In the end, it is true, the momentarily painful may lead to future pleasure and the momentarily pleasurable may lead to future pain, but when a man has to act, he is not impelled by either pleasure or pain but by his knowledge of the consequences of his act. It is knowledge which is involved here and not emotion, and that knowledge may be that a pleasant good or a pleasant evil will ensue if one makes a given choice, or that an unpleasant good or unpleasant evil will ensue from it. But how one is to interpret the speech of Socrates is far from clear, since Plato may have had in mind merely an exhibition of his master's skill at convincing a Sophist while he was still a young man.[26]

The insistence upon the goodness of the rational life is seen in Plato's use of nature as a norm. For it is the nature of men to be rational; that is what distinguishes them from the other animals. And the fact that some men are irrational simply implies that some men are unnatural. Though Plato does not use these words, yet he argues as if he were assuming that the end of life is the realization to the full of one's essential nature, and one's essential nature is the idea of the natural class to which one belongs. We shall see this argument reappearing more overtly in Aristotle.

[25] On the aetiology of pleasure and pain, see *Timaeus* 64d and *Gorgias* 497.

[26] The problem of interpreting this passage is discussed, as so many other exegetical problems are, by Paul Shorey in *What Plato Said* (Chicago: University of Chicago Press, 1933), pp. 129 ff.

That some things which exist are not natural but contrary to nature is difficult for us to accept, for we are more inclined than he was to think of our classes as statistical aggregates and not as perfectly homogeneous. Homogeneous classes ought not to contain any members which deviate from the norm, for if they did so deviate, how then would we know to what class they belonged? The problem of classification, and hence of identification, is all-important in the Platonic philosophy and we shall discuss it below. For the time being, we can simply say that to Plato classes were established by Nature and not by custom or convention, and that they were spatiotemporal expressions of the eternal ideas or archetypes. That in itself conferred goodness upon them, for it was inconceivable to Plato that Nature could be bad. The problem was to determine what was natural and what not.

V

That problem was tackled in his meditations on logic and epistemology. We find him saying in *Phaedrus* that there are two principles which we must learn if we are to think clearly. The first (265d) is "that of seeing and of bringing together into one idea things which are scattered about here and there, so that by defining each thing one may clarify that which one wishes to explain." The second (265e) is "that of cutting things up into kinds at the joints in a natural manner, and not undertaking to break up any part like a bad carver." These natural divisions are determined by the ideas, each of which is separate from all others.[27] When then (270d) we are studying the nature of anything, we must first discover whether it is simple or complex; second, if it is simple, we must see what power it has of acting or of being acted upon; third, if it can be acted upon, we must ask

---

[27] This is true even of the most general ideas, Being, Identity, and Difference. See H. Cherniss, *The Riddle of the Early Academy*, p. 55. This should be recalled if one is tempted to read a hierarchy into Plato.

by what; fourth, if it has many forms, i.e., belongs to many classes, we must number them and in each case put the same questions which we put in the case of simple things. We have then the following categories in accordance with which we may ask questions: the categories of simplicity and complexity, of action and passion, of cause or agent and perhaps of effect. To these must be added Plato's conception of explanation, for without it logic in his opinion would be sterile.

That explanation must always be teleological appears as early as *Phaedo* (97d), if *Phaedo* really is early, in the passage where Socrates gives us something of his intellectual history. Having pointed out that he had been delighted by hearing that Anaxagoras had explained the order and the cause of all things as the action of mind, since that would mean that all things were arranged in the way which would be the best possible for them, he then expresses his disappointment at discovering that all Anaxagoras had done was to assign as causes "airs and aethers and waters and many other such absurdities" (98c). Such materialistic explanations are not explanations at all, since they would give as causes of Socrates' sitting in jail his bones and joints and muscles, whereas the real reason is that the Athenians have condemned him and he has decided that it is right for him to sit still and await the execution of his sentence. What he wanted was some reason to believe that if, for instance, the earth was in the center of the universe or flat or round, it was better for it to be so than otherwise. The question now becomes that of what is meant by *better* in this context.

In *Timaeus* we have a myth, not of creation to be sure, but of the cosmic order, and there if anywhere one might expect to find this concept clarified. At the very opening of the myth (28a), we find that an eternal model of a work of art, if copied, will always be beautiful, whereas a temporal model will give rise only to something which is not beautiful. The universe must have been modeled after an eternal archetype, for it was made by God and (30a) God "wished that all things should be good and nothing evil as far as possible" and took all that was disordered and brought it into order. But the orderly is the rational, and "for this reason he established intelligence in the soul, and the soul in the body . . . so that the work he was undertaking might be most beautiful and naturally best" (30b). One of the criteria of perfection is unity (31a). But this unity is the unity of an organic being, a living creature, and hence it must have parts. But since the most perfect form of a physical object is spherical, the universe must be in the shape of a sphere. (33b).

"Best" then is synonymous with "the rational" and the rational is (1) eternal, (2) logically prior to its exemplifications, (3) autonomous, in the sense of depending on nothing else for its existence. Hence when we have hit upon the ideal nature of anything whatsoever, we have come back to logical form or idea or class concept, which will be unified and eternal and, for that reason alone, good. But at the same time such ideas, since they each have their own identity, are different from all other ideas, and to the categories of unity and eternality we must add that of difference. In Plato's own language, the most general categories are the Same, the Other, and Being.[28] And presumably all ideas are therefore self-identical (the Same), different from all others (the Other), and really exist (Being). Hence one of the main purposes of logic is to discover through the application of the categories what is eternally the same and really existent. For the things which we perceive in this life are never the same from moment to moment, differing from what they themselves have been, and, since they are in this state of flux, have no "real being."

The inability, or perhaps the unwillingness, to conceive of anything transient as real is at the heart of the rationalistic tradition and, as we shall see, forced subsequent philosophers into further and further retreats from perceptual experience. The acceptance of time as a reality which cannot be derived from anything prior to it is modern. The *archai* of the pre-Socratics, the gods of the poets, the Ideas of Plato, the Laws of Socrates, were all believed

[28] Cf. the discussion of Being and Unity in the *Sophist* 244–45.

to be eternal and immutable, and it was their immutability alone which sufficed to prove their ultimate reality and goodness. Time for Plato was "the moving image of Eternity" (*Timaeus* 37d), though he never explained how motion could be generated out of the immovable, and though one might have true opinion about temporal matters, one could not have knowledge of them. Logic then was concerned exclusively with the everlasting pattern of change, not with change itself, and the technique of logical thinking had to conform to the demands of eternal being. These demands were implicated in the three categories which we have mentioned.

For instance, as is well known, one of Plato's devices for analyzing thoughts was that of dichotomy. Since the Same and the Other exhausted all possibilities, a thought could always be contrasted with its negation. This is the French technique of *de deux choses l'une*, of the *reductio ad absurdum* in geometry, foreshadowed in the fragments of Parmenides. We have already mentioned some of the difficulties involved in this. But this does not exhaust Plato's logical technique. We find in his three categories the so-called Laws of Thought which were to be made explicit by Aristotle. The Law of Contradiction is entailed in the distinction between the Same and the Other, for if an idea has an enduring character, then it cannot be other-than itself. No reference is made to respects and times, since an idea is all of a piece and does not exist in time. The introduction of the specification of respect and time by Aristotle freezes the objective fact as of a certain date and thus nullifies its temporality. This, as I say, is unnecessary in the world of ideas. The Law of Identity is entailed in the permanence of the ideas: once one has grasped their nature, they are always self-identical. The Law of Excluded Middle is entailed in the only element of diversity admitted among the ideas: each being whatever it is, it cannot be anything else. There is no middle point between identity and difference. Once these three laws are granted, they can be used in the world of time to direct our thinking. For everything in the world of time is an image of items in the world of ideas and one's logical task is to return to the ideas themselves from their incorporation. When dealing with their incorporation, one has to purify it of all chance impurities and then hope to uncover the idea itself. For we can recognize an instance of an idea without knowing the idea itself.

It should not be forgotten by those who wish to understand and not merely find fault with Plato that he was looking for real and not nominal definitions. Thrasymachus in the first book of the *Republic* is not only willful but downright wrong in defining justice as "the advantage of the stronger" (338c). For Plato cannot bring himself to believe that positive law is identical with what we have come to call divine law. In this he would have been on the side of Antigone and against her sister Ismene. Yet Antigone identified as divine law what after all may only have been tradition or custom. In the long run it may well be that we all follow in her footsteps when we obey our consciences but, if we were Platonists, we would still try to do what followed from given definitions. Thrasymachus could ask Socrates what difference it would make whether he was sincere in his beliefs or not (*Republic* i. 349a), and Socrates was able to answer that it made no difference since he was merely following the argument itself, wherever it might lead. Yet he comes to the point where he has to grant that it leads him to seeing no signs of justice whatsoever. And what can he mean by that except that most people would agree with him? So we too should probably say that it is unjust to have one law for the powerful and another for the weak, regardless of what happens from time to time. Plato would then ask whether our feelings arise from our verbal definition of justice or from our knowledge of the nature of justice. His own answer would be obvious.

There is no system of logical procedure given in the dialogues, no treatise on terms, laws of thought, definition, division, inference, and fallacies. Plato's logic must be formulated from his practice. But the need for textbooks in logic was growing as Athens became more of a commercial and trading center, with a mixture of people with various traditions of civic rights. The activities of the Sophists alone would have been enough to make men more and more conscious of forensic tricks, and it was natural for a philosopher to believe that clarity and consistency of thought would expose them. It was perhaps naïve also to believe that when exposed they would lose their charm, for the mistakes of the fathers seem often like wisdom to their children. We sometimes wonder how the Athenians could have turned so deaf an ear to Demosthenes and forget how lightly we ourselves took the threats of Hitler. It was ironical enough that, once Athens was conquered, the tutor of the conqueror's son produced the first disquisitions on logic.[29]

[29] We are far from maintaining that we have listed all of Plato's contributions to philosophy and repeat the warning given in our preface: This is not a history of philosophy. The *Timaeus* alone in one sentence (29e) stated what A. O. Lovejoy has called "the Principle of Plenitude," the consequences of which fill the pages of *The Great Chain of Being* and were elaborated throughout the centuries in treatise after treatise. The myth of the Soul as Charioteer in *Phaedrus,* the problem of *Meno,* the myth of recollection and of innate ideas, the doctrine of Love, the political works, all have had their echoes in philosophy, science, theology, and art. But in our attempt to develop the fortunes of rationalism, we have had to neglect everything which did not bear upon them. This is not a book about individual philosophers but about the history of selected ideas.

CHAPTER IV

Aristotle

THE RATIONALISM OF ARISTOTLE led him to construct a world which was similar to Plato's in some respects and vastly different in others. The world of ideas was matched by Aristotle's world of reason, but whereas the former was a set of propositions, intellectual in their nature, open to contemplation, the latter was a fixed set of events which might be named the Order of Nature. Both worlds were eternal and invariable, but there was more of a tendency on Aristotle's part to look for the eternal in the temporal than there was on Plato's. Neither trusted sensory observation to give one the truth. In Plato, as we have seen, one might have true opinion about the perceptual world but no knowledge; in Aristotle one could grasp particulars through observation, and by some process, never clearly defined, universals would emerge out of them, but he too maintained that there was no knowledge of particulars. He introduced a concept which occupies no place in Plato's system, the concept of chance. To Aristotle chance was a genuine cause of events in spite of the fact that one could neither foresee its action nor formulate any laws about its effects. He also introduced a new vocabulary to describe change, a vocabulary which has survived into our own times, and by the invention of such terms as potency and actuality he seemed to many to explain why change proceeded as it did. And whereas in Plato logical processes were utilized, as they must be by anyone who reasons, but left unsystematized, in Aristotle they were codified into a set of rules for thought. Perhaps the most important point of agreement between the two men was their common acceptance of teleological explanation. We shall now follow our procedure of beginning with the distinction which Aristotle, like his predecessors, made between appearance and reality.

I

Like his master he was looking for that which was permanent in the world, and instead of finding it in some material substance, or in atoms, or mathematical principles, or in the Ideas, he found it in a set of laws which were universally applicable. He assumed —he did not prove—the split between what things would be like if they were organized rationally and what things appear to be like to observation.[1] This assumption is inevitable unless one is prepared to accept all the diversities, conflicts, and exceptions to law of the world of observation and to give up the search for general laws. The most important of Aristotle's laws was what one might call the Law of Natural Development.

According to this principle, everything which exists in time, inanimate as well as animate, develops or changes in a set manner from what he called matter to what he called form. The form of anything was in all probability a descendant of the Platonic idea, but instead of existing apart from the thing of which it was the form, it was found in normal experience embedded in the matter from which it emerged. The familiar example of this is the development of the chick out of its egg or of a tree out of its seed. By

[1] For a study of what Aristotle took for granted, see G. Boas, "Some Assumptions of Aristotle," *loc. cit.*

applying the terminology of potency and actuality to such processes, Aristotle gave his readers the impression that occurrences were simply the uncovering of the permanent. If one says that the oak is potentially in the acorn, the statue potentially in the marble, the chicken potentially in the egg, one has the feeling that development consists of nothing more than pulling the rabbit out of the hat: it was there all the time. There were two types of evidence for the theory of actualization. Cabbages did come out of cabbage seeds and not out of radish seeds. All living things developed in accordance with a predictable set of stages. There might of course be interruptions, of which we shall speak later, such as someone's frying an egg before it turned into a chicken, but for Aristotle that which happened, as he constantly said, "on the whole" or "for the most part" determined the rule. He was not strictly obedient to this principle as a matter of fact, for he first subtracted human interference from the course of history and imagined a world as it would have been if people were not always upsetting the natural development of seeds and eggs. At the same time he did recognize that something else, which he called Chance, was as likely to upset events as human beings were. But of that too, more later.

The second bit of evidence came from art. The architect builds a house according to plan and the builders fashion the wood and other materials to realize the architect's plan. Were Nature to build a house, he says, she would do it in the same way as the architect does. Each step in the process of building is as it is because of the idea which the architect has in mind and which he uses to control the activity of the carpenters. Similarly the physician has an idea of curing a disease, the idea here being a plan of action, and puts it into practice in his profession. It is realized or actualized when the patient recovers and health is the form of the cure as the chicken is of the egg or the oak of the acorn. Now here two things must be distinguished. First there is the general Law of Development, that all change proceeds from matter to form. This applies to all kinds of change, growth, qualitative change (alteration), motion, and quantitative change. Such changes all pass from one polar antithesis to its opposite, for things can change only into that which they are not. But in the second place the form of each change is the purpose of the change and, when that purpose is accomplished, one has the final term in the various kinds of process. That there is such a purpose in all changes is assumed. What the purpose is in each kind of change is observed.

The form then of any process is the end term. But the word in Greek could be either *shape*, or *goal*, or *purpose*. In the case of the architect a shape or pattern becomes a purpose and it is easy to see why all purposes which are the making of *things* might be called shapes, since such purposes are realized in material form. Furthermore, the shape of the matter is changed as the purpose is brought to fruition. But in some processes, such as thinking, which proceeds, according to Aristotle, without the utilization of any bodily organ, there is no material shape which is changed and we have two possible ends or forms, the pattern of thinking itself and the solution of the problem about which one is thinking. But the term, matter, also suffers a change in meaning. For since thoughts are not caused by or generated from material things, certain psychological states have to serve as matter to thought. Sensations give rise to ideas which in turn become matter in relation to the purified thoughts about thought. If one can keep one's mind on the problem which one is trying to solve, then one can say figuratively that the answer is the form which is emerging out of one's thoughts as the solution progresses. No trouble ensues from the figurative use of these two terms so long as one remembers that they are figurative and not literal.

It is easy to see what Aristotle means when he says that the house is the purpose of the architect or the statue the purpose of the sculptor. It is also easy to see why such purposes may be called ends, since they terminate the processes involved. But in what sense of the word is the chicken the purpose of the egg or the oak the purpose of the acorn? The answer in Aristotle

(*Physics* ii. 8) is that natural events are always regular and that if the chicken were not the purpose of the egg, it would not appear on the whole when the egg is properly hatched by a hen. Nonpurposive events are random. If we see a man walk down a street with regular stride and buy a newspaper every morning, we predict, as we see him leave his house, that he is on his way to buy his paper. But if today he emerges from his front door and moves to the right, tomorrow comes out and moves to the left, today buys a paper and tomorrow sits dreaming on a bench in the park, and so varies his behavior from day to day, we have no evidence of any purposiveness in what he is doing. He appears to be aimless. Similarly if hens' eggs turned into a variety of animals instead of turning into chickens, we might say that anything was to be expected of such capriciousness, but, as we know, there is a regular sequence of events to be predicted and the prediction is on the whole justified.

But unfortunately there is one difference between Aristotle's notion of purpose and ours. It is true that we should insist that a given end be reached, or at least sought, if we are to call a course of behavior teleological. But we should also say that a given purpose may be realized in a variety of ways, that a man of purpose who meets with an obstacle to his usual course will go round the obstacle, climb over it, or otherwise try to circumvent it. If the man on his way to buy a newspaper finds that the street is torn up for repairs, he will look for another street; or if he discovers that he has no change in his pocket with which to buy his paper, he will try to make change; or if his special paper is sold out, he will go farther to find a newspaper stand which still has it in stock. We should be likely to maintain, I imagine, that the steady repetition of a given set of processes was evidence more of mechanism than of teleology. It may be replied that, judging from Greek art, the Greeks were more tolerant of standardization than we are. Otherwise we should not be able to date statues as typical of a certain period, or to identify their subjects. And it is true that the variety of Greek sculpture and architecture does not seem very great, though we have little to go on. On the other hand Greek hortatory literature was often given over to urging the Greeks to conform, for which there would have been little reason if they were not subject to deviation from the norm and "individualism."

We also believe that a person's purpose must be clear to him as he acts, if he is acting purposively. It is his awareness of what he is trying to do which guides his behavior, not simply the repetition of a set of acts. One may acquire habits which become compulsory, second nature as Aristotle calls it, and which are performed with no purpose whatsoever in mind. But in what sense of the word can one say that an acorn has that sort of purpose as it grows? When Aristotle says that moving bodies seek their natural position, he surely does not mean that they seek it as a conscious being seeks something. Earthy bodies always fall to earth and aerial bodies move into the sphere of air, flames mount upward and rain falls down, but if we say that they strive to do these things, do we actually mean anything more than that they do them regularly? The persistence and constancy of natural law is something in which we all believe, with modifications, but we have purged natural science of its teleological language largely because it is superfluous.

Be that as it may, in Aristotle the form, being the purpose, determines the nature of any event. Things, one may say, are what they are for. This is important, since it gives Aristotle a clue for making correct judgments of right and wrong. It goes without saying that the purposes of things are only those purposes which they normally attain, that is, when they are not interfered with by chance or force. Until a person has matured, he has not achieved his purpose of being a man, and consequently a baby, child, or youth is not yet what he "really" is. What a thing really is was given a name which has survived in English through its Latin translation, the essence. Its essence is contrasted with its accidents. The accidents are those properties which may or may not appear in a thing and are thus a matter of chance. The essences of things, however, are prescribed by Nature and do not vary; they take the place of the Platonic ideas but are always incorporated.[2] They too are class characters, not the characters of individuals. No individual in itself has an essence; it has an essence only as a member of some natural class. In fact in the order of Nature there is only one individual, the Unmoved Mover, who later was to turn into God. I find no evidence that Aristotle ever raised the question of what purpose was achieved by the existence of individuals. The question which was to be raised by some of the Christian fathers, of why God should have created the world, meaning why forms were incorporated, was never raised by Aristotle. In Plato the Demiurge, who of course did not create but organized the world out of pre-existing matter, did so because he wished all possibilities to be realized. But Aristotle (*Metaphysics* 1003a 2) expressly denies that all possibilities can be realized. Yet he nowhere, to the best of my knowledge, explains what the barriers are to the realization of any form. In the Order of Nature it is clear that conflicting ends could not exist, but in that order the conflict could consist only in logical contradiction. An irrational man would be such a contradiction since man is a rational animal. An irrational man would be either a child who is not yet rational, or an insane person who has lost his reason, or an anthropoid barbarian who is not "really" a man. There are no forms in the Order of Nature corresponding to such creatures. But in the world of experience another principle is at work limiting the realization of forms.

Certain kinds of matter cannot be the locus of certain forms. It is impossible to realize a physical shape in liquids or gases. Whatever chemically differentiates a hen's egg from a sow's ovum makes it impossible for a sow to give birth to a chicken. In the biology of Aristotle himself, the female produced the matter and

---

[2] This may explain why a man like Cicero found it difficult to distinguish between the philosophies of Plato and of Aristotle. He says, for instance, that there was only a difference in name between the Peripatetics and the Old Academy. *Abundantia quadam ingenii praestabat, ut mihi quidem videtur, Aristoteles, sed idem fons erat utrisque et eadem rerum expetendarum fugiendarumque partitio* (*Academica* i. 4. 18). Cf. i. 6. 22.

the male the form, so that we should have to transform our example to read: It is impossible for a boar to beget a chicken or for a cock to beget a shoat. There are also certain attendant conditions which are needed if a form is to be realized, such things as moisture and warmth. Finally there are certain causes at work in whose absence nothing will happen. These agents bring about the effect as the sculptor carves his statue or the physician cures his patient. Aristotle calls these agents "efficient causes." But though we may be willing to admit the necessity of the proper matter, the proper conditions, and the proper agent if a form is to be made actual, we still do not know why a possibility, which presumably means something for which the proper matter, conditions, and agent do exist, is not actualized. What prevents it? Clearly, if we knew what prevented a possibility from being realized, we might remove the obstacle or at least imagine conditions under which it could be realized. When we do not have this information, we say that accidents or chance prevented its realization. But does this mean anything more than that things have not happened according to rule?

Now there can be no accidental or fortuitous events in the Order of Nature. There all ideas are linked together by logical necessity and presumably it is possible to express all such linkages as a series of propositions which follow logically from their premises. For Aristotle makes a good bit of the importance of logical and natural priority. Thus if he says that the form is naturally prior to the matter, the hen to the egg, he means that one could not tell what the matter was aiming at until one knew its form. And since the world is everlasting, without beginning or end, and processes go on repeating themselves cyclically, the natural priority of the form is logical priority too. For temporal priority is never absolute, but determined within a series of events abstracted from the total cosmic history. One should visualize the Order of Nature as a logical map in which all possibilities are laid out in logical order like a system of Euclidean geometry in which every inference has been deduced and put in its place. On such a map there would be no temporal dimension whatsoever, and the adjectives "prior" and "posterior" would be figurative, if their primitive meaning is chronological. If all went well, there would be a parallelism between logical and causal order. Premises would be parallel to causes and conclusions to effects. But unfortunately all does not go well. For the incorporation of a form is also its degeneration. As Plato saw that no geometric figure or other ideal was ever perfectly exemplified in experience, so Aristotle saw that no process of actualization was ever exactly as it ought to be. In both cases the trouble lay in the nature of matter, though how matter, which has no properties whatsoever except that of becoming something, could effectuate anything, even deterioration, was not explained.

It may seem incredible that any man should make so sharp a cleavage between appearance and reality as I have indicated. It will seem the more incredible, if that adjective is susceptible of comparison, to those who have been indoctrinated with the Hegelian formulas of intellectual history. To them it is essential that Plato's successor take a point of view diametrically opposed to that of his master, and consequently they have interpreted the relation between the Order of Nature and the world of observation as that of a pattern embedded in the latter. It is true that Aristotle insists that all forms exist in matter, that none are off by themselves, while at the same time insisting that the Unmoved Mover, who might have been expected to be the form of the world, does exist apart from that of which he is the form. If the Order of Nature in its fixity and invariability is to be found only in its incorporation, then there should be no deviation from what-ought-to-be in what-is. But unfortunately for the neatness of the theory Aristotle did admit that what-is is often disorderly, that accidents prevent the realization of potentialities, and that monsters upset the regularity of classes. This made for better sense rather than for greater consistency. And since the disparity between the two worlds has been obscured by most historians, we shall dwell a bit longer on it here.

To begin with we have on the one hand a world which is real, which is rational, and in which logical necessity is the rule. It is real because it is permanent. It is rational because it consists of ideas which are linked together either as species and genera or as groups of genera which can be subsumed under one or more of the ten categories.[3] Its structure is determined by logical necessity in that certain ideas are believed to imply others. On the other hand we have the world in which we live from day to day and which is the world of appearance, of observation, of causality. It is a world of appearance because things in it do not enter our consciousness as linked together in permanent series, but are seen to be so linked only after they have been purified into logical concepts. It is the world which we observe, in that our contact with it comes through our senses and to Aristotle sensory perception is not knowledge (*Posterior Analytics* i. 31). Moreover, there is no knowledge of individuals (*Metaphysics* 1003a 13). And finally the events in it are produced by causes which may or may not succeed, though unless chance intervenes they will. To introduce a dangerous formula, dangerous because it may be misleading, one can say that in the Order of Nature formal causes always terminate events; in the world of observation accidental traits may terminate them. To return to our eggs, in the Order of Nature chickens always come out of eggs; in the world of observation the eggs may terminate on the breakfast table.

It requires little in the way of argument to show that one could not have a science of the accidental, except a science combining statistical manipulations with the laws of probability. But though Aristotle is willing to say that the natural is that which happens "on the whole," a phrase which sounds like a statistical generalization, he means by it simply that we poor men have no other

[3] In *Categories* iv. 1b 25, the categories are listed as follows: substance (a man, the horse), quantity (two cubits long), quality (white), relation (greater than), place (in the agora), time (yesterday), position (sitting, lying), state (shod, armed), activity (to cauterize), passivity (to be cauterized). In *Metaphysics* 1017a, the list is reduced to eight. The categories are the most general things that can be said about anything, are not deducible from one another, and indicate questions which may be asked about any subject.

means of detecting it. I have no statistics on the destiny of eggs, but I imagine that in the United States more end up as food than as chickens. But it should be recalled that Aristotle is thinking of nature as it would be without the interferences of human beings. Clearly, if there were no human beings, there would be no breakfasts, and one may doubt whether snakes and rats eat so many eggs that one could identify the final cause of eggs as furnishing food for reptiles and rodents. Hence we can eliminate statistics, which, as a matter of fact, had to wait until the seventeenth century before being discovered. In Aristotle's own words (*Metaphysics* 1064b 30),

We say either that everything exists always and from necessity (and we use the word "necessity" not as we do when speaking of things caused by force, but in the sense in which it is used when speaking of logical demonstration) or that it occurs for the most part, or else neither for the most part nor always and necessarily, but as it happens. For instance, it might be cold in dog days, but this happens neither always nor for the most part, but it might happen sometime or other. The accidental then is that which occurs neither always nor from necessity nor for the most part. We have then told what the accidental is, and wherefore there is no science of it is clear. For all science is of that which always exists or exists on the whole, but the accidental is of neither sort.

That things do happen in general with steady recurrence is of course granted by Aristotle, but at the same time the recurrence is interrupted and an accident may replace an essence as a final cause.

When interruptions to the rule occur, the human mind asks why. We take it for granted, as Aristotle did too, that the rule ought never to be disobeyed. Hence when one observes the accidental occurrences in the world of observation, one imagines that a cause for them can be found. Now frequently it looks as if a cause could be found in individual events, as when a man drops dead in his youth of cardiac failure or a vegetable is eaten before it goes to seed. But in all such cases we read into the event a class of causal linkages of which we already know something.

If we did not know that death came as a result of cardiac failure, or of something similar, we could not qualify the sudden death in question as a case of anything whatsoever: we should simply see the young man drop dead. So too with the vegetable. We happen to know that some vegetables are edible and that their nutritive value causes people to eat them from time to time. In all such explanations we first integrate the observed event into a larger class of events which has all the characteristics of a universal. If one lumps all such occurrences together into one class and asks why natural potentialities are not always realized, one has to invent some blanket term to cover them as an aggregate. In the past that term was "chance" and it was said that chance was the name which covered our ignorance of causes. But it is now known, if not generally accepted, that it is also the name for the combining of several causes acting together in a genuinely unpredictable fashion. For in order to have any science, we must untangle from the mass of observations certain regularities, to which either we or tradition gives a name. The planets and the sun in our solar system would be an excellent case in point. For the planets are well separated from one another and the Law of Gravitation applies within a very small margin of error to their movements round the sun. We think of them as isolated beings of enormous size cut off from the gravitational fields which emanate from them, as well as from whatever gases form their atmosphere. It is true that they are not so independent in their motions from one another as children are led to think, but their reciprocal attraction and repulsion are calculable, given their masses and distances. When we come down to earth, however, we find it harder and harder to untangle causal series which will be independent of all others. Hence we have developed laboratory techniques which permit us to single out those events which we want to study. But outside the laboratory the events intersect, collide, swerve from their normal course, and if we do not, or cannot, anticipate the collisions, intersections, and swervings, we call the events accidental. As a matter of fact, since every event which actually takes place is an individual event, and since knowledge is always of groups of events, the most improbable event is the occurrence of anything individual. We would do better to define "chance" as that which never ought to occur but frequently does. A chance event is an event for which there is only a proper name. It is the event for which there is a multiplicity of co-operating causes, not the event for which there is no cause or the event of whose cause we are ignorant.

Aristotle personified Chance as if it were some sort of general cause instead of being the name for a large class of events. The reason which he gives for their not being subject to demonstration is that they always occur as accidental, not essential, causes (*Physics* 196b 23) and that they occur "contrary to what happens always or on the whole" (197a 20). Yet one can recognize a chance event. And indeed he devoted a whole chapter of his *Physics* (ii. 5), to defending chance as a cause, and devoted the preceding chapter to attacking people who deny this. But here trouble ensues, for he also maintains that a cause is always existentially distinct from that on which it acts (the patient), and even to know that is to know something about the unknowable. If that is pressing a point too much, let us take one of Aristotle's own examples of a chance event. In the *Metaphysics* (iv. 30), he cites the case of a man being driven by a storm at sea to a place to which he did not intend to go. Here chance is that cause or set of causes which was not implicated in the patient's purpose. If the storm blew the ship off its course, the storm was the cause of the man's being where he did not intend to go. Thus in this example a chance event is also an event which is "conditionally necessary." The ship in the instance cited was driven to the island of Aegina, so that the event in question was a dated, localized, historical event. One could predict that because of all the islands between Greece and Asia Minor, a ship which was driven off its course by heavy winds might hit one of them. But one could not predict that that particular ship on that particular day would be so driven off its course as to hit that particular island. There is no class of events called "The ship which put off from the Piraeus on May 1, 350 B.C., and which was driven by a storm to Aegina." Hence there was no way of inferring anything about it. After it had happened, one could absorb it into various classes of events. At that time one could apply logic to whatever classes one had in mind and make various inferences from what one knew of them. No individual event is any rarer than any other, for none occurs more than once. It is kinds of events which are rare.

The world of observation is then a world which is not only unknowable, though perceptible, but also the world of chance. We have a situation in which an eternal world is set over against a temporal world, unity against multiplicity, immutability against change, universality against particularity, logical necessity against causality, including chance as a cause. But there was another conflict between the two worlds which arose in part out of the traditional Greek admiration for that which is according to Nature. Nature is purposive and good, whereas the unnatural is, whether purposive or not, bad. The question arises of how a network of timeless beings, a map, can in itself be either purposive or unpurposive. Where nothing whatsoever happens, no purpose can be achieved. But when Aristotle talks about natural ends, he switches from the primary meaning of "nature" as an order, to its exemplifications in the world of observation. Here processes do go on and some purposes are achieved regularly. Nature as the Order of Nature is, one might might say, the universal end or purpose of all things; that is, all things make for order, strive to exemplify order, and the order which they strive to exemplify is the realization of forms. But in that case one wonders how anything could be called unnatural. And the only answer seems to be, "When chance intervenes, an unnatural purpose may be achieved." But this is merely substituting one word for another.[4]

If I overemphasize this, it is because of the custom which his-

---

[4] It will be found that most of the acts which are called unnatural are performed by human beings, or caused by the desires of human beings. But why should human beings be unnatural?

torians seem to follow either of maintaining that Aristotle "bridged the gap" between Plato's Ideas and their incorporation or else of maintaining that everything in Aristotle can be found in his master. The gap between the universal and the particular, between the eternal and the temporal, is bound to be dug whenever a philosopher reasons. If the timeless were simply that whose rate of change is very slow, the case would be different. But there is every reason to believe that in Aristotle the eternal is the logical as opposed to the causal, the timeless as opposed to the historical. He does not say that in our experience we collect a large number of instances of something or other and then gradually see a uniformity of behavior in them. On the contrary, though he gives experience its due, he realizes that his class concepts cannot be simply more or less uniform ways of behaving. They must be absolutes, like the primitive terms in mathematics, and he wants them to emerge out of experience. This brings him back face to face with the problem of *Meno*.

Nor is it right to say that all this can be found in Plato. The theory of potencies and actualities, the doctrine of the Unmoved Mover, the notion of inherent teleologies, to say nothing of a dozen other theses, are far from being Platonic. The closest approach to the doctrine of potencies in Plato is the use of the word "to participate," but the participation of the particulars in the universals is not the development of the universals out of the particulars. There is no Unmoved Mover in Plato, not even in *Timaeus*. The Demiurge in that dialogue is the organizer of pre-existing matter, acting as an architect, not as the beloved object. The purposes in the cosmos are those of the Demiurge, not of individual beings, except in so far as the individual beings are themselves complicated instruments, which is true of human bodies. One does not have to be either a Platonist or an Aristotelian, as the old saw would have it, but if one is an Aristotelian, one cannot also be a Platonist.

II

Aristotle is a philosopher whose method is among the clearest. He states his methodological assumptions without evasion and in full consciousness of what they determine. Whether they are based on his metaphysics or are simply harmonious with it, I do not know. But since they have become an integral part of the philosophical tradition, which includes the scientific, and were not seriously questioned until the Italian Renaissance, I list them herewith. They form as complete a system of rational method as exists and it was by discarding one or more of them that rationalism began its decline.[5]

First, Aristotle assumed that things are arranged in serial orders. This is a cardinal principle for Aristotle and he lists the kinds of order in three different works, the *Categories* (xii), the *Metaphysics* (iv. 11), and the *Physics* (viii. 7). Though the lists are not all alike, none of them mentions logical order, except in so far as the relation between genus and species or premise and inference is logical order. This is worth noting, since later philosophers, especially the Neoplatonists, were to make much of arranging all classes in a single series running from most inclusive to least. Examples of Aristotle's serial orders are temporal, causal, and what he calls "natural." To be prior or posterior in time and in a causal series is easy enough to understand. To be prior or posterior in nature is harder. In the *Metaphysics*, as just cited, he gives as an example of natural priority the relation between subject and attribute, the former being naturally prior to the latter. Presumably the subject could exist without the attributes, but not the attributes without the subject, though just what meaning one could give to a subject without any attributes is obscure. Yet this is very important, for the substratum is also naturally prior to its qualities and one might imagine him to be saying that there exists a substratum which has no attributes. But I think it is fair to say

---

[5] I refer again to my "Some Assumptions of Aristotle" for a detailed study of these assumptions.

that in this unique case he means nothing more than that the qualities of the substratum may change, while the substratum itself, in its own nature, no more needs to have these qualities than any others. The substratum, like the subject of a sentence, is a grammatical necessity. We have to have a noun to which attributes and qualities can be given. We shall see below how the substratum, the being without qualities, became in later thought Nonbeing, Matter, Ugliness, and Evil, potentially anything, actually nothing.

That which is prior in nature may be posterior in time. For the form of a thing is temporally later than its potency and yet naturally prior. It is prior in the sense that it directs, guides, controls the development of the potency, as the artist's aim guides his artistry, but it is not overtly present until the process of development is finished. Therefore it is necessary that one know what a thing's nature is before attempting to know it, for otherwise one might confuse one of its accidents with its essence. The essence, being a characteristic of the class to which a thing naturally belongs, is not determined by convention, but is an inherent trait of the class over which human beings have no control. It is this feature of things which makes it possible for a man to begin where he will and be assured of finally reaching the "real nature" of that which he is studying. Epistemologically the universal is prior to the particular, but in the order of the acquisition of knowledge, the particular is prior (*Metaphysics* iv. 11). If there were no fixed species, there would be no assurance that starting with particulars we should end at one form rather than at another. But since the form or essence of things is established "by nature," there is a possibility of laying down rules which will lead to its discovery. These rules include that of looking for what happens on the whole.

There are, Aristotle admits, varying degrees of regularity. The circular movement of the heavens is the most regular. Then come the combinations of the elementary qualities, the hot-cold, the moist-dry. These are followed by the motions of the elements themselves which may be displaced by force, but always return to their natural positions. Then the plants, animals, and finally men and their works. I have found no explanation of why these degrees of regularity should obtain; they are simply observed to exist. One cannot introduce as an explanation the amount of matter present in each type of change, since the works of man, such as politics, include no handling or use of material tools or organs. Degrees of regularity are simply there to be observed and the scientist must regard them as stubborn facts. For this reason such sciences as ethics and politics can never be so certain as physics.

The one control over observation is repetition, for only by repeating one's observations can one discover what happens for the most part. There is nothing in the corpus to suggest that Aristotle anticipated either the Baconian or the Millsian technique of experimentation, in spite of his appeals to experience when he is criticizing his predecessors. The story which Pliny tells of Alexander's sending back to his tutor specimen plants and animals from Asia seems to be the source of the legend that Aristotle made great collections of data before generalizing, as indeed he may have done, though how he could generalize about the breeding and movements of animals from dead specimens is a bit difficult to imagine. It is, however, true that his works contain collections of scientific and pseudoscientific data and can be used as source books of political constitutions, sophistic arguments, and the habits of animals. But it should also be remembered that he did not believe perception to be knowledge. One uses the evidence of the senses to study the sensible, he says in the *Nichomachean Ethics* (1104a 13), but the sensibles are "mixed conglomerates" from which arise "the knowledge of the elements and first principles through analysis" (*Physics* 184a 21). Perceptual evidence can obviously be used to confute a purely *a priori* argument, if the argument implies that certain perceptual effects ought to occur. But Aristotle also uses perceptual evidence to prove, for instance, the earth's sphericity (*De caelo* 295b 20), and the existence of qualitative change (*De generatione et corruptione* 314b 12). And he overtly lays it down as a rule that "we should rationally assert only what we see occurring in many or all cases" (*De caelo* 279b 18). One cannot reach the true universal in this way, but observation can always reinforce purely deductive reasoning.

Aristotle, as we have said, believes that sensory perception is always of particulars, whereas scientific understanding is of universals. The universal (*Posterior Analytics* i. 31) can be abstracted from a large number of particulars, for at least in this passage it is present in them. This will work for sensory qualities, *red, sweet, loud, round*, but will not work for universal ways of behaving, for, as we have suggested above, there is no way of being sure that our statistical similarities are natural if we rely on observation alone. Judging from some of his examples, he was aware that wood is used for building and that reason is used for cheating, and though he does not compare the numbers of natural occurrences with those of unnatural, perverse, or unusual occurrences, he must have had as much common sense as his critics, for he says that understanding is not acquired through sensation: "the universal and that which occurs in all things it is impossible to perceive" (*Post. Anal.* i. 31). Moreover scientific knowledge, as distinguished from perception, is always knowledge of the *why*. The *why* in this case is not the teleological *why* but the *why* of antecedent causation. Completed knowledge for Aristotle is knowledge of the four causes of all events and he nowhere asserts that perception is more than the first step toward such knowledge.

Aristotle also takes it for granted that nothing can come from nothing (*ex nihilo nihil*). This principle, which has been interpreted in a variety of ways, in him means primarily two things: (1) that material objects cannot be created out of nothing, (2) that nothing happens without a cause if the event is "in accordance with nature," but chance too is a cause. Both usages limit possibilities: not everything can happen. This is his version of what used to be called the Uniformity of Nature. It is a methodological rule which we all use in some form or other, for if anything can happen without restriction, then science is impossible. But at the same time we can give no reason why men are always born of men and wheat of wheat, to cite a criticism which Aristotle made of Empedocles. If we find nonwheat being born of wheat, or wheat being born of nonwheat, we call the produce a mutation or a special kind of wheat (or nonwheat) or deny that its parent stock was really wheat or, following the alternative, nonwheat. Our vocabulary is our initial help in such matters. It all boils down to the problem of classification, or, if one prefer, to that of the identification of what is essential. If whiteness is an essential trait of swans, then black swans are not really swans and that is the end of the story. This may seem silly, but there are still human beings who think that skin color is an essential character of *Homo sapiens*. Aristotle thought that it was rationality.

I have said that both interpretations of the principle *ex nihilo nihil* are to be found in Aristotle. But two different methodological traditions grew out of his works. On the one hand those scientists who took the preposition *ex* seriously insisted that no explanation was complete until a material identity had been established between cause and effect.[6] This involved their reducing all problematical situations to material substrata: the human being is identified with his body, physical objects with their masses. Thus what Poincaré called a cascade of equations could be established. The successes of this mode of scientific thinking are too well known to require exposition here. The second interpretation, which is more frequently found in Aristotle, becomes teleology. No complete explanation can fail to state the purpose of any event. But here events which were ostensibly purely material were invested with motivations which normally could have been attributed only to human beings. Fire and the other elements must *seek* their natural positions; the planets must move in circles, because circles are perfect shapes; the universe does not wish to be governed badly; the organs of the animal and vegetable bodies

---

[6] See Emile Meyerson, *Identité et Réalité* (2d ed.; Paris: Alcan, 1926).

are instruments for good ends.[7] The famous Table of Opposites (*Metaphysics* 986a 22) is also a table of goods and evils, and when we learn that Nature always does the best possible thing, we also learn that since the upward, the clockwise, the forward directions are better than the downward, the anticlockwise, and the backward directions, we are not surprised at which way the heavens move. And since we are told to the point of satiety that Nature does nothing in vain and that she is also good, we can see why teleological explanation answered all scientific questions.

Another principle assumed by Aristotle was the Principle of Parsimony. This rule is usually phrased: Entities should not be multiplied beyond necessity. For methodological practice the entities in question are first selected by the questions which they raise. If we ask why certain stellar bodies move and others are fixed, we have already made a classification which rules out of our answer anything other than causes of motion. We consequently must know beforehand what the causes of motion are and see to what extent they are applicable to the planets. Looking at the heavens, we see a vast variety of perceptual differences and the one reason why we pick out the differentia of motion is that we presumably thought that all stellar bodies ought to be stationary. (Historically the question is raised because our predecessors raised it and we were not satisfied with their answers.) The multiplication of entities is relevant then to the problem which has been asked about a delimited subject matter. In Aristotle's case this particular problem was solved by his conclusion that there must be a divinity resident in each planet who kept it on its circular path. He could maintain that he had observed the Principle of Parsimony, in that all planets were asserted to move in circles about the earth and that each divinity was behaving in the same way.

A better example of his use of the principle is in his criticism of Anaxagoras (*De caelo* 302b 21), where he points out that there

---

[7] But those inclined to sneer at Aristotle should remember that purposive behavior was identified by him with regular behavior.

is no need to postulate an infinity of elements since a finite number will give the same results. Again, when he is discussing the kinds of locomotion (*Physics* 243a 16), he reduces the four kinds, pulling, pushing, carrying, and twirling, to two, pushing and pulling. Carrying can be explained as a form of pulling or pushing, since the vehicle on which something is being carried is itself pushed or pulled. Twirling consists of pulling one part of a body and pushing another. Thus carrying and twirling are unnecessary. The application of this principle amounts to the simplification of observation. It does not reduce the observed factors to "appearance" in the sense of "unreality," but it does reduce the number of basic factors which must be studied by the scientist. This intellectual simplification of the world is neither more nor less than that. It means that we can understand the events which interest us more easily than we could if they were as various as they seem to be. But to erect a metaphysics upon such simplification seems unwarranted.

Yet it was standard operating procedure to transfer the technique of understanding to the structure of the world. As late as Copernicus, and indeed later, we find such slogans as, "Nature always follows the simplest course." And in our own time we find epistemologists maintaining that if we can explain sensory qualities as the effects of air waves or light rays upon sensory end organs, then only the waves and rays are real, oddly enough reviving a dictum attributed to Democritus to the effect that only atoms and the void are real. But this is analogous to saying that if one is hit in the head with a stick, only the stick really exists but not the pain. Explanation is not annihilation. Now in Aristotle we have the phrase (*Metaphysics* 1076a 3), "Things do not wish to be governed badly." And by "badly" Aristotle means, "by a multiplicity of rulers." "Things" of course mean the universe, and to his way of thinking there is one pattern in accordance with which all events take place. But it is probable that he also thought that a pattern or direction or set of laws presupposed a cosmic mind responsible for them.[8] And that cosmic mind turns out to be the Unmoved Mover, a descendant of the *Nous* of Anaxagoras. The Unmoved Mover of Aristotle moves by the force of attraction, "as the beloved attracts the lover," to use Aristotle's own phrase, which in turn recalls Plato's *Symposium*. It is an idea which had the noblest of fortunes, terminating as it does Dante's *Divine Comedy*. It is interesting that two of the greatest intellects that Greece ever produced should have been so naïve as to put the weakest of forces at the heart of the cosmos.

All generation, according to Aristotle, is either combination or separation, and in the long run what are combined or separated are the irreducible simples. Consequently, though the whole is always prior to its parts, compounds should always be resolved into their elements as a first step in understanding them. Strictly speaking, the only complete analysis is that of material substances into the elements, which in turn are analyzable into the opposing elementary qualities of the hot and the cold, the moist and the dry. Aristotle makes no claim to being able to analyze everything that far; such ability is simply a theoretical possibility. Nor can he show us exactly how such an analysis would proceed, for the only tests he had for the presence of any elementary quality were perceptual. One can feel heat and cold, wetness and dryness. One similarly can see the natural motions of upward and downward, which indicate the presence of fire and earth on the two extremes, water and air in between. The rest is purely dialectical. For instance, air arises out of fire when fire loses its dryness, for since qualitative change is always between opposites, the only quality which can take the place of dryness is wetness. One never sees air being produced out of fire or water out of air, but logically— verbally?—that is what must happen if analysis is reliable.

Such logical analysis appears also in a work like the *Politics*. States must be ruled by either one ruler, a few rulers, or many rulers, an idea which is also in Plato. This analysis is superficial, as must be obvious, since "a few" is vague enough to require fur-

[8] Cf. Newton's General Scholium in the *Principia Mathematica*.

ther precision. Be that as it may, and it may be that Aristotle was simply relying here on the actual monarchies, oligarchies, and democracies with which he was acquainted, the analysis is presented as a logical operation, and indeed it makes sense to oppose the one and the many, even if it does not make much sense to insert the few in between. Again, he says that a state must be governed for the sake of the ruler or for the sake of those who are ruled. If we know what "for the sake of" means—I do not say that we do know this—then we need no empirical investigation to see that these are the only two possibilities. In general Aristotle in his analyses relies on opposition, and his basic opposites were qualities and their "privations," for the absence of a quality, such as dryness, is its privation, wetness, and this is just as perceptual as dryness itself. One of his favorite oppositions is that between agent and patient, and *to act* and *to be acted upon* are among the ten categories. One might imagine a third possibility, that of simply existing without either acting or being acted upon, but I recall no Greek thinker who followed that lead. Yet in Greek there are two verbal forms which might have aroused curiosity in the mind of so grammatically oriented a thinker as Aristotle. I refer to reflexive verbs and the middle voice. In the former case it looks as if something were both acting and being acted upon, and in the latter, though the sense is active, the form is not.

Verbal as such analyses appear to be, they clearly are not exclusively verbal or there would have been an analytical possibility for every form of word. They were thought of by Aristotle as reflecting the actual state of affairs. If something happened, then there must have been an agent to bring the change about, a patient to be acted upon, and a passage from one condition to its opposite. The four kinds of change, genesis, destruction, locomotion, and alteration (qualitative change), all exhibited these traits. Matter was always moving toward form, unless accidents happened, and that in itself was opposition. Genesis and destruction, being either composition or disintegration, were clearly movements from being to nonbeing or from nonbeing to being. Locomotion had to be from one direction to its opposite except in the case of the planets, for even if air, for instance, moved in the plane of air, it could only move from left to right or right to left. Qualitative change was always the appearance or disappearance of "floating qualities" and each had its opposite. Analysis thus mirrored the fundamental character of natural change.

Another and equally important methodological rule was the denial of action at a distance (*De generatione et corruptione* 322b 23). This implies that whenever a change is effected, the agent must actually touch the patient. The one exception to this seems to be the changes produced by the Unmoved Mover, but He acts only metaphorically (324b 14). Now if agents touch patients, then the tendency will be for the scientist to explain all changes as changes in material things, for it would seem to be impossible to touch anything immaterial. And if contact is established between two material objects, *A* and *B*, if *A* touches *B*, then *B* also touches *A*. In generalized form this might read: When an agent acts upon a patient, the patient reacts upon the agent. Because of this possibility, Aristotle takes the trouble to point out that we can touch something without being touched by it. "We say sometimes that a man's grief touches us but not that we ourselves touch him" (323a 32). This pun is far from convincing, though it does give us an example of an effect without a complementary effect. Our pity for a friend's grief may leave him cold, for he need know nothing about it. He need, moreover, have done nothing to let us know of his grief: we may have learned of it at second hand. In view of this sort of exception, it would perhaps be best to conclude that no action at a distance applies only to action upon material bodies.

These are the most important of Aristotle's methodological rules and as a group determine the bulk of his conclusions. They suggest, it is hoped, the vast distance between the world of science and the world of experience. That there is serial order in the way our experiences come to us or are concocted by us is undeniable, but it is simply spatiotemporal order. Nothing in raw experience is seen to be the cause of anything else; causality is a relation which we discover after reflection upon the confusion of daily life. If this were not so, there would be no need for all the proverbs which urge men to think about the effects of their desires, appetites, emotional crises, aspirations, or lack of them. Nothing in perception is evidence of anything else until it has been shown to be so. The perceptual world is a phantasmagoria of colors, sounds, and other sensory data, jumbled together as far as anyone can tell in a hit-or-miss fashion. We have to learn that smoke means fire, that clouds mean rain, that acorns mean oaks. Such meanings are not written in raw perception. Daily we see things coming from nothing: green emerging from blue and yellow pigments, the rainbow appearing in the sky, flowering plants coming out of hard pellets in the ground, arms and legs moving after an act of will. The enunciation that nothing can come out of nothing was hailed as a great discovery by Lucretius and Lucretius was not a savage. As for Nature's always following the simplest path, how complicated is the development of a child in the womb, how varied the shapes of leaves, how diversified the human face! To discover the simplicity and uniformity underlying such phenomena and others like them was the work of scientific giants, not the undisciplined observation of what was taking place before the eyes of all. There is nothing apparently uniform in the tremendous diversification of species, over 700,000 kinds of insects alone, and probably about a million animal species as a total. Could not the goddess Nature have satisfied her love of simplicity by less diversification? And as for analysis, it would not be needed if our daily life were analytical. James's buzzing confusion does not merely surround our infancy; the buzzing diminishes solely because we become used to it. Similar remarks could be made about action at a distance. When a soldier obeys a command, is the effect due to contact? If so, the contact has to be discovered; it is not apparent. The probability is that human beings were more empirical when they believed all natural events to be produced by divine command, as light appeared by the command of God. For as late as Newton scientific laws were thought of as divine legislation by scientists as well as by the rest of us.

Each of Aristotle's methodological principles is an intellectual simplification of experience. Each operates for the sake of intellectual satisfaction, and if it brings in its train pragmatic values as well, that makes it all the better. As a group, they establish the rules of the game, rules which need not be followed at all if one does not wish to follow them. A childlike mind can get along pretty well as far as the ordinary business of life is concerned. He will have need of some causal information, of knowing the regularity of the seasons and the sequence of day and night. But the causal information he requires need not go much beyond folklore. If he knows what seeds produce what plants, how animals are bred and what they eat, he can live. For he can also accept all the disasters of life with a shrug of the shoulders or a cry for forgiveness to his gods. Men have lived surrounded as they thought by capricious divinities whose nature it was to do things which could not be understood. If you think that a dance will produce rain when you need it and the dance fails, you can always say that the rain god was displeased either with you or with the dance, or that your enemies had danced a counterdance, or that one of the dancers had made a false step. I doubt that many people have found their faith weakened by the failure of their prayers. It might in fact be considered vulgar to expect God to be influenced even by a contrite heart. For how could an immutable will be influenced? No, the introduction of the rules as they were codified by Aristotle was the introduction of order into our ways of thinking. They gave us an intimation that we were not living in a chaos.

But it goes without saying that the belief in gods and miracles and the inexplicable and the wonderful did not die out because of the teaching of even a great philosopher. It is almost a truism that the more technical a philosophy, the fewer the people who will see its reasonableness. Intellectual history shows an interplay between folklore and science, religion and philosophy, and there is never any saying which will predominate. By incorporating into their methodologies the element of purposiveness, Plato and Aristotle became acceptable to the early Christian fathers, and in fact, after the time of Eusebius, his phrase, the *praeparatio evangelica,* was taken in all seriousness. *Timaeus* became Christian evidence, though the Demiurge was far from being the Biblical God.[9] Aristotle's *Metaphysics,* when it was rediscovered in the Middle Ages, turned into Christian theology, though his Unmoved Mover created nothing and his cosmos had neither beginning nor end. But the philosophy of the atomists, much more in keeping with post-Renaissance science, went underground after the eclipse of Roman civilization. The very name of the greatest atomist, Epicurus, became a synonym for all that was reprehensible in morals and religion.

III

Whereas Plato thought that human life was of no great moment and that his fellow Athenians were of less than average intelligence, Aristotle on the contrary seems to have been fairly well satisfied with things as they were. He recognized the existence of evil, but he thought that he could eliminate it in the life which was of interest to him, namely the life of leisure. In fact that life was the only life worth living. The child, the woman, the slave, the barbarian, were all beyond the pale. Though he may be said to have thought of the state in organic terms, the lower orders existed for the sake of the higher, and not, as in both the *Republic* and the *Laws,* for the sake of an ideal justice of more than human value.

There is no feeling in Aristotle of the tragedy of life. Though his chapters on tragedy are of the greatest interest historically, at

[9] For the differences between the two, see F. M. Cornford, *Plato's Cosmology* (London: Paul, Trench, Trubner, 1952), pp. 35 ff. In this connection it might be worth recalling that even serious scholars have interpreted Vergil's Fourth Eclogue as a Messianic prophecy.

least in their influence on Renaissance literary criticism, via Horace, even they exhibit no sense of the inevitability of suffering, no sense that the very fact of being born into a world inherently hostile to human aspirations is pregnant with tragedy, no world-weariness, no pity for the sufferings of others, no insight into the vanity of human wishes. He was capable of pronouncing one of the most fatuously optimistic of assertions: "In the natural course of events the true and just are stronger than their opposites" (*Rhetoric* 1355a 20). But if the natural course of events is the ideal order of nature, there is no distinction between truth and falsity, justice and injustice, which is relevant to it. And if it means that human history as it develops exhibits more and more truth and justice, one cannot but marvel at his blindness to Athenian history. Was Philip's conquest of Athens a revelation of greater truth and justice? Was the history of that city after the Peloponnesian War a march toward greater truth and justice? Or was Aristotle simply talking for the sake of saying something encouraging, as some nineteenth-century writers looked forward to the effect of evolution on social misery?

There can be little doubt that to Aristotle the life of the Athenian gentleman was in no need of critical appraisal. It was a standard by which all life could be judged. Since some men were born incapable of reasoning, nature intended them to be slaves. Since some men, mechanics and laborers, have souls "perverted, as it were, from their natural condition" (*Politics* 1342a 22), let them work for men whose souls are not perverted. Even the kind of music which should be played to them and to free man should be different. Manual work is fit only for slaves (1277a 35) and furthermore no man can live a virtuous life who engages in it (1278a 20).[10] This is attenuated by his opposition to legal slavery, as it existed in his civilization. He was presumably always talking of natural slaves, those men who are born without reason.

What then does he admire? He has laid down certain axioms defining his set of values and they are worth listing here.

---

[10] Cf. *Metaphysics* 981a 30 and 981b 17.

First, the superiority of the final cause and end of a thing (*Politics* 1252b 34; *Metaphysics* 982a 14). If the end of man is the life of reason, then the fact of its being the end confers value on the life of reason. This will be the life which is lived "in accordance with nature," for it is the nature of man to be a rational animal. The *Nichomachean Ethics* tells us what such a life would be like. The program gives us a good example of taking a traditional slogan and endowing it with rational significance. Goodness then is woven into the texture of the things and is not given to them by human desires and aversions. Our failure to achieve goodness is attributable to our failure to understand the essential nature of humanity. This entails the idea that goodness is a value uniform through the whole of a class. What is good for the class of men is good for all men, as it is in Plato, and the claims of the individual are nullified. The reasonableness of the ethics which follows is based on the possibility of the unnatural. If all men were natural, regardless of their peculiarities, then each man would have the right to be whatever he is. Alcibiades, Crito, Phaedrus, Charmides, are all different, perhaps radically different, yet each would be as good as his neighbor and it would be absurd to dispraise Alcibiades for his intemperance or Phaedrus for his love of sophistic rhetoric. If some of these differences on the other hand were unnatural, and if the unnatural is bad, then one could condemn them justly and strive for their elimination. To thine own self be true, is not an Aristotelian slogan.

Second, we have the superiority of the self-sufficient (*Politics* 1253a 1). This again is an absorption of a traditional value into a theory of value. The self-sufficient, the *autarkic*, as a mark of superiority is found throughout Greek ethics, and is one of the marks of God's pre-eminent superiority in Plato. As a standard of goodness it appears even in Christianity (Acts 17:25). To reach self-sufficiency became the goal of all the ethical schools, and they differed only in their techniques of reaching it. But there was a curious paradox involved in preaching both conformity to the natural end of a class and self-sufficiency as well. Man in

Aristotle was defined as a social animal. If he was to live a natural life, he must live in a society. Aristotle's society was an organization of social and economic classes in which the lower orders, as I have said, existed for the sake of the higher. But just as no form can be realized apart from its appropriate matter, just as the reason depends upon sensation and appetite, so the higher orders of society depend for their very existence on the lower. How then can any member of such an order be self-sufficient? The later moralists, as I trust we shall see, understood this problem and advocated withdrawal from society. Aristotle does not seem to be aware of the conflict.

Third, we find him asserting the superiority of the whole to the part (*Politics* 1288a 26). In Stoic philosophy this was to lead to the inference that an individual must play his part in the cosmic drama and submit to his fate. In Plato's *Republic* the same principle implied that each man was to fit into the class for which his psychical nature had best equipped him. But Plato's state, though an organic whole, was a whole composed of groups and not of individuals. Aristotle's state might have been any one of three types, monarchy, aristocracy, or constitutional democracy; he was not engaged in setting up one ideal republic. But he always thought of society as a collection of households and was bitterly critical of the totalitarianism of Plato. Within each household there was a head, a petty monarch, very much like the man of the family according to Saint Paul (Eph. 5:22–24). These heads of households were all equal and their relations to one another are left unorganized. Aristotle uses this principle of the superiority of the whole in discussing monarchy (*Politics* iii. 17), where he says that the man of great virtue who is fit to rule is as the whole to the part. The active reason, since it is the final cause of the human being, and the Unmoved Mover, the final cause of the cosmos, are both in the position of kings and thus represent the whole. But in the *Metaphysics* (1023b 26) he distinguishes between natural wholes, none of whose parts are missing, and "a universal which contains its members so that they form a unity." A natural whole would be exemplified by individual plants and animals. The whole man is better than any of his parts and Aristotle probably was thinking here of the parts as the three parts of the soul, not the various parts of the body. For it is the soul's unity which composes the man who may be considered to be good or bad.

His fourth criterion of goodness is naturalness. For a man to be natural or to live in accordance with nature was for him to realize that end which was his essence, namely rational animality. The technique of discovering that which is natural is twofold: (1) you look for that which happens on the whole or for the most part, as we have already seen; (2) you look for the genus and differentia of the class of beings in which you are interested. We have already spoken of the difficulties involved in applying the first technique. The second contains as many, if it is supposed that genera and differentiae are determined by nature rather than by convention. For how is one to discover to what natural class human beings belong, unless one has already a preconceived classification of things from which men are to be differentiated? To common sense it is obvious nowadays that men are a kind of animal. Yet there are still people who would pronounce such a classification monstrous. Men, they would say, are between the angels and the animals and the differences between men and beasts are such that each forms a class by itself. If men are *sui generis*, they are indefinable. If they are a kind of animal, then we start with the idea of a class to which they may be naturally assigned. But then how do we discover their differentia? The ancients themselves knew this problem. Was man a featherless biped, an animal which laughs, a tool-making animal, the one animal perpetually in rut, the one animal with a sense of sin? These and more have been used as definitions of man, though not all by the ancients. Which type of differentia is one to choose? If Aristotle chose rationality as man's differentia, it was because of tradition to begin with and because he was interested in psychical data. When he was writing his *Politics*, he could define man as a social animal. In any event man's rational animality was his essence, determined, Aristotle thought, by nature, not by convention, and hence to live in accordance with nature was to live a life controlled by reason. This he thought was a realizable ideal. Presumably one had simply to know psychology, political science, and logic to become aware of sophistic fallacies and the dangers of a passionate life, and then one could live rationally. For the rational life would be the happy life.

Aristotle's final criterion of goodness was the mean. That one should do nothing in excess was an inherent part of the Greek tradition, but Aristotle saw that the determination of the excessive is no simple problem. One's natural tendency is to give in to a desire or appetite. He also knew that the tendency to give in fed upon itself. He pointed out in so many words that ethics is not an exact science, and one sees his standards of the good life more clearly here than elsewhere. The *Republic* follows the lead of reason to the bitter end. If private property and the accumulation of wealth induce men to buy power, though they do not know how to use it properly, then private property must be done away with. But, says Aristotle, how can a generous man make gifts to his friends if he has no private property? If pride in family, says Plato, induces men to put their sons in positions for which they are unsuited, then away with family life. But the family is the element of society, retorts Aristotle, and cannot be done away with without wrecking society. Wreck it then, says Plato, for it does more harm than good. But such logical constructions apparently repelled a man like Aristotle. The Middle Way is the safest —and therefore the best. At this point a knife-edge was inserted into the heart of rationalism, a knife-edge which would go deeper and deeper as the years went by until the whole technique was destroyed.

There was no place in Aristotle's logical or metaphysical system for the mean. As we have said, the Law of Excluded Middle annihilated means. A thing must be positive or negative, good or bad, black or not-black. Consequently, when faced with the status of the mean, he said that it stood as an extreme to each of the extremes. This of course would not do logically, since the extremes are in opposition, and if, to take one of his examples, courage is a mean between foolhardiness and cowardice, then it cannot be the antithesis of both. The whole idea of a mean, derived from arithmetic and applied to morals, is a metaphor and doubtless a useful one, but Aristotle is not too proud of it. He introduces it apologetically (*Nichomachean Ethics* 1104a 10). But he does use it here and there in the form of related standards, such as excessive size, symmetry, regularity, when he says that revolutions spring from a disproportionate increase in any part of the state (*Politics* 1302b 34), when he speaks of the self-destructiveness of extreme democracy and oligarchy (1309b 23) and the planning of cities (1330b 22). Its use is further evidence of his conservatism: he disliked the idea of both the plutocrat and the pauper, of the roaring boor and the long-faced anaesthetic spoilsport. His discussion of the virtues is the revelation of a man justifying his prejudices with an air of rationality. And since his prejudices are also shared by most of us, these treatises seem to us to be among his best.

IV

The end of life is happiness, according to Aristotle, and the purpose of his ethics is to lay down the rules for attaining it. Happiness is identified with the realization of man's essence and that, as we have said, is his rational animality. Man is a recapitulation of the animate kingdoms, vegetable, animal, and human. His vegetative nature appears in his appetitive and nutritive faculties: like a plant he feeds and reproduces his kind. His animal nature appears in his sense organs. His human nature is expressed in the development of these faculties into reason. Thus the human soul has both rational and irrational parts and, as all virtue is excellence in the sense that one's inherent potentialities are realized, each of the two parts of the soul has its peculiar virtues.

The vegetative and animal souls have their excellence in the right habits. These habits are instilled by drill, not by sermonizing, for neither plants nor animals understand sermons. So the child who has not attained the age of reason must be drilled into forming the right habits, not reasoned with. We have two tendencies in regard to our lower nature, the tendency to give in and the tendency to refrain from giving in. When we satisfy our natural appetites properly, we are being liberal, and when we refrain from doing so, we are temperate. These two tendencies in later ethical writings were to be called desire and aversion, and the emotions accompanying them were called love and hate. The virtues of the irrational soul were called by Aristotle the ethical virtues as contrasted with those of the rational soul, called intellectual.

The rational soul had two functions, that of reasoning about truth and falsity and that of reasoning about future conduct. When the soul speaks the truth, knows how to reach the truth, can make the proper inferences, it has the virtue of wisdom. When it plans properly for the future, it has prudence. Thus the four cardinal virtues for Aristotle were liberality, temperance, wisdom, and prudence. The two intellectual virtues were fostered not by habit but by teaching. And, in the strict sense of the word "logic," the treatises on how to instill the intellectual virtues are in the *Organon.* Hence the major hortatory parts of the ethical books deal with the ethical virtues, not with the intellectual. When then people speak of logic as the art of thinking, they are talking good Aristotelian. Thinking for him had a moral value; it was not moving little black marks, unrelated to fact, about on a piece of paper. It was in no sense of the word what would nowadays be called pure or formal logic.

In forming the right habits, we are urged to avoid extremes. This appears even in satisfying those desires which are given to us by nature, such as hunger, sexuality, play, irascibility, and so on. As we have said above, all such virtues are a mean between two extremes. Temperance is a mean between licentiousness and insensibility, wittiness a mean between buffoonery and boorishness, just as courage is a mean between foolhardiness and cowardice. But these means are not mathematically determined, since some extremes are closer to the mean than others. Foolhardiness, for instance, is more opposed to courage than cowardice, licentiousness more opposed to temperance than insensibility. To reach the mean involves experiencing the emotions indicated (1) at the right times, (2) on the right occasions, (3) toward the right persons, (4) for the right causes, and (5) in the right manner. The truly courageous man learns through habit to act in the right way, to recognize the right times, occasions, persons, causes, and manners, by second nature, that is, automatically. He learns to know what is and what is not done. He absorbs the code of a society and does not have to think when an occasion or cause calls for a display of courage, wit, or any other virtue. A contemporary American, for instance, who is courageous will not participate in every movement for reform, but if he is properly educated, he will support, let us say, the Bill of Rights, regardless of appeals which are made to him to refrain and let well enough alone. The Jew or Christian who believes in his religion will not steal either ideas or property from his fellows. Thus a well-knit society is constituted in which a set of standards for good conduct is drummed into one from babyhood on, and when one reaches maturity one is no longer aware of what one's standards are. One simply lives in accordance with them. This, I gather, is the Greek idea of a gentleman, the man who is fair and good, and it is far from being a contemptible ideal in any society. For if every situation demands rational analysis before action is taken, there will be no action.

To form such habits, to acquire such an education, demands that there be teachers, and somewhere or other there must have been someone or other who thought out the code and put it in order. That someone for us is Aristotle, but for the men who were trying to live according to the code it had to be someone no longer known, so that it would have the sanctity of tradition.

Regardless of who it was, an intellect was needed to think out the kind of times, occasions, causes, persons, and manners on which the virtuous emotions could be indulged in, so that the ethical virtues were in the long run as determined by the intellect as the intellectual virtues were. The fact that my courage is not planned or stimulated by me but by my teacher, does not imply that a reason, and not simply instinct, was guiding me. The arrow which finds the target, as Thomas Aquinas says somewhere, is guided by the reason of the archer and the beast which acts rationally is guided by the reason of the Creator. So the gentleman who acts spontaneously, doing the right thing without stopping to take thought, is substituting his masters' reason for his own—his masters', his ancestors', or his gods'. By doing so he preserves the integrity of his society and, when he says that something is right or wrong, he knows that dates and places have nothing to do with it. This kind of gentleman is as faultless as a machine; ethical commands turn into descriptions when applied to him.

Unfortunately such exquisite perfection is helpless when the ancestral situation changes. One can walk in the path of one's fathers only so long as the path is level and has no turning. Any codification of laws, whether statutory or customary, eliminates dates and places, and raises the historical to the heights of the eternal. Ethics is usually distinguished from both psychology and sociology; the ethicist searches for those standards which are binding on all men and all societies. It was the Sophist who emphasized the relativity of standards, but the course of European ethical thinking has been opposed to relativism. Aristotle was apparently not aware that he was rationalizing either his own desires or those of his social class. When he noted a difference of opinion among Greeks and Persians or Greeks and Barbarians, the Greeks were right and the others were wrong. According to classical ethics, both pagan and Christian, one man could be right and the whole world wrong. This may be the reason why no system of ethics has ever been practiced. When this remark is made, however, the ethicist replies that he is describing what ought to be, not what is.

Let us suppose that he is right and that Aristotle, since we are talking about him, was also right in his particular description of what ought to be. What is to happen when times change and radically new problems confront men? Suppose it were true that private property had been abolished. Could a man be generous then? Would the fact that generosity would no longer be needed, in the sense that all men's needs were satisfied, be a substitute for the feeling of generosity, the willingness to give things away in order to please a friend? Is there no inherent value in the making of gifts? Is the regret that one is unable to confer pleasure on someone of whom one is fond an ignoble or trivial emotion? To take another example, suppose the time came when some theory of eugenics were put into practice. Only the beautiful, the strong, the very intelligent, are allowed to have children and the rest of us are sterilized. We have the compensation of dreaming of a beautiful, strong, intelligent race of men coming along to take our place—if the laws of probability work out as the eugenicists are optimistic enough to think they will—but we also live a dreary life, with no children to comfort our old age or to work for. We become halfmen. But so far we have been speaking only of the possible goods which might be lost. How is the virtuous man to meet new problems when he has been drilled only in the solution of old ones? How can he challenge the totalitarian state if he has been accustomed to living in a democratic state? How did Aristotle's ethics fit men to adjust to the Macedonian conquest? How would it fit men to meet the challenge of Christianity, of the industrial revolution, of the present Age of Belligerency?

It is clear that Aristotle never faced this type of problem, for he probably thought, as most of us do, that we are the human race and that our civilization is human civilization. Yet the discovery of the revolutionary changes of history is not new. The ancients believed that there had been a succession of very different ages in their past. Some believed in progressive deterioration of moral and other values, some in progressive improvement. Aristotle himself indicates a belief in cycles in which all ideas are rediscovered. Yet it is hard to find a philosopher whose literary remains show any serious use made of such ideas. On the contrary, those of whom we know anything always assumed that the end of life was the same for all men and that the good would always be the same in the future as it had been in the past. This is all the stranger in that when they were talking about foreigners, Egyptians or Persians or Scythians, they saw very clearly that their goods were not the Greek goods. Yet they had such superb confidence in the rightness of their own ways of thinking that they concluded that civilizations which were different from their own were just ignorant or wrong. Moreover not even the Sophists, so far as we know, who capitalized on such moral diversity as was expressed in the *Double Words*, ever asked why people should disagree so profoundly. The remaining evidence shows only that they knew of the differences and decided that the good was determined by Custom, not by Nature.

So it may not be surprising that Aristotle contented himself with a life for the sophisticated Athenian. The life of reason could be attained by following a few simple rules. First, depart from the extreme which is the more opposed to the mean. Second, pull away from your natural inclination. Third, when the attainment of the mean is impossible, choose the lesser evil. This amounts to little more than the first rule, except that sometimes one is confronted with two possible courses of action and can actually see that one is the better, whereas in following the first rule, one does not see the alternative with any clarity and knows only that one has a tendency toward an extreme which is more opposed to the mean than its opposite is. Thus a man may have an appetite for strong drink which he knows will lead to alcoholism if satisfied. He can choose between indulgence or self-denial, both of which are extremes. He should choose self-denial, since it would lead to a state closer to temperance than self-indulgence would.

But all this implies that one has the power to choose in accordance with rules whose reasonableness one can understand. To see the better and follow the worse was a psychological possibility to

Aristotle, as it was to Plato, since the only determinism which they recognized, outside of the material world, was that of actual corporeal restraint. If you cannot swim, you cannot survive for long in the water, nor can you be blamed for not jumping in to rescue a man struggling in the waves. And if you are fettered, you cannot move. But so long as you are not in chains, there is no reason why you should not make any decision which seems right to you. If you really see the better, you can pursue it. Your will in other words, not very clear words however, is free. The feeling of man's impotence had not as yet weakened the moral fiber of the Greeks, though it was soon to come. The Choice of Heracles was a free choice, neither inevitable nor predictable. Furthermore, as will perhaps be clearer when we come to discuss the contributions of Stoicism, if society or family or friends were a burden to your freedom of choice, you could always shake them off. In Aristotle this last possibility was no problem, for he was talking only about the man who was already free and an absolute monarch in his little world.

Happiness, which is the end of the moral life, is in the first place an activity of the *nous*, the reason. The reason is that mental faculty for which all the other faculties exist. It is the end of man, his final cause. Moreover, when a man is thinking, he is not utilizing any of his bodily organs and is thus liberated from the body. Since it is activity, it is inherently good, for to act is better than to be acted upon (*De anima* 430a 18). To be acted upon is obviously to be subjected to external influences and it would appear that the ideal of Aristotle was to provide for a maximum of freedom from such influences. They for their part have their function fulfilled in bringing us messages from the objective world in the form of sensations. But the sensations themselves turn into ideas, once they enter the human mind and the active reason combines and distinguishes between them to make the material of thinking. When, however, Aristotle comes to describe the processes of thought and of knowledge, we find that to know is to know the causes of things (*Metaphysics* 994b 29). These causes, as everyone knows, exhaust all possibilities of cognition, and when we know them, we need search no further for the truth. But Aristotle also realized that it is impossible to find a single premise from which all knowledge might be deduced, for the sciences, each of which "deals with a single genus" (*Posterior Analytics* 87a 38), are as distinct in their subject matters as are the genera themselves. At the same time, when we are engaged in thinking rather than in sensing, we are confronted with universals, not with particulars, and we contemplate a set of ideas which are more widely applicable than any others. We know, in other words, the most abstract ideas that exist. It is this contemplation of the general ideas which is the activity of the *nous*. It is not doing anything in the sense of acting upon anything, as an efficient cause might act upon matter; it is simply looking, so to speak, and seeing.

The active reason, moreover, is completely separate from the body. In the famous passage in the *De anima* (430a 10) which describes it, it is said to be separate, impassive, and unmixed in its essential nature. It thus when active amounts to man's entire liberation from all terrestrial concerns except that of understanding, for it is understanding. This being so, happiness as the activity of the *nous* is the most continuous activity. Strictly speaking, it ought to be thoroughly continuous without interruption, for since it is timeless, it should not appear now and then disappear. Aristotle does not, so far as I know, ever explain the paradox of turning on and off our intellectual powers. That we can contemplate the eternal ideas now and not contemplate them later can only be explained in the assumption that contemplation is a temporal affair. But Aristotle will not permit the ingression into the mind's pure activity of anything temporal. Similarly, when he says that the active reason—the term is not his—is immortal, he must mean, if he is consistent, that while we are active, we enter into a timeless world. But that means only that we are, while in a temporal world, capable of thinking about eternal objects. Thus a mathematician may think about his mathematical beings, which are certainly not subject to change, while still carried along on the stream of history. But if there is a distinction between the knower and the known, it might be possible for the former to be in time and the latter to be eternal. Unfortunately Aristotle takes the position that when the *nous* knows, it is identical with its objects. Hence both ought to be in the realm of the timeless. But in that case the problem remains of how it would ever suspect that temporal things also existed. And if the *nous* becomes identical with its objects, does it become fused with the Unmoved Mover when it knows Him?

In the third place, happiness, such as he describes it, is the most pleasant form of activity. There is a clue to why this should be so in an observation in the *Nichomachean Ethics* (1157b 16), to the effect that "nature seems especially to flee from the painful and to seek the pleasant." This dictum is not developed in Aristotle, as it was in Spinoza, and he makes little use of the hedonistic norm. Nevertheless, if he is to be taken seriously, one has a right to infer that, since the reason is the final cause of man and therefore his nature, to bring it to realization ought to prove especially pleasant. He distinguishes between psychic and bodily pleasures (1117b 28) and argues that the bodily are worse than the psychic because they bring us closer to the beasts (1118b 2), and this may be evidence that he took his dictum as seriously as we do. On the other hand, since a good many men prefer an animal to a specifically human life, and prefer it because it is pleasanter, on the principle that nature is what happens on the whole, they might be thought of as more natural than the Sages. Praise and blame are properly given only to acts, he says (1109b 30), which are within our control and psychic pleasures accompany only voluntary acts. Perhaps he means to say that when we are living the life of reason, we are more in control of ourselves than when we act as beasts.

Finally, and here the traditional criterion of goodness enters, happiness is the most self-sufficient of our activities. When we are thinking about thinking, we are independent of everything external to us. Even our subject matter is absorbed into ourselves and we are at last free. We are in need of nothing; we possess all desiderata. But—and unfortunately there is always a *but*—only a few men within a society can ever attain such happiness. Mechanics and laborers, as we have seen, are excluded. So are children and natural slaves. For the activity of the *nous* requires leisure and, he says (*Politics* 1269a 34), it is generally granted that in a well-governed state there should be leisure from the necessities of life. Hence only a few people within a state can ever be happy, and the very structure of the state, since the end of states is happiness, is determined by the needs of a very small part of the population. This does not prevent his saying that the good forms of government have regard for the common interest, but apparently he believes it to be to the common interest that free men with leisure should be allowed to spend their time in abstract thought. There is no passage in the corpus which explains why this should be so, and since few men outside of the Lyceum cared much about his opinions, living their lives as they saw fit, I suppose that he was never faced with this question. Since philosophy seems to have been practiced, as it is today, in cloistered communities, it seldom touched the people whose interests it analyzed, whose practices it often condemned, whose desires it deprecated. The gap between ethics and cultural anthropology is as wide today as it was in the fourth century B.C. and ethical conclusions are as unrealistic. The nineteenth century, for instance, because of the industrial revolution, the spread of colonialism, the growth of cities, was a time when moral problems took on a cogency which they never had had before. Up to that time the teachings of the Church sufficed to remind men of the possibility of sinning. But in the nineteenth century philosophers became aware of new sins, the sin of permitting one's brothers to live in degradation and misery, the sin of mass warfare, the sin of exploiting helpless savages, the sin of keeping women in servitude, and the sin of attaching privilege to birth. Yet the influence of the books was very slow in making itself felt and ethics remained a topic of classroom conversation rather than an exhortation to reform.

V

The ethics and politics of Aristotle remained within the school but his logic gained widespread influence very soon after its promulgation. It was based, as everyone knows, upon the subject-attribute proposition and the problems which it arouses lie rooted in that form of discourse. For when we say that *All men are mortal*, we are not merely attributing a property to a class of beings, but by one of those puns of which philosophers have always been fond, we also classify the group called men within the group called mortals. The Greek anti-intellectuals saw this difficulty and some of the Sophists apparently utilized it in their arguments. If you say, *This apple is red*, you may be made to identify this apple with the color red; you may be made to classify this apple in the class of red things; you may simply attribute the property of redness to the subject, this apple. Even when men saw the nonsense of identifying the subject with the attribute, they still argued over whether the copula, *is*, meant inclusion in— or when negative, exclusion from—a class or whether it was simply the announcement of the subject's possessing a given attribute.

As far as the special forms of argument elaborated by Aristotle go, the syllogism, the confusion was of little importance. For whether one says that all men belong to the class of mortal things or that they have the attribute of mortality, anything which can be said about the class of mortal beings or which is implied in being mortal can be said about men. Similarly with two classes which are mutually exclusive, such as the class of mammals and the class of invertebrates or the proper attributes of each kind of being, if *No S is P*, then clearly nothing implied in the predicate can be attributed to the subject, nor can any member of the appropriate class be also a member of the class to which the subject belongs. This formulation gave one the basis of classification. And Aristotle, who was a great inventor of names, established a relationship between certain classes, the species and the genus, which has survived to our own day. A genus was a class of classes and the included classes were the species. It should be noted that Aristotle did not classify genera into "higher" groups such as families or orders. That came later. The species were differentiated from one another by a definite property called the *differentia*. Thus *man* belonged to the genus *animal* and was differentiated from the other members of the genus by the property of *rationality*. Though no man is a horse and no horse is a man, they do share the common generic property of animality.[11]

The two propositions mentioned are universals. But there were also two particular propositions, one affirmative and one negative: *Some men are wise* and *Some men are not tall*. These immediately invoke doubts. Does the assertion that some men are wise imply the assertion that only some men are wise and that therefore some are not wise? Or, if it is known that some men are wise, can it also be true that all men are wise? At this point experience enters into play and logic as a purely formal enterprise loses its purity. For the predicate *wisdom* in itself gives one no ground for inferring its presence or absence anywhere whatsoever. To assert that some men are wise is not to contradict the assertion that all men are wise, nor does the assertion that some men are not wise imply that none are wise. "Some" here seems to mean something like "as far as I know," or "within the limits of my experience." But what have you or I to do with the case, since all that we are doing is to pronounce the assertion? Is the logician trying to tell the truth in the sense of factual truth, or is he simply trying to see the implications of certain ideas regardless of what we may or may not think about them? It is likely that for Aristotle logic was a guide

---

[11] To avoid a possible, if not probable, misunderstanding, I am not identifying this classification with that of Linnaeus or any other modern taxonomist.

to correct thinking and not a formal science, a nonempirical identification or differentiation or interrelating of terms. For there seems to be no recognition on his part of the distinction between formal and material truth, except when he is discussing fallacies. He wants the premises of his syllogism to be true to fact and not simply possible forms of propositions. The question of how we know that all *S* is *P* is for him a reasonable question, especially since experience gives us only particular propositions. Our "alls" are always restricted to what we have discovered. As we have seen, even when he is speaking of that which is natural, he is careful to say that the natural is that which happens for the most part. And furthermore he restricts knowledge to the apprehension of universals and maintains that though particulars can be observed, they cannot be known.

Since the typical Aristotelian proposition is of the subject-attribute form, the relational proposition cannot be absorbed into his system. In daily life we argue that if *X* is greater than *Y* and *Y* is greater than *Z*, then *X* is greater than *Z*. One can reinterpret the Aristotelian into relational forms, but the reverse is impossible. Inclusion in a class, like qualification, is a relation, but some relations are not either inclusion in a class, or qualification. Plato saw the difficulty of erecting relations into qualities in *Theaetetus* and elsewhere and Aristotle made no attempt to do so. One can see *redness*, but what sensation corresponds to *redder-than*? It was later maintained, by the English Platonists, that all relational assertions were projections of human judgments into the external world; the relations might exist between the ideas but could not in the nature of things exist among objects. Why Aristotle did not tackle this problem is not known, for he must have realized that we are constantly judging things to be greater than others, to the right or left of others, to be better than others, to be equal to others. He had little knowledge of mathematics or he might have tried to translate a geometric proof into syllogistic form. And if he had, he would have failed. The most ordinary operations of arithmetic, such as addition and subtraction, are not syllogistic.

And surely he must have added and subtracted columns of figures.

The classes of which Aristotle was thinking were set up by nature, not by man, and that is why through logic one could reach conclusions which were true to fact. But there is no natural class of beings which are simply *equal to* or *greater than* or *to the right of*, but all relations involve a term to which a given term stands in the relation in question. Relative or respective words are incomplete without one or more *relata* and sometimes derive their meaning from their *relata*. To be the brother of someone implies that one is a male, though the sibling relation obviously may obtain between members of either sex. This of course is simply traditional usage, for just as some languages distinguish between aunts and uncles on the father's side of the family and those on the mother's side, so it would be possible for a language not to distinguish between brothers and sisters linguistically and to call them both siblings indifferently. But in any event relations bind things together regardless of linguistic peculiarities, and cannot be found in the absence of that which they bind. There are no things which have the quality of being brothers and which are only children. There are no things which are great unless there is something than which they are greater. This would cause no difficulties if Aristotle had accepted as the primary form of the sentence the relational sentence, or, better still, had accepted two kinds of primary sentence, the attributive and the relational. The former would assert the possession of attributes such as perceptible qualities, the latter relations which could be observed but which were not perceptible qualities.

The drive for unity was probably the force determining what he could do. Just as incommensurables, such as the diagonal of the square, were scandalous (and in our own time we have retained the term "imaginary numbers" as if they were not so real as integers), so relations seem to have been an intellectual puzzle. I see no way of explaining why this should be so, for after all the ancients showed enough courage in tackling problems worse than that. We must simply accept it as a fact that they confined their attention on the whole to classes set up largely on the basis of perceptible qualities or properties in the sense of what a subject might do or suffer. Their logic induced them to look for entities which would be of the nature of *things*, not processes or events, and even when they investigated something like light or heat, they had to find a *thinglike* being which would behave as light or heat. The material thing was their intellectual model, and this is especially true of Aristotle, who explained qualitative change as the presence in a material object of a quality which could move about in space, occupying now this position, now that, without undergoing any internal change. The formation of the elements, for instance, is interpreted on this basis, the primary qualities of heat, coldness, wetness, or dryness coming and going instantaneously. No explanation was given for their appearance and disappearance except in the case of the privative qualities, the cold and the wet, which took the place of their respective opposites, the hot and the dry. To be cold was simply to be not-hot, and to be wet was to be not-dry. But why anything should lose its dryness or hotness was left unexplained. That a privation should be perceptible seems curious, but it is worth noting that when it was a question of the problem of evil in early Christian times, this type of answer was given: evil is the absence of good. There is no question but that this mode of thinking greatly simplified science according to the Principle of Parsimony. But it is a question whether it was not oversimplification.

We have frequently said that classes according to both Plato and Aristotle were established by nature, not by convention. This is of special importance in Aristotle's logic, for it meant that definitions were real, not nominal, and that logic was a branch of metaphysics. Aristotle knew that all things fell into a set of categories, as we have mentioned above. These were the most general of all predicates. There are obviously more kinds of things that have quantity of some sort than weigh ten pounds, more kinds of things that are in time than exist at this moment here. They are known by a special faculty, the somewhat over-worked *nous*, which in this context may be named intellectual intuition. The ten categories were logically independent of one another, as we have said above, and this made it impossible for an Aristotelian either to attempt to unify all science under one scientific procedure, or to establish a logical hierarchy with one category at the apex and the others under it in some logical order. Moreover, there is no science of merely spatial beings or merely causal beings or merely passive beings; the sciences each deal with the things included in a single genus. Thus there could be a science of zoology or physics, for these would study respectively animate beings or beings moving in space. Aristotle was neither an epistemological nor a psychophysical nor a substantialistic monist. He accepted difference, as Plato also did, as one of the fundamental features of the universe.

The ten categories were in the final analysis ten types of order. And though there was no conviction on Aristotle's part, as we have said, that each could be studied separately as a type of order, nevertheless they were intuited separately. Each initiated problems of definition at a minimum and one finds discussions of almost all of them scattered here and there in the corpus. Space, for instance, was finite in extent; time was the measure of motion; change was always the actualization of potencies; there need be no passion correlative with every action, and so on. The kinds of order were all distinct from one another. But just as Socrates heaved a sigh of relief when he discovered that Anaxagoras had introduced a cosmic mind into the world to set things going, so Aristotle said that he seemed like a sober man in comparison with his predecessors. His cosmic mind became the Unmoved Mover in Aristotle, and it was he who kept the world in order by the force of attraction. It will not do to say that the Unmoved Mover is simply a name for the order which is exemplified in nature, that He is a personification of the Order of Nature as contrasted with the world of observation and chance. For Aristotle is definite about the separateness of the Unmoved Mover, as indeed he is about the separateness of the active reason in man. There must be an agent and a patient wherever there is change and the motions of the planets are a form of change, just as the growth of a seed into a plant is. There must be one agent, since the "world must not be governed badly." The universal agent must be entirely active and incapable of being acted upon. He is the governor of the cosmos and, as a ruler, he must be external to that which he rules. He must have no potentiality in him, since if he had, he would not be complete and perfect. Therefore he must be completely actual. Furthermore, he must be immaterial, for no material thing is eternal.[12] How such a being could cause in any reasonable sense of that word temporal and mutable effects, when one also assumes that there must be some similarity between cause and effect, is mysterious. If the Unmoved Mover were simply that toward which the whole creation moves, He would stand as a sort of Platonic idea of the whole, never realized but always potentially there. That is not, however, Aristotle's point of view. Finally, though the Unmoved Mover turns into God, He is not the creator of the universe, as the Biblical God is, nor is He the Demiurge of *Timaeus*. He is loved by everything below Him but He gives no love in return. How could he who lacks nothing love his inferiors? The perfect soul could no more love than hate. Like the Gods of Epicurus, He is impassive and totally uninterested in anything beyond Himself. His life is the life engaged in thinking about thinking. The attempt to fuse such a being into the being of a personal, anthropomorphic creator, judge and eternal father of us all, was bound to be an intellectual failure. It was, however, a great emotional success.

[12] When he wrote *Metaphysics* xi. 6, Aristotle either forgot or had not yet said that all potentialities need not be realized. For on that principle a material object, though capable of changing, would not inevitably change.

Supplementary Note

It is always difficult, and sometimes impossible, to prove a universal negative proposition. But I have searched through the works of Aristotle in vain for a proof in which he uses the syllogism. His demonstrations sometimes are based on simple observation, especially when he is criticizing an opponent, sometimes are enthymemes, but I have yet to find a syllogism except as a sample of a type of reasoning. The opening of his *Metaphysics* (xi. 1) is an argument which is of a certain importance in the system. To avoid errors, I am quoting Ross's translation. Chapter 1 begins as follows: "Substance is the subject of our inquiry; for the principles and the causes we are seeking are those of substances." This is his topic sentence. He continues, "For if the universe is of the nature of a whole, substance is its first part; and if it coheres merely by virtue of serial succession, on this view also substance is first, and is succeeded by quality, and then by quantity." The first part of this argument may be rephrased in syllogistic form as: All wholes are such that their first parts are substances; the universe is a whole; therefore the universe is such that its first part is a substance. But this is not the way in which Aristotle actually does argue, and the hypothetical clause which introduces his argument is not used to form even a complete hypothetical syllogism. The second portion of the argument is straightforward dogma and he does not attempt to prove the order of the categories of quality and quantity. He continues, "None of the categories other than substance can exist apart." This is a premise. But this is backed up simply by the opinions of those whom he calls "the old philosophers" and by those of his contemporaries who "tend to rank universals as substances." In other words he is giving some reason, that of authority, for holding to the exclusive ability of substances to exist apart. He then moves on to say that there are three kinds of substance: one that is sensible, which is divided into two kinds, the eternal and the perishable, and a third which is immovable, that is, unchangeable. This classification is based again on the opinions of other philosophers; it is a restatement of their positions. He then proceeds to say, "Sensible substance is changeable," and asserting that all change proceeds from opposite to opposite from intermediate points and not from all opposites but from contraries, "there must be something underlying which changes into the contrary change." If one ask why, he replies, "For the contraries do not change." This concludes the chapter as we have it.

Again, not one of these arguments is syllogistic, and when they are hypothetical, they are not hypothetical syllogisms. They can all be rephrased in the form of syllogisms, it is true, but then any argument, if one is willing to go to the trouble, can be twisted about to turn predicates into attributes. But the insertion of such words as "such that" or "of the nature of," though useful for the task of rephrasing, are cumbersome and unnecessary if one is thinking of conviction. It is no better to say, All things that change are such that they have an underlying substance which undergoes the change, than it is to say, If a change occurs, it is due to a subject which changes. I do not say that this is very intelligible, for what the underlying subject is which changes is less than clear. But if one understands the meaning of a *subject of change,* then the simpler sentence is as useful in the argument as the more complex sentence.

This single chapter may not be typical of the corpus as a whole, but I think that it is a fair sample nevertheless of his proofs. Aristotle is one of the few philosophers who is careful to state his premises and he leaves it to his readers to see the relevance of his conclusions to his premises. When one comes to a man like Sextus Empiricus, one sees the various forms of syllogism in use, as well as traditional forms of nonsyllogistic proof. But in what we have of Aristotle, who brought the syllogism into the light of day, it is strange to find him making little or no use of it.

CHAPTER V

The First Break in the System

═══════════════════════════════

THE RATIONAL STRUCTURES of Plato and Aristotle, whatever their weaknesses, were cemented by the mortar of logical consistency. Where they failed, all rationalism must fail. The breaking point comes when the rationalist tries to deduce existence from essence, or, in more ordinary language, when the philosopher tries to show that the world of perception is as rational as that of logic. The premises of a mathematical system can include an axiom or postulate to the effect that its inferences are exemplified in experience, but even then one is bound to discover that the exemplifications are imperfect. Where numbers are involved as exemplified in quantities, the arithmetical operations are never found to be perfectly incorporated, and where it is a question of geometric forms, these two fall short of what mathematics demands of them. Both Plato and Aristotle nevertheless accepted the material, or empirical world, as an integral part of their philosophic architecture, and if they put the blame on matter itself, what else was there to take it? Reason cannot operate without generalities. The tantalizing approximations of experience to perfection had to be interpreted as a block to man's intelligence, but they were a block upon which one could rise to an ideal world, the world of Ideas in Plato, the Order of Nature in Aristotle.

There were at least two ways of escape from this situation, if one wanted to escape. One, which was taken by Plato's successors in the Academy, was refusing to admit the need of studying so haphazard a set of beings as those found on earth. The other was just the reverse, that of denying the ideas altogether and of taking matter and its behavior as ultimate. This was the escape attempted by the early Stoics and Epicureans. Neither escape was successful. The conflict between essence and existence could not be resolved with the means available in the fourth and third centuries. A possible third way out lay in the simple denial of any hope of success and it was not long before the skeptic way was followed even by the later members of the Platonic Academy. It should be admitted that the writings of the early Academics and those of the first Stoics and Epicureans exist only in quotations found in such writers as Diogenes Laertius, Stobaeus, Philo Judaeus, Sextus Empiricus, Eusebius, and the Romans, Cicero and Seneca, all of whom wrote several centuries later than the men whom they were quoting and all of whom quoted them for their own purposes. One can use one's imagination to guess why they said the things they are quoted as saying but after all one can only guess. Thus one can see the seeds of skepticism in Plato and imagine why they flowered in the Middle Academy. It is also possible to guess that some of the details of Stoic and Epicurean cosmology were invented to serve as a foundation for an ethics, though one approaches dangerously near to mind reading in saying so. Where several of the later writers agree on what they attribute to an earlier thinker, one has some evidence that what they report is reliable, though their agreement may simply be due to their using a common source. Let me then frankly admit that what is said in this chapter is often taken from secondhand sources, as it must be, and that, even when a direct quotation is used to prove the authenticity of a man's doctrines, the quotation is out of context. We are in short back in the position in which we found ourselves when speaking of the pre-Socratics.[1]

I

1. The disciples of Plato seem to have continued the school named after the estate of their master, the Academy. The first director of the Academy was Plato's nephew, Speusippus, and since his one surviving work is on the Pythagorean theory of numbers, it has become customary to think of him as rebellious to his master's teaching, rejecting the theory of ideas and modifying his epistemology. Yet like all philosophers, except those who refuse to budge out of a very limited field, he must have made the usual distinction between the world as it seems and the world as it really is. If it be true that for Plato's idea of the good he substituted a unit, the One from which the *archai* or first principles of each other type of thing arose, then it may be inferred that he introduced into Platonism a form of Pythagoreanism which was to be developed later by the Neoplatonists.[2] This would look as if he tried to fuse all the ideas into the One. Yet he is reported by Aëtius to have denied that the divine *nous* emerged from the One or from the Good, but to have said that it was *sui generis* (fr. 38). There is clearly a confusion of two basic metaphors here, the first being explanation on the basis of the source from which things

---

[1] For the reliability of our sources for this period, see E. Zeller, *Stoics, Epicureans, and Sceptics,* trans. by Oswald J. Reichel (London: Longmans, 1870), chap. 4. Zeller still remains the most critical of the historians of Greek philosophy and, because of his copious footnotes, one of the most helpful. One must always be grateful to the compilers of fragments, but in the long run these compilations are anthologies of scattered quotations and the interstitial tissue has been fabricated by the compilers themselves. Could one reconstruct the works of Shakespeare out of quotations in Bartlett?

[2] Fr. 33a, from Aristotle's *Metaphysics* 1028b. All fragments of Speusippus are quoted from and numbered with the numbers of P. Lang, *De Speusippi Academici scriptis* (Bonn: Georg, 1911).

come into being and the other the end toward which they tend. Plato's idea of the good was the end and goal of all things, not their supernatural origin. The relevant fragments do not help us clarify this matter and the most that one can say is that they show us a philosopher who did not shrink from a pluralism of kinds, the sort of pluralism which is found in Aristotle's theory of the categories.

Now by starting with the idea of unity, on the ground that everything of which we can predicate any attribute is a unit of thought, we would not inevitably draw good and rationality, magnitude or mentality, out of it. Whatever the interrelations of such ideas, they were set up for psychological or historical reasons, not for logical. The idea of the good in Plato was as the sun, that which illuminated and gave life to everything. But when the figure of speech is examined, it turns out to mean concretely that the best way to understand things is to discover their purpose. This we saw above in discussing Socrates' criticism of Anaxagoras. This way of thinking by Aristotle's time was traditional and remained so until the Italian Renaissance. Hence one might question the position of the Good in the cosmos, that is, its primacy over all the other ideas, but one could never deny its ultimate importance as a clue to explanation. But when the order of things was reversed and a philosopher tried to explain the origin of things as coming out of a source, then the details of the genetic process became a problem. One can understand that any process is regular by looking at it, and if purpose is equated with the constant attainment of a goal, then purposiveness could be read into all processes which were regular. But why anything should give rise to anything else is more mysterious. We can observe sequences but we cannot observe the details of genesis. To explain the world as the product or the creation of a single source is to revert to mythology, the mythology of the primal egg or of the creative god. The nature of Speusippus' idea of genesis was a puzzle to Aristotle (fr. 48c). It becomes a greater puzzle when we read that Proclus, who, it must be admitted, is not the soundest authority, said that

Speusippus made a distinction between the genesis of ideas in thinking and the actual creation of things (fr. 46). For this would seem to imply that the two orders, that of thoughts and that of things, were distinct not only in existence but also in origin, which would make it impossible for all things to have emerged from the One. Whether Speusippus himself was aware of the puzzles he had introduced into philosophy, one cannot say, but that one of his contemporaries felt them, is undeniable.

2. Next in line in the Academy was Xenocrates, who was a bit more faithful to the teachings of Plato. He apparently accepted the theory of ideas, but derived them all from the One and the Indefinite Dyad.[3] His use of such numerical terms for his ultimate principles repeats the Pythagorean strain and presumably his two worlds were the world of mathematics and the world of numbered things. This may simply mean that if we are to understand the world of observation, we must have recourse to mathematics, that the world is fundamentally a mathematical world. The two terms, the One and the Indefinite Dyad, would then be names for the assumed fact that plurality is as real as unity and that, if we start with a monism of source or origin, we shall never be able to explain why it should have become diversified. To call the One the source or origin of the world is dubious poetry and ambiguous science. As poetry it stirs one into feeling that above or beyond or within the clearly perceptible variety of experience is some sort of homogeneity. But homogeneity may be of substance, as when one maintains that all things are material, or again it may suggest that all events are describable in one sort of law, whether mechanical or teleological, or in the third place that all things were produced out of a common source, as in the Hesiodic myths, or that all things have some common quality, such as beauty or goodness. But the efficacy of such a word as Unity depends upon the freedom it gives one to imagine the various possibilities it permits.

[3] Fr. 26 (from Theophrastus) in Richard Heinze, *Xenocrates* (Leipzig: Teubner, 1892). I shall use Heinze's numbering throughout.

But if one is a philosopher as well as a poet, one will naturally ask for more precision or at a minimum put certain questions to oneself about how any uniform origin could produce such multiplicity. And if one is certain, as Xenocrates seems to have been, that the process is one which is intelligible, that is to say, rational, one will immediately suspect that a unit existing by itself alone would never change. The ancients took it for granted that change, not immutability, was a problem. If then the One became somehow or other diversified, there must have been some cause of the diversification. That cause was presumably the Indefinite Dyad. But there is also the possibility that by the Indefinite Dyad was meant indefiniteness or plurality.[4] If that interpretation is correct, then Xenocrates may simply have thrown up the sponge and consented to a duality of *archai*, the interplay between which was responsible for the existence of the things which exist. In view, however, of some of his other reported opinions, it seems more likely that he thought of duality as a numerical principle which could actually be divided by an "active" force, the One. This is of course metaphysical mythology, but not unusual in this and subsequent periods. If Xenocrates could say that the soul was a self-moving number (fr.60), he would not stop at other expressions the sense of which is mysterious. There is, for instance, a passage in Stobaeus[5] quoting Aëtius to the effect that Xenocrates made the One and the Indefinite Dyad gods, the former being male and the latter female (fr. 15). If he actually believed this, then the union of the two would be thought of as sexual and out of it would come the world of things.

This fusion of mythology and metaphysics was destined to great fortunes, for not only did Paganism turn its gods into philosophic principles, but Judaism in the work of Philo, and Christianity in that of the early Fathers did the same. To call Plato's Demiurge or Aristotle's Unmoved Mover by the name of Zeus

---

[4] See Heinze, *op. cit.*, p. 11.

[5] I use the Wachsmuth-Hense edition, cited by volume and page. The passage mentioned here is in Vol. I, p. 36.

was not merely a literary device, but may have arisen from the feeling that the ancestors of the race or the early poets, such as Homer and Hesiod, were philosophers talking mythological language. As eighteenth-century poets personified all sorts of abstractions, so did the ancient philosophers and it is no more strange to find the One or the Dyad transmogrified into gods than it is to find pictures of Truth as a naked woman holding aloft a mirror, or Hope as another clinging to an anchor. This tendency was recognized even by Cicero, who was far from being the keenest mind in antiquity, when he said[6] that people call that which comes from a god by the name of that god, wherefore Terence said,

> ... *sine Cerere et Libero friget Venus.*

Does this mean only that Love grows cold without food and drink? One's answer will depend on what one means by "meaning." But Cicero also notes the reverse process, the deification of abstractions. He points out that on the Capitoline Hill stand temples to Faith, to Mind, to Virtue. Should one be inclined to scoff at this, one might think of our own deification of the *Logos*, of *Sophia*, of Providence, of the Way, the Truth, and the Life, and even of Eternity ("I saw Eternity the other night . . ."). One bleeds the life out of a god by identifying him with a metaphysical abstraction; one vivifies an abstraction by deifying it.

The One and the Dyad then may well have been divine to Xenocrates, and the Cosmos as a whole possessed of soul. But to this Xenocrates seems to have added one more detail which was developed, though not because of him, some centuries later, the detail that the souls of things could be arranged in a scale of perfection, running from the upper heavens down to earth. According to Aëtius and Plutarch, Xenocrates believed that Zeus is the supreme god situated in the heavens, whereas Hera is in the air, Poseidon in the water, and Demeter in the earth (frs. 15, 24). But

---

[6] *De natura deorum* ii. 23. 60–61. Cf. *De legibus* ii. 11. 28. The quotation is from Terence's *Eunuchus* (iv. 5. 6).

since the same author attributes to Plato, Pythagoras, and Chrysippus, along with Xenocrates, the notion that Typhon, Osiris, and Isis are great *daimones* surpassing us in power, but not having a pure—unmixed—nature, since they feel pleasure and pain, it may be well not to give too much credit to his exegesis.[7] It would be interesting to know where Plutarch got his information, for so far as Plato is concerned there is no justification for it in the extant dialogues. Since we have no writings of Pythagoras, we cannot say whether Plutarch is right or wrong, and as for Chrysippus, we shall come to him later. Meanwhile we may profitably keep in mind the remark of Zeller, that "historians did not hesitate to attribute to the founder of the [Stoic] school all that was known to them as belonging to its later members, just as everything Pythagorean was directly attributed to Pythagoras, and everything Platonic to Plato."[8]

3. Meanwhile the philosophic atmosphere was thickened by the appearance of early Stoicism, the founder of which was Zeno of Citium. Whatever he may have written was completely lost by the sixth century A.D.,[9] and historians usually base their accounts of his life and works on Cicero, Seneca, Diogenes Laertius, and Plutarch. Whereas the Academics made their distinction between reality and appearance on the basis of epistemology, Zeno seems to have made his on the basis of causal power. The earliest testimony to this is found in Cicero (*Academica* i. 11. 39), who says that according to Zeno there was causal efficacy only in material objects. This is a flat denial of the earlier principle that matter was inert and incapable of acting. For Zeno and the Stoics in general causation was the kind of thing which we observe when material things come in contact with one another and a dynamic disturbance occurs. Their basic image then is drawn from crude experience—and I am not using "crude" in a disparaging manner. We no longer know why they laid down this revolutionary prin-

---

[7] *De Iside et Osiride* xxv. 360e.
[8] *Op. cit.*, pp. 53 f.
[9] See Simplicius in *Cat. schol. in Arist.* 49a 16.

ciple, but in view of the dominance of Platonistic and Aristotelian antimaterialism, it must have taken daring to do so. For by matter they meant, as Diogenes Laertius tells us (vii. 135), that which occupies space in three dimensions, a view which he attributes to Apollodorus, but which there is no reason to suppose was held exclusively by him. They were so confirmed in their materialism that they maintained that even things which do not seem to be material, like the virtues, were nevertheless made of matter. Seneca, a late authority to be sure, but one sympathetic to Stoicism, goes so far as to say (*Epistle* cxvii. 2), "We believe that which is a good is corporeal, because the good does something; whatever docs something is a body." Thus, he contines, wisdom is corporeal. The soul too and God are bodies and there is nothing which is immaterial.

The fact that they had to argue to the materiality of certain things is evidence that such things did not appear to be material. The realms of appearance and reality were thus reversed by them and what had been real in previous philosophies were now only apparent. But, like all substantialistic monists, they should have faced the problem of why reality disguises itself. Yet, again like their fellow monists, they did nothing of the sort. Instead they endowed matter with precisely those properties which observable matter does not seem to have. And hence whatever benefit they might have derived from choosing an empirically knowable substance as their reality, they lost. For they ended up with three-dimensional matter on the one hand and metaphorical or metaphysical matter on the other. It surely could not have been believed that the matter which was day and night and the seasons[10] was the same as the matter which was sticks and stones. It is therefore more likely that the early Stoics meant to say that the causes of all such things, including the virtues and vices, were corporeal.[11] To identify reality with the cause and appearance with its effect is common practice. But even if our virtues and vices

---

[10] Plutarch *De communibus notitiis* xlv. 1084a–d.
[11] Cf. Zeller, *op. cit.*, p. 126.

are conditioned, for instance, by our endocrine glands, they are not identical with them, any more than a bottle of whisky is identical with a headache.

If there is one property of matter more noticeable than others, it is that it exists in masses cut off from other masses. This had been utilized by Democritus and was to be noticed again and utilized by the Epicureans. But the Stoics were not atomists and, if they were thinking in terms of macroscopic objects, some means must be provided for making more than a collection of them into a universe. These men were not unaware that things hang together and that the cosmic story is not simply a story of random collisions and reboundings. To explain this they introduced into their system a substance called the *pneuma*, translated into Latin as spiritus, the history of which is an interesting case of inversion of meaning. The *pneuma* in Stoicism was definitely material, for it pervaded all space and accounted for that unity which they believed to exist throughout the cosmos. At the same time they spoke of it as divine. Hippolytus reports both Zeno and Chrysippus as saying that God was the *arche*, the source and origin of all things, and "that he was the purest of all bodies."[12] Just what he was pure of is not told us, but no doubt he was thought of as a very thin substance capable of penetrating everything.

If the question is raised of just why the Stoics felt that they had to have a single material substance omnipresent, why they could not simply have deduced or otherwise justified their belief in the concurrence of all natural laws without attributing it to any agent, the answer must be that everyone continued to think that acts must have agents, just as transitive verbs must have subjects and objects. It is of course true that no one to this day has ever succeeded in logically demonstrating such a concurrence, either in the form of a series of deductions from a single self-evident premise or in the form of showing that all laws are mechanical or teleological or electromagnetic or whatever other forms of law there may be. The kind of unity of which such philosophers write

[12] *Philosophoumena* i. 21. I quote from Diels, *Doxographi graeci*, p. 571.

is a dream which evaporates when examined. But dreaming such dreams did not cease with the extinction of classical philosophy. It must also be remembered that human beings have little to go on beyond the solar system and in the classical period of our history the solar system was the universe. For all the fixed stars were studded in the same sphere and there was nothing beyond them. This formed a cosmos with observable boundaries and also with observably demonstrated laws. Moreover, as one can easily see, the inhabited world was the Mediterranean basin edged with the wilderness and the river of Oceanus. Such facts have no logical significance, if one will, but they do have great psychological influence. One cannot find premises beyond the range of one's potential experience. If that experience gives us a world with the earth at its center, with planets circling round it at regular rates of speed, if added to that is a ring of cities and states located on the shores of an inland sea, then it is reasonable to think in terms of a few simple laws governing this limited and easily imagined world. Moreover everything was done by man power. Men not only wielded axes and hammers, but they piloted ships, built houses, and, what is more, felt the expenditure of energy in their muscles. It was not extraordinary that they should have thought all work to be done by a workman and that if there was a single task which was the government of all things in an orderly fashion, there must be a single director of the task, a director everywhere present and everywhere efficacious. The *Pneuma* or Spirit was that director, and when one felt religiously inclined, one called it God; when scientifically inclined, one called it *Pneuma*.

One could consequently pile up the synonyms for the Spirit, calling it not only God, but also Law, Mind, Soul, Nature, *hexis*.[13] The world as a whole, says Cicero (*Academica* ii. 37. 119), is wise, has a mind which changes all things, moves all things, and rules over all. It did not take long, but how long we do not know,[14] for

---

[13] See Themistius *De anima* 72b.
[14] For a good synopsis of the Stoic conception of the cosmos as a whole, see Diels, *Doxographi graeci*, Arius Didymus, **29**, p. 464.

the Stoics to speak of the cosmos as a Great Animal, the macro-cosm which we reduplicate in our own make-up. But an animal was supposed to have that kind of unity celebrated as *organic*, the unity of a complicated machine contrived to accomplish a given purpose and for the accomplishment of which all its parts are as they are. In a fabricated machine, it is the wisdom and foresight of the inventor which determine its character. In the human body, it is the soul which in its turn is governed by the Reason. In the cosmic animal the *Pneuma* is the ruler, not located in any single part of the universe, analogous to our brain, but permeating it throughout. Since the *Pneuma* is not identical with that which it governs, but is present within it, the Stoic metaphysics should not be called a pantheism. All things are not God, but God is in all things. Thus, in spite of themselves, the Stoics had to retain a dualism between agent and patient, between God and the world, between soul and body. What the Spirit accomplished was some-thing which "ordinary" matter could not accomplish and, as the attributes and properties of it were multiplied, it became more and more unlike ordinary matter. When, for instance, they identified it with Fire, they recognized that it was not like the fire with which we are acquainted on the hearth, for that destroys things, whereas the divine fire preserves them.[15]

The ambivalence of the early Stoics toward their Spirit comes out very clearly in the famous *Hymn to Zeus* of Cleanthes, which, since it is not too long, we quote.

> Most glorious of immortals, you of many names, ever omnipotent,
> Zeus, ruler of nature, governing all by law,
> Hail! For it is man's duty to address himself to you,
> For we are your children, being, as it chances, the sole image of one,
> Whatsoever mortals live and move about the earth,
> Wherefore to you shall I sing hymns and your power shall I for-ever celebrate.

[15] According to Arius Didymus (Diels, *Doxographi graeci*, 33, p. 467), Zeno said this; according to Cicero (*De natura deorum* ii. 15. 40), Cleanthes did too. If they are right, it was part of early Stoicism.

You and none other does the cosmos, circling round this earth, obey
Whithersoever you lead, and willingly is it led by you.
These have you as servants in your invincible hands,
The forked lightning, fiery, everliving;
When it strikes, all nature trembles.
By it you guide the universal *Logos*, which pervades all things,
Mingling with both the greater and the lesser stars;
As you have been and are supreme ruler of them all.
Nor is any deed done on earth against your will, O Lord,
Either in the high and divine heaven or on the sea,
Save that which evilmongers do in their madness.
But you know how also to render the even odd,
And to bring order into the unordered, and the displeasing is pleasing in your sight.
For so have you brought all things into unity, good with evil,
That the universal *Logos*, ever-being, has become one.
When the evil flee from it, they become
Miserable, and those of good men who always yearn for the possession of wealth
Neither see the common law of God, nor listen to it;
But evildoers again and again strive indecently for something else,
Some possessed by passionate zeal for fame,
Some turned to craftiness in complete disorder,
And others to the shameless and voluptuous deeds of the body,
Hastening in all ways to become the opposite of the good.
But Zeus, giver of all gifts, shrouded with dark clouds, you of the bright lightning,
Free men from endless misery,
Which you, Father, may expel from their souls, and give us the power
To be governed by your mind, trusting in which you govern all things with justice,
To the end that honoring you, we may share in your honor,
Hymning your works continually, as it is fitting
For a mortal, since there is no better prize for men
Or for gods, than ever to celebrate the universal law in justice.

In this poem Zeus is anthropomorphic, governing the universe as a lawgiver; his omnipotence is limted only by the deeds of ignorant and evil men. No one reading this *Hymn* would ever think that Zeus was simply a kind of very thin matter, uniform in nature, something like a gas so rarefied that it had spread into all the crevices of macroscopic objects. Since he is immutable, his government never changes.[16] Why he has no power over the deeds of evil men is not clear, but it may be that this foreshadowed the idea that evil was not really real. In general the Stoics identified the regularity of God's rule with Fate. As early as Chrysippus the world-reason was asserted to be that "according to which all things which will come to be in the future will come to be, and those which are coming to be, come to be."[17] Every event is strictly determined and Aristotle's admission of chance into the world is flatly denied. This would seem to imply man's impotence and indeed the Stoics made a great deal of the necessity of bowing to fate, accepting the will of God as irresistible, playing the part given to one in the cosmic drama. It does not follow that, because general laws can be formulated, describing the behavior of a class of things, the individual members of the class contribute nothing to the events in which they participate. For the very fact that such laws are general prevents their including in their formulation the individual traits of the members of the class being described, and no individual thing or event is characterized exclusively by the general traits of the class in which it happened to be located by a scientist. Yet what the thing or event actually does may be determined by just those traits which are not included in the general law in question. Hence when Cleanthes excludes from God's competence the maleficence of the ignorant, he could justify this by saying that ignorance may extend to any field and that in the field of which a man is ignorant, he will act blindly, as determined by one of his individual and peculiar traits. So a man ignorant of the Law of Gravity might jump off a cliff

[16] The thoughts expressed in the *Hymn to Zeus* could profitably be contrasted with what Cicero reports of Cleanthes' theology in *De natura deorum* i. 14. 37: *Cleanthes . . . tum ipsum mundum deum dicit esse, tum totius naturae menti atque animo tribuit hoc nomen, tum ultimum et altissimum atque undique circumfusum et extremum omnia cingentem atque complexum ardorem, qui aether nominetur, certissimum deum iudicat.*

[17] Diels, *Doxographi graeci*, p. 323.

with evil results. There is no evidence that Cleanthes did argue in this fashion. But there was no logical paradox in the Stoics' preaching both universal determinism and free will, free will to the extent of resignation to the universal order. The decision to be resigned is an act of will and is determined by the individual himself; otherwise it would be irrelevant to ethics. But of that more below.

The history of the cosmos, as conceived by the Stoics, is of little interest to us here, for it had practically no influence in subsequent philosophies. Yet it may be worth while to point out that the fire which was God and which was therefore preservative was also at one epoch in cosmic history destructive. That epoch was the time of the universal conflagration, called by the school the *ekpyrosis*. This conflagration reduced all things to their elemental stuff which is, as far as is discernible, the primordial fire or God. The length of the period between one conflagration and another was called the Great Year, the length of which varied according to the calculations of various writers. But that there was a Great Year and that after the *ekpyrosis* a new cycle began, were integral parts of the doctrine. Some Stoics even went so far as to say that exactly the same individual things and events would recur in each cycle. But this led to detailed debates which need not be introduced here.[18] However bizarre the notion may seem, there are two arguments in its favor. First, if matter is indestructible and there is to be a universal conflagration, then there is no reason why anything other than what has happened in the past should occur after the conflagration. If, as Leibniz was to say, this is the best of all possible worlds and God is good, then if the world is to be destroyed, its reconstitution is the only possible thing that can happen. Second, as Nietzsche was to argue, if the number of things—or possibilities—in the universe is finite, then sooner or

18 The best-known modern version of the Great Year is of course Shelley's chorus from *Hellas* beginning, "The world's great age begins anew." A less well-known but very clear account is in George Moore's "My Mother's Funeral," in *Memoirs of my Dead Life*. Vergil's Fourth Eclogue is perhaps the best-known ancient poem based on the theme.

later the combination of things out of which the present universe arose will recur. Both arguments may have flaws, but they are rational arguments nevertheless.

The real world then, as opposed to the world of appearance, was a world without beginning or end, undergoing indefinitely repeated cycles of birth and decay. It was a world infused with a fiery substance which, though material, nevertheless was divine and had all the characteristics of a wise and providential God.[19] Its main resemblance to the world of appearance was the absolute determinism which controlled the events happening in it.

4. Like the Stoics, the Epicureans set up a world vastly different from the world of appearance. But whereas no one can be sure of the source of the Stoic theory, since it has but faint resemblance to anything that went before, one knows that Epicurus got his idea of reality from Democritus. In one of the famous Democritean fragments, we are told that sensory qualities exist by convention and that in reality there are only atoms and the void. It was his form of atomism which was taken over with certain modifications by Epicurus. Like the Stoics, the early Epicureans maintained that only matter was real, but unlike them they did not endow matter with the properties of the soul. On the contrary, they argued, if all is matter, then purposiveness must be ruled out of real existence as appearance. One can explain all events as motions of the atoms in the void. And the atoms themselves have only the properties of shape, size, and weight. The number of atoms is indefinite and empty space is unbounded.

We are then to picture what one might call the scientific cosmos as a great snowfall of atoms moving downward through infinite space. But since Epicurus also seems to have held that all atoms would normally fall in straight lines and with equal velocity and therefore never meet, he introduced the postulate that there occurred a fortuitous swerving in their fall from the straight

---

[19] Strange though this may seem to us, it should not be forgotten that even a zealous, if "erroneous," Christian, Tertullian, believed that both the human soul and God were material.

path.[20] Because of this swerving, the atoms formed larger conglomerates and eventually macroscopic objects. By a counterprocess conglomerates of atoms might disintegrate, and the cosmos becomes the scene of continual and endless birth and decay.

The swerving of the atoms is usually thought of as a blemish on a theory of beautiful simplicity. But it will be observed that the introduction of the swerve had as its logical source the fact that conglomerates of atoms actually existed. Since they would not exist if all the atoms fell in straight lines and with equal speed, something must occur to explain their existence. Epicurus could have argued that some atoms fall faster than others and that the faster ones would overtake and link themselves to the slower. But deceleration of fall in the opinion of Epicurus was a problem and had itself a cause, namely, resistance to or by other material objects. Similarly, following Galileo, we are taught that a moving body would continue to move in a straight line indefinitely if it did not meet with the resistance of the air or some other medium producing friction. He could, to be sure, have invested each atom with an inherent velocity running from the very slow to the very fast, or with inherent paths running from the straight line to, let us say, the circle. But each of these hypotheses would have created difficulties of its own and he posited the swerve perhaps as the simplest assumption. It was of course an element of chance, but chance had been made legitimate by Aristotle, whatever the Stoics may have believed, and it made little difference whether one introduced it into the order of nature or the world of observation. If chance events happen, as they did in Aristotle, on the level of experience, why not proceed further and permit them to enter into the world of reality?[21]

Like the Stoics, the Epicureans had to face the problem created by the existence of an apparently immaterial being, the soul. Epicurus assumed that he had but to explain psychical phenomena

---

[20] See his *Letter to Herodotus* (43) in C. Bailey, *Epicurus* (Oxford: Clarendon Press, 1926), p. 24.

[21] *Ibid.*

as the behavior of very subtle atoms, the lightest and swiftest of all bodies. Both schools held to the concept of the soul as something contained within the body, a substantial not a functional soul. This psychic substance escapes from the body at death and, like a gas, is dispersed into the surrounding atmosphere. Thus any hope or fear of immortality is eliminated. And just as there is no reason to believe in immortality, so there is no reason to believe in a divine providence, no use for prayer, and, though the gods exist, they have neither creative power nor power of interfering in human affairs. They are made of ethereal matter, are perfectly happy, and therefore unconcerned with human history. The Epicurean gods are exemplars of what men would be if men were perfectly happy and perfectly beautiful. Moreover, the gods have no more reality than men or than the other physical objects which surround us. They exist indeed, but they are composed of atoms as every other existent thing is and have no privileged ontological status.

The beauty of Epicurean metaphysics is the beauty of any materialism. It is the simplest account of the things that are, employing the fewest assumptions. In temper it is very similar to the metaphysics of a man like Hobbes, in that Hobbes too had to grant so much difference to the mind and whatever is in it that to all intents and purposes it became a different kind of matter. The smooth subtle atoms which compose the human mind and the bodies of the gods are of course material particles. But since they can do things which other material conglomerations cannot do, it has to be admitted that at least new activities, vastly different from those exhibited by ordinary physical objects, are their portion. I refer obviously to knowing and feeling and wishing. I am not saying that Epicurus was condemned to a substantialistic dualism. I am simply saying that he held a functionalistic dualism. If he could have stated the conditions under which psychic phenomena would occur, and if those conditions were velocities and atomic shapes, or whatever other properties atoms might be said to have, then he would have given a materialistic explanation of the rise of such peculiar behavior. But since the peculiar behavior was found only in gods and men, he would have had to conclude that there existed two radically different kinds of being, one which was subject to the laws of physics in its gross behavior and one which was subject to the laws of psychology.

5. The one school of philosophy which showed little if any development was that of Aristotle. The Peripatetics showed an amazing fidelity to the doctrines of their master, and until we come to Alexander of Aphrodisias, who lived in the third century of our own era, we see no important change. Aristotle's immediate successor in the Lyceum, Theophrastus, wrote copiously and we are indebted to him for most of our knowledge about the early philosophers. His book on plants is a valuable contribution to botany and his *Characters*, which we shall mention below, influential in the history of literature. But otherwise there is little to report on the contributions of the Peripatetics to the rationalistic tradition. It was perhaps enough if they kept alive the teachings of the school's founder.

II

We turn now to the method used by the various philosophers whom we have been discussing in the establishment of their metaphysical views. These methods were, to be sure, inherited for the most part, since by the fourth and third centuries philosophical inquiry had been pretty well ritualized. There are, however, certain methodological details which it may be worth while pointing out.

1. Little is known about Speusippus, but there is one fragment which, though tantalizing in its brevity, suggests a doctrine which was revived by Hegel in the nineteenth century. Eudemus, presumably the pupil of Aristotle, is reported as saying that Speusippus maintained the impossibility of defining anything unless one knows everything (fr. 31b). This is corroborated by

another fragment, from Philoponus (fr. 31c), in which Speusippus says that nothing can be defined or divided unless one knows everything, since he who would know the nature of a man or a horse or anything else, must know all things which are not men or horses or whatsoever may be in question, so as to know how they differ from them. In other words, every term contains within it the negation of all its contraries. To know what man is requires knowing what not-man is. In the Middle Ages this principle was phrased as the famous *Omnis determinatio est negatio*—all determination is negation—the acceptance of which bound one to the conclusion that any term which denoted the whole of things, any universal predicate, would be meaningless. We have no evidence that Speusippus made anything of this principle, but it may well have been the reason why he denied that the divine *Nous* is identical with the One and the Good but said it had its own nature (fr. 38). For if his ultimate principles had been fused into one, there would have been no knowing them. The knowledge—or definition—of the good can be acquired only by contrasting the good with the not-good, of the one only by contrasting it with the not-one, of the *nous* only by contrasting it with the not-*nous*. But once again, is he talking about contraries or opposites? Do we contrast the good with evil or with everything that is not-good, the red, the sweet, the tall, the salty, and so on? If he did mean this, which seems absurd, then he would have set himself an impossible task, for not only is the number of such qualities much too large for any human mind to survey them, but also, though red is not-good, some red things are good.

In view of this it may be possible to interpret a fragment of his (fr. 32a) which discusses homonyms and synonyms. Here we find him distinguishing between words which express "the *logos* of the essence" of something and those which are simply names. Synonyms are words which express a common essence; homonyms do not. But what is the *logos* of an essence? If we call both a sea lion and a lion animals, the word "animal" expresses an essence which the two beasts have in common, but the word "lion" does not. Yet to comprehend the common nature expressed in the word "animal" is to know much more than the word "animal." It is to know the not-animal thoroughly in order to explain just what constitutes animality. If this is so, then we see also that the *summum genus* is inexplicable, since there is nothing with which to contrast it, and so is the individual, since the individual has too many properties and qualities to make definition possible.

It may have been because of such difficulties that Speusippus wrote the book that is referred to by Athenaeus as the *Book on Similarities*. This seems to have been, as far as one can judge from the references which are made to it, a kind of taxonomy. Just what the principle of division was I have not been able to determine, for one has simply the information of what plants and animals were classified together. To learn (fr. 19) that "Speusippus in the second book of his *Similarities* placed the *kestra* [the garfish] and the *saura* [lizard?] together as of one kind," is not very illuminating, since we do not know what he thought was similar in them. But it is at least reasonable to infer that by his exhaustive classifications he hoped to provide differentiae for all classes of things and thus to provide a sufficient basis of the kind of knowledge which he required. He is quoted (fr. 94) as having said that philosophy is the desire for knowledge of the things which are everlasting, a state of contemplating the true as true, the truly rational care of the soul—a description which was far from novel but which marked him as still some way a Platonist. But we have no fragment which tells us much of anything about the nature of contemplation, whether it is a purification of perception, a recollection of prenatal experiences, or direct apprehension of Platonic ideas. In one fragment (fr. 29) from Sextus Empiricus he is quoted as saying that "some things are sensible, others noetic, and of the noetic the criterion is the scientific reason, but of the sensible it is scientific perception. Now scientific perception," says Sextus, "he assumed to have been established as a participant in rational truth. For just as the fingers of the flute player or harpist have technical skill not in themselves and brought to perfection previously, but perfected through practice according to rational methods, and as musical sense has a power of apprehending the harmonious and the discordant, not as self-creative but the result of rationality, so too scientific perception, though by nature non-rational, takes over through scientific practice the function of accurately penetrating to the underlying substance."[22] This would give to perception powers which Plato was unwilling to grant it, and if we are to take seriously the power of sense to penetrate to the underlying substance, sense has more than an access to right opinion. It has also the power of attaining knowledge. This comes from practice; but it comes. Therefore it would look as if perception could reach reality, surely a startling enough conclusion to find in a Platonist. But if Plato's nephew and successor could hold so revolutionary a point of view, it was not strange that the Academy should later diverge even farther from the tenets of the dialogues.

2. Though testimonies to the philosophy of Xenocrates are found as early as Aristotle, one has but the barest evidence of his method of discovery. He had maintained, as we have seen, that the soul was a self-moving number, and in Aristotle's *De anima* (404a) we come upon the statement that those who thought of the soul as self-moving, "all seem to have assumed the initiation of motion to be a peculiarity of the soul, and that all other things are moved by the soul, and the soul is moved by itself, because they see nothing moving which is not also moved." The source of motion was apparently much discussed and Aristotle in his *De motu animalium* (698a 8) lays it down as an axiom that the source of motion in self-moved living beings must be itself unmoved or at rest. If the soul moves, it must be moved either by something else or by itself. Why choose the second of the alternatives? The probable answer is that Xenocrates agreed with many of his contemporaries and successors that only material things could be acted upon. The soul, being immaterial, must be active, and, if it moves, must have the source of its motion in it-

[22] Sextus Empiricus *Adv. math.* vii. 145–146.

self. But why should he have called it a number? Alexander of Aphrodisias, thinking about this, asked whether it was odd or even, whether it was four or six, if even, or five or seven, if odd, which may show that by his time the idea seemed absurd.[23] Aëtius attributes to Pythagoras the idea that number moves itself and says that Xenocrates agreed with him (fr. 60). The self-motion of number may very well be the productivity of numbers in creating new numbers "out of themselves" as spiders seem to reel out their gossamer. When the first nine numbers "flow" out of the Monad, the Monad is pictured as creating them out of itself. Similarly in our own time we hear of ideas arising "by the sheer force of logic," as if logic were a power resident in a proposition which could propel or ejaculate new ideas from its own being. Neither number nor the soul is material, and both could be taken as good examples of the activity of the incorporeal. This is a fairly wild guess, but the terms of the discourse are so foreign to our ways of thinking that only wild guesses will make sense out of them. When one is dealing with philosophers who say that the One is male and the Dyad female, that there are invisible *genii* below the moon, that the equilateral triangle is akin to the divine, the scalene to the mortal, and the isosceles to the daimonic (because the daimonic has at one and the same time the nature and passion of a mortal and the power of a god) (fr. 23), that there are lucky and unlucky days (fr. 25), one uses the *raison du coeur* to explain what they are driving at or abandons the puzzle. The one method which seems safely attributable to Xenocrates is that of uncritical analogy.

In his argument that all being could not be identifiable with the One, his argument is clearer. If Being were the One, it would be an individual. But it is not an individual, since all things *are*. This means that *being* as a predicate is distributed among all things and thus is fractured and cannot be one. It will occur to the most naïve mind that there is a distinction to be made between dis-

---

[23] See Mullach, fr. 41.

tributing a quality among a number of subjects and distributing pieces of a material substance. But apparently this distinction did not strike Xenocrates as very forceful, if it occurred to him at all. For, according to Porphyry, he also says that being could not be divided *ad infinitum*, but sooner or later one would reach atomic particles of being (fr. 45). Because of this difficulty, which would leave some things that are without any being, he turned to another hypothesis which appears to have interested the commentators, the hypothesis of "atomic lines" out of which planes and solids could be constructed. Planes can be thought of as classes of lines and solids as classes of planes, or, if one prefers, a plane could be thought of as a line of which all points are moving in the same direction and solids as generated by planes similarly moving.[24] This idea could at most suggest a way of defining the plane and the solid; it could not create them in space or give them existence.

It would look as if by "being" Xenocrates meant "existence" and that in the back of his mind was the further notion that existence was the occupancy of space. It is always dangerous for a historian to attempt the exploration of mental hinterlands; it is wiser to limit oneself to the foreground. But in *Timaeus* Plato had shown the Demiurge constructing the world out of geometric solids, but he was building an ideal, not a material, world, and Plato was careful to posit at the outset as irreducibles both the Same (Identity) and the Other (Difference). These would correspond to unity and multiplicity. Xenocrates may have been doing the same, for we have only comments made by men discussing Aristotle's physical theories to guide us and the opinions of Xenocrates are introduced into the discussion only because Aristotle objected to them. Simplicius, for instance, commenting on Aristotle's *De caelo* (139b), brings in Xenocrates' theory of atomic lines and distinguishes between geometric and physical

---

[24] It may be asked whether the second hypothesis does not beg the question, for how would one identify the directions required? But Xenocrates should not be blamed for this. The suggestion does not come from him.

lines, a wise distinction. He points out that the latter are not only length, as they would be in geometry, but also that they have breadth and some height. Surely Xenocrates must have known this. Granting him as much good sense as his opponents, one interprets him as trying to give a purely logical account of existence, saying in effect that if to exist means to occupy space, then the smallest unit of existence would be an atomic line, out of which planes and solids could be built by geometric devices. In our own time no less an intellect than Einstein distinguished between axiomatic and applied geometry, and by the latter he meant a geometry exemplified in physical phenomena. Thus one might say that the top of a table corresponds physically to a geometric plane, though it is not a geometric plane, but at the same time it is treated by us as if it were one. I attribute a similar point of view to Xenocrates, largely on the basis of a comment by Philoponus (fr. 44) to the effect that Xenocrates agreed that an actual division of anything into infinitesimal parts was impossible—"he says that the cutting up of magnitudes to infinity is possible potentially, but not actually"—also an opinion of Aristotle. On the other hand, we do not know whether Xenocrates agreed with Aristotle that all potentialities need not be actualized, or with Timaeus in the dialogue named after him that they must be.

All then that we can say about the method of Xenocrates is that it was dialectical and not empirical. He tried by pure deduction to give an account of the natural world. He apparently first laid down the most abstract ideas which he could reach and then proceeded to infer from them the nature of everything implied in their nature. In making this attempt he ran counter to the direction of his most eminent contemporaries, the early Stoics and Epicureans, for they seem to have begun with the evidence of perception and worked backward to generalities.

3. The viewpoint of common sense as shown in the early Stoics is illustrated by their basic axiom that everything is material. By the material they meant that which could act and also

be acted upon.[25] This axiom denied the equally popular notion that only the immaterial could act and that the material was passive. Action and passion to the Stoics were motions and motions were observable only in material objects. If then a cause is that which is responsible for all change, all change will be reduced to motion, and it logically follows that matter, the only thing which moves, is also the universal cause. This in turn reduces the number of kinds of change, which in Aristotle were four in number, to one, locomotion. Consequently the Stoics had to find a method which would permit them to explain all changes in the world as caused by something material which was mobile and which could produce motion in other things. That something was, as we have seen, the *Pneuma*. The logic in this is simple: develop the characteristics of a material body such that it can penetrate everywhere and be a universal cause; attribute to this material body properties which are adequate to the effects for which it is to be made responsible. Solutions of this problem were restricted by the assumption that causal relations could subsist only between similars.

But the Stoics seem also to have realized that the simple assertion that the *Pneuma* was the universal cause would not work unless it could also be asserted that it actually had the power to do what was required of it. Since it was what we would call a gas, it could move about like the wind, though the wind is not self-moving. But it also could be seen to have varying degrees of strength, and the concept of *tonos*, which we retain in the phrase "muscle tone," was helpful in explaining its behavior. Cleanthes is said by Plutarch[26] to have maintained that "the impact of fire is the *tonos*, and if it should be sufficient in the soul to accomplish its appropriate task, it is called force (ἰσχύς) and strength (κράτος)." It gets into the nerves—or possibly sinews—and determines whether a man should act or not and also how he should

---

[25] See Plutarch *De communibus notitiis* xxx. 1073e. Cf. Zeller, *op. cit.*, pp. 121 ff.
[26] *De Stoicorum repugnantiis* vii. 1034d.

judge.[27] Here the *Pneuma* takes on the role which the animal spirits were to play in physiology down into the nineteenth century. If we overlook the picturesque details of Stoic physiology and psychology, it is clear that the school accepted the consequences of their materialism. Once they had laid down their basic premise, they were prepared to follow through and, as we know, they ended up by making the soul, the ideas, the qualities, even truth and God, all material.

But what they meant was that the causes of everything were material and the one gap in their reasoning was the proof that an effect is substantially what its cause is. That there was always similarity between cause and effect was, as we have said, common knowledge, but obviously if the similarity was not limited, it would amount to identity. One does not prove the substantial identity of two things by saying that one is the cause of the other. But one consequence of Stoic materialism was clearly seen and accepted. That was universal determinism. The idea of causation was itself obscure and has remained so, but the Stoic did not doubt that no accidents occurred in this world, no miracles, nothing logically absurd. There was never a break in the causal chain. But then if this is so, and there are a finite number of possibilities, it would seem likely that we have a model for the universe as a whole in the objects which surround us. These objects form units, cohering together, whether they are inanimate or animate. The tension and distention which are exhibited by the *Pneuma* must be reduplicated in all things, and the cosmos becomes a unit similar to human beings, but on a grander scale. The notion of the Great Animal is seen to follow, if not with rigid logic, at least with psychological plausibility, from the notion of universal determinism. For why should the determinism in larger things be any different from that in small? We have learned that this does not follow and that it is risky to extrapolate the type of events which we find in limited areas into more extensive areas without manipulation. The analogical method is too apt to break down—

[27] Stobaeus, Wachsmuth-Hense edition, Vol. II, p. 62.

witness theology. Nevertheless it requires an admirable boldness of imagination to project the limited experience of mankind into the world as a whole. In fact, there seems to be no reason to believe that the world is a whole at all, in the sense that things about us are wholes. Such doubts, however, do not seem to have occurred to the Stoics.

In view of their axiom of universal determinism, it was to be expected that the Stoics would explain the rise of knowledge as an effect produced in us by external causes, rather than as an exfoliation of innate ideas. Zeno thought of perception as a sort of imprint made upon the soul by material forces and Cleanthes is said by Sextus Empiricus (*Adv. math.* vii. 228) to have likened it to an impression made upon wax, one of the most lasting similes in the history of epistemology.[28] Once the impressions were made, they could linger on, as in Hobbes, and become memories, and, in accordance with a principle laid down by Aristotle (*Posterior Analytics*, end) then turn into "experience."[29] But this could permit the possibility of every man's having his own set of truths and truth ought to be interpersonal. To avoid the complete individuality of truth, they first posited a kind of irresistible impression (the cataleptic datum) which cannot but be true. We have only to be aware of one to apprehend its truth. Such data are analogous to self-evident propositions. That men have such experience cannot be denied, but on the other hand there is no evidence that the Stoics provided any reason why some impressions should be cataleptic and others not. For if both the cataleptic and the non-cataleptic are produced in us by the same causes, why should some be truer than others? The Stoic here was faced with the same problem which confronted David Hume when he made the distinction between impressions and ideas and then simply said that ideas were faint copies of impressions. But Hume at least believed that all impressions were true.

---

[28] The simile is used to describe memory by Aristotle (*De memoria* 450a 23). Cf. *Theaetetus* 191d.
[29] See Plutarch *Placita* iv. 11. 900b.

The Stoics with more logic also turned to the *consensus gentium* as a criterion of truth. I say with more logic since if everyone has the same impressions, everyone will agree, and if impressions are in any way a test of truth, uniformity of impressions will give one at least an interpersonal set of ideas. If all people believe in God, then God must exist, for it would be unlikely that everyone would have a set of false impressions. Cicero in his *De natura deorum* (ii. 2. 5) uses the argument in the following way: "Unless we had an idea understood by us and grasped in our minds," says Lucilius, "so unwavering an opinion"—as the belief in God—"would not remain in them or be confirmed year after year, nor could it remain fixed in men over so many centuries and ages. Surely we see other opinions fade away as fictions and vain fantasies during a lapse of time. Who would believe that Hippocentaurs and the Chimaera ever existed? What old woman could be found so senseless as to fear those portents which were once believed to exist in the lower regions? As the days go by the inventions of fancy disappear, but the judgments of nature are confirmed." This is to be sure Cicero speaking, not an early Stoic, but it gives a reason for accepting the *consensus* which does not contradict anything which we know of the early Stoics.[30] If beliefs come from cataleptic impressions, and some beliefs are repeatedly expressed over the years, it would look as if the same cataleptic impressions were experienced by the great mass of people. Foolish and superstitious ideas then are identified with those which only a few people believe in. The same argument in different words is repeated by Seneca in his *De beneficiis* (iv. 4. 2): "He who says [that the gods do not exist] pays no attention to the voices of those who pray or to those all about him who with hands raised to the heavens call for blessings on individuals and the state. Surely this would not be so, nor would all mankind have joined in this madness of addressing the dumb and ineffectual deities, unless we knew of

---

[30] In fact, an examination of the sources of the fragments which von Arnim has collected in his *Stoicorum veterum fragmenta* (Leipzig: Teubner, 1903–1905) shows that he relied heavily on Cicero.

their benefactions, sometimes given without being asked for them, sometimes in response to prayer, great and timely help which obliterates by divine intervention threats of great size." This begs the question, to be sure, but forgetting that, we can see that the argument is based on common belief. People would not continue praying if they did not believe that their prayers were effective; they do continue praying; therefore they do believe that their prayers are effective. Then comes the leap: therefore their prayers are effective.

Now Cleanthes himself is represented by Cicero (*De natura deorum* ii. 5. 13–15) as using four proofs for men's belief in gods: (1) our foreknowledge of the future, (2) the benefits which accrue to man from a temperate climate, the fertility of the soil, and so on, (3) the awe inspired by lightning, storms, rain, snow, and the like, and (4) the uniform motion of the heavens. The first three are the psychological causes of the belief and may be that which establishes the *consensus,* but the fourth is used to establish a familiar argument: where there is regularity, there is a cause and the only reasonable cause for the regularity of the heavenly motions is a god. Chrysippus, however, used, if we may trust Cicero once more (ii. 6), another argument. "If there is anything in nature," he says, "which the human mind, man's reason, his force, his power could not produce, surely that which brings this about must be better than man. But the things of heaven and all those things the order of which is everlasting cannot be brought about by man. Therefore that by which these things are brought about is better than man. But what would you call it other than God? In fact, if gods do not exist, what could there be in nature superior to man? In man alone is reason, than which nothing is more excellent. But that there be a man who thinks that there is nothing in the world better than he is, is foolish arrogance. There-fore there is something better. Therefore God exists."

A diligent search through the remains of the Stoics will show that the argument from the *consensus gentium* is not frequently found and that no Stoic ever hesitated to criticize views which were very widely held. For instance, probably no idea was ever more general than that goodness is pleasure. And yet the Stoics vigorously combated hedonism. How many people would have agreed that overcoming the emotions was essential to the good life? But though their appeal to the *consensus* was not usual, it could easily be made harmonious with their theory of knowledge.

The use of the cosmological argument is less understandable. In the phenomenon of adaptation they saw added proof of the existence of God. They seem to have believed that everything whatsoever was made for the use of something else, which gave them a well-knit cosmos. The gods existed for the sake of one another, the animals for our sake, witness horses and hunting dogs. Cicero goes so far as to say (*De natura deorum* ii. 14. 37) that according to Chrysippus, "just as the shield's cover is made for the sake of the shield, the sheath for the sword, so throughout the world all things are made for the sake of others, for example, the fruits and grains which earth produces for the sake of animals, animals for men, the horse to pull our wagons, the ox to plow, the dog to hunt and guard us." The particular things which are in the world need not be perfect, but the whole is perfect (ii. 14. 38–39). There is nothing antimaterialistic in such beliefs but they are not justified by an appeal either to the traits of a universal *Pneuma* or to universal determinism.

The Stoics also were given to allegorical interpretation of myths and legends. In this they followed common practice, a practice which is also found in Plato and Aristotle. When the philosophers wanted to quote Homer or Hesiod, as we quote the Bible or Shakespeare, they did as we do, and gave their texts a meaning which they put into them themselves.[31] One uses allegorical interpretations when for one reason or another one wants to retain a text which on the surface does not make sense. Such texts are usually sacred. In the case of the ancient myths, one could either discard them or try to show that they "really" meant what one

[31] Cicero ridicules this practice among the Stoics in *De natura deorum* i. 15–16.

believes to be the truth. The truth is naturally one's own philosophy. What value lies in proving that other people agree with
one is dubious. But I suppose that we all like to imagine that we
are mouthpieces for the wisdom of the race even when the expression of that wisdom sounds foolish. There runs through
European thought the barely concealed feeling that human nature as a whole is not wrong, and if one believes in a *consensus
gentium*, one finds it in the hidden meanings of myths and folklore. Allegorical interpretation eliminates the disagreements among
men whom one respects for one reason or another. Philo Judaeus
was to rely on it for his interpretation of the Pentateuch, the early
Fathers for their interpretation of the Bible as a whole, and in our
own day the psychologist, Jung, used it when he wished to call
the Collective Unconscious to the witness stand.

To make an allegorical interpretation one must first possess the
key. And the key must be the literal translation of the symbols in
the supposed allegory. If Seneca says that the ancients did not believe that Jupiter hurled thunderbolts but meant by the name
"Jupiter" simply the ruler and guardian of the universe, the "mind
and spirit of the world,"[32] it is because he does not believe in a
thundering Jupiter, does believe in a ruler and guardian of the
universe, and wants to believe that he has the backing of tradition.
By etymologies which are usually false, Zeus can be turned into
the cause of all things, Hera into air, Hephaestus into fire, and
Poseidon into water. It would have been much simpler to maintain that we moderns are more intelligent than our ancestors, but
that would display *hybris*. The difficulty appears when one asks
why, if all knowledge is a sublimation of sensory impressions, the
sublimation does not express itself in uniform symbols, why
Homer and the mythographers had to conceal—or were even able
to conceal—their meanings in symbols which were so obscure.

4. The Epicureans agreed with the Stoics in basing their
method on sensory observation and also in their use of the dictum

---

[32] *Quaestiones naturales* ii. 45. 1.

ex nihilo nihil.[33] We have already (Chapter 1, II. 6) pointed out the various interpretations of the dictum and shall not repeat them here. But deriving all knowledge from sensory experience also could be interpreted in at least three ways: (1) that every sensory perception is equally reliable, which no one took seriously; (2) that all ideas have their roots in sensory perception; (3) that all knowledge must be checked for its correspondence with sensory experience. In Epicurus the two possible sources of knowledge were reason and sensation. But pure reasoning had to be about something; it must operate on propositions which are furnished to it by some other faculty, intuition, revelation, perception, imagination, memory. Sensation itself is always true in so far as sensory qualities are whatever they happen to be when experienced. That is, we cannot doubt that we see red when we see red, though we may not know whether it is caused by an external source or is a hallucination. The negative afterimage of green is red and we cannot fail to see the red when we are seeing it. But we can err in saying that the background on which we see it is actually painted with a dab of red pigment. Epicurus was not an adherent of the theory that the senses as such are always trustworthy; in short, he was not what modern classifiers of doctrines call a phenomenalist. Bailey points out in his study of the atomists and Epicurus[34] that even the cardinal principle, *ex nihilo nihil,* was tested by sensory observation, and yet sensory observation was also tested by rational or dialectical argument. If the dictum were not true, then anything could happen. If existent things could be destroyed, then everything would have disappeared. (It might have disappeared to be sure, but why would it have?) Yet we see things coming into being with no apparent source of their existence and we see things being dissolved into apparent nothingness. As Bailey points out, behind this lies the assumption that "the

[33] See Bailey, *op. cit.,* p. 21. Though Lucretius credits Epicurus with the discovery of this principle, it had long been in use, as we have said above. One of its clearest statements is in Aristotle's *De caelo* 302a 3.

[34] C. Bailey, *The Greek Atomists and Epicurus* (Oxford: Clarendon Press, 1928), pp. 275 ff.

sum of things always was such as it is now and always will be the same." Thus, though Epicurus was capable of saying flatly that "all sensa are true and existent, for there is no difference in saying that something is true or existent,"[35] at the same time he was not talking about sensory qualities but about things. Perception will tell us what exists and what does not exist, but it must submit to rational criticism. To say that a certain kind of knowledge is always true does not imply that there are no other kinds of knowledge which are true also. And Epicurus did admit that "anticipations"—of which more below—are feelings and are true. But on the other hand, no sensation could give us the principle itself of the validity of sensations. Our trust in perceptual knowledge is simply there; we all do trust it—until it plays us false. If we wish to know what the weather is like, we look. And if we wish to know whether a given substance is sugar or salt, we taste it. Perceptions are the source of all our images and, even in the atomic theory, Epicurus derived his ideas of what the atoms are like from perceptible shapes. But he did not hesitate to correct the impressions of the senses when reason demanded this.

The atoms, for instance, are imperceptible because they are too small to be seen. Though Epicurus was convinced that all reason owes its validity to sensation, he did not conclude that imperceptibles were nonexistent. A deduction or inference to be true must be corroborated by observation; that much will be accepted by anyone. If a theory, in other words, implies something on the perceptual level which is not found, then the implication may be consistently deduced but it will not be factually true. On the other hand, we know that any number of premises may be fabricated which will lead to conclusions which can be perceptually corroborated. Observation is a check on deductions since it can disprove them. But strictly speaking it cannot prove them. It can strengthen inference, make it more plausible, but that is all. The theory of the *eidola*, which Epicurus took over from Democritus,

---

[35] Sextus Empiricus *Adv. math.* viii. 9; cited by Bailey, *The Greek Atomists and Epicurus*, p. 237, n. 1.

was consistent with the facts of observation. If a visual object was throwing off little replicas of itself and they entered the eye, we could actually see the *eidola*. And we do see them. But the fact that I look into the garden and see a rose in bloom is not proof of the theory that little *eidola* are being sloughed off by the rose and entering my eye. If they were supposed to enter my eye and I did not see the rose, I should probably conclude that the theory was false, though, if my Epicurean opponent was pigheaded enough, he might retort that there was something the matter with my eye. But I am simply trying to point out that an "empirical" theory of this type does not limit one to the data of sense. Nor was Epicureanism so limited.

The method was helped by the introduction of "anticipations" (*prolepses*). This is of peculiar interest historically, for it is an early version of a contemporary theory of knowledge elaborated in opposition to the stimulus-response theory of perception.[36] *Prolepses* remain in our minds after we have had several similar perceptions and they lead us to anticipate the kind of experience which we are about to have. They explain the difference between looking and seeing, listening and hearing, and guide us in our interpretations of the data before us. For those data are highly ambiguous. The naked color blue in itself, not seen anywhere in particular nor as the color of any special object, may be the sky, a flower, mold, a symbol, cloth, and any number of other things. When we see a blue flower, we do not think that we are looking at the sky, for we do not anticipate finding the sky at the end of a stalk. The theory of the origin of *prolepses* as an accumulation of sensory data may well be false, and probably is false, but the use of the concept was helpful because something of the sort was needed. I have of course gone well beyond the Epicurean documents in expounding Epicurus' theory. Modern historians for that matter are not in entire agreement on what the theory entailed, nor are they on anything else in our intellectual past, but

[36] I refer to the various works of the Transactionalists. See G. Boas, *The Inquiring Mind* (La Salle: Open Court, 1959), chap. 1, for an account which tried to be sympathetic to their views.

I have merely tried to make it as plausible as I could. It is backed up by certain passages of Lucretius (v. 181–6 and 1046–9) in which *prolepsis* is treated as a plan of action. For the interpretation of a sensory datum may well be a plan of action, unless perception is simply the passive reception of imprints made upon us without our doing anything whatsoever.

That Epicurus paid so little attention to the application of rules of reasoning is perhaps not so astonishing as it might seem to the modern reader. Such a rule as the Law of Contradiction was accepted by everyone without criticism, for no philosopher was interested in simply listing the data of the five senses. Philosophy has as one of its major tasks the synthesis of what we know, its organization into some sort of system. There were plenty of skeptics in antiquity for whom such syntheses were dubious and indeed a waste of time. But Epicurus was not one of them. He knew that one had to go well beyond sensation if one were to form general propositions, and he had no hesitation in doing so. The strict application of the canon of perceptual validity would have led (1) to the acceptance of hallucinations and optical illusions as true, (2) to the rejection of any causal linkage between events for, as the skeptic said, we can observe contact but not causation, (3) to the rejection of such theories as those of the planetary bodies, for all that we can see are points of light at different positions in the sky, (4) to the denial of the existence of everything too small or too big to be perceived. Perception, in short, gives us the data and the checks on our reasoning, but it cannot furnish explanations of those problems which puzzle us. It may furnish us with models in terms of which we shall solve our problems. For instance, we are to explain all occurrences as far as possible in terms of colliding atoms. But if the simple laws of collision will not answer our questions, and if they entail conclusions which are observably false, then we are at liberty to introduce a new hypothesis to supplement them.[37] The swerving

---

[37] See Bailey, *The Greek Atomists and Epicurus*, p. 529, for examples of Epicurus' introduction of extra hypotheses.

of the atoms would be one case in point. If the atoms did not swerve, they would not form macroscopic objects. But they do form macroscopic objects. Therefore they must swerve.

Again, he objected very strongly to teleological explanations. If Lucretius is accurately reporting his master's views (i. 1021–8), Epicurus insisted that no purpose created the world; it was created by the collisions of atoms and by nothing else. The eye, says Lucretius (iv. 823–42), was not given us in order that we might see, nor was any organ of the body created for our use. The instrument creates its function; the function does not produce the instrument. This was in entire disagreement with the leading explanatory technique of Aristotle and obviously a denial of that part of *Timaeus* which dealt with the anatomy of the human body. It was clearly an attempt at rebutting the Stoics. Aristotle and indeed any kind of teleological explanation were much too useful to the early Fathers to be discarded and hence this part of Epicureanism, like its materialism, was doomed to extinction.

Neither the early Stoics nor Epicurus were, strictly speaking, rationalists if we mean that adjective to name men who were mainly interested in deduction. Both groups, while using the reason to criticize sensory perception, nevertheless admitted the use of nonrational sources of knowledge, such as the *consensus gentium*, allegory, perceptual data, and *prolepses*. One of the common weaknesses resided in their desire to prove ethical theses which are logically, if not psychologically, independent of natural science. It is true that we do not have their complete works, though as far as Epicureanism is concerned we have the great poem of Lucretius. But if the aim which he set himself of using his knowledge to alleviate our fear of death and of the gods is an integral part of the doctrine as a whole, then clearly the doctrine must be so oriented that it will accomplish that aim. The steady drift of philosophy toward a philosophy of life, religion, and ethics is an indication of how the rationalistic fiber was weakening. We shall see, I hope, how it weakened still further in the years that were to come.

III

1. If the earlier Academics had anything to say about the value of life, the remaining fragments do not show it. The so-called *Definitions* of Speusippus are simply commonplaces which exhibit about as much critical insight as the definitions of Alcuin in the ninth century and, moreover, they are probably spurious.[38] To learn that "virtue is the best condition, a state of a mortal creature praiseworthy in itself, a state in which one can be said to have achieved goodness, a just participation in the laws in accordance with which one's way of life is called serious, a state productive of good order," is not to learn much about the problems of fourth-century life as a philosopher might see them. One reads these platitudes with impatience, wondering how a close associate of Plato could have been so uncritical. They are, as a matter of fact, moral proverbs excerpted from or paraphrased from certain passages in the Platonic dialogues, edifying perhaps, but not very enlightening. Socrates would have torn them all to shreds.

The literary remains of Xenocrates are even poorer. His moralizing fragments (frs. 58–60) are the usual pronouncements about the identity of happiness and virtue, of wisdom and the knowledge of first causes and "intelligible being," of the distinction between theoretical and practical prudence, none of which are of much interest since they give us none of their author's reasons for believing in them.

When we come to the third member of the early Academics, Crantor, we find a few remarks which carry on a tradition which we have seen in the poets. It is the old comment on the misery of life which appeared as early as Homer (*Odyssey* xviii. 130): "Earth bears nothing more feeble than a human being." Quoted by Plutarch in his *Consolatio ad Apollonium* (vi. 104c), and therefore perhaps little more than a ritualistic thought to comfort one in grief, a passage supposedly written on the death of one Hippocles is nevertheless worth quoting if only to illustrate the

[38] See Lang, *op. cit.*, pp. 22 f.

strain of melancholy which goes through Greek literary history. It runs: "Of all the things which ancient philosophy says and prescribes, if we cannot prove anything else, this at least is certain, that life is often troublesome and painful. For if it is not of such a turn by nature, it is directed toward corruption at least by us. And hidden chance itself from afar and from the very beginning of life sees to it that we pass not one day in health. As soon as we are born, some evil fate is mixed with all. For your seed, being mortal, shares at once in the cause by which dullness of soul, diseases, cares, and death descend upon us from yonder. To what end do we turn to this point? That we may know that nothing novel happens to a man, but all of us suffer in the same way." This is a *topos* which became a favorite in later times, both in such pagan writings as the Pseudo-Platonic *Axiochus* and in the *Contemptus mundi* of the Christians. But as the theme is very well known, we shall not overburden these pages with more quotations, for they would all sound the same note: the heaviness of life and its futility.[39] We shall end simply by referring to a passage from Sextus Empiricus (*Adv. math.* xi. 51–9) purporting to repeat a parable by Crantor. If we imagine, he says (Mullach, fr. 13), a large theater on the stage of which the various goods appear, as if in an Elizabethan masque, to claim first rank, Wealth will present herself first. "I," she will say, "since I furnish adornment for all, both clothes for the body and shoes for the feet, and all utilities both for the sick and the well, all pleasant things in peace and the sinews of war, I deserve the primacy." And the Greeks with universal consent will award the prize to her. But then Pleasure will appear and say that she is friendship to one, love to another, good conversation, eloquence which steals away the intelligence even of the most prudent, and she will add that wealth is uncertain, ephemeral, and disappears in a flash. It is not riches, she will say, which are good but the pleasures which they bring. And the Greeks will shout that it is she who should have the crown.

[39] For references to numerous other writers repeating this *topos*, see Mullach's notes on this fragment, p. 147.

Then Health will come and in her turn be acclaimed, only to be followed by Virtue, who will point out that in her absence all goods melt away. "Hearing this, the Greeks will bestow the primacy to Virtue, second place to Health, the third to Pleasure, and the last place to Wealth." How much of a reflection on actual Greek life this is, we leave to others to decide.

2. One of the most revealing documents of the period immediately following that of Aristotle (middle fourth century) is the *Characters* of Theophrastus. For in the first place it recognizes that there is no such thing as a Greek type to which all Greeks should attempt to conform, and in the second that, though all Greeks speak the same language and have about the same education, they differ from one another markedly. These differences, expressed by the same word as that used originally to denote the marks made by an engraver, were not so finely differentiated as to distinguish individual from individual, but nevertheless did set up subclasses of human beings. These classes are the Ironical Man, the Flatterer, the Garrulous Man, the Boor (or Insensible Man), the Shameless Man, and so on.[40] How the characters were determined, Theophrastus does not tell us, whether they were innate, caused by peculiar education, or associated with certain bodily peculiarities, as might be suggested by physiognomical treatises. But apparently once they were established, they were ineradicable. There is a certain likelihood that the characters were believed to be caused or at any rate to accompany physiological peculiarities, for there was after all in circulation at that time the theory of the four humors which determined the four temperaments. That theory plus the theory of physiognomy might have been the explanation of this interesting work. We have in Plato men like the young Theaetetus, Charmides, Laches, Lysis, and Thrasymachus who seem to incarnate moral and intellectual traits. We have also his views as given in the *Republic* that men were born appetitive,

---

[40] See R. C. Jebb, *The Characters of Theophrastus*, edited by J. E. Sandys (London: Macmillan and Co., 1909), for text and translation with copious historical notes.

irascible, or rational. We have the long description in the *Nicho-macbean Ethics* of the Great-Souled Man. But I can think of no collection of character sketches so vivid and detailed in Greek literature before the *Characters*. The book is not a scientific treatise in any sense of the word and it would not do to take it too seriously. Each character represents an extreme, like the vices in the *Nichomachean Ethics*, and no virtuous character is described. But the introduction, though Jebb calls its opening "fatuous,"[41] does present a problem to anyone believing in the homogeneity of classes, national characters, or even *Zeitgeister*.

If the characters were ineradicable, there was little sense in trying to make men better than they were. The courageous man would be courageous, the coward cowardly, whatever instruction they might receive. The fate which drove Oedipus or Antigone to their doom would be replaced by character. If this work were a serious psychological treatise, Theophrastus could have reasonably argued that each type of evil person should be put where he could do least harm and each type of good man where he would do most good. So far as I know there is no work in which the consequences of the theory of characters were inferred with the interesting exception of literary theory. Writers of fiction try to make their personages intelligible. And the only way in which this can be done is by an imitation of the scientific technique of generalization. One can understand the Slanderer, the Hypocrite, the Hypochondriac, the Miser, the Misanthrope, but one cannot understand Napoleon, Talleyrand, Benedict Arnold, Cesare Borgia, or Woodrow Wilson—the list is purely fortuitous —until one has classified them. During the Middle Ages certain personages of religious history, St. Joseph, Herod, Judas, Mary Magdalene, took on fixed characters and were always presented as "true to character." Similarly a given individual, whether in history or in literature, turns into a type of character, and though Hitler was probably not a monster in his relations with Eva Braun,

---

[41] See his note to l. 1 of the Proem, *op. cit.*, p. 36. The Proem is probably unauthentic.

a monster he remains in our thoughts about him and a monster he will always be. The most consistent characters are in our mental hospitals, or ought to be there, for the exigencies of life demand a flexibility and plasticity of character which is the very opposite of consistency. Yet we still speak of men of character as men to be admired.

What the immediate effect of Theophrastus' *Characters* was, we do not know. But a reading of it gives one the impression of a clear-sighted man who could spot telling details of behavior and who could enliven for posterity the manner of his time. Of authors who remain, he was unique in avoiding the vague generalities of his contemporaries. We have to turn to Lucian and Plautus before we find anything comparable. He saw men neither as hopeless nor as generally happy, though in view of the type of men whom he depicted, he was far from being an admirer of the human race. For our purposes his importance lies in whatever effect he may have had in weakening the idea that men must be judged as members of a homogeneous class of beings, their lives to be appraised by their conformity to the class concept.

3. Though neither the Stoics nor the Epicureans were so gloomy as Crantor, neither had much liking for human life as it was being lived. Both sought an escape from the troubles of life in peace of mind, their main difference lying in the path which they laid out to their respective goals. Both were philosophers of escape, preaching, in brief, definite withdrawal into oneself, cutting off all ties of responsibility to others.

The Stoics were perhaps as contemptuous of their fellow men as the Epicureans. Chrysippus is reported by Plutarch[42] to have found no one in history deserving of the name of Sage. The opinion of Chrysippus is echoed in Seneca's saying that a really good man is as rare as the Phoenix (*Epistle* xlii. 1). When they are less contemptuous, they are equally skeptical. They had no illusions

---

[42] *De Stoicorum repugnantiis* xxxi. 1048 e. Cf. Cicero *Academica* ii. 47. 145 f.

about the ease with which a man could attain a virtuous life. Cleanthes[43] pictures man as "walking in evil" most of his life. If he ever becomes virtuous, it is late and as his life draws to a close. By teaching men could be made better, but the progress is slow, painful, and may never reach its goal. In fact, the Stoic insistence on the need for moral instruction would have been senseless if the founders of the school had had a high estimation of the value of life.[44] All ethical teaching is obviously based on the feeling that life as it is usually lived should be improved. No ethicist accepts life as it is; if he did, his teaching would be reduced to one command, "Do as you please." *Fais ce que vouldras* was all very well for the Thelemites, but it would have revolted Zeno and Epicurus.

This dissatisfaction with life was also shared by such a religious leader as Gautama Buddha or St. Paul. The first step toward regeneration was the great enlightenment which came to Gautama under the Bo Tree, that all life is suffering.[45] To St. Paul came the revelation of man's inherent sinfulness and the possibility of regeneration through Christ. Their solutions were clearly different, but they both agreed that terrestrial life as it was being lived was in desperate need of radical change. In contrast to these two religious leaders, the philosophers, both Stoic and Epicurean, were able to find a solution for life's miseries without supernatural assistance. They underwent no trance and obtained no revelation. Once a man knew what reality was, he could by giving it assent lift himself above the confusion and unhappiness of the mass of human beings.

The demand for peace of mind or for self-dependence may

[43] Fr. 529 (von Arnim, *op. cit.*, Vol. I, p. 120).

[44] Cf. Zeller, *Stoics, Epicureans, and Sceptics*, p. 255.

[45] See T. W. Rhys Davids, *Buddhism* (London and New York: Society for Promoting Christian Knowledge, 1890), p. 48, for the Four Truths: suffering or sorrow, the cause of suffering, the cessation of sorrow, the path leading to cessation of sorrow. The withdrawal of the Buddha from civic life is analogous to that preached by Epictetus. It will be noticed that "the Buddha declared that he had arrived at these convictions, not by study of the Vedas, nor from the teachings of others, but by the light of reason and intuition alone."

well be a sign that both schools thought mental perturbation and dependence on others were all too common. The period during which the early members of both schools were living was one in which the small city-state had to all intents and purposes lost sovereignty. How intensely the individual Greek felt this loss is problematic, for it goes without saying that what we know of the feelings of people comes from what has been written by them, and the only popular literature we have is folk songs, ballads, jokes, street-corner conversations, and letters to the editors of newspapers. But this type of thing in Greek is lost. The surviving literature, moreover, was bound to have been written by a few men living in cities and representative of no one but themselves. In a hundred years or so no one will know whether T. S. Eliot expressed the thoughts of the majority of his contemporaries or whether Norman Vincent Peale and the Reverend Fulton Sheen expressed them. Similarly, though we do know that both the Stoics and Epicureans formed schools, indeed philosophic sects, we have no way of knowing whether the mass of men paid them any heed whatsoever. Regardless of that, it is safe to say that the way preached by the Stoic was the way which he thought had been either abandoned by his fellow men or untried by them, and that this was the reason of their unhappiness. He never asked any of them whether indeed they were unhappy; he took that for granted. They should have been unhappy.

The main cause of man's supposed unhappiness is his unnaturalness. To follow Nature, as we have said frequently in this book, was a slogan which had been in vogue at least as early as the *Clouds* of Aristophanes (1078), and the two phrases, "according to nature" and "contrary to nature," were stock terms of praise and blame. Just what constituted the unnatural was always something of a puzzle, for after all in one sense of the word "natural" everything is natural. But there were at least two usual ways of determining the unnatural: by pointing to that which was abnormal in the sense of rare, and by first discovering the purposes of acts and things and then pointing to deviations from the attainment of that purpose. Thus pederasty in Greece at certain times was common enough to be made the butt of satirists and the target of criticism; so were love of fame and of money, ambition, love of possessions, and so on, in short, every form of "worldliness." The former could be called unnatural in that sexual relations were said to exist for the sake of procreation and obviously pederasty could not result in the begetting and bearing of children. Money, ambition, and so on could be called unnatural, since life could go on without them and the rational life might be frustrated by them. If man then was a rational animal, which no one seemed to doubt, then anything which might impede the exercise of reason was unnatural. But then nature took on an added meaning: the natural was to be found in the life of savages and beasts. If savages and beasts did not follow certain customs and seek possessions and found cities, those customs were contrary to nature. The most extreme form of this argument is seen in the legends associated with the Cynic Diogenes. The animals did not drink from cups, had no houses, wore no clothes, had no money. The philosopher therefore drank out of his cupped hands or knelt down and lapped up his water from pools and streams, lived in an abandoned wine jar, and wrapped a few rags about his nakedness to protect him from the cold. Men were consequently, in this form of naturalism, criticized for seeking superfluities. The simple life was enough. Moreover, by getting rid of superfluities, one also got rid of worry about retaining them. In the case of Diogenes, one also got rid of consideration for others and ordinary decencies. That the irrational animals were no standard for rational animals seems not to have occurred to the Cynics. And similarly there was no reason why the savage, who had according to theory no civilization, should be a standard for civilized man.[46]

The Stoic seldom went so far as the Cynic. But he too rejected many of the goods which other men cherished. Some of these they maintained were neither good nor bad, but indifferent. Ac-

[46] See *Primitivism in Antiquity*, chaps. 3, 4, 11, and 13.

cording to Sextus Empiricus (*Adv. math.* xi. 73), pleasure itself was held to be indifferent, Cleanthes maintaining that it was no more natural than decoration and therefore valueless. Pleasure may be attached to certain virtuous acts, but their virtue does not lie in the pleasure which they bring one. The value of an act is to be determined rationally. If the act achieves the purpose for which it was designed by nature, then it is good whether pleasurable or not. There could be no compromise with this principle. "Such teaching," says R. D. Hicks, "whether Christian or Stoic, is bound to divide the world of existing men into two opposing classes, saints and sinners, the wise and the foolish."[47] And the Stoics located most men among the sinners and fools.

The life according to nature would be a life according to reason, but to discover what such a life might be requires the preliminary discovery of how reason operates. If there are certain self-evident premises from which the reasoning process starts, then the problem is not too hard. But every school of moralists had its own self-evident premises. They might all agree that the fundamental trouble with the human race is lack of independence (*autarky*). But that is surely far from being self-evident. If life itself cannot go on without the co-operation of others, then one must conclude that life is downright bad and death is the one good, or that *autarky*, being an impossibility, is not the goal. Should one ask a Stoic why independence of all desires except those which can be satisfied by oneself is the end, no answer would be given. But how strange is a conception of human life which cannot be exemplified! The basic difficulty in it lay in the Stoic's individualism. Unlike the Platonists, the Aristotelians, the Epicureans, they emphasized the City of God, the cosmos in which every individual was a citizen and in which he must play his assigned role. This role he must freely accept, though in the long run he could not do otherwise. But to play a role in a drama, to fulfill one's obligations to a society whether natural or supernatural, is to recognize the demands of others. Yet the Stoic, as if

[47] *Stoic and Epicurean* (New York: Charles Scribner's Sons, 1910), p. 87.

he held that the drama was played on an invisible stage and in a private theater, addressed himself exclusively to the individual. Each man was to achieve his own salvation, his own peace of mind, his own independence of external goods. Surely to point out a conflict here is not to exaggerate. With appropriate emendations one of the clearest expressions of this conflict is found in the words of St. Paul (Acts 17:24–28) to the Stoics and Epicureans on the Areopagus:

> The God that made the world and all things therein, he being Lord of heaven and earth . . . neither is he served by men's hands, as though he needed anything, seeing he himself giveth to all life, and breath, and all things; and he made of one every nation of men for to dwell on all the face of the earth, having determined their appointed seasons, and the bounds of their habitation; that they should seek God, if haply they might feel after him, though he is not far from each of us: for in him we live, and move, and have our being.

The God of whom Paul was speaking is of course not the divine *Pneuma* of the Stoics, but, that aside, the tenor of the sentence is Stoic and the conflict of which we have made mention is clear. For if we live and move and have our being in God, then there is no way in which we can live and move and have our being in something else, God being all-inclusive. And if God gives us all things, then he gives us our way of life. Happily our purpose is not to provide an exegesis of Pauline theology and, for all I know, he may have made use of Stoic terminology for forensic purposes only. The sinner might have replied to St. Paul, I am what God made me, as he might have replied to Cleanthes, If I spurn the law of Zeus, that law is not universal, and if it is universal, then my behavior is conditioned by it. St. Augustine and Calvin were perhaps better Stoics than they knew. The Stoics might well have argued that even the City of God contains evil men, for all possibilities must be realized in a perfect world, but they had little cause to look down on them.

Another test of the rational is the discovery of the indispensable. If one is to live in accordance with reason, then one must discover the reason why one does anything whatsoever. And if there is no reason for doing it, one rejects it. The indispensable is relative to life itself, or to a happy life, or to an economic life, or some other sort of life. But in the Cynics it was that which could not be dispensed with if one was going to continue living. Pleasantness of life, living with one's fellows, living so as to meet with the approval of society, none of these or similar things counted. Diogenes was the great exemplar of the simple life of course; and to him if the animals could sustain life without drinking vessels, clothes, houses, that was proof that such things were superfluities and could be dispensed with. Crates, describing his "happy city," Pera, says that it has a fertile soil but is "squalid in every way," but "into it never sails a fool, nor a parasite, nor those who lust for harlots' bodies. But thyme it yields and garlic, figs and wheaten loaves; for such things men do not wage wars, nor take up arms for money or for fame."[48] The notion that only the indispensable was the rational continued from Cynicism into Stoicism until in Epictetus, as we shall see, to live rationally required the rejection of almost everything, including family and the state.

4. The attitude of Epicurus toward his fellow men was not much more friendly than that of the early Stoics. "I was never anxious to please the mob," he wrote,[49] "for what pleased them I did not know, and what I did know was far from their comprehension." His hatred of other philosophers was notorious[50] and he would not even admit his debt to Democritus. Yet his purpose in writing was to free men from two fears, the fear of divine intervention in terrestrial life and the fear of death. The theory of atoms accomplished both, or was supposed to. But why did he or his disciple, Lucretius, care whether the mob was freed from fear or not? If pleasure was to be the end of life and was to be found by oneself unaided by one's fellows, why worry about their fears? One had only to revert to the state of the "untaught

---

[48] See *Primitivism in Antiquity*, chap. 4, for Cynic primitivism in general.
[49] Bailey, *Epicurus*, 48, p. 131. Cf. fr. 58, p. 134.
[50] *Ibid.*, p. 226; but see **9.**

and natural animal" (Sextus Empiricus *Adv. math.* xi. 96) and follow instinct. Pleasure is the end because it is what all creatures seek until they are perverted by culture, from which he urges his pupil, Pythocles, to flee.[51] But again, if all men naturally and instinctively seek pleasure and if the good is what all men seek, then (1) why do they need any instruction on how to find it, and (2) why is it that so many men do not seek it? If he can say, as he does, "The source and root of all good is the pleasure of the stomach, and both wisdom and subtlety have their rise therein,"[52] this may be a bit of practical advice to men who turn away from the pleasures of eating or it may be a generalization of fact. In both cases it would be superfluous as a moral precept. It looks like a happy acceptance of human life as it exists. But unfortunately, no sooner had this been laid down as a basic principle than a distinction was introduced. The distinction was that between pleasures which are lasting, pleasures which are followed by pains, and pleasures which are greater than other pleasures. But once this is introduced, the attempt to found an ethics on observation fails.

Epicurus, moreover, himself realized that man in a state of nature required certain things which instinct would not provide. In the *Letter to Herodotus*,[53] he suggests an outline of cultural history which was to be filled in later by Lucretius (v. 780–1457). Just as Aristotle had pointed out that sometimes nature needs the help of art, so Epicurus says that after the beginning of human history our reasoning powers elaborated the hints given by nature, at times slowly and at others quickly. Thus language was first developed haltingly and only later did the various peoples consolidate their linguistic efforts and form national languages. This was done to avoid ambiguity and to clarify meanings. It may be presumed that this was an improvement of man's instinctive or untaught ways of communication and that Epicurus did

[51] *Ibid.*, p. 129, fr. 33.
[52] *Ibid.*, p. 135, **59.**
[53] *Ibid.*, p. 47.

not disapprove of clear thinking. Furthermore, knowledge itself, he held,[54] is a source of happiness, but not that knowledge which is likely to cause alarm or fear. These may arise from accepting folklore and from the irrational fear of death, both of which are common. Such a program is far from being a reversion to a primitive condition; it does not urge reliance on instinct or the ideals of the untutored mind. He insists (*Letter to Menoecus*) that even in the pursuit of pleasure prudence is the first and greatest good, "for from prudence are sprung all the other virtues."[55] But then oddly enough, the virtues are justified for the simple reason that they are the greatest source of pleasure. This is a far cry from the sensationalism with which he started, for after all if we have primary feelings of pleasure, such as the pleasures of the stomach, on which to build an ethics, why do we need any rational control of our appetites? The only answer that seems reasonable is that "the unexamined life is not worth living," an answer which, as we know, went back to Socrates. But the need for examination would never arise if one did not think that life as it is lived by the Many is unsatisfactory.

At times Epicurus emphasized the need for protecting oneself against one's fellows. In the list of his *Principal Doctrines*[56] one reads that to secure protection from men, anything is a natural good. But at the same time this is useless if "things above and things beneath the earth and indeed all in the boundless universe remain matters of suspicion."[57] One must retire from the society of the Many into quietude.[58] And yet he also preaches the desirability of living with others who "possess the power to procure complete immunity from their neighbors."[59] What such a community would be like is difficult, if possible, to imagine, for the mere fact of living with others would involve at a minimum con-

[54] *Ibid.*, p. 51.
[55] *Ibid.*, p. 91.
[56] *Ibid.*, p. 95, 6.
[57] *Ibid.*, p. 97, 13.
[58] *Ibid.*, 14.
[59] *Ibid.*, 40.

versation with them and that would mean dependence on them intellectually and, in all probability, disputes. In fact elsewhere he recognizes that friendship has its source in the need for help.[60] And in spite of this, he says that for the sake of friendship we must run risks.[61] He was himself, if his letters to his various friends are genuine, a devoted and enthusiastic friend.[62] Apparently friendship need not be a hindrance to *autarky*, "the greatest of all riches," the fruit of which is freedom.[63]

Epicurus then may be said to have assumed the same attitude toward life as his philosophic predecessors. He did not go so far as some of the poets, who thought it better never to have been born, and he did try to find a standard of goodness in the sensible world. But he could not bring himself to use that standard without qualification. His depreciation of life was based on social living; it is clear that like so many of his fellows he wanted as much freedom from dependence on others as possible. What there was in the loosely organized society which made it so burdensome, I do not know. But that it was burdensome is clear from the writings of all the moralists. The outcome was to be seen in early Christianity, which refused to admit any obligations to the society in which it developed, encouraged in early monasticism a flight from all worldly occupations, and then built up new social units which were more tightly bound together and disciplined than any that paganism had ever seen.

---

[60] *Ibid.*, p. 109, fr. 23.

[61] *Ibid.*, p. 111, fr. 28. Such fragmentary sayings are often mutually contradictory, for when they are genuine, they are quoted out of context. Thus fr. 8, from the *Symposium*, runs, "Sexual intercourse has never done a man good, and he is lucky if it has not harmed him," while fr. 10, from *On the End of Life*, reads, "I know not how I can conceive the good, if I withdraw the pleasures of taste and withdraw the pleasures of love . . . and the pleasurable emotions caused to sight by beautiful form." (Bailey, *Epicurus*, p. 123.)

[62] Bailey, *Epicurus*, p. 127 ff.

[63] *Ibid.*, p. 137, fr. 70, and p. 139, fr. 77.

IV

Accompanying any appraisal of life, there is likely to be a system of ethics. Just what the causal relation between the two may be we shall not attempt to ascertain, for there is no longer any way, so far as the ancients are concerned, of ascertaining it. We can see from the texts that *autarky* was what the ethicists wanted; their ethical theories tell us how they proposed to get it. But similarly it has been pointed out in many histories of philosophy, especially in those which follow Hegel's outline, that this period was peculiarly ethical and that the metaphysical speculations of Stoic and Epicurean were formed in order to justify their ethical teachings. There is, to be sure, a certain harmony between the two, but every philosopher who writes on more than one subject will strive to be consistent. Such consistency, however, is no evidence of either logical or psychological priority in the views which have been made consistent.

1. If one wishes to discover the ethical views of Speusippus, one must go to the *Definitions*, a work which can hardly be considered authentic, as we have pointed out above, though it is listed among his works by Diogenes Laertius (iv. 5). It thus was supposed to be genuine in the third century A.D. or thereabouts. To learn that "virtue is the best disposition [of mind]; a condition of the mortal animal praiseworthy in itself; a condition in accordance with which conduct is called good; a just community of laws; a disposition in accordance with which one's state of mind is called perfectly earnest; a condition creative of good order and obedience to the law" (fr. 21),[64] is not to gain much information about virtue's sources and the problems which men face in trying to be virtuous. There are over one hundred and fifty such definitions, of prudence, of justice, of temperance, of courage, and so on, of all the virtues which so many of Plato's dialogues attempted to define without succeeding. In fact the list

---

[64] I am using the text and numbering of Mullach here, since Lang does not quote the *Definitions*.

might well serve as the starting point for a Socratic interrogation. Justice, which the ten books of the *Republic* tried to define, is disposed of as "the harmony of the soul within itself, and good order of the parts of the soul in their interrelations; a condition which apportions to each according to its worth; a condition in accordance with which he who possesses it is inclined toward choosing those things which are right for him; a condition of life obedient to law; communal equality; a condition obedient to right laws" (fr. 23). These might well be the various answers given by some young interlocutor of Socrates as he strove to find one which would withstand his master's criticism.

Aristotle in the *Metaphysics* (1072b) attributes to both the Pythagoreans and Speusippus the idea that neither the best nor the most beautiful is in the *arche* or first principle, because the *archai* of both plants and animals are causes, and it cannot be truly said that the beautiful and the perfect are in them (fr. 34a, Lang). The reason is that the best and perfect are in the final causes of things and not in their seeds. This gives us Aristotle's reason for rejecting the theory that the good is in the beginning, not Speusippus' reason for believing it to be there. Speusippus might as well have replied that the perfect could not come from the imperfect nor the good from evil.[65] Moreover, if all change is from opposites to opposites, from below to above, from genesis to destruction, from good to bad, and so on, which happens to be Aristotle's own belief (*Categories* 15a), one would imagine that he would have welcomed what he thought was the inference to be drawn from Speusippus' theory, though to do so would have involved the denial of his own axiom.

According to Sextus Empiricus (*Adv. math.* xi. 4–6, fr. 76), Xenocrates agreed with the early Stoics in dividing things into three kinds, the good, the bad, and those which are neither. Whereas, says Sextus, most philosophers take this for granted, Xenocrates tried to prove it. "For if there is something distinct from the good and evil and that which is neither good nor evil,

---

[65] See Lang, frs. 35a ff.

then it would be either good or not-good. And if it is good, then it will be one of the three; and if it is not good, still it is evil or neither good nor evil. But if it is evil, again it will be one of the three. All existence then is either good or evil or neither good nor evil." This tells us nothing except that Xenocrates used a dialectical method in making his preliminary distinctions, whereas his contemporaries were satisfied to take them as self-evident. But he seems to have been addicted to such demonstrations. Aristotle (*Topics* 152a) refers to him as arguing that the happy life and the morally earnest life are the same, "since the lives most desired [or perhaps, desirable] and the greatest are one." This might be the start of an empirical ethics in which the desires of mankind would determine what would be taken as the good. But Aristotle continues by saying that this is no proof, since one kind of life might well come from the other, in his own system happiness demanding seriousness. I say this since there is another passage of Aristotle (*Topics* 112a) upon which Alexander of Aphrodisias (fr. 81) comments, "If the *daimon* of each man is his soul, as Xenocrates teaches, he would be happy who had a good soul. But the serious—or earnest—man has a good soul. Hence the serious man is happy." Apparently Xenocrates was also somewhat given to etymological arguments, a vice which often accompanies pure dialectic, for he says that just as to be happy (*eudaimon*) is to have a good *daimon* (fr. 81, l. 14), and to be unhappy is to have an evil *daimon*, we call the wicked *kakodaimones* (fr. 67). But there is no need to cite such passages, for they are more revealing of a type of mind than of a chain of reasoning. If taken seriously, then both virtue and vice would be laid at the thresholds of our *daimones*, which would help us to evade our responsibilities. But we have no reason to believe that he ever went so far as that. For the moral maxims which are assigned to him show no logical relation to any principle of determinism or indeterminism.[66]

2. In both the Stoics and the Epicureans on the contrary we

---

[66] Anyone sufficiently interested may find such fragments as 101 ff. worth reading.

have well-developed ethical systems. The Stoics' attainment of peace of mind could be both justified by their metaphysics and derived from it.

If the cosmos is an organic being, all of whose parts have their proper places and their specific roles to play, then mankind as a whole and each individual man as well must have theirs. What these roles are is determined by the whole and it is therefore foolish for any man to rebel. The universal determinism is responsible for whatever happens to an individual; he can only recognize its inevitability and submit. Thus if a man first accepted the Stoic metaphysics, he could be induced to resign himself to his fate. If on the other hand he looked for consolation, he could find it in the metaphysics. A kind of quietism would be the natural result of a belief in fate as the guiding principle of history, much like the quietism of Molinos. To accept the will of God and bow one's head before divine decisions is not an unreasonable program, however difficult it may turn out to be. It is not a program by which one could conquer the hostile forces of flood and drought, but nevertheless it is one by which one might win greater victories, those over oneself.

Stoicism, even in its earlier manifestations, contained the following main ideas: (1) the idea of the Great Animal, the Cosmopolis, or the organic universe; (2) thoroughgoing determinism, resulting in a series of events endlessly repeated in cycles; (3) the search for peace of mind as the greatest good; (4) the possibility of liberation from the emotions.

The idea of the Great Animal meant not merely that the whole cosmos was an organic unit, but that it had a soul as well as a body: it was alive. Its soul was the *Pneuma*, identified with God, and our individual souls were duplications of the universal soul on a smaller scale. Just as the *Pneuma* fitted means to ends, saw that all things served a purpose, however purposeless they might seem to men, so the individual souls had a guiding principle, rational in nature, in their make-up. Now whether the Stoics meant that things operated as units and the name for their unitary behavior was the *logos*, a name given because their behavior was rational, or whether they thought that the *logoi* were separate beings lodged within the human body, the bodies of all things that grew, and the cosmos as a whole, we cannot say with certainty. But the probability is that they cut off the *logos* existentially from that which it governed, for the notion that all change was caused by an agent acting upon a patient was too generally accepted for them to have rejected it. In any event, the individual soul, though part and parcel of the Great Animal, nevertheless contributed its share to the cosmic economy. When the Stoic urged men to be resigned to their fate, he was not involved in the controversy about determinism and free will, since he never asserted that anything was entirely passive. There is theoretically a kind of determinism which maintains that nothing causes anything within the whole of things, but the whole is somehow or other controlled by a power beyond it. But cosmic passivity was not a tenet of the Stoics. Since they did not believe in the reality of universals, each individual man was a reality, no matter how much he might resemble others. Therefore each man was a cause which acted not without motive or with wild caprice, but nevertheless he was responsible for what he did to a certain degree. "A certain degree" is vague and the early Stoics' remains do not tell us to what exact degree an individual was responsible. He would naturally be limited by his experience, for all ideas were derivative from perceptions. But he was certainly free to decide whether he would submit to the universal order or rebel against it, just as he was free to liberate himself from the enslavement of passion.

It may be worth making a slight digression here to clarify as far as we can this problem of determinism and free will. It may be laid down as an axiom that every item in an event contributes something to the outcome of the event. We recognize this in daily speech when we speak about the influence of the weather, the therapeutic effect of drugs, the need of nitrogen in the soil if plants are to grow, the effect of overcrowded slums on crime.

There is therefore no *a priori* reason why human beings alone should prove ineffectual. If I marry a woman because I love her, that love is a relation between her and me, not something apart from us which drives us into marriage. If I were different, or if she were different, regardless of the climate, sunspots, economic conditions, other people's opinions, the marriage would not take place. Such things would of course have some influence on making us what we are, but, given those influences, we exist as we are and are not zeros. Second, if I choose to read *Hamlet* instead of *Twelfth Night* and am asked why, I shall probably give some reason for my choice. This reason will not be the psychological cause of my choice, for in all likelihood that will be concealed from me. Nor will that reason be physiological causes, glandular secretions, sexual impotence, low metabolic rate, or what you will, even though such causes are perhaps present. They may be operative and determinative of my choice of play, but they belong to me, are an integral part of my psychophysical character, unless I turn out to be some sort of creature cut off from all else, a soul, psyche, consciousness, behavior pattern, call it what you will, which can miraculously act in entire independence of everything else in the universe. Such a being has never yet been discovered and has little chance of being discovered. There may be a conflict of motivations and purposes within me, but again they are part of me. If in part or as a whole they determine what I do, it is I who am doing it. No will could ever be so free as not to have to handle certain materials and work within their limitations. But again none could be so determined as to be utterly ineffectual. In short, universal determinism is the only hypothesis which makes it possible for a man to believe in the power of his decisions. It would be only in a world of lawlessness, of completely random occurrences in all areas, that a man could not count on carrying out his desires. Hence I confess to seeing no inner contradiction in the Stoic theory of the Great Animal and the commandment to reform.

The theory of cycles follows from the theory of universal determinism, unless there are infinite possibilities of change. But if these possibilities of change are finite in number, then sooner or later a given state of the cosmos is bound to recur.[67] The number of possibilities was thought of as much more limited than we would believe today, since in the first place the world seemed more limited in extent, second the kinds of causes seemed less numerous, and third the metaphor of the Great Animal induced men to think in terms of birth, growth, senescence, and death. The psychological effect of this was not only quietistic but sedative. What was the use of thrashing about in wild efforts to conquer other nations, to make great inventions, to plan sweeping reforms, if everything a man did was only a series of incidents in an endlessly repeated masque? The City of Zeus would go through its history in a determined, if not predetermined, fashion, and emperors and slaves, Greek and Barbarian, would all play their appointed parts in that masque. The interlocking events in the great cosmic biography would lead to each man's realizing that no one was inherently more important than another and might be expected to make men more sympathetic with one another. We have one thing in common, the *logos*, and our rational nature, which leads us to a common understanding of our citizenship in the cosmopolis, might also lead us to benevolence toward our fellow citizens. This appears more clearly stated in the works of the Roman Stoics, but it is inherent in Stoicism as a whole.

Once we have comprehended the vanity of most of our acts, we shall relax and peace of mind will be ours. Our perturbation comes from the emotions—anger, lust, ambition, and the like—and we can subdue them if we wish. They weaken our reason and cause us to see things in a false light. Once we have dominated them, we have, in the words of that later Stoic, Spinoza, clear and distinct ideas.[68] One of Zeno's pupils, Herillus, accord-

[67] This form of the argument was not that of the early Stoics, so far as I know. It was that of Nietzsche.

[68] Though the phrase was invented by Descartes, his Christianity got in the way of his becoming a Stoic.

ing to Diogenes Laertius (vii. 165), said that the end of life was knowledge. And since knowledge cannot be acquired if we are in the grip of passion, it is obvious that, according to his way of thinking, we must rise above our emotions in order to attain the highest good. The state of impassivity, *apathy*, may be called, and has been, a cold priggish attitude. Priggish it certainly was, for that was the inevitable fate of any purely individualistic ethics. A man who is out to save his own soul, and thinks he is succeeding, will, one imagines, feel himself holier than his fellows and look at them with only the mildest curiosity, somewhat as the gods of Lucretius looked down on struggling mortals. But it is not for one who has spent his life in teaching and studying to take the temperature of the scholar and depreciate it.

But the emotions not only enslave the reason, they are in themselves degrading. The Stoics never lost sight of the supposed fact that man was a rational animal, but they overlooked the animal part of his nature. The beast could not reason; he followed his sensations and images. Pleasure and pain are attributes of sensation, not of ideas, except in so far as we have ideas which cause us to feel happy. The Sage will feel a kind of agreeableness in his peace of mind, but that is not pleasure in the sense that eating and drinking are pleasant. Moreover, when one seeks knowledge, one seeks it not for the agreeableness of knowing something, but for the truth, whether agreeable or not. This complicates the theory. In Epicureanism pleasure and pain were sought and avoided, respectively, by all and could be thought of as natural signs of good and evil. But then the Epicurean had to distinguish between pleasures the enjoyment of which entailed subsequent pain and those which did not, between temporary and lasting pleasures, between the primary pleasures of the flesh and the higher pleasures of understanding.[69] In Stoicism one never seeks pleasure at all, for at best it is simply a by-product of sensations which, as far as Stoics are concerned, are but inchoate knowledge.

The fact that emotions should be overcome is no ground for

[69] See Epicurus *Letter to Menoecus* 129 ff. (Bailey, *Epicurus*, pp. 87 ff.).

thinking that they can be overcome. The emotions which are connected with social ties can be overcome by cutting the ties, and the Stoic seems to have thought that a good thing to do. That technique can be extended to all experiences with which emotions might be allied. In fact, since one might become enthusiastic or angry or depressed by almost anything, it might look as if most of life would have to be suppressed in order to become a Sage. And indeed at times it looks as if that was precisely the end of the Stoic program. Aristotle had laid down the life of contemplation as man's goal, contemplation of philosophic truths. The Stoic too could urge a man to spend his life in thinking about Providence, God, the *Pneuma*, the eternal recurrence, the cosmopolis, but actually how could one do this without a household full of slaves or servants who would carry on the ancillary work? Aristotle at least understood that happiness can only be attained by a man who enjoys leisure. The Stoics were inclined to believe that the attainment of wisdom is rare but, so far as I know, they never faced the fact of why it is rare. It is always easy to castigate human folly and ignorance; it is more difficult to propose a goal which all human beings can reach.

Before leaving the matter of Stoic ethics, it would be well to jot down, if only summarily, its resemblance to some forms of Christian ethics. Both Stoics and Christians believed that the City of God was more important than the City of Man, though the Christian was more willing to pay its due to the latter. Both believed that man was in need of salvation, but the Christian did not usually satisfy the need by rational discourse and contemplation. Both believed in the brotherhood of man, the triviality of national and social differences, the equality of all before the law, but the Christian lost little time in organizing an ecclesiastic hierarchy in which brotherhood counted for less than rank. The law became a mystery which only a few could understand, and one man finally became its interpreter. It has been pointed out by others that as the pagans had no orthodoxy, they could have no heresy; their diversity of beliefs was deplored perhaps, but never annihilated by sword or flame. The Stoics and Epicureans are the last pagan ethicists to give a rational account of moral values.

3. The ethics of Epicurus is even simpler than that of the early Stoics. Pleasure and pain are known to all and furthermore, as a standard of good and evil, are immediate sensations. They are, moreover, actually used by people as such standards: no one has to be persuaded to seek pleasure and avoid pain. If they exist, and of course they do, no theory of atoms, of a cosmic order, of determinism or indeterminism, of Platonic ideas, of lower and higher psychic faculties, is required to justify them. This form of hedonism is straightforward empiricism. Similarly it could be argued that the distinction between lasting pleasures which bring no pain in their suite, and pleasures which are followed by pain, is legitimate and in accordance with common sense. Men could easily understand that they lived for more than the passing moment and that they ought to consider the future as well as the present. It is true that if pleasure is the criterion of goodness, then a pleasure is a pleasure regardless of date, but it is also true that if pain is evil, a future pain is no less evil than one present. The trouble arose when one tried to find a pleasure which would not be followed by pain, for the mere cessation of a pleasure could be painful and there are none which last forever. Considerations of this sort would suffice to turn the Epicurean toward the alleviation of pain rather than the pursuit of pleasure.

The metaphysics of Epicurus was devised so as to relieve men of their two greatest sources of pain, fear of death and fear of the gods, as we have said above. This is now a commonplace of all histories of philosophy, but its significance as a historical influence has been perhaps underestimated. Though neither Epicurus nor Zeno nor Cleanthes could have known anything of the coming of Christianity, their philosophies were as useful as a preparation for its reception into the general body of opinion as could have been desired. We have already mentioned the similarities between Stoicism and early Christianity. But Epicurus was no less influential in changing men's minds about just those beliefs which had to be eliminated if Christianity was to be accepted. If he was right in thinking that "the ruling disturbance of men's souls" is the belief that the heavenly bodies are blessed and immortal and "nevertheless have wills and actions and causal influences" (*Letter to Herodotus* 81; Bailey, p. 52), combined with the fear of life after death, then Christianity also could profit by his argument that such fears were groundless. Belief in the gods was not eliminated by the Epicureans, and in fact Christianity, like other great religions, took over popular beliefs in a different and more acceptable form. But belief in gods who were interested in human affairs was eliminated at least among the thinking classes. God and the angels in Christianity, along with a host of evil powers, were very actively concerned with human life, and the fear of death was increased by that religion rather than diminished. *Post mortem* rewards and punishments must have been a potent argument used by Christian missionaries in inducing men to change their way of life. And that tradition has of course never died out. But the Christian, though fearing death and divine vengeance, was given a way of softening his fears. He had only to have faith and live a Christian life. There was nothing rational about the primary act of acceptance; it was justified by its pragmatic effects. Epicurus taught men to reason about the absurdity of such fears. His arguments were the last efforts of reasonable men to eliminate terrors arising from causes about which the human mind was ignorant.[70]

From today's point of view there seems to have been something naïve in such efforts. We have learned that human behavior is less influenced by argument than by superstition. To have learned that after death we cease to exist, since we are atoms which will be dispersed in our dying, and that nonexistent beings can feel neither pain nor pleasure, was rationally sound, once the premises were

---

[70] Why classical rationalism failed to triumph over what in its origins was superstition as great as that of any of the pagan rites and myths, is still an unsolved problem. People who are inclined to snap judgments about this would do well to read E. R. Dodds, *The Greeks and the Irrational* (Berkeley: University of California Press, 1951), esp. pp. 248 ff.

accepted. One could no more be punished or rewarded after death than one could enjoy or dislike an experience which one had never had. Similarly, if the gods are, like everything else, conglomerations of atoms which are "blessed and immortal" (*Letter to Menoecus* 123; Bailey, p. 82), we should believe nothing said about them which is inconsistent with a blessed and immortal life. Such beings are untroubled themselves and cause no trouble for anyone else, "for all such behavior is in the weak" (*Principal Doctrines* 1; Bailey, p. 94). To think that God, who of all beings must be free of wants, *autarkic*, could be pleased by anything men do or could wish to harm them, is to believe in a God who has the worst traits of His creatures. If the Sage on earth is the man who has peace of mind, then surely those ideal beings who are the gods must have so superior a peace of mind that nothing could move them. They are as good as nonexistent, as far as human destiny is concerned, except that they serve as models of a happy life. The Sage will live "like a god among men" (*Letter to Menoecus* 135; Bailey, p. 92), the gods being perfect examples of happy beings.

So far, so good. But if down within the lower reaches of the human soul there is a real fear of dying, of ceasing to be, the fear may be a form of wishing to continue to live as long as possible. What used to be called the instinct of self-preservation is strong enough to account for man's dread of extinction. We see this expressing itself in all our pathetic attempts to defeat the passage of time, in our last wills and testaments which strive to impose the decisions of the present upon the future, in memorials of one sort or another which may at least preserve a name, if nothing more, in written constitutions which are believed to retain a permanent meaning, in our praise of works of art as immortal masterpieces which last as masterpieces but a few years, in fact, in so many and such childish devices that one needs only a few examples to prove the point. But if this desire is real and as widely disseminated as one thinks, then it would be futile to try to eliminate it by argument. For the effectiveness of premises is in part psychological. They cannot in the nature of logic be proved, but must be accepted because of the plausibility of their implications. Though for centuries men have believed in the principle *ex nihilo nihil*, which would imply that the material universe had no beginning and will have no end, they have continued to believe in the story of creation. Similarly, since there was no proof that everything was a conglomeration of atoms and that only atoms and the void really existed, men might and, as it turned out, did reject that hypothesis in favor of one which would gratify their hearts' desire more fully. The Epicurean materialism was a beautifully simple theory and, what is more, in harmony with observation. It may well have led to peace of mind by removing the two main sources of mental disturbance. But if along with the fear of death went the hope of immortality, and with the fear of the gods the desire for a supernatural father, then it seemed to destroy as much good as evil. It was not the least intelligent of the Fathers who said, *Credo ut intelligam*. And one has only to contemplate the history of Catholic dogma to see that philosophy was bound to be vanquished in the battle with faith.

V

The main contributions to logic during this period were made by the Stoics, though, if we had more Academic writings, it is likely that the disciples of Plato would also be seen to have continued the logical tradition of their master. Speusippus' distinctions between homonyms and synonyms (Aristotle *Categories* 1a), his interest in definitions, his work in taxonomy, may all show that he was a logician as well as a metaphysician and ethicist, but since we have so little on which to base an opinion, we may as well pass over him lightly. The same may be said of Xenocrates and Crantor.

1. Epicurus, we are told, had little use for logic in any form. There is no fragment which attests this, but in the *Life* by

Diogenes Laertius (x. 31 ff.) we read that the Epicureans rejected logic and dialectic as misleading. Students of Nature have only to let things speak for themselves. The tests of truth are sensation and concepts (*prolepses*) and feelings and, to use the translation of Bailey, "intuitive apprehensions of the mind."[71] These require no further substantiation. They are true. They are the foundation of all knowledge and when we have to pursue knowledge of that which cannot be perceived, we must base our interpretations on phenomena (Diogenes Laertius, x. 32). Yet Epicurus admits that reason contributes something to knowledge and says that "all thoughts arise from sensations through coincidence, analogy, similarity, and synthesis" (x. 32). Just what reason contributes is no clearer than the difference between analogy and similarity. But it should not be forgotten that we are basing this on the writings of a very confused and frequently unreliable reporter.

We see an example of Epicurus' use of reason in the *Letter to Herodotus* (39). First of all he lays it down as an axiom that nothing is created out of nothing, for, if it were, then anything could be created out of anything indifferently. This is a rule of scientific methodology and preserves one from attributing effects to random causes. He had previously said that, in Bailey's words (*Epicurus*, p. 21), "we must keep all our investigations in accord with our sensations, and in particular with the immediate apprehensions whether of the mind or of any one of the instruments of judgment, and likewise in accord with the feelings existing in us, in order that we may have indications whereby we may judge both the problem of sense perception and the unseen." The use of the *ex nihilo* is to be applied to problems of the "unseen." But it seems clear that Epicurus thought it was justified by sensation or at least by some sort of experience, since all our ideas are based eventually on sensation. But no such principle could possibly be based on sensation, immediate apprehensions, or feelings, since by

---

[71] See his Appendix to *Epicurus*, pp. 259 ff., and Appendix III to *The Greek Atomists and Epicurus*, pp. 559 ff., for the meaning of this phrase.

their very nature these experiences are those of an individual person definitely dated and localized. Uncriticized experience moreover shows us daily things which seem to be created out of nothing, chickens coming out of eggs where previously there had been nothing but a gelatinous mass of albumen and yolk, plants coming out of hard seeds which have neither leaves nor flowers, compounds coming out of elements, and the only reason why we do not accept the judgments made on the basis of such experiences is that we have accepted the principle *ex nihilo* before we have enjoyed the experiences in question. The person who has not already accepted the principle believes wholeheartedly in creation *ex nihilo*, and the reason why Epicurus had to formulate it was precisely because such people existed. They base their judgments on what they see, not upon a critical investigation of what is obvious to any eye. If the principle, moreover, were actually "in accord with" sensation or the other forms of immediate experience, there would be no reason to announce it with such solemnity, for all such experience, he says, is equally true. On the other hand, in his *Principal Doctrines* (23 and 24; Bailey, p. 100) he grants that some sensations are false.

His second principle is that nothing is destroyed into nothing, and his argument here is, again in the translation of Bailey (p. 21), "if that which disappears were destroyed into that which did not exist, all things would have perished, since that into which they were dissolved would not exist." Regardless of the possibility that the consequence might not follow, unless one accepted a further axiom that all possibilities must be realized, it is again clear that Epicurus is utilizing a purely dialectical argument. No possibility of that sort could be corroborated by any experience, for there is no experience so sweeping that it encompasses all possibilities. One can argue to a probable consequence of the present situation; we are used to doing it in practical matters. We can say that in the past we have found certain causes followed by certain effects and that, in order to eliminate the effects, we must eliminate their causes. As a common-sense rule of thumb, nothing could work better, but the rule itself is no part of immediate experience, but at most a crude generalization from the experiences of many similar sequences. To what degree and in what respect they must be similar in order to be a sound foundation for induction is another matter into which we need not go here. But we do not seize upon any kind or degree of similarity as a basis for induction. Some similarities seem relevant to our problem and some do not. One of the similarities between certain animals is the "element" in which they live, but we no longer find it wise to classify them according to their habitat into terrestrial, aqueous, aerial, and perhaps even igneous animals, though in popular speech we still speak of birds, beasts, and fishes. Be this as it may, the principle which unexamined experience shows us continually is destruction, and it has taken centuries of criticism to convince the naïve person that when a piece of paper is burned, its substance is not destroyed. For, say what one will, the visual paper is destroyed and, if there was printing upon it, that is destroyed too, and all the argument in the world to the effect that the carbon which was in the cellulose of the paper still remains cannot convince one that nothing has been destroyed. This principle is as *a priori* as any other rule of methodology.

His third principle echoes an argument of none other than Parmenides, surely one of the least empirical of philosophers. It runs (Bailey, p. 21), "The universe always was such as it is now, and always will be the same." So far this might be interpreted as an antique version of the nineteenth-century principle of the Uniformity of Nature. But the Uniformity of Nature in its usual presentation was equivalent to the belief that the same causes always produce the same effects. But this is not exactly what Epicurus meant, for in another place (*Letter to Pythocles* 87; Bailey, p. 59) he admits that sometimes there are several theories which harmonize with phenomena.[72] He is talking about "the

---

[72] The reasoning in this passage, as in those just discussed, seems to me so vague that I have preferred to quote Bailey's translation rather than translate afresh. In this passage in particular I fail to grasp the argument. He says, "When one accepts one theory and rejects another, which harmonizes just

whole" and argues that "there is nothing into which it changes: for outside the universe"—i.e., the whole of things—"there is nothing which could come into it and bring about the change." So the Eleatic reasoned that the universe could not move, for there was no place into which it could move. It could not change, for it would have to change either into itself, which would not be a change, or into something else, and there is nothing else. Epicurus' argument is equally dialectical, in fact, verbal. For if the universe is the whole, clearly there is nothing leftover. The question is what meaning one could give to the term, the whole. As a matter of fact, the parts of the whole might move about in the empty space between them and thus produce all sorts of changes which had never existed before. The meteors which hit the earth are within the whole, and when they change the earth by their impact, they change the whole. But we are simply indicating the limits of Epicurean empiricism and what we have said suffices for our purpose.

Regardless of whether one thinks highly of logic or not, a philosopher is bound to do some reasoning and Epicurus cannot be censured for using the tools of his trade. He can, however, be criticized adversely for not having seen how far he was departing from his first principles. What logic he had resembled Dewey's logic of inquiry, perhaps more fittingly called epistemology. Here he introduced some new ideas which, though they were not of much influence in the classical period, are of interest today. The main idea of this sort is that of the *prolepsis* or anticipation. It is his reply to the problem of *Meno*. A *prolepsis* seems to be an anticipation on the part of a man of the nature of what he is looking at or for. It is, Diogenes Laertius reports Epicurus as saying

---

as well with the phenomenon, it is obvious that he altogether leaves the path of scientific inquiry and has recourse to myth." Why? If a second hypothesis harmonizes just as well as a first with phenomena and the harmony with phenomena is the standard for the acceptance of a hypothesis, then on that basis alone we have as good a right to accept one as the other. Bailey's commentary on this passage, though detailed as far as textual problems are concerned, does not appear to me to discuss this particular point.

(x. 33), "a memory of what has frequently appeared before one." We say, for instance, "Such and such is a man." When the word "man" is spoken, this memory image or concept arises before one and one recognizes what is meant. "And we could not seek that which we are seeking unless we had previously known it" (x. 33). If we are asked, Is that object a cow or a horse? we have to know what each looks like before we answer. But similarly, when we want to know what something is, we first have to have an anticipation of what we ought to find, a hypothesis of what the object will look like. The *prolepsis* thus takes the place of the Platonic idea recollected from prenatal existence.

If Epicurus had other views about dialectic or logic or methodology, his literary remains give us no evidence of what they were. He probably assumed the usual methods of reasoning to be valid, simplified them, refused to discuss their subtleties, or the problems internal to their structure, and let it go at that. What we are told of the Stoics is somewhat different.

2. Zeller concludes his estimate of Stoic logic with the words, "The whole activity of the Stoics in the field of logic was simply devoted to clothing the logic of the Peripatetics in new terms, and to developing certain parts of it with painful minuteness, whilst other parts were neglected."[73] Every student of the history of ancient philosophy is indebted to Zeller not only because of his exhaustive research, but also because of his extraordinary ability to organize the ideas which his research had revealed. At the same time it must be remembered that what seemed important to a man writing in the middle of the nineteenth century does not always seem so to us and that what seems unimportant to him may take on new importance to us.

In the first place their distinction between the *logos* unexpressed and the *logos* which is expressed, the meaning of a term and the term itself, seems at least to me of a certain value. It is true that Aristotle in the *Posterior Analytics* (i. 10. 76) had distinguished between the outer word and the word "within the

---

[73] *Stoics, Epicureans, and Sceptics*, p. 118.

soul," and he may have meant by that distinction exactly what the Stoics meant by the λόγος προφορικός and the λόγος ἐνδιάθετος. If so, let the credit be his. The importance of the distinction is that it does away with the belief that logic has to do only with little black marks on a piece of paper, the outward sign of the meaning, and is not concerned with thoughts. The old-fashioned notion of logic as the art of correct thinking seems to be rooted in this conception and, instead of dealing with assertions the only interest of which is their form, the logician is forced to turn his attention to judgments made by human beings on specific occasions. When this distinction is grasped, then it becomes understandable that the logician should also be busied with criteria for factual truth and not merely with formal consistency. In the words of Sextus Empiricus, quoted by Zeller (p. 72, n. 1), it is the possession of the inner word which differentiates man from the lower animals. The beasts too have sounds which they utter for certain signals, but they do not think.

It is the meaning of the outward signs which is interpersonal and uniquely incorporeal. It makes it possible for two people to mean the same thing when using different sounds to express it. And though I have found no text to justify this, it follows that the overindividuality of meaning is what makes the *consensus gentium* a court of appeal. For if the meaning of terms and judgments were corporeal and individual, no two men could ever agree except by accident and the possibility of all men having common notions would be very slight. Now the mere fact that all men do share certain beliefs is no proof of their being right, but the Stoics saw in the irresistibility of ideas a criterion of their truth. If all men, one might argue, feel the irresistibility of the same ideas, that must be because the individual differences of language, sensation, images, and whatever else might differentiate one man's experience from another's, have been canceled out. These differences would be corporeal or rooted in matter. The residue, being immaterial and the same in all minds, would turn out to be that which was universally believed. But if the force of conviction is a test of truth, such beliefs would have to be true.

The difficulty does not lie so much in our doubts concerning universally held beliefs as in the process by which highly individual experiences could at last eventuate in highly similar beliefs. For the Stoic maintained that all ideas arose from sensations, just as the Epicurean did. Out of sensations arose images, according to Zeno (fr. 55; von Arnim, Vol. I, p. 17), which were impressions made upon the soul (fr. 58). But in order to impress itself upon the soul, a thing must exist, and the forceful, the *cataleptic*, impression or image is the impression of an existent thing and hence true. To such images we give assent (fr. 61). The difference then between opinion and knowledge is simply the degree of firmness or strength. Opinion in the doctrine of the Stoics, says Sextus Empiricus (fr. 67), is the weak and false assent given by us, whereas knowledge (fr. 68, from Stobaeus) is "the steadfast and strong and unalterable *catalepsis*" of the reason (*logos*). A *catalepsis* carries along with it the suggestion of a seizure. The soul which has a *cataleptic* image is seized by it, cannot resist it, is vanquished by it. There are unfortunately no fragments which give in any detail the process by which meanings are distilled out of sensory material, for not only must they lose their personal character, but they must in some sense of the word be the active judgment of the mind which makes them. The activity of the mind may be an illusion, to be sure, and perhaps the most reasonable interpretation of the doctrine is that when the interpersonal residue of sensory material has been produced in the mind, we have the illusion of activity. We think that we are making a judgment, expressing meanings of our own, but in reality the judgment is making itself in us.

In the second place, their doctrine of the categories included an item which was to have great influence in the early years of the Christian period. That item is the subordination of the categories in a definite series. The ten categories of Aristotle were independent of one another and no logical hierarchy could be set up among them. The Stoics' most general category was that of

Being, undifferentiated into kinds, later called *Something*, equally undifferentiated. This was then differentiated into *Underlying Substance, Quality, Manner,* and *Relation.* These would appear to answer the questions, What is the material? What sort of thing is it? What kind of thing is it? To what is it related? If then I say, This substance is square in respect to shape when seen from in front and is to the left of that object, I have successively refined my description and made it as a consequence more definite. Moreover the subordination of the categories appears when I realize that I cannot talk about a substance without giving it some quality, and that the quality will be of a certain kind and that the object in question will not be cut off from everything else but will be related to other things. It will also be noticed that one can begin with *Relation* and work backward, for if *A* is to the right of *B*, it will be because it is a spatial object, and if spatial, it will be of a certain kind, and if of any kind, it will be a substance. This ties in with the Stoic conception of the organic universe in which everything is tied to everything else. The conception is not yet that of a hierarchy of existence; it is rather that of a reticulated universe. But nevertheless the belief in the possibility of subordinating the categories was of great help to those later philosophers who, for one reason or another, believed in a cosmic hierarchy.

These two features of Stoic logic would alone make it of historical importance, though they are not the only elements in the doctrine which have interested historians of logic. We shall rest content with pointing them out since they became integrated into the tradition with which we are concerned. But meanwhile doubts were being developed about each of the ideas which we have been describing, and we shall now turn to the rise of skepticism.[74]

---

[74] For a thorough study of Stoic logic and its innovations, see Benson Mates, "Stoic Logic," *University of California Publications in Philosophy,* XXVI (1953), which not only points out its differences from Aristotelian logic, but gives detailed outlines of its formal structure, accompanied by comparisons with modern theories.

CHAPTER VI

Reason *vs.* Reason

AS IN ALL CIVILIZATIONS, so in the Greek, there had been a long tradition of nonrational belief expressed in myth and realized in religious practices. Fear of the gods and of semidivine powers of earth and sky made itself felt in various rites which are known to every student of ancient religions. Recent investigations into cultural anthropology have discovered the survival of barbarous superstitions among the Greeks as indeed among modern Americans. Sometimes such superstitions were rationalized as symbolic of deeper truths, though in what sense one truth is any deeper than another has never been satisfactorily explained. Sometimes they were held openly as literal accounts of supernatural forces which could influence the lives of men for better or for worse. If we may judge by our own times, there is a nostalgia even on the part of the more sophisticated members of a society for the practices of one's early forebears. As in the history of an art obsolete instruments become beautiful in and for themselves, so it looks as if in the history of ideas the loss of literal truth is balanced by the acquisition of figurative truth and what once was a straightforward statement of fact turns into a metaphor. When one surveys the history of civilization in Europe, one gets the impression that nothing is lost, but that ideas, institutions, and artifacts are retained by investing them with what I can only call a new significance. If one's ancestors loaded a scapegoat with their sins and put it to death, their children give a god the same horrible function. The survival of armies and their use in settling international disputes, in spite of the clear fact that almost all members of society think of them as ineffectual tools and of their acts as abominations, is as good evidence of the conservation of obsolete instruments as any that could be found.

What is even more curious is that there seems to come a time in the history of a people when the conflict between ideas which can be held with some show of reason and those which are grounded in folklore eventuates in the victory of the latter. One would imagine that when a certain state of education had been reached, folklore and superstition would surrender and thought disciplined by philosophy would take over. But on the contrary the rational way of founding belief seems always to be conquered by the irrational or the nonrational, and such phrases as "the traditions of the race," "the ways of our fathers," "the cry of the blood," are pronounced with such solemnity and heartfelt conviction that they seem to mean more to those who hear them than the theorems of scientists and the syllogisms of the philosophers. Whether this is because people require the sentiment of close attachment to the past, however obtained, or because reason cannot answer all the questions which we ask of it, I do not know. What explanations I have seen all turn out to be the question rephrased in declarative form. Such terms as the Collective Unconscious, the Spirit of the Race, or the Social Memory do have an emotional aura which gives them an explanatory appearance. But one might just as well say that a symbol is retained even when what it used to symbolize is rejected, as to say that it has a deeper meaning stored up in the memory of the people as a whole.

That the intellectual climate of Greece changed after the days of the early Stoics and Epicureans, that the critical powers of an Aristotle or a Plato became ineffectual in the third century B.C., is common knowledge.[1] But an intellectual climate consists in what people, flesh-and-blood individuals, believe and express. There is no society which ever existed in which all its members were agreed about everything. A cross section of the most enlightened society of today would show a stratification of belief running from the most savage superstition to the most critical philosophies. But nevertheless there is a statistical predominance of certain shared ideas at any time and in any society and it is that which determines the climate in question. One has only to read the newspapers of the United States to see that scientific knowledge is far from having gained a foothold in the minds of most of the people. Pseudosciences, such as astrology and folk medicine, race prejudice, savage religious rites, are probably embedded in the lives of more people than a cool appraisal of evidence. It would be folly to think that higher education could uproot these growths. In the very nature of things higher education can never be spread throughout a whole population. Even if everybody is capable of understanding the more difficult branches of the sciences and philosophy, someone has to do the work of a society, and in actuality more people, vastly more, have to do it than can be engaged in mathematics, astronomy, physics, logic, chemistry, and their companion studies. The educated class never controls a free society, for in the first place it has not the numbers, and in the second, its special work is too absorbing of time and energy to permit political and social control.

But also there is something self-defeating in the rational scrutiny of any area of inquiry. Reasoning is based on premises, on basic metaphors, on ritualized methods of verification, and all of these may turn out to be shaky foundations on which to build a way of life. From one point of view all philosophy is skeptical. Philosophy asks questions not only about the nature of things, the an-

---

[1] See E. R. Dodds, *The Greeks and the Irrational*, p. 248, for an excellent brief statement of both the disease and attempted explanations of it.

swers to which are the natural sciences, but also about beliefs, experiences, traditions, customs, which are accepted with docility by the people in general. Xenophanes was a skeptic about the theological beliefs of his contemporaries; the Milesians doubted the veracity of their sensory impressions, for otherwise they never would have advanced such a view as that everything was water, or air, or some primordial mixture of things; Heraclitus doubted the stability of what seemed permanent; Socrates doubted the customary definitions of the various virtues; Plato doubted the veneration in which the poets were held; the Sophists were notorious doubters of ethical and political traditions. As soon as a man criticizes sensory experience, he is properly called a skeptic. Philosophy and science as well, for, as everyone knows, there was no distinction between the two in ancient times, feed on doubt. If nothing were doubted, there would be no science and rational inquiry would cease to exist.

But there is another type of skepticism, which is a criticism of knowledge itself, any sort of knowledge, and which in its extreme form maintains that we cannot arrive at the truth. It is an old story, which needs no repetition here, that such skepticism is self-refuting, since it holds to the truth of at least one proposition, the invalidity of all knowledge. But most skeptics have maintained a more limited form of doubt, holding that most knowledge is subject to severe criticism and yet that some beliefs, if only that life requires the holding of certain assumptions, are accepted either for their pragmatic value or for the peace of mind which they will bring one. Sometimes it has been said that such assumptions fit in with the general experience of the race or tribe or social group with which one's lot is cast, and that was more or less the position of Aristophanes in his caricatures of Socrates and Euripides. Sometimes, as in the case of William James, it is held that one has a right to believe in certain ideas, such as the existence of God, though no sound proof could be given for it, on the ground that a man who believed in God would live a better life than one who did not. James never explained how a person could be induced to believe in something which he knew could not be proved. The Abbé Bautain maintained that what one could not justify by reason could be justified by faith. Tertullian in the second century, speaking of the Incarnation, pronounced the famous sentence, *Credo quia ineptum*, as if anyone could believe in something which was based on evidence but only a saint could believe in the logically absurd. Kant was to say that though a belief in the existence of God, the freedom of the will, and the immortality of the soul was contrary to reason, yet we needed such beliefs in order to live a moral life. He never doubted the possibility of being moral in the world as described by science. But it is questionable that, when one reaches such beliefs, one is induced to change one's mind by demonstration. The beliefs in question, vague as they are in meaning, are ground into one in childhood and the force of habit makes one cling to them with devotion.

Again, the idea that the experience of the race as a whole is worth more than the experience of any individual is not an implausible doctrine, assuming that one knows what racial experience is. If all people have believed in gods, incest taboos, the superiority of their own tribe to all others, then such beliefs may be held to be identical with common sense. Common sense was said to be the test of some truths by the Stoics, the French Traditionalists at the end of the eighteenth century, and the Scottish philosophers who followed Reid. But this differs little from the notion that the value of a work of art is to be determined by something called the Judgment of Posterity. When a literary critic says that Homer, Vergil, Dante, and Shakespeare have always been admired and that therefore they are among the greatest of Occidental poets, what is he doing other than basing his opinion on the collective opinion of a group? The appeal to authority in religious, ethical, and aesthetic matters is a commonplace, nor does the appeal actually involve counting each and every nose, but only those noses which have been sniffing at the questions at issue. There is no logic in this, to be sure; if there were, no one would appeal to authority, to tradition, to common sense. No serious person ever maintained that in matters of fact, such as the shape of the earth, the atomic weights of the elements, the velocity of light, the average rainfall of Java, one should look in the books and see what mankind has always thought about them.[2] But in matters of policy, questions of better and worse, there is a certain justice perhaps in first discovering what the consensus has been. If there has been a consensus, it may be wise to follow it, if only for the sake of social peace. And if social peace is more desirable than discussion and the steady illumination of the problems of life, then there is all the more reason to pursue it.

There are some problems, such as the squaring of the circle or the invention of a perpetual motion machine, which have been proved to be insoluble. People who persist in working for their solution are usually given bad names. No one at the time of my writing these lines, to take another type of example, has discovered a formula for the occurrence of the prime numbers, but still, one imagines, there are mathematicians working away at one. It has not by any means been proved that such a formula is undiscoverable. To refuse to bother one's head about the former type of problem would be wise; to turn away from the latter would be foolish. But periodically there have appeared on the philosophic scene men who, contemplating the disagreements of philosophers, have maintained that there was nothing but sorrow to be gained from such investigations, and they saw no value in making themselves miserable over matters which could only eventuate in misery. Socrates, for that matter, when he turned away from cosmological questions to ethical questions, presumably did so because the former could do nothing toward the betterment of life. Whenever men put peace of mind ahead of the search for truth, regardless of the field of inquiry in which it is to be found, they take much the same point of view. If the proper study of mankind is man, its propriety is measured by its proximity to man's immediate problems. If at the present time someone says that it

[2] No one, that is, except the Legislature of the State of Tennessee.

would be more important to work for international peace than to explore the interplanetary spaces, he would not be saying anything foolish. But if the two major adversaries could use their energies in traveling through the heavens, it might divert their attention from killing off the human race. Unfortunately what they learn from their astronautical adventures will probably be put to military use anyway and one can understand the attitude of Candide in such cases, cowardly as it may appear.

There was, then, in Greek tradition much that would make for skepticism. There was the criticism of the senses which proved misleading in many situations: that form of skepticism was part and parcel of scientific inquiry. There was also skepticism about traditional mythology; the treatment of Homer as a mythographer whose stories must be interpreted allegorically is evidence of this. We have already referred (Chapter 2) to the debate between Apollo and the Furies in the *Eumenides* of Aeschylus, which illustrates the ethical problems which the favoritism of the gods aroused. Euhemerus, whose writings are lost, explained away the gods as culture heroes whose benefits had been so great that men deified them after their death.[3] Among the sayings of Socrates we find the famous sentence interpreting the oracle which had pronounced him the wisest man in Greece: he was the wisest only because, whereas others knew nothing but thought they knew something, he alone knew nothing and knew that he knew nothing. In the early Platonic dialogues he is portrayed as a questioner, not as a dogmatist. But the very method of the dialogues, with its pros and cons, its satirical intention, its failure often to reach any solution of the problem which it had set out to investigate, could

---

[3] Later, rulers rather than culture heroes were deified during their lifetime. Dodds, *op. cit.*, p. 258, n. 32, gives the Greek text of a poem written by Hermocles on the occasion of the deification of Demetrius Poliorcetes.

It runs:
> Other gods are far distant,
>   Or have no ears,
> Either they exist not or pay no heed to us,
>   But you we see before us,
> Not wood nor stone, but real.

lead men to take a skeptical attitude toward many questions. Moreover, if all we can know is that with which we were endowed before birth, then why do more than try to bring that endowment into light? Finally, if knowledge is the contemplation of eternal ideas embedded in sensory objects, why do more than look and see? I am not saying that Plato himself would have approved of any of these inferences; in fact, I am fairly sure that he would have disapproved of them, but that does not mean that others took his point of view. In fact, as we shall see, his own school, the Academy, became the stronghold of skepticism.

The kind of skepticism in which we are interested here is that which results from a rational criticism of reason itself. This form of skepticism could not but fortify the other types.

I

Skepticism as an accepted name for a philosophy is usually said to begin with the mysterious figure of Pyrrho, one of the many ancient philosophers who did no writing. A fourth-century figure, his one aim seems to have been peace of mind. The earliest testimony to his philosophy, if we omit the eulogies of his disciple, Timon, comes to us from Cicero, who lived about three hundred years later than the man whom he was discussing. Cicero is not an exceptionally gifted thinker; he was after all a lawyer, a man who wrote in his book on duties (*De officiis* ii. 51) that one need have no scruples against defending a guilty person unless he be nefarious and impious. "The Multitude desire this, custom suffers it, humanity indeed permits it." And he adds, "I should not dare write this, especially since I am writing about philosophy, except that it had been in agreement with that most serious of the Stoics, Panaetius." To his way of thinking Pyrrhonism had long been exploded.[4] If so, there would seem to be no pressing reason to mention it, and indeed Cicero tosses the Skeptics aside as he does

---

[4] *De officiis* i. 6; *De finibus* ii. 35, v. 23; *Tusculanae disputationes* v. 85.

the views of everyone with whom he happens to disagree.[5] Yet there are hints of what Cicero believed to be the tenets of Pyrrhonism here and there. For instance, he tells us (*Academica* ii. 130) that according to Pyrrho, the Sage does not even feel those things which are indifferent morally but lives in a state of apathy. In the *Tusculan Disputations* (ii. 15) we learn that in agreement with Zeno and the dissident Stoic, Aristo, he held that pain was indeed an evil but that other things were worse. In the *De finibus* (ii. 43) we are told that he again agreed with Aristo in saying that there was no choice between the best of health and the most serious illness, that (iii. 11) all things were of equal value, that (iii. 12) the *honestum* "was not only the highest good but also the only good," that (iv. 43) Pyrrho's conception of virtue leaves nothing whatsoever to be sought for, though it might be replied that if peace of mind or apathy is the end, then we ought to seek for peace of mind.

Such snatches are not very rich in content. They tell us simply that according to a person who thought the views discreditable Pyrrho was essentially a moralist, that he saw nothing to choose between one value and another, and that virtue (the *honestum*) was the one and the highest good, though if it were the one good the adjective "highest" would be replaced. We have then to turn to a later authority and happily possess one in Sextus Empiricus, who not only did not think Pyrrhonism an exploded and rejected doctrine, but actually believed in it. Since Sextus lived in the latter part of the second century A.D., something must have occurred to keep the life in skepticism for one hundred and fifty years after the death of Cicero. A partisan of a philosophic or other doctrine is not usually its best historian, but in the absence of anyone else, we must rely mainly on Sextus.

---

[5] See, for instance, his treatment of Epicurus. In *De natura deorum* i. 72, he speaks of Epicurus, *Quae . . . oscitans halucinatus est;* in ii. 46, he says that he was a person *non aptissimus ad iocandum minimeque resipiens patriam;* and earlier in the same work (i. 61) he asks, *Quid dixit quod non modo philosophia dignum esset sed mediocri prudentia?* But the indexes to any edition of Cicero will provide copious examples of his sectarianism.

Sextus opens his *Outlines of Pyrrhonism* by saying that there are three main kinds of philosopher: the Dogmatists—Aristotle, Epicurus, the Stoics "and some others"—who believe that they have discovered the truth; the Academics, Clitomachus and Carneades, to whom we ourselves must add Arcesilaus, who maintain that it cannot be grasped; and the Skeptics, who continue to seek it. Hence the skepticism which is upheld by Sextus is not the denial of the utter impossibility of knowledge. The skeptical way of thinking may be called (i. 7) either "investigative" or "suspensive" or "dubitative," from its persistent search for answers, its suspension of judgment, or its habit of doubting. It has taken the name of Pyrrhonism from Pyrrho's more weighty and more manifest application of the method. The Skeptic is essentially the man, he says (i. 8 ff.), who can test appearances by judgment and suspend judgment when there is no more probability on one side of a question than on the other. Appearances are simply sensory impressions, our perceptions, and they are opposed to noetic objects, our concepts. The distinction between sensation and thought was obviously traditional and was to continue into postclassical philosophy. But Sextus is thinking of the judgments which we make about perceptions or on the basis of perceptions, not on the sensory components of perception. If, for instance, we have come to a conclusion which is a generalization from a number of sensory impressions, we then test a new experience by applying to it that generalization in order to see whether the two agree or not. This process of comparison, Sextus is careful to say, may be applied to two impressions or to two judgments as well. In short the agreement between impressions, judgments, and generalizations is the test for reliability which he uses most frequently. This is surely an acceptance of the Law of Contradiction in extended form and, when utilized as a criterion of reliability—or truth for that matter —it turns reason against itself.

It is at this introductory moment that Sextus (i. 12) gives us the reason why the Skeptic behaves in this manner. He does so "in the hope of attaining calm" (*ataraxia*), a term also used by the

Epicureans. Presumably the ancient philosophers were more subject to unrest and perturbation when confronted by unsolved problems than the moderns. "Men of great innate ability, since they were troubled by the conflict in things and doubting which side they ought to agree with, came to seek what is the truth about things and what falsity, so that by the decision they would acquire calmness of spirit. The source of the skeptical program is above all the confronting of every proposition with an equally true proposition, for from this we believe we come to the point of no longer dogmatizing."

Pyrrho's disciple, Timon, is reported by Eusebius, via Aristocles (*Praeparatio evangelica* xiv. 18. 2), to have believed that there were three subjects of inquiry: (1) What sorts of things exist? (2) What attitude ought we to take toward them? (3) What benefit is there in them for us? Now one might imagine that the inevitable answer to the first question would be at least a classification of things, let us say, into material and immaterial, animate and inanimate, terrestrial and celestial. But not at all. Pyrrho, if Timon is right, was thinking of good and evil, and he replied to the question by saying that things appeared to be equally "indifferent and unstable and undecided" and "because of this opinions are neither true nor false. Consequently one ought to put no faith in them but be without opinion and without inclinations and unmoved, saying of each thing that it no more is than is not, or that it both is and is not, or that it neither is nor is not. Those behaving in this way, says Timon, will benefit by attaining first the ability not to speak and after that calm of spirit." It will be obvious that the epistemology behind this attitude is not unlike that of Gorgias, though the motivation is quite different. But Timon, as reported by Eusebius' report of Aristocles, gives us none of Pyrrho's reasons for his beliefs and we can only guess at them. One thing stands out, however, and that is that once again knowledge of the unstable seems to be impossible. Knowledge is still thought of as a mirroring of a stable object. Plato was willing to go as far as saying that one might reach true opinion of the sensible world, but even Aristotle, so often hailed as a great empiricist in contrast with his master, maintained that there could be no knowledge of particulars.

The indifference of things, their instability, and their lack of "decision" in all probability meant that one thing was no better than another, no more fixed in the realm of Goodness than in that of Evil, no more capable of inducing one to decide in its favor than against it. For if what he was seeking was calm, to be attained by silence, he was not thinking of the metaphysical character of things but of their relation to the good life. That may justify Cicero's statement of the indifference of good health and serious illness, to which we have already referred. Men may prefer health to sickness, but in the scheme of things one is as good as another. So the Stoics preached resignation to whatever befell one; one might as well be resigned, since there was nothing which could undo the past. The apathy or calm or silence which resulted might seem like a kind of bovine stupidity, but, according to Diogenes Laertius (ix. 69) whom I quote reluctantly, among the Skeptics it resulted in gentleness. This quality of gentleness was the absence of anger and the refusal to condemn anything. When achieved, it was not much different from Stoic apathy; but it resulted from an entirely different cause. For the Stoic, like Spinoza later, reached his goal by understanding the causal law; once you knew why things happened, you would lose all emotional disturbances concerning them. You would neither rejoice over nor regret whatever might happen. But the Skeptic, believing that such understanding was always illusory, since it could not really be reached, accepting the inevitable state of ignorance, ceased to worry.

This did not prevent Timon, whatever may have been true about Pyrrho, from castigating other philosophers in the most scurrilous manner. It was he apparently who invented the story that Plato had bought the books on which he based the *Timaeus* and to which he made no acknowledgment.[6] Zeno the Stoic is

[6] This is reported by Aulus Gellius, iii. 17.

described as a fussy old Phoenician woman in the shadowy gloom; she limps along holding her little fish basket, with a mind less able than a musical instrument which no one is playing (Diogenes Laertius, vii. 15).[7] In fact, Eusebius reports Aristocles as saying that Timon railed at all philosophers except Pyrrho (*Praeparatio evangelica* xiv. 18. 6). This is hardly a spirit of either calm or gentleness. Moreover, in spite of his skepticism, in his *Indalmoi* (*Images*), as quoted by Sextus (*Adv. math.* xi. 20), he speaks as any other philosopher, saying, "Now I shall relate how things appear to me, possessing an account which is a correct criterion of truth, telling how the nature of the divine and the good lives forever, from which the most balanced life proceeds for mankind." One wonders whether the emphasis in these lines is put on how things appear to Timon or on the correct criterion of truth. Since the verses are quoted by Sextus, it is unlikely that they are presented in a wrong light. He cannot be claiming an insight into a truth which transcends appearance, and if he is simply telling us what criterion is embedded in phenomena, then it seems unlikely that they would give us any evidence of an eternal divinity or goodness. Moreover, in another fragment (Diogenes Laertius, ix. 105), he is quoted as saying, "But appearance prevails over all, whatever its source." Putting the two passages together, we may perhaps interpret them as maintaining that whatever criterion of truth exists, it will be found in appearances, and that one can base a theology and ethics on appearances which will supplant that based on dogma. But this is a fairly wild conjecture and is offered as no more than that.

---

[7] Literally, this is "less able than 'what-you-will'" and is usually translated as a musical stringed instrument. The word is used, according to Liddell and Scott, "when one is uncertain about a word." But, assuming the meaning of a musical instrument, a musical instrument is stupid unless someone is playing it.

II

Athenian philosophy in the Middle Academy developed another skeptical tradition. We have seen how the Early Academy went in for metaphysical constructions whose foundations were largely allegory and number mysticism. The Middle Academy, whether because its members were disgusted with such vaporous phantasms or because they thought they were reverting to what they believed to be the true spirit of Platonism, turned to doubt. Sextus (*Outlines of Pyrrhonism* i. 1. 3) distinguishes between the Academics and the Pyrrhonists on the ground that the former flatly denied the possibility of reaching the truth, whereas the latter kept searching for it. Cicero in his book on the Academics (i. 4. 17) maintains that both the followers of Aristotle and those of Plato had "composed out of the fertility of Plato a certain fixed formula of doctrine, and this in fact was full and copious as well, but on the other hand they abandoned the Socratic manner of discussing problems in the light of universal doubt and the refusal to assert anything. The result of this was what Socrates would in no way have approved of, a certain art of philosophizing and an order of subjects and outline of doctrine." Arcesilaus, the first of the skeptical Academics, may have been reacting against this dogmatism. For in the treatise *On the Nature of the Gods* (i. 5. 11) we find Cicero presenting Arcesilaus as one who followed Socrates in giving forth no positive assertions.[8] If, in spite of Cicero's weaknesses as a historian, we accept his accounts, we may also attribute to Arcesilaus the view that all sensory appearances are false (*De natura deorum* i. 25. 70). If all such appearances are false, then we might be expected to turn to purely conceptual knowledge, such as might be thought to be discoverable in mathematics, in their place. But this was not the way of Arcesilaus.

On the contrary, whether because he did not accept the Intel-

---

[8] He is also inconsistent with what he said elsewhere—or what he was going to say—that Skepticism was an exploded doctrine; and he continues by adding that, though in *Greece* it had no longer any adherents, yet *usque ad nostram viguit aetatem.*

ligible World at all or because he thought all ideas were derived from perceptions, he simply maintained that we must suspend judgment (*Academica* ii. 18. 59). For what would be more absurd than to give assent to the unknown? In fact, he is reported, again by Cicero (i. 12. 45), to have maintained that "nothing whatsoever can be known, not even that which Socrates had retained"— to wit, that he knew he knew nothing. "Thus all things he thought were hidden in darkness, nor is there anything which can be either perceived or understood, wherefore nothing ought to be either asserted or approved of and one must always restrain one's rashness and prevent any lapse from restraint, for such rashness would be too obvious, should something either false or unknown be asserted, nor is there anything more shameful than for assent and approbation to run ahead of knowledge and perception. To this way of reasoning he was faithful, so that, arguing against the opinions of all men, he induced most to accept his point of view; consequently, when equally strong points were found for both sides of the same question, it was easier to withhold assent from either."[9]

It is clear that when a man says that appearances are false, he must have some criterion of falsity. But it might also be argued that, if one has a criterion of falsity, one must also have a criterion of truth. When Arcesilaus withholds assent from propositions both sides of which are equally probable, he is only being prudent; there is simply no sense in accepting or rejecting a proposition if the evidence *pro* is equal to the evidence *con*. It is certain, as Aristotle says, that you will be alive or dead tomorrow, but it is not certain which you will be. Today the chances are that you will more likely be dead than alive tomorrow, but after all we need not stickle at that. In such a case no assent can be given to either

---

[9] Though it reduces Cicero's authority as a reporter, it should be pointed out that he then proceeds to say that this point of view is in harmony with that of Plato, "in whose books nothing is affirmed and many things presented on both sides of a question." The second clause is accurate, but how would the first apply to the *Symposium, Timaeus, Republic, Laws, Phaedrus, Ion, Apology, Crito,* or *Phaedo?*

alternative and suspension of judgment is certainly appropriate. But if we maintain that all knowledge is false, we are saying something quite different. I am merely raising the question of how one knows that it is all false rather than true.

On the other hand, once one has accepted the Law of Contradiction, one has at least a criterion for distinguishing between consistent and inconsistent sets of propositions, and if one is convinced that two propositions are contradictory or imply contradictory conclusions, one has at least that much ground for refusing to give assent to the pair. That fact alone would not prove that neither of them was true or false, for of two contradictory propositions, one may well be true. But if, alongside of their evidence of contradiction, a person also knows that the probability of each being true or false is the same, then all he can do is to reserve judgment. The matter is complicated by the question of the status of perception. Perceptions are always of individuals, never of universals, *pace* Santayana. This was agreed upon by all. Assuming that one would be able to put such perceptions into words, a manifest impossibility, for some words in any declarative sentence are bound to be universals, then one could not have any knowledge of a perceptual nature and no perception could ever contradict another. If at this moment I am suffering from the heat, that clearly is not contradicted by the proposition that earlier today I did not suffer from the heat or that later today I shall not suffer from the heat. Hence if Arcesilaus really believed that all phenomena were false, he may simply have meant that none was truer than any other, since all of them, when verbalized, would have to include date and place and respect. And since no two dates and places and respects, when attached to a given individual, are ever the same, clearly one would have to revise one's theory of truth in order to call any of them true or false.

Arcesilaus, we are told by Sextus (*Adv. dogm.* i. 150 f.), did not lay down any criterion. Combating the Stoics with their notion of self-evidence, the cataleptic image, he pointed out that fools as well as sages find certain beliefs self-evident and compelling. If the *catalepsis* occurs in a case of perception, it is worthless, since one assents not to perceptions but to judgments. One cannot assent to anything which says nothing, and *red, hard, sweet* are inarticulate until they are incorporated into judgments. But the Stoic doctrine did apparently maintain that the cataleptic images were perceptual and the proper thing for the Stoics to do was to withhold assent. But at the same time Arcesilaus maintained something which is almost incredible in view of what we have already said. For he went on, again as Sextus tells us (i. 158), to hold that in all matters of choice and rejection, the wise man will follow that which is "reasonable" (*eulogos*) and that in so acting he will follow the right course. "For happiness comes from wisdom, and wisdom resides in right living, and right living is whatever is done with a reasonable justification. He then who pursues the reasonable will follow the right course and be happy."[10] But we are given no indication of what the reasonable was or how it was discovered. This in fact gives some support to Sextus' comment that in reality Arcesilaus was a dogmatist (*Outlines of Pyrrhonism* i. 33, 234) and induced his pupils to doubt in order to instill into them "the dogmas of Plato." As the Chimaera of Homer (*Iliad* vi. 181) was a lion in front, a serpent in the rear, and a goat in the middle, so, said Aristo the Stoic, Arcesilaus was Plato in front, Pyrrho in the rear, and Diodorus the Megarian in the middle. This may well be a just estimate of him.

III

Carneades, a second-century figure, was also "head" of the Academy. There is a story in Lactantius (*Inst. div.* v. 14) to the effect

[10] C. J. De Vogel in her *Greek Philosophy, a Collection of Texts* (Leyden: Brill, 1959), par. 1105, p. 199, says, "Surely this is not what was taught by Arcesilaus, but we may infer from the passage that A. replied to Stoic opponents saying that sceptics do have a rule for practical life in the eulogon, and that happiness, *which according to the Stoics is the end of life*, depends on it, since it is attained by phronesis." (Italics in text.) Arcesilaus may not have taught that happiness was the end of life, but the weakness of his position lies in his use of any criterion of choice whatsoever.

that when Carneades was on a mission to Rome, he debated on the nature of justice in the presence of Galba and Cato the Censor. On one day he gave all the arguments in favor of justice and on the morrow all those against it—one would like to have seen the faces of his Roman auditors as he did this. If the story has any truth in it, he would have been a sort of Sophist to whom argument was a game and truth a matter of little importance. This may have been the case, for according to Sextus (*Adv. dogm.* i. 159) he maintained that there was absolutely no criterion of truth whatsoever, neither reason, nor perception, nor imagination. "For all these deceive us collectively." But here again he does not tell us what he means by "false" or deceptive, or how, if there is no criterion of truth, one could possibly tell whether anything is false or not. One learns that one is deceived by testing a statement with what one knows is true. And, as a matter of fact, in practice Carneades did have a criterion of truth, for he admitted that the main trouble with perception was that sometimes its objects were true and sometimes false. It was our inability to tell which is which that puzzles us. This inability arises from our failure ever to penetrate the perceptual screen to whatever it is which it conceals. But he does believe that it conceals something. If there is no self-evidence in any of our perceptual experiences, then clearly we have to devise some criterion which is not embedded in perception. To the Stoics that criterion was the cataleptic impression. To David Hume, who took much the same starting point as that of Carneades, it was the vivacity of impressions as contrasted with what he called ideas, faint copies of impressions. To Descartes it was the clarity and distinctness of our ideas, grasped apparently by the "natural light." But none of these solutions would have been satisfactory to Carneades, for the simple reason that they too are criteria relative to the observer, fools being as convinced of the truth of illusion as sages are dubious of it.

Carneades was not willing to leave the field to fools and sages indifferently. He admitted that, as we have said, all images (sensory impressions) are images of something—this he must have taken for granted—and that something is both the sensible object (that from which the image comes) and the perceiving mind (that in which it occurs). But from here on his discussion, as presented by Sextus (i. 168 f.), becomes more cloudy. In relation to the perceived object, the image may be true or false, "true when it is harmonious with the perceived object, false when it is discordant with it." The crux of the matter is our ability to spot the harmony and the discord. Whether this is accomplished pragmatically, that is, by acting as if the presentation was harmonious and seeing what happens, I do not know. The example he gives is that of Orestes' mistaking his sister, Electra, for one of the Furies. But this will not do, since there was no way for Orestes *while seeing the girl* to know that she was not one of the Furies. We, who are on the outside of the situation and know that he was suffering from a hallucination, can easily tell that the experience was hallucinatory. But this begs the question. Carneades had no difficulty in saying that the hallucination was not harmonious with the object, that is, with Electra, but Orestes was not confronted with both his sister and his hallucination at the same moment and hence could not make the comparison, even if he had known what tests of harmony to apply. Hence Carneades reverts to something very like the Stoic cataleptic impression, if not identical with it. If the impression is obscure, owing to the smallness of the object or to its distance or to the weakness of one's vision, then it cannot be trusted; if it is forceful and clear, then it is the criterion of which we are in search. But again, while one is presented with a perception, it will appear obscure only in reference to other similar impressions which were clearer, but that takes us well beyond the immediate experience in question. Carneades seems to recognize the extension of experience in time, for he says, once more in the words of Sextus (i. 173 f.), "when it is extended, one impression becomes more probable and more vivid in kind than another." It would seem then that, as in Hobbes, the repetition of a given kind of impression reinforces itself, presumably on the analogy of a habit. To paraphrase the conclusion, one might say that a repeated impression, remembered to be like others, leads us to project a sort of objectivity into it. It becomes true. But this again is not unlike the theory of *prolepsis*. "In fact," he concludes, "our judgments and our acts are tested by what happens on the whole."[11]

To this general criterion Carneades adds others. First (i. 176), he recognizes the fact that no impression occurs in isolation, but always in a context. It will be both probable and linked to others.[12] Thus one does not simply see a man, but one also perceives his complexion, size, shape, motion, speech, in surroundings of air, light, day, heaven, earth, friends, "and all the other things." When all these appear to be harmonious, we believe the more strongly in what we see. The harmony here might seem to be the harmony between the whole cluster of impressions; for instance, if we see the man in the daytime, we ought to be able to see also the color of his eyes, or if we see Socrates surrounded by other men, they ought to be his friends. But this is not the meaning of Carneades. On the contrary, he says that we know already what to expect of Socrates, and the harmony in question is that between what we are seeing now and what we expected to see. Sextus' own example is drawn from his profession, medicine, and he points out that no diagnosis is made on the basis of one or two symptoms, but from a concurrence of symptoms. But here again one first knows what symptoms to look for, the concurrence of which is a sign of the disease which one suspects the patient to have, and the harmony is between one's *prolepsis* and what is before one. This is doubtless a reasonable procedure, but it must nevertheless be pointed out that it could never arise out of immediate perceptions by themselves.

---

[11] Cf. the frequently repeated Aristotelian slogan that the natural is that which happens on the whole. Since the truth is that which happens "according to nature," the criterion of Carneades is not much different from the Aristotelian idea of the natural. My use of the date of a man's experience in criticizing Carneades' criterion of harmony is derived from A. O. Lovejoy's *The Revolt against Dualism* (2d ed.; La Salle: Open Court, 1961).

[12] R. G. Bury's translation in the Loeb Classical Library is "irreversible." But, though his knowledge of Greek is much greater than mine will ever be, the sense of the passage is that a perception occurs grouped with others.

Furthermore, if one is going to invoke the aid of memory or learning, then one has to devise some criterion of its truth also.

A third test, which is more trustworthy and the "most perfect," produces judgment. It is contextual and is applied bit by bit. One runs through all the details of the configuration of impressions to see whether any of them are possibly false, as if one were applying the fourth stage of the Cartesian method. These details include the ability of the judge to see clearly, the medium in which the object is seen, and the object itself. The medium may be too dark, the distance at which it is seen too great, the time of looking at it too short, and so on. To cite but one example (i. 187), a man entering a dark room sees a coil of rope and jumps over it thinking it to be a snake. But finding that it does not move, he starts to think that maybe it is not a snake. But then he reasons that snakes sometimes are motionless when cold, and tests his tentative conclusion by poking at it with a stick. He then decides that it is not a snake after all. Here once more the judging subject has an idea in his mind of what a real snake should be, sees something which looks like a snake, tests it by his already-acquired knowledge of how true snakes behave. His perception is whatever it is; it is his judgment which turns out to be false. But its falsity is not demonstrated by any immediate experience; it is demonstrated on the contrary by the consistency of a set of judgments. The situation is as if he had framed the following set of propositions.

(1) I am seeing a snake.
(2) But this object is motionless and all snakes move.
(3) But snakes are motionless when cold.
(4) Yet when poked with a stick, a snake will move.
(5) I poke it.
(6) It still does not move.
(7) Therefore it is not a snake.

In what sense of the word this exhibits a harmony of images, I leave to others to decide. Yet Carneades, in view of his sorites proving that there are no gods, would surely have rejected my version of his argument.[13] He apparently thought that what was discordant was the complete set of impressions and not the judgments based upon them.

We should perhaps say a word about Carneades' sophistic arguments, which are also reported by Sextus, but as they add nothing to the development of the tradition whose evolution we are attempting to describe, we shall omit them.[14]

IV

It was generally believed that without sensory impressions there would be no judgments, that in the final analysis all ideas are based upon perceptions. But perceptions were notoriously untrustworthy. Aristotle in his *Metaphysics* (1009b) had indicated some of their weaknesses, and Aenesidemus in the first century B.C. proceeded to systematize the bases of their untrustworthiness in his famous *tropes*. Carneades had said that color changes according to the percipient's age, state of health, whether he is dreaming or awake, the time of day, and so on (*Adv. math.* vii. 411–414). But Aenesidemus gives us a series of details which were incorporated into the epistemologies of almost every thinker who doubted the truth of sensory impressions. They are listed in Sextus (*Outlines of Pyrrhonism* i. 14. 36) and in Diogenes Laertius (ix. 79–88). We suspend our prejudice against the latter for this occasion and cite his version of them, since it is more detailed than that of Sextus and does not disagree with it. Perceptions then vary among individuals because of the following individual differences.

(1) *The difference among animals in regard to pleasure and pain, the harmful and the helpful.* "From this it may be concluded that they do not have the same impressions [as we] and that therefore in such arguments [as those about pleasure and pain] one should adopt a suspension of judgment."

---

[13] See the sorites in *Adv. dogm.* iii. 182.
[14] See *Adv. dogm.* iii. 138 ff.; also, Cicero *Academica* ii. 29. 95, 30. 98.

(2) *The natures of men and their peculiar temperaments.* "Thus Demophon, the butler of Alexander, was comfortable in the shade but shivered with cold in the sunshine."

(3) *Conflicting impressions of two or more senses.* "Thus an apple will look green but taste sweet and have a pleasant color. [Cf. Sextus *Outlines of Pyrrhonism* i. 94.] And the same shape, because of the difference in mirrors, seems different." In short, to what sense is one to give preference? Which mirror reflects the true shape?

(4) *Fluctuations in disposition,* such as health, disease, sleeping, waking, joy, grief, youth, old age, courageousness, fear. All of these will influence our sensory impressions, and every perceiver has some disposition of which he cannot rid himself.

(5) *Education, customs, traditional beliefs, national conventions, and philosophic assumptions.* These give rise to different notions of beauty and ugliness, truth and falsity, good and evil. They determine our ideas of the gods and the genesis and destruction of all phenomena. In short, no perceiver can emerge out of his educational background and see everything afresh and as if for the first time. His judgments therefore will be determined by that background and are in themselves no more than a reflection of it.

(6) *Mixtures and compounds.* Nothing appears purely or in accordance with its own peculiar nature. It is always in the air, in a certain light, in moisture or dryness, heated or cooled. But all these details influence the way the object will be perceived and it cannot be perceived entirely removed from any physical environment.

(7) *Distances, positions, places.* The size, shape, smoothness, straightness, and color of objects vary with the distance at which they are seen, the position in which they are placed, the angle from which they are viewed. This, by the way, is pretty good proof that the Greeks knew more about perspective than their medieval successors.

(8) *The quantity and quality of an object,* whether it is hot or

cold, its velocity, whether its color is pale or variegated, will all determine the way in which it will be perceived.

(9) *If an object is familiar or strange or rare*, it will be perceived differently from the way in which it would be perceived if it were commonplace. Aenesidemus exemplified this by earthquakes and sunshine: people who are used to earthquakes do not wonder at them, nor do we wonder at the sun since it shines during the day and we are used to it.

(10) *The relation of things to one another*, the light in relation to the heavy, the strong in relation to the weak, the better to the worse, the up to the down, determine how we shall perceive them. Many of our perceptions are precipitated out of relational schemata and we overlook the fact that when we feel something to be heavy, it is because it is heavier than something else which we are accustomed to. Thus nonrelational terms have their origin in relations. The comparisons we have made are forgotten and we judge the terms out of relation.

These ten tropes are grouped into three types by Sextus (*Outlines of Pyrrhonism* i. 14. 38): one which is based on the perceiving subject, whether an animal or man, whether this sense organ or that, whether the subject is healthy or sick or otherwise; the second, which is based on the object about which a judgment is being made, its quantity and qualities; the third, on a composition of the two, for such matters as spatial relations and mixtures are dyadic relations subsisting between subject and object. Sextus then proceeds to investigate in detail the various tropes. Though his arrangement of them is not the same as that of Aenesidemus, we shall roughly summarize what he has to say in his order, thus making reference to his text easier.

Of the differences among animals, in so far as these differences affect perception, one may infer, he says (i. 14. 40), that since some are produced spontaneously from fire (the salamander?), others from putrid water, others from vinegar, others from mud, others from rotting meat—my list is incomplete but will serve as a sample—it is likely that the dissimilarities and differences in mode of birth should produce equal dissimilarities and differences in what they perceive. The same would be true of animals produced through sexual union, or animals born from eggs or born alive, like men. Why this should be true may seem puzzling to the modern reader, but it should be remembered that the element, earth or water or air, out of which an animal is spontaneously produced would determine its "nature" and the question of whether we perceive like by like was by this time settled in the affirmative. Thus, though I am embroidering upon the text of Sextus, an earthly animal would be less capable of perceiving fiery, aqueous, and aerial things than an animal in which those elements were congenital. As for the animals, like men, who are born through sexual union, they come into the world predominantly either hot or cold, moist or dry, though some contain all the elemental qualities. Even men, it should not be forgotten, may be predominantly sanguine or melancholy, bilious or choleric, though the other humors will usually be present also. To do full justice to Sextus, one can say that if he failed to point this out in detail, it was because his contemporaries took it for granted. The question of how anyone knew whether the various origins of animals determined their perceptions or not, we can omit discussing. It was one of those *a priori* principles which even skeptics do not question.

As for differences in sense organs and other organs, he points out that men who suffer from jaundice say that what we see as white, they see as yellow, and men whose eyes are bloodshot see the same things as blood-red. "Since then of the beasts, some have yellow eyes and others bloodshot eyes, and some have transparent eyes and others eyes of other colors, it is likely, I think, that they perceive colors differently" (i. 14. 44). He then mentions a case of negative afterimages, the supposed nocturnal vision of some animals, optical illusions, such as those produced by pressing on one eyeball. Since mirrors can distort visual objects because of their diverse shapes, so the lenses of the eyes must change them also according to their shapes.[15] Hence it is likely that dogs, fish, lions, and men have visual perceptions which vary in size and shape. Similar differences should be expected in the case of the other sensory organs, for they all differ in their constitution. We can also learn something of the varieties of perceptual experience from the likes and dislikes of the various animals (i. 14. 55). "Sweet oil appears very pleasant to men, but to beetles and bees it is intolerable; olive oil is beneficial to men, but when it is poured on wasps and bees, it is destructive; sea water to men is a disagreeable and poisonous drink, but fishes find it very agreeable and potable." Pigs prefer to wallow in the mire rather than to bathe in clean water. Some animals eat grass, others bushes, others are shrub eaters. Some live on seeds, some on flesh, some on milk. The paragraph is a compilation of all the curious feeding habits, repugnances, desires of the various animals, which were of so much interest to the ancients, who seem to have thought that according to Nature food should be uniform and behavior as well. But concludes Sextus (i. 14. 58), or Aenesidemus through Sextus, "If the same things are unpleasant to some and pleasant to others, and the pleasant and unpleasant reside in perceptions, then different perceptions arise in animals from the underlying objects." We see once more that the existence of an underlying object was not doubted.

This being so, we retain our ability to express our human impressions, but we have no evidence of the "nature" of things and must suspend judgment about it. For we have no way of appraising our impressions as superior to those of the beasts in so far as they are reliable witnesses to reality. In fact, there is reason to doubt their superiority in all cases. The dog, for instance (i. 14. 64), has more acute vision than we have, better olfaction and hearing. Moreover, it chooses the agreeable and avoids the disagreeable; it possesses the art of hunting; it recognizes friends and

[15] Visual impressions were generally supposed to be a function of a beam which flowed out of the eye and met a beam which emanated from the object.

distinguishes between them and strangers—witness the recognition of Odysseus by his dog Argus—and it can also reason, using "the fifth complex indemonstrable syllogism." Then follows one of the most famous animal stories in European intellectual history, used constantly to prove the intelligence of the beasts well into the seventeenth century.[16] The story was originally told by Chrysippus. A dog tracking his prey comes to a triple fork in the road. (For reasons not given, the prey in question held to the road instead of darting off into the woods.) The dog sniffs down the first branch without scenting his quarry, then the second with similar results, and then without sniffing dashes down the third. He therefore must have said to himself, "My prey went by this road, or by that, or by the third; it did not go by the first two; therefore it must have gone by the third, and I do not have to sniff at the road to prove this." But this is not the end of canine talents. The dog can relieve his suffering, removing thorns from his pads and when a foot hurts, he raises it and limps along on the three others. He knows enough to eat grass when he needs an emetic. He is in short as virtuous and intelligent as man and, as far as his sensory powers are concerned, he is better-equipped than we are.

So much as a sample of the comparison between men and beasts. But we next come to differences among men, who differ from one another in both soul and body. The argument is the same. Individuals vary as much in what they perceive and in what they like as men and beasts do. Who then is to be chosen as the critical man? What individual has perceptions which are the standards for all perceptions? Not only that, but there is a striking disagreement among the testimony of the various senses themselves. Paintings look to the eye as if they were in relief, but to the touch they are felt to be flat. Honey tastes pleasant to some but it looks unpleasant. Most objects, moreover, are likely to be a complex of different sensory qualities. The apple, cited by Diogenes Laertius, seems smooth, odorous, sweet, and yellow.

---

[16] See G. Boas, *The Happy Beast* (Baltimore: Johns Hopkins Press, 1933).

Does it have all these qualities in itself, or has it one quality which varies according to the sense which perceives it? The issue becomes still more complicated when one brings in the condition of the observer, conditions which may be natural or unnatural: age, motion or rest, confidence or fear, grief or joy. All such conditions are accompanied by perceptions which are peculiar to them and once more we are in the situation of not being able to set up one condition which is more authoritative than any of the others. Are the young man's perceptions or the old man's correct, the well man's or the sick man's? Since there is no way of finding a person who is not in some condition at the time of perceiving something, it is a hopeless task to select any single condition as determinative of truth. There is hardly any need to go painfully through the long list of individual variations in perceptions for they all come down to the same thing: perceptions vary with a set of circumstances which are inescapable and of which none are uniform. The only reasonable solution is suspension of judgment.

There are two or three observations about this argument which are of some interest, for the dispute still is pertinent in empirical circles. First, if we really are confined to our impressions which are so variable, where did the idea of a permanent underlying or real object come from? That things have their own nature independent of anyone's perceptions is never doubted by any of the Skeptics. They simply conclude that, whatever it is, it is unknowable. Assuming that their premise of what R. B. Perry felicitously called the egocentric predicament was true, would it not be impossible for anyone to have the idea of such a nature? Upon what would it be based? Certainly not upon the stream of perceptions. Yet we do have the idea. If, however, all ideas reflect perceptions, it must come from perceptions. And it cannot do so.

Second, what is the basis for the argument that we are confined to the perceptual screen? This is a universal proposition and, if Aenesidemus is right, there could be no grounds whatsoever on which such a proposition could be erected, and, what is more, there would be nothing but accident which would ever give anyone the idea that universal propositions existed. Each man would be confined to his own special idiosyncratic world nor would he ever discover this, since even the people with whom he might be talking would be merely his perceptions, as far as he could tell. To know that people vary in what they see according to age, health, acuity of perception, and so on, is to have compared them with one another, to have accepted *bona fide* their reports on what they perceive, to have communicated with them as if they were as real and independent as one is oneself. But the moment one communicates with another person, one accepts at least the possibility of interpersonal meanings of both terms and sentences. It would seem wiser to follow Pyrrho and learn to say nothing. Certainly it would make no sense to say that what I taste as sweet you are tasting as bitter, for there would be no evidence of the existence of any one thing which would be sweet or bitter, of anything, that is, which might be the "underlying object" in which such qualities inhere. At most one might conclude that two tastes have been reported on a given occasion.

Third, regardless of underlying objects and real natures, it seems to be assumed by Aenesidemus that there ought to be agreement in our reports of what we severally observe. There ought to be some way for men to "get together," as if it were anomalous for a group of human beings to have conflicting impressions. But ever since the publication of the *Double Words* it had been known that people neither believe nor feel the same things. The Skeptic could at most note this and perhaps indicate the conditions under which the differences arise. This would be a protopositivism and no question about the reference of the observations to anything beyond or below or above them would be relevant. But apparently the tradition that all qualities inhered in stable external objects was too strong to be resisted and, by accepting it, the Skeptic was confronted with a problem which did not emerge from his positivism but from the tradition against which it was a protest. The Skeptic, it would seem, should not have suspended judgment about real natures, but should have denied their existence. As far as the ethical problems were concerned, the question of good and evil, justice and injustice, that is still being debated in terms which Aenesidemus himself laid down. But here again, one might reasonably ask why anyone should imagine that all men ought to find the same acts good and evil. That there might be more chances of social harmony if men did agree in their moral judgments—and acted in accordance with them—is probably true. But, if one is laying down the foundations for a system of "values," it seems absurd so to construct it that it will conflict with all the facts of valuation which are known.

To return now to Aenesidemus, he was not satisfied with denying the interpersonal validity of perceptual judgments; he also attacked the current methods of causal explanation. As reported by Sextus (*Outlines of Pyrrhonism* i. 17. 180), this concept can be tested by Eight Tropes. First, since all causal explanations deal with unperceived beings, there is no perceptual evidence for them. Presumably here he is assuming that "real" causes, or perhaps the causal influence itself, the transmission of power from cause to effect, are never perceived. Similarly Malebranche and Hume were to deny the empirical nature of causation some centuries later, a denial on which Kant was to build still later. Second, there is a tendency always to look for one cause of each type of event, whereas there is always the possibility of explaining any event in a variety of ways. For instance, though Sextus gives us no examples of a multiplicity of causes, if a man is shot down in the street, is the cause of the shooting, which could not have occurred unless the assassin happened to meet his victim, to be found in the chain of events which brought the assassin to that spot at that time or in that which brought the slain there? Is it to be found in the psychological condition of the assassin or in something done previously by the victim which brought on that condition? If we define the cause as that in the absence of which the event would not have occurred—we are talking here of a particular event and not of a class of events—one can see that the number of such things is very great and any one of them would do. Third, the causalists assign to orderly events causes which are not ordered. This would seem to rest upon the assumption of a parallelism in the order of causes and effects, or it may mean simply that in a series of events which occur in a determinate order, such as the fall of rain and subsequent growth of vegetation followed by decay, the Dogmatists who are under attack introduce one cause for the fall of rain, such as the intervention of Zeus, another for the growth of the vegetation, such as some vital principle in the seeds, and a third for the decay of the vegetation, such as the summer's drought. In this case, if it be one of which Sextus or Aenesidemus would approve, the first series is orderly, one factor following another in observable regularity, whereas the second is disorderly in that three different and unrelated causes are invoked. Fourth, the Dogmatists project into the unperceived world the linkages of the phenomenal world, whereas no one knows—or can know—how the world beyond phenomena proceeds. Without accepting the distinction between phenomenal and subphenomenal worlds, one can see that there is always a tendency to universalize the formulas which describe the known world so that they will be applicable to that which lies beyond its frontiers. Thus it seems strange and indeed incredible to some that the dynamics of the macroscopic world, the world of billiard balls, should not be true of the subatomic world. It has been pointed out by Hunsaker[17] that in the early period of aeronautics it was taken for granted that, since air was a fluid, it would follow the same laws as water. But it was discovered that the laws of hydrodynamics could not be transformed into those of aerodynamics. The "unknown" in these sentences of mine is clearly not the unknown of Aenesidemus, but the principle may well be the same. Fifth, and this seems too severe a criticism, the Dogmatists "explain things according to their own hypotheses about the elements, rather than according to common and generally accepted methods" (i. 17. 183). But

---

[17] See Jerome C. Hunsaker, "A Half-Century of Aeronautical Development," *Proceedings of the American Philosophical Society*, XCVIII, No. 2 (1954), esp. p. 122.

what common and generally accepted methods were there in the first century B.C.? Or, if it is Sextus who is in question, in the second century A.D.? It seems a bit unfair to blame a theorist for trying to apply his own methods since he believes them to be right and proper. Sixth, and this was to be repeated by Bacon, they neglect negative instances. Seventh, they are often self-contradictory. Eighth, and this too was one of Bacon's criticisms of his contemporaries, they try to explain the unknown by things equally unknown.

Whether Aenesidemus was attacking a particular school of philosophers, as Bréhier thought,[18] the Stoics and Epicureans, or all aetiological explanation, need not disturb us. For there are no details available on other types of explanation dating from this period, though we may surmise that Peripatetics and Platonists still existed and published their thoughts. We can see by an examination of his criticisms that he believed (1) that all explanations should be confirmed by observation; (2) that one should admit the possibility of multiple causes; (3) that the causes assigned to a series of events should exhibit some order, though not necessarily the order of the problematic events; (4) that one should work from generally accepted hypotheses; (5) that attention should be paid to negative instances; and (6) that an explanation should be at least as certain as that which is being explained. We shall see below that Sextus attacked the very idea of causation and shall postpone a discussion of his personal views for the time being. But as far as Aenesidemus is concerned, the questions which emerge from his criticisms are (1) whether causality is observable or not, and (2) whether there are any generally accepted methods. We shall see that Sextus himself did not believe in the possibility of observing causation, and if the Stoics and Epicureans disagreed with this, and if the Peripatetics were still teaching and writing—and they were— and since primitive Neoplatonism was flourishing along with all

---

[18] See Emile Bréhier, "*Pour l'Histoire du Scepticisme Antique*," reprinted in *Etudes de Philosophie Antique* (Paris: Presses Universitaires, 1955), p. 185.

sorts of theological and pseudotheological schools, and since the new allegorical method was being extended from the interpretation of texts to the interpretation of nature, and since belief in sacred texts which by their very nature were incontrovertible was spreading, then if the criticism comes from Sextus, he must have been thinking only of his own empirical method in medicine. But the germs of this chaos were already present in the time of Aenesidemus.

The remaining critical comments of Aenesidemus need not occupy us much longer. He argued against the objective existence of good and evil on the ground of man's disagreement over what they are. Men all agree (Sextus *Adv. math.* xi. 42) that the good is what appeals to them, but they differ on what this is. They agree that a woman should be well formed, but disagree over what beauty of form is.[19] And indeed one might think that at least in matters of sexual attraction taste would be uniform. Analogous disagreements pervade the whole area of valuation, and since the good is what men find good and there can be no superhuman standard of goodness, then arguments about the "nature" of good and evil are futile. Nothing could be true in the opinion of Aenesidemus unless most people agreed about it. This was as true of matters of fact, the sensible world (Sextus *Adv. dogm.* ii. 8), as of matters of policy. He was willing to assert, in spite of his Ten Tropes, that "some things appear to all in common and some only to an individual," and the former are true. But he does not, as Sextus reports, tell us what such things are. As Bury points out in the introduction to his translation of Sextus,[20] "Aenesidemus was not consistent in his Scepticism." This is

---

[19] This might seem to be one of the strangest features of human nature. Leaving the Greeks out of the discussion, one has only to look at a series of paintings of the female nude, from Botticelli, through the Mannerists, Rubens, Boucher, Ingres, Delacroix, Courbet, to Matisse and Picasso, to see how taste in women has changed. See, for example, the illustrations in Kenneth Clark, *The Nude, a Study in Ideal Form* (New York: Pantheon Books, 1956), esp. chaps. 3 and 4. It is true that Sir Kenneth is speaking of ideal form as contrasted with real nakedness. But actually a reference to the book is superfluous, for if anything is commonly accepted, it is that men's taste in women varies.

[20] Loeb Classical Library, Vol. I, p. xxxviii.

no doubt true, but some of the blame may lie on the shoulders of his reporter.

V

It is with a sense of relief that one turns to a man whose writings are extant in bulk and for whose views we need not turn to secondhand reports. The works of Sextus Empiricus (second century A.D.) have survived in large measure and were frequently copied. Since skepticism was one of the most potent forces in the breakdown of ancient rationalism and therefore as part of the *praeparatio evangelica*, a person who would understand exactly what happened to the intellectual life of the pagans would do well to study Sextus with care. We shall not repeat all of his arguments in detail, but confine ourselves to those criticizing the criterion of truth, the "real" existence of good and evil, and the concept of causality. For clearly it is these three which are the main supports of any rational philosophy.

To begin with, Sextus makes a distinction between what I shall call validity, that is, logical consistency, and truth (*Outlines of Pyrrhonism* ii. 12. 138). This distinction is easily grasped, for we can all construct syllogisms, similar to those used by Sextus, which exhibit no formal fallacies and yet are not true to fact. Sextus' example is, "If it is night, it is dark; but it is night; therefore it is dark." This argument is valid, but since it actually is not night, the conclusion, though it follows from the premises, is false. But Sextus goes further and tries to show that the categorical syllogism is always a *petitio principii* (ii. 13. 163). He gives this example: "Socrates is a man; all men are animals; therefore Socrates is an animal." "If it is not immediately evident," he says, "that everything which might be a man is also an animal, the universal premise is not accepted, nor shall we grant it in the argument. But if it follows from the fact that a man exists and is also an animal, and therefore the premise, 'All men are animals,' is admittedly true, then at the same time that we say that Socrates is a man, we also agree that he is an animal too, so that this very argument suffices, 'Socrates is a man; hence Socrates is an animal,' and the premise, 'All men are animals,' is superfluous." This criticism was to be repeated in the nineteenth century by John Stuart Mill. Its cogency, as is well known, depends on whether we take the major premise in extension or in intension. If in extension, we should theoretically have to include Socrates in our survey of men before we could phrase the universal proposition. But if the meaning of "man" is "rational animality," we might not know that humanity implied animality, and, since no one ever argued in this fashion anyway when he wished to discover something, but engaged in syllogisms exclusively as a technique of exposition, the categorical syllogism could still serve as a corrective of thinking. But Sextus is looking for formal arguments which are both valid and true at the same time and which also imply conclusions which were not evident at the start, but emerged from the premises (ii. 12 143). This has turned out to be a demand impossible to satisfy, unless one reduces all formal reasoning to sets of tautologies. In such reasoning one substitutes terms for other terms with which they are synonymous and produces, as in the words of Henri Poincaré, a cascade of equations. But no such arguments have existential import, though one can of course always insert an existential postulate as one pleases.

Sextus also attacks all five forms of Stoic reasoning, hypothetical syllogisms in the affirmative, hypothetical syllogisms in which the minor is denied and therefore the major, disjunctive syllogisms with both an affirmative and a negative minor, and conjunctive syllogisms with a negative major. These too seem to Sextus to beg the question (ii. 13. 159). Thus if we argue, "If it is day, it is light; but in fact it is day; therefore it is light," the antecedent either is agreed upon or is not self-evident. But if it is not self-evident, it will not be accepted; if it is evident, then why go to the trouble of drawing the conclusion from it, for the conclusion is superfluous? Hypothetical syllogisms then suffer from the same weakness as categorical syllogisms, and this could, as a matter of fact, be tested by rephrasing them in the categorical form. Sextus makes no apologies for using hypothetical syllogisms in his proof of their circularity.

The question then resolves itself into finding some criterion of the truth of direct apprehensions or perceptions. We have already seen how Aenesidemus handled this question. Sextus adds little if anything to his predecessor. The problem is stated in this form (*Adv. dogm.* i. 25): Does there exist a criterion of things directly perceived or grasped by reasoning, and next is there a way of demonstrating by signs or by proof the existence of things not evident? If no such criteria exist, then the best we can do is to suspend judgment. Man, he says, is a truth-loving animal and moreover the most comprehensive philosophic schools act as arbiters on the most important problems. We have a vital interest then in discovering a criterion if one can be discovered.

The criterion, he says (i. 29), has two references, first to our acts, second to our assertions.[21] Taking them up in that order, Sextus emphasizes the fact (*Outlines of Pyrrhonism* i. 11. 21) that the Skeptic does not deny that the appearances are appearances of underlying objects; the question is whether the latter are what they appear to be. He orders his life in accordance with the phenomena in the following fourfold set of rules. First, he is guided by Nature; second, he is under the control of the emotions;[22] third, he conforms to traditional customs and manners; fourth, he is taught by the lessons of the arts. The guidance of Nature is the guidance of perceptions and thought; the control of the passions is exemplified by our giving in to hunger and thirst; tradition leads us to regard piety as good and impiety as bad; the arts in which we are skilled have taught us to apply them as useful. "But," he says (i. 11. 24), "we say all these things un-

---

[21] In *Outlines of Pyrrhonism* ii. 3. 15 ff., three references are given.

[22] ἐν ἀνάγκῃ παθῶν. Bury translates, "in the constraint of the passions," but does this mean "disciplining the passions" or "being constrained by the passions"?

dogmatically." The first two rules are clearly descriptive: we cannot live without perceiving things and thinking about what to do; nor can we live without eating and drinking. The second two, however, are regulative: we ought to follow tradition and we ought to profit from the arts. We recognize the demands of our nature as men and we have the power to modify our behavior for our good. But all this is only a *modus vivendi* the end of which is "calm *(ataraxia)* both in our opinions and in the moderation of our feelings toward the inevitable." Since he does not believe that anything is good or bad *by nature*, he remains unperturbed and does not worry about the course of events, taking calmly what the gods provide. The Dogmatists, on the other hand, make themselves miserable not only by arguing, but also by pursuing the good and avoiding the bad. The Skeptic is not in a state of absolute calm, for (i. 12. 29) there are certain experiences which are inevitable, such as feeling cold and thirst. But even here he is less disturbed than those who believe these evils to be rooted in the natural order. The Pyrrhonic tradition of seeking peace by the suspension of judgment thus continues unbroken. But even in its origins it was a surrender of the reason to the irrational.

The achievement of suspension of judgment arises through "the opposition of things" (i. 13. 31). The Skeptic opposes phenomena to other phenomena, thoughts to other thoughts.[23] Phenomena are opposed when one notes that a tower which appears round at a distance, appears square close at hand. Thoughts are opposed to thoughts when the argument to the existence of Providence from the order of the heavenly bodies is met by the reflection that the good often fare badly and the evil well. From here he passes on to an exposition of the Ten Tropes. These in his opinion show not only that there is no such thing as self-evidence of the truth, but that, since all thoughts derive from phenomena, there can be no self-evident premises of formal arguments. For if there is no way of knowing that two people are experiencing the same

[23] The *nooumena* of which he speaks are not of course Kant's things-in-themselves.

thing, regardless of their verbal reports, how can we know whether their judgments mean the same thing? And in view of such perplexity, one can only suspend judgment.

The criticism brought against the Skeptics of that day as well as of our own is that Skepticism is a self-refuting theory. If nothing is true, then Skepticism itself is not true. But Sextus clearly did not hold so extreme a form of Skepticism. He knew what a self-refuting position was (ii. 13. 185). But "since we do not think that any reasoning is certain and do not in every way say that those [arguments] in accordance with formal rules are not certain but that they appear probable to us," we are not in a condition of self-contradiction. "Those [arguments] that are probable are not necessarily certain" (ii. 13. 187). The probability of which he is speaking is of course not calculable probability, but psychological probability, i.e., that which seems plausible or convincing. What he is trying to avoid is dogmatism, by which he meant the conclusions of the systematic philosophers which went well beyond phenomena. Such conclusions he lists (*Adv. dogm.* i. 46) in so far as they concern the nature of a criterion. The list shows that philosophers are divided on this question, as they are on all others. But differences in opinions do not prove that none of the different opinions is right. At least one of his examples, that of Xenophanes, shows that the philosopher in question was not doubting man's ability to attain truth in every field, but only in regard to "reality." It is interesting to see how the notion of the two worlds survives even in those writers who believe that one of them is unknowable.

Sextus, as we have said, also turns his critical powers on the conception of causality. He follows his usual technique, to begin with, in pointing out the general disagreements about the meaning of the concept (*Outlines of Pyrrhonism* iii. 6. 13). He points to the three kinds of causation, which oddly enough correspond roughly to what is demonstrated by three of Mill's canons: "effective" or conclusive causes, the presence and absence of which are followed by the presence and absence of the effects, and variations in which are followed by variations in the effects; accessory causes, which accompany other causes, being insufficient in themselves; and associate causes, which contribute a slight influence to produce the effect. He is still thinking of causation in terms of force exercised upon a patient, if one may judge from his examples. It is only the first type which is of any interest, since the other two, which might have been conditions without which the first type would be inoperative, turn out to be nothing more than efficient causes of less than sufficient power. Sextus is willing to grant "that the existence of causality is probable" (iii. 5. 17), for, he says, "How could there be increase, decrease, genesis, destruction, motion in general, each of the physical and psychical effects, the ordering of the whole cosmos, and all the other things if they did not occur in accordance with some cause? And even if none of such things exists in the natural world, we shall say that it is because of something that they appear to us in every way to be such as they are not. Furthermore, anything could come from anything whatsoever, were there no cause. For instance, horses might come from flies, perhaps, elephants from ants." Other absurd events are cited to show that there is an order in nature, repeated series of regular events, which to him, at any rate, require explanation in terms of something to which their regularity is attributable. There is, to be sure, a paradox here, but one which has been overlooked by all who use natural order in, for instance, the cosmological proof of the existence of God as a First Cause. For traditionally, when things move regularly in what has been established as their normal condition, no reason is sought: reasons are asked when the regularity is interrupted. But when philosophers begin to talk about the world as a whole, the cosmos, the universe, Nature as a single system, then the regularity seems to demand an explanation. Sextus is aware that he is speaking of a special kind of causality, the cause of universal order, for he immediately proceeds to criticize the concept of causality when it is applied to things this side of the whole.

"It is impossible," he says (iii. 5. 20), "to conceive of a cause

until one has apprehended its effect as the effect produced by it."
For when we say that something is a cause, we have to think of
what effect it is the cause; it cannot just be a cause of anything
in general. And furthermore, when we think of something as an
effect, we have already in the back of our minds that of which
it is an effect. Thus, to use an example of our own, if we think
of rain as a cause, we also are thinking of that which it causes, e.g.,
the sprouting of seeds; and when we say that the seeds have
sprouted as the effect of something, and are not simply observing
that they have sprouted, we have already supplied the rain in our
minds as the cause. We are caught again in a circular argument,
for we have broken up a long event into two parts, the first of
which we call the cause and imagine that it exists as if cut off
from other things, the second of which we call the effect since it
has been cut off from the first. This can be done since, to revert
to our example, it may rain without any germination of seeds, as
in the late autumn, though the seeds, we may grant, will not
germinate without rain or some other form of moisture. My language may well be anachronistic, for it looks as if Sextus was
thinking of separated causal and effected beings, not of incidents
in a total event. But the principle is the same and the criticism well
taken, if we are willing to grant that we are dealing with our idea
of causality and not with any specific causal series. On the other
hand, Sextus does examine the relative dates of cause and effect
(iii. 5. 25 ff.). People say, he continues, that the cause must exist
either prior to the effect or simultaneously with it or after it. The
third possibility he dismisses as ridiculous, though the teleological
tradition might have given him pause, for the final cause never
exists until the event is completed, except "potentially." As for its
priority, causation is a relation—of two terms—and things which
are related have to be thought of together. (But do they have to
exist together, synchronously?) But if the cause has to exist along
with the effect, then it cannot bring the effect into being, for it
would have to exercise its causal power before the effect came
into being, in order to be its cause. The upshot of all this is that

we have no clear idea of causality and should suspend judgment when it is being discussed.

One might imagine that Sextus had already given the Dogmatists enough to occupy them, but he had not yet finished. Among the other dogmas which he attacked was the idea of motion as something caused by movers. This involves us in an infinite regress (iii. 10. 67), for whatever thing causes another thing to move must also be in motion, motion which will demand its moving cause in turn, and so on. I have found no discussion of the Unmoved Mover as a cause which acts by attraction and we may perhaps take this as evidence either that Sextus had not read *Metaphysics* xi, or that he thought the idea frivolous, or that he was unable to combat it. Nor have I found any reference made to Aristotle's thesis that something can touch something else without being touched by it.[24] If he had accepted the former of these ideas, he might have found a way out of the infinite regress. By accepting the latter thesis, he might have been able to accept also the idea of an unmoved mover, for if a mover is untouched, it is unmoved and the regress stops at it. I put more emphasis on this than may seem reasonable, but I do so because it is another indication of how little interest Sextus has in Aristotelianism. In fact, the references in his works to Aristotle are very few. Nor are they to what we think of as the salient doctrines. For instance, he is referred to as saying that length without breadth is conceivable,[25] that a Thasian existed who thought he always saw an image of a man walking in front of him.[26] He gives (*Outlines of Pyrrhonism* iii. 19. 137) Aristotle's definition of time as the measure of motion or rest, but is not sure that it does not come from Strato; he quotes him (*Adv. dogm.* i. 7) as saying that Zeno the Eleatic was the founder of dialectic and that Empedocles first studied rhetoric. He says that along with Theophrastus and other Peripatetics, he distinguished between the criteria of per-

---

[24] *De generatione et corruptione* 323a 33.
[25] Cited nowadays as fr. 29 (Rose); Sextus *Adv. dogm.* iii. 412.
[26] From *Meteorologica* iii. 4; Sextus *Outlines of Pyrrhonism* i. 14. 84.

ception and of the intelligible (i. 217); that the number of Aristotle's adherents is as great as that of the Epicureans (i. 328); that Aristotle said that the conception of gods arose from men's observation of psychic and celestial phenomena (iii. 20).[27] He makes a reference (ii. 33) to the *Physics* (iv. 5) and to *De caelo* (270b 6), and (ii. 37) to *Categories* (15a 14), on the six kinds of motion (or change). But in general his references show no detailed knowledge of Aristotle, and several of his references are from secondary sources. This may be an indication that Aristotelianism was a philosophy which had lost its hold on men's imagination by the end of the second century A.D., in spite of Sextus' remarks on the number of its adherents. Bréhier seems to be right in thinking that the target of his attack is the Stoics and, after them, the Epicureans.

If that is so, one of the reasons why he is interested in attacking the idea of causality is that the Stoics with their deterministic metaphysics and the ethical views which they based upon it would find their whole intellectual structure undermined if causality were proved to be unsubstantiated. The Epicureans were less vulnerable, for they believed in chance, though they made little of it. Their thesis that everything could be explained as falling atoms rested upon the hypothesis, announced much earlier by Democritus, that only atoms and the void were real. As a matter of fact, this doctrine should have proved helpful to Sextus, since it showed that our perceptions never tell us anything reliable about reality. But since it was held as a dogma and could not be proved, Sextus refrained from accepting it, as he refrained from accepting any dogmas about imperceptibles except as working hypotheses or as conventions which might or might not be true. Regardless of that, one can see that by his attacks on all metaphysical theories, on criteria of both perceptual and intellectual knowledge, on the doctrine of causality, he opened the door for any kind of nonrational belief that might care to enter. If there was any one thing which the rationalists stood for, it was the pursuit

[27] Again a supposed fragment (fr. 10 in Rose).

of reason whithersoever it might lead them. From the days of Xenophanes down to Cleanthes and Epicurus, philosophers had found the one corrective to unfounded opinion, superstition, and dogmatism in the rigorous application of the rules of logic, as they knew them, to any thesis that might be advanced. The skepticism of Sextus was itself a rationalistic technique and, whatever he may have said against the weakness of syllogisms and other logical devices, he himself used them all when he needed them. There was nothing else, other than flat dogmatic assertion, that he could do. But the hunger for rationality and the love of truth were not so strong as the desire for escape, peace of mind, calm, and possibly salvation, and these could not be found in reason. Reason could tell one whether such ends were worthwhile perhaps, but it demanded a kind of devotion which was fatiguing, disturbing, and difficult.

It is curious that the first uses of the rational method, as found in Socrates and the Eleatics, possibly even in the early Sophists, seem to excite the Athenian intellectuals rather than to depress them. Though argument was used for satirical and destructive purposes, as it always has been, it was, at least among philosophers, a help to the creative imagination, restraining it when it tended to become too fantastic and yet suggesting new roads upon which it might venture. We know too little about the Milesians and the Pythagoreans to say more than that they translated the ancient myths of cosmic birth and decay into rational language. But when we come to the figures of Heraclitus, Parmenides, and Democritus, we meet with that independence of mind which seems to us characteristic of the great scientific investigators. The double role of reason, that of criticism and that of construction, was played wholeheartedly by them, and apparently the mere fact that a belief was traditional did not give it special plausibility. The same may be said of both Plato and Aristotle. One may not accept the theory of Ideas, but the problems which it strove to answer remain our problems; they are not simply quaint notions that some antique thinker fabricated as one would tell a story or write a poem. If we still read with fascination the Platonic myths, it is not with the same kind of interest that we read the myths preserved in Ovid's *Metamorphoses;* on the contrary, we have an uneasy feeling that they embody in concrete form philosophic ideas too difficult to expound in scientific language. And as for Aristotle, it would be insulting to any possible reader of these words to point out for him the contribution of the *Metaphysics,* the *Nichomachean Ethics,* the *Politics,* or even the *Poetics,* to the incorporated thought of the West. None of this means that the ancient rationalists saw our peculiar problems, to say nothing of solving them. But they did establish the rules of the game which we are still playing. Aristotle, for instance, clarified certain methodological assumptions which are rejected only after the most careful analysis.[28] It is not out of a sense of piety to the past that we go back to him and to his master, but rather because we cannot avoid using their methods and puzzling over their problems. It is not so much a matter of their having found the right answers; many of their conclusions are absurd. But granted their premises, the conclusions usually follow. Moreover, the premises are intelligible. We know what Democritus meant by atoms, just as we know what Aristotle meant by purpose. The atoms of the former are not the atoms of Dalton nor are the purposes of the latter the purposes of Freud. But the meaning of the two terms is clear and what follows from their use is not shrouded in clouds of metaphor.

I am far from suggesting that reason creates its own premises, provides its own data, spins out of itself the questions which it tries to answer. I understand fully that no system of thought can be erected without basic metaphors, without observation, without the perception of problems, without myth, if one wishes. Even a mathematician has to know what he is trying to demonstrate before starting the process of reasoning. But nevertheless the rationalistic method is the only one which is self-correcting. By

[28] See G. Boas, *Some Assumptions of Aristotle,* pp. 8–30.

accepting as a rule of thought the Law of Contradiction, for instance, there is no escaping its power. One turns it upon oneself from moment to moment to restrain the flights of the imagination, to discipline one's power of invention, to supervise one's conclusions. The Skeptics did good service no doubt in calling men's attentions to fallacies both formal and material, but they did not and could not prove the unreliability of all knowledge. Nor did they even see the weakness of their own position. As a matter of fact, skepticism is symptomatic of a state of mind rather than a philosophic position. No one of any philosophic importance had maintained that there was absolute certainty to be found in his tenets. Most philosophers had recognized the indemonstrability of premises, the relativity of sensory perception, if not the difficulties in the notion of causality. But they had at least the courage of their convictions and continued the pursuit of truth. Philosophy began to totter as soon as someone gave it a moral, rather than an intellectual, purpose. For when one engages in an intellectual enterprise for peace of mind, the good of the state, or the greater glory of God, one tends to lose sight of one's errors and easily lapses into dream. This is amply illustrated in the rise of philosophic sects, the acceptance of authority, the justification of sacred texts.

CHAPTER VII

The Acceptance
of Authority

▭▭▭▭▭▭▭▭▭▭▭▭▭▭▭▭▭▭▭▭▭▭

THE DIVERGENCIES OF BELIEF which led so many of the
Skeptics to their skepticism increased as the cultural dominance
of Athens declined and that of Alexandria and then Rome grew
more vigorous. The one philosophic school which seems to have
maintained itself as a sect with orthodox doctrines was that of the
Epicureans, for the *De rerum natura* of Lucretius proposed no
thesis which Epicurus himself could not have subscribed to,[1]
though it dates from at least two hundred years after his death.
We have seen how the school of Plato developed into a form of
Skepticism which differed only in detail from that of the Pyr-

---

[1] See E. Zeller, *History of Eclecticism* (*Philosophie der Griechen, dritter
Teil, erste Abteilung*), trans. by S. F. Alleyne (London: Longmans, 1883),
p. 26: "Though many deviations from pure Epicureanism are perceptible in
Lucretius, on closer inspection they will be found to refer to traits which
merely concern the form of the poetic presentation, but do not affect the
scientific theories. The same may be said of other philosophers among the
later Epicureans concerning whom tradition has told us something."

rhonists. As for the Stoics, their later disciples, if we count men like Seneca among them, took their sustenance wherever they found it to their taste. Unfortunately Zeno and Cleanthes had no sacred bard who, if only because of the beauty of his verses, preserved a systematic account of what doctrines they upheld unanimously. The works of outstanding Stoics, such as Panaetius and Posidonius, have come down to us only in mutilated form.[2] When we come to Epictetus and Marcus Aurelius, not to speak of Seneca, their interests were so largely ethical that it is next to impossible to untangle their metaphysical doctrines from their sermons. But this is typical of the period with which we are at present dealing. When men maintain that the purpose of philosophy is to teach a prudent way of life, they cannot be expected to dwell on topics which would serve only to upset one's peace of mind. At the same time it is only fair to remember that if anything does survive of ancient philosophy, it is thanks to the Church Fathers, and they, it goes without saying, were not interested in preserving error except to the extent that it would serve as a horrible example to Christians.

In contrast to the capitulation of the Skeptics, the later Stoics maintained their faith in reason, but it was the reason of their intellectual ancestors, not their own. With due allowances made for the lost works, we can say definitely that in the writings of Epictetus and Marcus Aurelius the reason of which they speak is either a supernatural order, Nature, God, or Fate, which was the termination of the reasoning of their teachers, or simply a catchword which they use when they want some ground for their ethical ideas. One seldom finds any chain of reasoning in either man. In short it is not unfair to say that Stoicism had by their time become a religion whose basic tenets never were to be questioned. They used the word "reason" continually; but what they

---

[2] Ludwig Edelstein is now at work on an edition of the fragments of the latter. His article, "The Philosophical System of Posidonius," *American Journal of Philology*, LVII, 3, No. 227 (1936), 286 ff., gives one a synthetic account of what is left of the man whom Strato called "the most widely learned among our philosophers" (xvi. 2. 10).

meant by it was more frequently "authority" or "tradition" than logical processes

I

1. In the fourth book of his *De finibus*, which is Cicero's refutation of Stoicism, we find him objecting to the "asperities of style and roughness of manners" of the Stoics, but making an exception of Panaetius who "shunned their gloom and sourness" and was "gentler in his doctrines and clearer in his speech" (iv. 28. 78), but who, interestingly enough, "constantly quoted Plato, Aristotle, Xenocrates, Theophrastus, and Dicaearchus." If Cicero is to be trusted, Panaetius was also a confirmed eclectic. He abandoned the old Stoic theory of the *ekpyrosis* (Ps-Philo *De aeternitate mundi* xv. 76) and held that the world was indestructible. We are also told, by Epiphanius (*De fide* ix. 45), that he did not accept divination and said that theology was nonsense, though Zeller rejects this.[3] He argued against the use of astrology on the grounds that twins, who must have the same horoscope, nevertheless led different lives (Cicero *De divinatione* ii. 42). He also rejected the [Platonic] theory of the immortality of souls (Cicero *Tusculanae disputationes* i. 32. 79), on the ground that whatever is born must perish and souls are born, as is proved by the fact of pain, for whatever feels pain is susceptible to sickness and whatever may become sick may also die.[4] Thus he was no orthodox Stoic. In fact from what remains of his opinions, he was a moralist, a cultivated man of parts, without much to offer in the way of metaphysics.

2. The investigations of Edelstein help us to a clearer understanding of Posidonius. The goal of philosophy, according to him, was threefold: to lay down the presuppositions of knowl-

---

[3] *Op. cit.*, p. 51, n. 4.
[4] Cicero, in spite of his admiration for Panaetius, proceeds to show that his criticism of Plato is unfounded.

edge, to discover general, not special, statements, and to understand the whole, not the individual. He visualized the world as the product of two *archai*, one of which was active, the *logos* which was resident in matter, the other passive, matter utterly without quality, the substratum which in Plotinus was to be potentially everything and actually nothing. This matter was the substance and stuff of all things, but is known to us always as of some shape and quality. The distinction between the Two Worlds in this thinker arises from the way things are presented to us and the way in which they are in themselves. We make a distinction between the essence of things and their matter, but in reality there is no such distinction. One is always in danger of reading too much into a statement of this sort, but it looks as if Posidonius realized the importance of sharply differentiating between our intellectual construction of the world and the world itself, not simply that knowledge is different from its object—for almost anyone would be willing to admit that much—but that we use formulas, apply images, to the objects of knowledge which are our own and not pictures of that which we are trying to understand.

Just how far he believed the reason to be creative of forms or patterns of thought, we do not know. But that the schemata in which we envision things are ours and not contributed by the things which we know seems to have been one of his fundamental principles.[5] The resemblance between this idea and Kant's theory, both of space and time as forms of perception and of the categories as projections of our methods of understanding, is striking. Moreover, it will be noticed that God, whom Panaetius identified with the active *logos*, but who is nevertheless contained in matter, is also substance without form,[6] whereas in Aristotle the active reason, like the Unmoved Mover, is form without matter. But this makes God a universal *noumenon*, not apart from the phenomena in existence, but entirely apart from them in our

---

[5] Edelstein, *op. cit.*, p. 290.
[6] *Ibid.*, p. 292.

thought. Diogenes Laertius (vii. 148) emphasizes the pantheism of Chrysippus and Posidonius together, saying that they both believed the real nature (οὐσίαν) of God to be the whole cosmos and the heavens, but we can put little confidence in this report, since he had previously said that, according to Posidonius, the heavens were the guiding force of the cosmos (vii. 139), which would mean no more than that, as in Aristotle, the sphere of the fixed stars was the ultimate cause of all change this side of the Unmoved Mover. But for every metaphysical fragment, there are several ethical fragments, so that we can assert nothing firmly about the metaphysical and epistemological views of this philosopher until the critical edition, promised by Edelstein,[7] is published.

3. When we come to Epictetus, we find little about appearance and reality. He represents that orientation of metaphysics toward theology which was to supplant the kind of philosophy for which the classical philosophers were the spokesmen. In discussing Providence, a favorite topic of the Stoics, he is not satisfied with rational proofs but insists on bringing in simple everyday experiences also as evidence supporting the cosmological proof of a provident Deity. In his *Discourses* (i. 6) God is no longer that omnipresent spirit infusing all things, binding them together in sympathetic and organic union, but is clearly a creator. If He had made colors, he says, and not our visual power, what good would it have been? If He had given us eyes and nothing to see, that would have been equally futile. And if He had made both but had not created light? "Surely from the very constitution of the things which have been perfected we are used to showing that it is in every way the work of a Creator (τεχνίτου) and in no way put together without a plan" (i. 6. 7). Here we have a conception of God which harks back to the Demiurge of *Timaeus*, not to either the Unmoved Mover, or the Lawgiver of Cleanthes, or the cosmic *Pneuma*, or the happy gods of Epicurus, remote from all earthly interests. In fact, when he begins to speak of God's creating animals for human food, for farming, even for making cheese (i. 6. 18), one begins to wonder

[7] *Ibid.*, p. 322, n. 131.

whether one is not reading Bernardin de Saint-Pierre in Greek translation. Appearance and reality have now become the City of Man and the City of God. Anticipating Marcus Aurelius, he says (i. 9. 1) that one is not a citizen of Athens or of Corinth, but of the cosmos, "the greatest and noblest and most extensive of all . . . a society of men and God . . . [from Whom] the seeds have descended not merely into my father or my grandfather, but into all things that are generated and grow on earth, and above all into rational beings, for they alone happen to commune with God, since they are linked to Him in the harmony of reason" (i. 9. 4).

The same dualism, moreover, which is seen in the two Cities, reappears in the dualism between soul and body. Plato in *Gorgias* (493a) had said that the body is our tomb, playing upon the words *soma* and *sema*, and quoting two lines from the *Phryxus* of Euripides[8] which ask whether we are not dying as we live and living when we have died. Death thus in the minds of many thinkers was a release of the soul (the "vital principle") from its prison. But in spite of Plato's play upon words, he gives us a Socrates who does not treat his body with contempt, though he does refuse to be its slave, who is not an ascetic, though he is not a voluptuary either. By the time of Epictetus, the status of the body had changed. Despite Stoic materialism, the body is one of the main obstacles to freedom; it is beyond our control. The *Encheiridion* (1, 2) opens with a distinction between those things over which we have power and those over which we have no power. The latter include along with property, reputation, and business, the body. He even goes so far as to say that "disease is an impediment to the body, but not to our power of choice, if we do not give in to it. Lameness is an impediment to the leg, but not to our power of choice. And say this when anything happens to you, for you will find it an impediment to something else, but not to yourself." Or again, in the *Discourses* (iii. 22. 21), "My poor body is no concern of mine. Its

---

[8] There is some question of the source of these lines. See the commentary of Dodds in his edition of *Gorgias* (Oxford: Clarendon Press, 1959), p. 300. But Dodds assigns them to *Phryxus*.

parts are nothing to me. Death? Let it come when it will, either to the whole or to a part of it." If you keep the body clean, as you would keep a tool clean and free from rust, that suffices (iii. 1. 43). The care of such things is no task for a free soul, but belongs to Another, as he terms God. And in spite of his having said that the body should at least be kept clean, he also says (Stobaeus, Vol. V, p. 1105) that we tend it though it is the dirtiest thing that exists. Suppose we had to do for our neighbors' bodies what we do for our own? [9]

In the views of Socrates the body is that which must be controlled lest it overpower the soul. He is depicted in both the *Apology* and the *Symposium* as one who could withstand bodily pleasure not by denying the demands of the body, but by temperance. But in Epictetus the body has become an alien thing, a piece of flesh which one can completely reject. Free yourself first, he says (*Discourses* iv. 1. 111), from the most trivial things, a pot, a cup, then a tunic, a little dog, a horse, a bit of land; then free yourself from your body, its members, your children, your wife, and your brothers. Egotism and asceticism could hardly go further. The soul is thought of as something utterly alien to the body, as it is to material possessions and other people. Wife and family are impediments to one's freedom; therefore they should be rejected as if they were old drinking vessels or domestic pets. Like the body, they contain the soul as in a prison. The body in turn, like them, is simply part of the natural order to which, it appears, the soul does not belong. That wife and children too have souls and that they might reject their husband and father for the sake of their own freedom do not seem to occur to Epictetus. It is his own freedom which alone matters. The mind is free to give assent (iv. 1. 66 ff.), to withhold it, to despise death, to refuse to do something, to desire or not to desire. And presumably he never stopped to think of how our thoughts are distilled from our sensations, of

[9] Using Diogenes the Cynic as an exemplar, he also says that the body can show that the simple life is not injurious to it (*Discourses* iii. 22. 86 ff.). One wonders what difference it would make whether the body were injured or not.

how our desires would have no object were it not for our bodies, of how death itself is the death of the body. His dualism is so complete that he overlooks the bodily origin of the psychic life. So complete a dualism was no part of the rationalistic tradition. None of the four dominant schools preached either sensualism or asceticism, for they all understood that giving in to desire or refusing to give in was equally extreme. They saw the ethical problem as that of coping with temptation. "Nothing in excess" was the acknowledged motto of the *Nichomachean Ethics*, and in the remains of Zeno and Epicurus we find similar slogans. Just as Plato realized that the appetites must have their day in court, and even in his ideal republic made a place for the appetitive class of men, so Epicurus, when he posited pleasure as the norm of the good, knew that our love of pleasure must be moderated by the rational consideration that it might well be followed by pain. Zeno is reported by Diogenes Laertius (vii. 10) to have defined a *pathos* as an "irrational modification of the soul contrary to nature, an exaggerated desire." But, if Cicero is not mistranslating Zeno in the *Tusculan disputations* (iv. 2 and 47), what he meant by a *pathos* was perturbation, a violent emotional drive, and not any bodily sensation whatsoever. And Plutarch insists (*De virtute morali* iii.) that according to the Stoics, the passive and irrational part of the soul is not cut off from the rest of the soul but should be under the control of rational judgment. The extreme asceticism of Epictetus derives more directly from Diogenes the cynic than from the early Stoics.

Another fundamental difference between the dualism of Epictetus and that of the school to which he is usually assigned lies in his conception of God. God in early Stoicism is the *Pneuma*, the cosmic spirit which pervades the whole universe, and if some doctrinal name must be given to this idea, the traditional name of pantheism is the most appropriate. But God in Epictetus descends from the Demiurge of *Timaeus*. He is referred to frequently as *Another*, as if his name were too holy to be mentioned. He is the Creator who "has made the sun and the fruits [of the trees], the seasons, the society and communion of men with one another" (*Discourses* iv. 1. 102). As Oldfather points out in his translation of the *Discourses*,[10] just as Job says, "The Lord gave and the Lord hath taken away," so Epictetus says (iv. 1. 104), "Did He not bring you forth? Did He not show you the light? Did He not give you fellow workers? Sensations? Reason? And as what did He bring you forth? Was it not as a mortal? Not as one to live on earth with a little flesh and to contemplate His order to join with Him in His procession and festival for a little while?" We are all begotten of God and He is the father of men as of the gods (i. 3. 1). What then is God's nature? "It is likely," he says (ii. 8. 1 f.), "that where is the essence of God, there is that of the good. What then is God's essence? Flesh? Not at all. Land? Not at all. Fame? Not at all. Intelligence, understanding, right reason. Here therefore solely is the essence of the good to be sought." It is probably an inference from this that makes him exclude animals from partaking of God's nature (ii. 8. 10). The Cosmopolis is a society of God, the gods, *daimones*, and men. The rest is God's creation. The similarity between this and the Christian conception of the relation of God to man and the rest of the universe is striking and it is easy to see why pagans who accepted this type of philosophy could also accept Saint Paul.

4. The *Meditations* of Marcus Aurelius were written almost a century later than the works of Epictetus. Between the two men came Seneca, but in view of the hopeless confusion of his thoughts, there seems to be little reason to include him in a study of this sort. His influence was great, to be sure, and eclecticism such as his is also an evasion of logical responsibility. But his type of mind, like Cicero's, was that of the amateur philosopher and there is no evidence which I have been able to unearth of his having made any contribution to the progress of our subject. He does exemplify the breakdown of rationalism but he is simply an example of it. His doctrinal position might be almost anything. The Emperor was of course an entirely different type of man. His meditations were

[10] Loeb Classical Library, Vol. II, p. 278, n. 2.

apparently jotted down during his campaigns in Dacia, and if they show nothing else, they illustrate how Stoicism could become a solace rather than primarily an intellectual discipline.[11] That the two outstanding Roman Stoics who have survived should be one a slave and the other an Emperor is in itself significant, for it symbolizes that brotherhood of man in the City of Zeus of which the Christians were to make so much. The very idea of a cosmopolis was based in part on the rejection of the distinction between Greek and Barbarian, and in the contrast between these two thinkers one finds a similar rejection of the distinction between men of low and high social station. It took very little time for this attitude to disappear, for as soon as the Church became an organization rather than a collection of individuals whose bond was their common beliefs, rank had to be introduced and therefore also a hierarchy of both power and prestige. One might reply that, regardless of all that, all men were equal in the sight of God. But men were not dealing with one another as if they shared God's sight. Marcus Aurelius himself did not abdicate and there will always be some question of the extent to which he applied his religious ideals. Fortunately that is not a problem which we have to solve in this book. This is a study in the history of a few ideas, not a series of biographies.

The two worlds of Epictetus are to be sure reproduced in the *Meditations*. But it is interesting to observe that here the alternatives are clear-cut and overtly stated. It is a matter either of atoms or of God. "Either Providence or atoms," Marcus writes (iv. 2), "and from abundant evidence it is clear that the cosmos, as it were, is a city." What the abundant evidence is he does not tell us nor does he tell us why the alternative is atoms and God, that is, Epicureanism and Theism, for traditional Stoicism had been no less materialistic than Epicureanism. He may be thinking of the element of chance in the latter and the strict determinism of the

---

[11] The text of Marcus Aurelius is notoriously difficult and in many places corrupt. I have therefore not hesitated to make full use of C. R. Haines's excellent edition, translation, and notes in the Loeb Classical Library, though, it goes without saying, my interpretation of the work is my own.

former. For, if he wished to believe in Providence, he could hardly believe also that the future was not determined. He was faced with the same problem that confronted some of the early Fathers when they tried to reconcile the dogma of free will with the dogma of God's knowledge of the future. This comes out more clearly when he states the premises of his philosophy (x. 18). "If not atoms," he says, "then nature, which brings order into all things." But the order here is not a causal order but a teleological order. "The worse are for the better, and these for one another." In a third place (viii. 17) the alternatives are not atoms and God, Providence, or Nature, but atoms and the gods, both of which were retained by Epicurus. A fourth statement of the case (ix. 39) is clearer still: "Either from one intelligent source all things as in one body flow together and the part ought not to find fault with what happens for the sake of the whole, or there are atoms and nothing other than a medley and a scattering." But again Epicurus was able to conceive of a world made of falling atoms and neither a medley nor a scattering. For the swerving of the atoms did not destroy the prevailing order. It was in fact introduced to account for the conglomerations of atoms which comprised the macroscopic objects.

More difficult to understand is the combination of the idea of a source from which the order flows and the idea of a whole which embraces everything. One would imagine that such a whole would include the source itself and in any pantheistic system this would be true. Later, in the Italian Renaissance, Bruno and later still Spinoza were able to use the phrase *Deus sive Natura* without obvious compunction or apology and, as early as the ninth century, Erigena made nothing more than a verbal distinction between the creative and the created. But Marcus Aurelius retained the distinction as an orthodox Christian would have done, and God was excluded from the order of nature as its creator and preserver. In that event one might have expected him also to raise the question of how we could know that which transcended the natural order and to have ended perhaps in some form of mysticism, if not in the negative theology. But he either did not see the question or had no answer to it. And he even went so far as to suggest (x. 6) that the cosmos is not subjected to any external power. I may be reading too much into this, for in this place he is talking of a power which might injure the cosmos, but the total phrasing is such as to make one believe that the cosmos is all-inclusive and that therefore there is no power beyond it. A rationalist, aware of his intellectual technique, could not have upheld both positions, for one can scarcely say that the cosmos contains both God and the world and also that God created the world and is outside it.

Marcus also believes that his tightly organized cosmos is good. That it might be evil does not occur to him. There is no more proof given, or attempted, in the *Meditations* that what is "according to Nature" is good than there was in his earlier predecessors. Someone might have suspected that the natural was bad and that salvation was to come from resisting nature. Marcus seems to have been incapable of conceiving of the cosmic animal as anything but good. "For nothing is harmful to the part which is helpful to the whole" (x. 6). Yet, again as in Epictetus, many a part was permitted to suffer and even to die and was urged to accept suffering and death on the ground that they were mysteriously of advantage to the Whole. What advantage could there be to the whole in the death of a man if that man was an integral and indeed a necessary part of the whole, as an arm or a leg might be necessary to the complete man? Did not the whole suffer from that loss? In reply one could only be told that, whether one knew it or not, all was for the best. But what the best was was never revealed.

The confusion of ideas becomes even clearer when one considers his conception of the role of the human body. The body (iii. 3) is but the vessel which contains the soul:[12] "On the one hand are intelligence and a *daimon*, on the other earth and gore." The dualism here is existential not merely qualitative, for death is

---

[12] Haines refers his readers to Saint Paul (I Thess. 4:4) along with other authors for this commonplace. In *Meditations* iv. 41, Marcus Aurelius quotes Epictetus' remark, "You are a little soul bearing up a corpse."

the emergence of the "little soul"—Hadrian's *animula?*—from its shell or husk, as a baby emerging from its mother's womb. The sheath or body is simply that which surrounds the "hidden thing within us" (x. 38). Our organs are the instruments of the soul, differing from the workman's tools only in being attached to the body. When they are cut off from the cause which moves them and halts their motion, they are like the weaver's shuttle, the writer's pen, the charioteer's whip. If one asks why the microcosm differs in this respect from the macrocosm, in which all forms a single whole, the answer is not forthcoming. Marcus Aurelius switches his point of view at this point as Epictetus does. When he wants to preach resignation, the cosmos becomes a Whole of which the individual is but a small and trivial part; when he wishes to emphasize the goodness, the admirable order of the cosmos, he introduces the creator and legislator of the whole as a being outside it. So when he is interested in moral counsel, he will think of the human being as a material vessel enclosing an immaterial soul which will escape at death. But when he is thinking of the relation between soul and body, the body becomes a tool or set of tools for an end which it is incapable of achieving. It is the less honorable and mortal part of a man which must be kept in a position of subordination to the more divine portion (xi. 19). It is irresistible to ask why God should have given us bodies since they seem to be only a hindrance to the good and an obstacle to the moral life. One might imagine that if bodies are instruments, they would serve some purpose in a purposive universe. One can hardly think of Marcus Aurelius as a Roman Fichtean to whom the overcoming of one's opposite was the very essence of morality.

The vagueness of his conception of the universal order appears once more when he speaks of our role in the Cosmopolis (vi. 42). We are all fellow workers in the achievement of one goal, some of us intelligently, some blindly. The difference would seem to indicate that, whether we know it or not, we work toward this single end, for he goes on to say that even the man who grumbles and seeks to hinder this purpose co-operates in accomplishing it. "For the cosmos has need of such too." And yet he also urges one not to play the part of the clown in the comedy, a part which is bad in itself but is not without significance in the play as a whole.[13] But why not? the clown might ask and ask it reasonably. And how can I avoid playing the part which Nature or God has assigned me? I did not write the play nor may I change my lines. If the grumbler co-operates in the order of the Cosmopolis, why not the clown? To resist might well be to deny the role which has been given me. There is surely little consistency in preaching both resignation to God's commands and also resistance to them. The problem becomes the more puzzling when one reads that all things are intertwined "and the union is sacred and hardly anything is alien to anything else. For [everything] has been harmoniously arranged and together forms the one cosmos. For there is both one cosmos made of all things and one God pervasive of all, and one substance and one law, a reason common to all intelligent animals, and one truth, if in fact there is one final purpose of all things of the same kind and of animals sharing the same nature" (vii. 9). Here we have first the proposition of the interconnectedness of all things to form a single whole. That whole is permeated by God, so that here the God who is outside of creation is forgotten and we revert to Stoic pantheism. The argument to the existence of one law, substance, reason, and truth seems to be based upon the single purpose which may be attributed to all things belonging to one class. This would seem to imply that everything in the universe is homogeneous, though the universal genus could be broken up into various species, each with its own purpose, but the specific purposes are nevertheless "harmonious" with the general purpose. This harmony would be shown in the life of the Cosmic Animal. But once again, if that is to be accepted, then must we not also accept the inevitability of whatever occurs as part of that life?

How then could there be alienation of an individual's purpose from the universal purpose, from God's purpose? How would it

[13] See Chrysippus, fr. 1181 (von Arnim, p. 339).

be possible for anything to happen contrary to nature? Why should the body, inferior to the soul, distract the soul from the truth, the law, or the good? Such questions are not faced by Marcus Aurelius. For, as a matter of fact, he has no philosophic system in the sense of a reasoned body of propositions. The *Meditations* are a set of religious dogmas, the inconsistency of which is no more disturbing to its author than prayer would be. The philosophy he accepts was accepted prior to the writing of the *Meditations;* their author had already accepted it before he jotted down his beautiful and moving thoughts. They were written for himself, as their title indicates, not as arguments but as directions to the good life. Their premises were accepted as authoritative, and if they were inconsistent, that was nothing that need disturb anyone. Just as Christians were able, and indeed in one case, delighted, to work from mysterious logical puzzles, so the two Roman Stoics whom we have been discussing saw no need to criticize the thoughts which their masters had expressed. Acquiescence in paradox could go little farther. How little we shall see later.

II

In neither Epictetus nor Marcus Aurelius is there more than a hint of their method. They both proclaim the supremacy of reason as the Stoic's guiding principle, but it is hard to find more than one or two passages in which reasoning plays any part. Both men are assertive. They know what they believe and their dicta are simple pronouncements, not arguments. Whether they are talking to themselves or to their pupils, they are not critical of their assumptions or inferences. These works are not works of discovery but of exposition. This does not save them from the objection that they are inconsistent, but it would be unjust to accuse them of proceeding from dogma, since they do not seem to attempt anything more. One might almost say, and this would certainly be true of the Emperor, that their words are a kind of prayer, communion with themselves as representatives of the divine. They are exercises in self-investigation, examinations of conscience.

The Stoic tradition was to them what the Biblical tradition was to be to the Christians. To them it was a matter of faith and as such something the questioning of which would be absurd. When Marcus Aurelius flatly says that the alternatives are atoms or God, he surely cannot be intending to analyze the logical possibilities. He is talking in rhetorical terms and he would only have needed to stop and think in order to realize that there were nonatomistic philosophies which were not Stoic and also not pantheistic or even theistic. The great historical misfortune was that Aristotle had called his Unmoved Mover God, and the Demiurge was sufficiently like the Creator to mislead even Christians into thinking of him as Yahweh. One imagines that the impetus to turning philosophy into religion was the increasing feeling of personal insecurity as city-states vanished into kingdoms and kingdoms into empires. The Multitude naturally continued their pagan habits and it made little difference to them whether Apollo turned into Saint Sebastian and Orpheus into the Good Shepherd or not, for the metamorphosis was slow enough not to seem revolutionary. There were enough similarities between the rites of the new religion and those of the old to soften the transition. It is always a small group of intellectuals who symbolize an age for historians of culture and for us it is bound to be the surviving philosophers. We have no way of knowing how much Epictetus and Marcus Aurelius were read by the general public. There is no mention of either, for instance, even in Eusebius who went out of his way to find anticipations of Christianity. Yet we can say that as far as the intellectuals were concerned, the insecurity was real and the acceptance of dogma probably a comfort. For just as in Lucretius the dominant note is that of removing fear, so it is in both of our Roman Stoics.

It is interesting to observe that in Marcus Aurelius the problem of truth becomes that of avoiding mendacity. It is no longer a question of the criteria of truth—he knows what the truth is both substantively and constitutively. The substance of truth is Stoicism and its constitution the order of nature. There is no problem here. But there happen to be people who do not tell the truth. "The liar," he says (ix. 1), "is impious towards the same divinity [Nature]. For the nature of the whole is the nature of reality. And in fact reality (τὰ ὄντα) is closely related to all things that have been. And again the same is called truth and is the first cause of all truths. Accordingly he who lies willingly is impious inasmuch as he creates disorder by making war against the order of the cosmos. For he is making war who has conducted himself so as to be in opposition to the truth. For having begun to conceive of things by the grace of nature, through his neglect he can no longer distinguish the false from the true." It would look then as if the apperception of the truth is a gift of nature, not of education, and here Marcus Aurelius may simply be referring to the cataleptic impressions, though this is a conjecture on my part. The truth is a reflection of the things that are, but what is error? How is it possible? There is no clear answer to such questions, for in one place Marcus Aurelius says that one should speak "from within oneself" (xi. 19),[14] but does this mean "by the *lumen naturale*"? Does he believe that we have innate ideas obscured by sin? Is he thinking of some sort of natural intuition? It is next to impossible to tell, unless one makes the historical guess that he is thinking of Plato's reminiscence or the Stoic doctrine of self-evidence. Yet, even if one of these guesses were correct, we should still be in a quandary about the injustice of Nature, the divine, which endows one man with better insight than another. Nor is the problem solved by a reference to the guiding principle or to reason, for we are still left with the paradox of being told to follow Nature or reason or the guiding principle and the fact that it is possible not to.

Epictetus is reported to have said (*Discourses* ii. 11) that we come into the world without any innate concepts of mathematics or music, but can learn them through training. But on the other

---

[14] Haines translates "from the heart," in Pascalian terms.

hand, we do have innate concepts of goodness and evil, fair and foul, the honorable and the dishonorable, and other moral values. These we can apply to individual cases in which such concepts are relevant. But they can be wrongly applied because of the differences in individual opinions. The conflict here is the old Platonic one between opinion and knowledge. And we are asked to seek a standard which is higher and more authoritative than opinion. That standard is revealed by philosophy. "To philosophize is this: to look into and establish firmly the canons; but to use them once known, this is the work of a fine and good man" (ii. 11. 24 f.). The philosophic program is expanded a bit in the lesson to Naso (ii. 14). The philosopher there should make his will harmonious with the occurrences of things "so that nothing that happens occurs against our will nor cause anything which we wish not to occur to occur" (ii. 14. 7). But since Epictetus does not believe that a man can actually determine the course of events, it turns out that all that he is preaching is resignation or an imitation of God. Knowing the nature of God, we can be godlike. But do we not participate in the nature of God since we are all parts of God? If Epictetus had included a fall from grace in his philosophic anthropology, his exposition, though more mythological, would have been more plausible. He could then have explained why it was possible for men to be in error, to have opinions which were not true, to fail to apply their innate moral concepts. But he does not use the myth of the Golden Age or any other myth of man's cognitive degeneration to explain man's present position. In fact, he does not seem to see the problem. His one prayer is to submit to God, to become like God, to be led by God (ii. 16. 42).[15] How intimately he fused his two Gods, the Creator and the Cosmic *Pneuma*, there is no way of telling now, but in all probability he did not appreciate their duality.

Our innate moral concepts may help us in questions of policy, but on what are we to rely in questions of fact? Epictetus has no hesitation in replying: Logic (i. 17). But the only hint he gives us

[15] Contrast the prayer of Socrates at the end of Plato's *Phaedrus*.

of the procedures of logic is its power of making distinctions. The
value of logic lies in the definitions which it enables us to make.
It will establish the criterion of truth for us. Whether it does this
by the method of dichotomy or otherwise, we do not know. He
mentions (i. 7) the use of equivocal and hypothetical premises, the
method of questioning, as, I suppose, in the Socratic dialogues, as
aids to the moral life. The purpose of logic, he says (i. 7. 5), is to
state the truth, to eliminate the false, and to suspend judgment
when things are not evident. It will teach us the operations of
causality and be a defense against sophistry. But he lays most emphasis upon the criticism of premises and their use in argument.
For it is by the careless acceptance of premises that a man is led
astray. All this has a moral purpose and Epictetus shows no interest in the theory of logic itself. He has accepted a logical technique, that of his school, and discusses it only in so far as its use
may serve the good life. This is strikingly clear when he is discussing error. Error, he says (ii. 26), lies in self-contradiction,
and when a man has come to perceive his inconsistencies, he will
learn to avoid them. For a man who has been shown his logical
errors will abandon those acts which flow from them. That acts
flow from ideas is assumed by him as by practically all the ancients. The traditional psychology of action is intellectualistic. He
granted (iii. 6) that in former times more progress had been made
in the theory of logic than in more recent times. Much labor, he
says, is being expended upon the solution of syllogisms, but in the
old days as much was spent on keeping the guiding principle
(τὸ ἡγεμονικόν) in accordance with nature. I take it that this is a
criticism of the contemporary playing with formal arguments,
such as that of *The Liar*, which figures in the *Discourses* at least
four times, but which is supposed to go back to Chrysippus.[16] With
such examples of logic Epictetus has no patience and he seems to
believe that an examination of their premises would solve them.
They have awaited, however, the appearance of Russell's "theory

[16] See *Discourses* ii. 17. 34. This sophism arises out of trying to answer the
question of whether a man who says that he is lying is telling the truth.

of types" before even a reasonable number of logicians would admit that some progress toward their solution had been made.

It is fair to say that in the works of these two men the reliance upon authority had become an integral part of their method of thinking. It was Cicero after all who first reported the *ipse dixit* of the Pythagoreans and gave credence to the idea that the ancient philosophers had both a secret and an exoteric doctrine,[17] the former of which was imparted exclusively to members of their schools. The first two centuries of the Christian period were also the time in which lives of the philosophers were being elaborated, based largely on gossip, and one would imagine that their thoughts were some sort of expression of their personal behavior in abstract language. It was the period of apocryphal letters and sayings and anecdotes, for it seems to have appealed to the men of this time to attach any abstract idea to a historical incident. The technique continued throughout the Middle Ages, to be sure, and it may have had an earlier beginning than I think, though it does not go back much before the first century B.C. A philosophy seems to have been appraised by the kind of life which its supposed founder lived and it is interesting to observe that the synoptic gospels, for instance, tell us more of the deeds of Jesus than of His actual thoughts. But this was not peculiar to Christian literature. The author of the life of Apollonius of Tyana even used the performance of miracles to prove the divinity of his hero. Thus for one cause or another men had begun to think that in the biography of a man lay a philosophy and a philosophy which was in some sense of the word truer than his recorded ideas. This reinforced what tendencies may have existed to turn to authority as proof, to substitute reverence for a great man for argument. And though both Epictetus and Marcus Aurelius believed that any man can become divine by leading the rational life, they both turned to exemplars of the rational life rather than to arguing their case from general principles. Diogenes of Sinope, Socrates, even the mythical Her-

---

[17] See G. Boas, "Ancient Testimony to Secret Doctrines," *loc. cit.*, pp. 79 ff.

acles, became concrete specimens of the good life and by pointing to them, one avoided the labor of argument.

It cannot be denied that an example is often more persuasive than an argument. And if one believes that a way of living is in itself a philosophy, then surely one may be excused from using a specific life story as if it actually were a philosophy. The ideas of your exemplar then become authoritative and his ideas are extracted from the pattern of his behavior. But it may also be true that men turned to biographies, as if they were arguments, because of their predominant ethical interest. Perhaps the best way to teach others ethics is precisely by example, thus vivifying the lessons which one hopes to inculcate in one's pupils. For it is by no means obvious that ethical problems can be translated into general terms, that a situation in which a man has to make a choice between two courses of action is typical of anything beyond itself. We have learned the difficulty of situating crimes, for instance, under the traditional rubrics of the law, and the names which we have for the virtues and vices are never of much help when we come to judge our own acts or proposed acts. But if one can point to an incident in the life of a saint and recognize in it one's own problem, then it is somewhat easier to say, "I shall act as he acted." This is surely understandable. But it is far from being rational. The rationalist requires a set of categories under which he can subsume his entire subject matter. If he cannot find them, he is forced to capitulate to experience, authority, revelation, or simple feeling.

III

1. There are certain desiderata in life upon which Epictetus lays greatest emphasis. These are freedom of choice, freedom from the fear of death, freedom from the demands of the body. These freedoms are lodged in the human will which has control over some things, though not over all. The things which are under

our control (*Encheiridion* 1) are psychological, ideas and choices on the whole. The others are things which are either bodily states or things which are entirely external to the individual, in his words, "whatsoever are not our deeds." By means of his extreme psychophysical dualism, Epictetus is able to argue that we need never submit to the demands of externals, that our psychical states are ours to govern, that nothing and nobody can force us to assent to a false proposition, to make the wrong moral choice, to fear anything or to hope for anything if we do not wish to. He argues (*Encheiridion* 1) that "if that which is slavish by nature you should think to be free, and alien things to belong to you, you will be impeded, grieved, in turmoil, and you will blame gods and men, but if only what belongs to you be yours, and alien things you believe to be alien, no one ever will constrain you, no one will impede you, nor will you blame anyone, you will not reprove anyone, nor will you do a single thing involuntarily, you will have no enemy, no one will harm you, for there will be nothing harmful to prevail over you." The ethical problem then is solved first of all in recognizing what is one's own and what is not, and then by freeing oneself from any involvements with the latter. This will entail sacrifices, such as the sacrifice of eminence in society and of wealth, but if one looks at these things calmly and replies to their call, "You are mine," then one will be free.

This puts a man into a position of solitude (*Discourses* iii. 13). But, says Epictetus, Zeus too will be alone at the *ekpyrosis*, but he is self-sufficient and so ought a man to be. This can be brought about by thinking of the divine order of the world and of our relation to it. And, lest anyone say that we are dependent on the good will and protection of Caesar, Epictetus replies by pointing out that, though Caesar has done away with wars, brigandage, and other evils which are under his control, he still cannot free man from natural disasters, such as earthquakes and lightning. Nor can he give us freedom from the torments of love, of sorrow, of envy. This freedom can be obtained only by exercising the reason, which is the spokesman for God (iii. 13. 12)—when a man can say to himself, "Now no evil can touch me: for me there is no thief, for me no earthquake; all is full of peace, all is full of tranquillity (*ataraxia*); every road, every city, every companion on the road, neighbor, fellow man, is harmless. *Another* supplies food, *Another* whose care it is, *Another* gives us clothing, *Another* has given us perceptions, *Another* has given us concepts. And when He does not furnish necessities, He will signal your retreat, will throw open the door and will say to you, 'Go forth.' Where? Into nothing fearful, but to that from which you were born, to friendly and kindred things, to the elements. Whatever was fire in you, into fire will it pass, and whatever was earth, into earth, whatever was spirit into spirit, whatever water into water.[18] No Hades or Acheron or Cocytus, no Pyriphlegethon, but all will be full of gods and *daimones*." A man who thinks thus is neither alone nor without help. But, says someone, "What if I should be attacked and murdered?" "Fool," replies Epictetus (iii. 13, 17), "not you, but your little body."

Nothing could be a clearer affirmation of the independence of a man's soul of his body than that. For here as elsewhere Epictetus is thinking of a man's slavery to his body. As in Lucretius, one of the dominating fears of man is seen to be his fear of death. No doubt everyone fears death and recoils from danger to life. The death penalty has always been the most serious of penalties for the most serious of crimes and one can see how even Socrates, as given us in the *Apology*, felt the need of pointing out how death was nothing to be feared. Yet the ethical treatises written after the triumph of Christianity never put so much emphasis upon freedom from fear of death as the pagans did; they put it rather on freedom from sin. For the acceptance of death by martyrdoms, as well as the promise of immortality, must have had some effect in changing men's minds on this point. Vice among the pagans is not so much disobedience to the commands of the Creator as betrayal of one's nature as man. And the fear of death, if it was

---

[18] Cf. Eccles. 12:6, 7, and the committal service in the *Book of Common Prayer*.

universal, was assuaged not by promise of reward in heaven, but by the promise of a peaceful mind on earth. "Of what sort do you imagine the good to be?" asks Epictetus (iii. 22. 39). And the answer comes immediately and without hesitation, "Serenity, happiness, freedom from restraint." But these can be obtained by a man alone and only by a man's own efforts. God has provided us with an example of such a man. "Look at me; I am homeless, stateless, poor, without a slave; I sleep on the earth; I have no wife, no child, no paltry residence, but earth alone and heaven and one poor wrap. And what do I miss? Am I not free from pain; am I not without fear; am I not free? When has any man among you seen me failing to satisfy my desires; when have I deviated from my course? When have I reproached god or man; when have I blamed anyone? Has any one of you seen me with downcast face? And how do I stand before those whom you fear and admire? Is it not as if they were slaves? What man seeing me does not think that he is seeing his own king and master?"

This clearly is a picture of the typical Cynic, rather than the Stoic. But to Epictetus the life of Diogenes is an ideal.[19] In fact Arrian devotes a whole chapter to Cynicism as the proper way of life (iii. 22). Chrysippus in one place is treated simply as a writer whom men like to boast of having read (iii. 2. 13), whom they quote to great effect (iii. 21. 7), but whose teachings they do not apply (*Encheiridion* 49). The early Stoics are usually treated with respect, but there is little use made of their writings. It is anecdotes of exemplary lives of which Epictetus is in search, anecdotes of Socrates, of Diogenes, and of course of Heracles, whose labors and whose choice at the crossroads had become standards of good behavior. All such anecdotes illustrate the personal freedom of the men and the god concerned, and in the case of Heracles, his power of endurance. Their freedom lies in their fearlessness in the face of death and of rulers, their willingness to do without those pleasures ordinarily thought to be precious, their acceptance

---

[19] See *Discourses* i. 24. 6; ii. 3. 24; iii. 2. 11, 21. 19, 22. 57, 80; and esp. iii. 24. 64.

of a life without physical comforts. Such comforts were thought of as chains from which a man must liberate himself, yet nowhere is there any clear indication of how the reason proceeds to show that they are chains. The *amor habendi* may indeed result in a man's devoting his life to its satisfaction, but so may the *amor scientiae* or even Saint Augustine's *amor amandi*. But to Epictetus, as we may have seen, the man himself is something different not only from his body, but also from his emotions, and, whatever the power of choice or the reason or the will may be—and nowhere are they sharply defined—they can presumably act in isolation from every other faculty which was normally considered to be part and parcel of the human psyche. To detach the reason as a separate thing and to liberate it from all perceptions and concepts seem to leave it nothing to do. For it is all very well to give it logic as its province, but logic requires premises to work from. There can be as much logic in selling goods, in attracting women, in getting food, as in doing mathematics, if one wishes to be logical. Hence the use of the word "reason" and of "the rational life" is not informative, unless one is also told what one is to reason about. The distinction between those things which are in our control and those which are not is a rational distinction, to be sure, and it can be made without any reference to existent beings. But the moment one cites examples of each type of being, one has filled in the blanks by observation, tradition, or simply fiat. Similarly the distinction between the natural and the unnatural is logical, in the sense that, if one knows that the two antithetical classes exhaust the universe, then one can make the distinction without appealing to experience. But is the exemplification of each class equally rational? Not in Epictetus. For him such identifications are purely a matter of tradition. When, for instance, he is discussing the education of our desires (*Discourses* i. 12. 15), the best that he can do is to say that we should learn to desire "each thing as it comes about." But this is simply resignation to the course of events, whatever that may turn out to be, much as a Christian would resign himself to the will of God. "How do they come about? As He who organizes them has ordered. And He has ordered summer and winter and abundance and want and virtue and vice and all such opposites for the harmony of the whole" (i. 12. 15). And again, the poor man who is asking for a precise statement of the nature of such distinctions can only look into his own experience, for what it is worth, and to common opinion. Thereupon he might just as well resign himself to being whatever he is without remorse.

2. Marcus Aurelius also accepts the tradition of what things are good and what bad or indifferent. The destiny of man is to live the life of a citizen of the Cosmopolis, the City of Zeus, and to that extent he may have followed the reasoning of his Stoic forebears to their conclusion of a universe in which all parts were interrelated to form a whole. Good and evil are terms to be applied only to such things as are under our control (vi. 41) but there is little if any mention of the freedom which this usage will bring us. To Marcus Aurelius it is not freedom which is the goal of man's striving; it is rather apathy. His emphasis is upon cooperation. His first commandment to himself (xi. 18) runs, "What is my position in relation to men? We have come into being for the sake of others. . . . The worse are for the sake of the better and these for the sake of one another." This is far from Epictetus' command to seek isolation from all, even from one's wife and children. But the slave had had to live for the sake of others and knew the price. The Emperor could do so freely. The ninth commandment reads, "Kindliness is unconquerable, if it be genuine and not offered with a smirk or with hypocrisy. For what can the most insolent of men do to you, if you pursue the road of kindness to him and, if possible, address him gently and teach him mildly at the very moment when he is undertaking to do you harm, saying, 'No, my child, we have been made for other things. I shall not be harmed myself, but you are being harmed, my child.' . . . But this must be done not ironically nor reproachfully, but tenderly and without carping in your soul. And not as in school, nor that a bystander may admire you. But as if you were alone with him, even

if some others are present." No comment is needed to prove that in such a passage Marcus Aurelius is taking his citizenship in the City of Zeus seriously. If the Emperor paid more attention to his fellow men than to his freedom, it may have been because he was already free.

Evil, he says (ii. 11), is inevitable and so are evil men. But it comes about through the same laws which bring the good into existence and it is our duty to submit to the will of God. Evil will not continue to exist forever (ix. 35), for so long as the world is in a state of change, both good and evil must exist. The thought here goes back historically, whether Marcus Aurelius was aware of it or not, to Aristotle's theory that change is always between opposites, so that if good is to be changed, only evil can take its place, and if evil is changed, it will be replaced by good. If that is a universal law, and therefore inevitable, one can only bow to it and be resigned. One is neither angry nor resentful; one is calm. This is apathy (xi. 10). Apathy then applies to one's reaction to other men's deeds. One is not asked to be apathetic to them as men, to feel neither love nor friendship toward them. The very opening of the *Meditations* is an acknowledgment of benefits received and of gratitude and affection of the benefactors. He was not a man who was trying to make disciples; he was teaching himself alone. When one reads his testimony to his family and friends for their benefactions, one sees a modesty and a self-effacement which he may not always have manifested as Emperor, but which he cherishes as moralist. Yet here too he looks back to exemplars of good behavior in individuals which he wishes to copy, not to a chain of reasoning which might justify such behavior. It is possible that this custom of taking a historical personage as exemplar derives from the Platonic dialogues and the role which Socrates played in them. The *Nichomachean Ethics* makes nothing of this but is an argument from beginning to end. But even in the dialogues Plato does not simply relate anecdotes of Socrates; Socrates is there to analyze and criticize men's arguments and definitions.

So that it is rather the Xenophontic Socrates who is the source of this tradition.

To justify it one might say, as we have intimated above, that an ethical theory which is not incorporated in a human being is abstract and empty. Do not tell us what we should do, but show us someone doing it, might seem to be the plea. It would then be the task of the philosopher to draw off from such lives the general principles which they exemplified. The impatience with theory which comes out in Marcus Aurelius in such ejaculations as (ii. 2), "Throw away the books. Be no longer distracted by them. It is not allowed."[20] It is this type of thinking which two thousand years later we find in Emerson when he says, "An institution is but the lengthened shadow of a man." It is understandable that a Stoic with his idea of an organic universe should believe that every man has an individual part to play in the cosmic drama and that these parts should "stand for" something. Just what they stand for is none too clear, but one may guess that they symbolize a philosophy of life. This philosophy need not be expressed in words, for just as the characters of Theophrastus did not first lay down a program consciously and overtly and then proceed to carry it out, so the Sages could live as if they had a clear-cut program, so thoroughly incorporated in their lives that one had only to know them at first hand in order to understand what their program was. It would then be the philosopher's enterprise to express in rational language as far as possible just what these lives or characters stood for. We shall have, it is hoped, a clearer idea of this when we discuss Philo's interpretation of the lives of the Patriarchs.

That a man's position in civil society may influence his character is suggested in the lines (vi. 30), "Watch out lest you be Caesarified, lest you take that dye, for it can happen. Hence take care that you remain simple, good, pure, dignified, unadorned, a friend of the just, god-fearing, kindly, vigorous in good works. Fight to remain such as Philosophy has wished to make you. Fear

[20] Cf. iii. 14, viii. 8.

the gods; save men. Life is short. There is but one fruit of life on earth: a righteous disposition and social practices." And he adds immediately, "All this as a disciple of Antoninus," followed by a character sketch of his father. This sketch shows us Antoninus as a man who above all fulfills his duty as the guardian of his people, obeying his guiding principle which tells him that his lot in life has been assigned by a power higher than himself and that he must accept it willingly. The difference between this conception of ethics and that of Epictetus is once more striking. It is true that both thinkers would have said that all men should follow Nature, listen to their guiding principle, obey the commands of God. But to Epictetus an emperor was no different from a slave and, just as a slave could attain the good life by cutting himself off from all commitments to other men, so should the emperor. He does not, to be sure, discuss the problem in these words, probably because he saw no occasion to counsel his rulers. He was talking to the lower ranks of society and Caesar to him was simply another of the many obstacles to the acquisition of goodness. Yet he gives no thought to the possibility that a man might have duties here on earth analogous to those which might befall him in the City of God. To Marcus Aurelius one's earthly lot could not be disregarded. If the gods had placed you on a throne, you were to think out your duties as a ruler and fulfill them. But again, it should not be forgotten that he was talking to himself and not to a group of pupils. Nevertheless there must have been a temptation to murmur against a fortune which made his leading the philosophic life more difficult than it would have been for a commoner. If there was such a temptation, it does not show itself in the words of his *Meditations* as we have them. Other sovereigns have abdicated: Tiberius, Charles V, Diocletian, Christina of Sweden, and these have done it for the sake of a life which they found more rewarding than that of a ruler. It might have occurred to Marcus Aurelius too that the life of an Emperor was incompatible with that of a Sage, that men were not made to be ruled by other men, and that he was usurping the power of God. But if such thoughts occurred to him, he said nothing about them, and seems to have believed that the dangers of maleficence could be alleviated by practicing the virtues of hard work, kindliness, keeping an even temper, and so on.

There is finally much less on the subject of the fear of death in Marcus Aurelius than in Epictetus. Death to the Emperor is simply an inevitable occurrence and neither to be encouraged nor resented. A man, he says (iv. 41) quoting Epictetus, is but a little soul carrying a corpse, and when the time comes to lay down the burden, he does so. One does not hasten the end (v. 33), but neither does one regret it. The time of death is fixed by nature (xii. 23) and, regardless of what comes after death, its arrival is to be accepted calmly. It is absurd to think that a man should continue to live forever, since it is a universal law that all things change (ii. 17). Since we are as much a part of the universe as everything else, we must accept the same fate as everything else. "It is in accordance with nature, and nothing evil is natural" (ii. 17). Now it may be that as a soldier Marcus Aurelius was himself willing to meet death as inevitable and that he was not so aware as a civilian might be of the common dread of it. In any event he does not harp upon it as one of the evils against which he must fortify himself. He mentions death frequently enough to show that it was one of his preoccupations. But unlike both Epictetus and Lucretius, it is not one of his major problems.

He has no set views on what will happen to the soul after the Releaser sets us free (xii. 36). It may be another life; it may be extinction (iii. 3). If it is another life, it may be one with a different kind of perception and indeed a different way of living. The soul may be released into the air and become diffused into the cosmic *Pneuma* (iv. 21). It might be agreeable to survive, but, if we do not, that is because Nature has willed it otherwise (xii. 5). Now a man who has such vague and tentative views on what happens after death is not one who has spent much time worrying about it. For a person to whom death was a daily fear would sooner or later make up his mind about what was to be feared or hoped for. Here too, it is reasonable to believe, his profession and his civil position made the fear of death less poignant than it would have been for one who was not constantly on the field of battle and not supreme ruler over an empire. But aside from all this, it is worth noting that we have here a man who believes firmly that goodness can be achieved here on earth with little thought of an afterlife. I emphasize this because in the ethical tradition of the Christian period it was frequently maintained that only a belief in an afterlife could justify doing good and avoiding evil. Such a belief was a postulate of the practical reason in Kant and since his time philosophers have used all their ingenuity to show that, in some sense of the word, we survive our terrestrial life. Usually, it is true, that sense is a strange one which, if taken literally, would prove of little compensation for the miseries of earthly living. To survive in the memory of our fellows, for instance, is not quite what a Christian wanted who had read the Book of Revelations and had found sustenance in it. To share in the fulfillment of the communal purposes of mankind may again be called immortality, but it is not the personal survival which frees one from the burdens of the flesh. Philosophy is full of curious reinterpretations of traditional vulgar beliefs and those concerning immortality are among the most curious. To read Marcus Aurelius and see how little he busied himself with such speculations is to see, one thinks, that the matter was not of primary importance to him. Nor need it be to anyone.

IV

1. Both Epictetus and Marcus Aurelius were saved from such fancies by their low opinion of the life which surrounded them and its trivialities. If Epictetus thought of the soul as bearing up a little corpse, that was because he despised the claims of the body which his fellow men submitted to too eagerly. He had nothing but contempt for the man who was nostalgic for Athens and the

Acropolis (*Discourses* ii. 16. 32), for had he not the sun, moon, and stars to contemplate? "If you understand the Governor of all things and carry Him within you, would you still long for stones and an elegant rock?" (ii. 16. 33). He ridicules the man who seeks position in Rome (i. 10). He sees the life of most people as nothing more than a waste of time. "How else do they spend the whole day but in counting, disputing, consulting about a little bread, a bit of land, and such questions of prosperity?" (i. 10. 9). They follow their sensory impressions rather than the reason (i. 28. 28) in the most important questions and employ their reason only in small matters. They are in a state of panic in matters of basic importance (ii. 1). They live in dread of Caesar (ii. 6. 20). They rush to diviners from cowardice (ii. 7. 9). They descend to the level of the beasts because of the domination of their bellies or from lust (ii. 9. 4). They fear death and exile when all that they have to fear is fear itself (ii. 16. 19).[21] They love to display their learning (ii. 17. 34); they go to school for the wrong purposes, not to cure their souls, but to boast of their education (ii. 31. 15). Epictetus is far from being opposed to studies, such as rhetoric and logic (ii. 23. 46), but is opposed to thinking that they unaided can improve a man. He finds too much insincerity about him, too much "counterfeit baptism" (ii. 9. 21).[22] Most of us, he says, relating the parable of the market, come to market to buy and sell, whereas only a few come to see it, to study its purposes, its constitution, and its promoters (ii. 14. 23). Those who contemplate are the wise.

Unlike Marcus Aurelius, Epictetus sees the spectacle of the world through black glasses. Whatever he may think about calm and apathy, of fulfilling one's role without protest or resentment, he himself in at least one striking passage reveals his fundamental discontent. Speaking of Socrates' ability to put an end to strife and to educate others through questions and answers, he adds that

[21] Is a reference to F. D. Roosevelt's Chicago speech superfluous?

[22] I take over the translation of Oldfather in the Loeb Classical Library. A Parabaptist is a man who is baptized and is yet unregenerate. See Oldfather's note on this passage.

this gift is a dangerous one to be exercised in Rome (ii. 12. 17). He relates what would happen there if one should try the Socratic method. One would reach the point of inducing one's interlocutor to admit that his soul was his most precious possession. One would then ask whether it is being properly cared for by the man himself or by someone else. "Thereupon emerges the danger that first he will say, 'What business is that of yours, my fine friend? Are you my lord and master?' And then, should you continue to question him, he will double up his fists to punch you. Of this sort of things I was once myself a zealot, until it sent me into my present condition." At least Epictetus was willing once in a while to give voice to his sense of humor.

But the futility of teaching others was not merely exemplified in his own life. "Did Socrates persuade all his associates to have a care for their souls? Not even a thousandth part of them" (iii. 1. 19). Yet he continued to pursue his mission. But since men are weaklings (iii. 5), drunk with a sense of their own importance and their love of power (iii. 7. 29), swollen with pride (iii. 14. 11), desirous of praise (iii. 23. 24), false philosophers (iii. 24. 38), "Epicureans and perverts," what hope has a real philosopher of curing them? "What else do these men want but to sleep without interference or constraint and to arise at their ease to yawn and wash their faces, then to write and read what they wish, then to play the fool somehow or other, applauded by their friends, regardless of what they may say, then to start off for a stroll and, after walking a bit, to bathe, then to eat, then to lie down for a nap, to stretch out on such a bed as is fitting for such men—how should I put it? But one can judge for oneself."[23] The picture, harsh as it is, is not harsher than that painted by Juvenal.

2. Marcus Aurelius, though much less acid in tone, also gives us no pleasant appraisal of life. Physicians, astrologers, philosophers, generals, tyrants, whole cities, like Helike, Pompeii, and Herculaneum, have perished after their cures, predictions, disquisitions, slaughters, and rules, and now lie buried in the dust,

---

[23] *Discourses* iii. 24. 38; cf. iii. 22. 26.

though all were concerned with warding off this fate (iv. 48). All is in flux: "All that you see will rapidly pass away, and those who shall see its passing will in their turn also rapidly perish" (ix. 33). If one has been a citizen of the Great City for five years, it is as good as a hundred (xii. 36). For most of our cares are vain and whether life be short or long is no measure of its goodness. Why not then, one wonders, relax and, practicing the art of resignation, accept the futility of human effort and look upon the spectacle without abusing it? But this is not the way of the Roman Stoic. Things are so mysterious that they are hard to understand "even for the Stoics" (v. 10), and the things which men value highly are such trash that one finds it difficult to tolerate the most accomplished men or even to live with oneself.[24] "Hence in such gloom and filth and in such a flux, both of substance and of time, of change and of things which are changed, what there is to be praised, or to what we can give serious thought, I do not know. On the contrary, one should console oneself by waiting for one's natural dissolution and not be vexed by loss of time, but comfort oneself quietly in these considerations: first, that nothing will happen to me which is not in harmony with the whole, and second, that I can do nothing in opposition to my god and *daimon*. For no man can force me to stray from them" (v. 10).

But death as a release into the cosmos is not the only justification for welcoming death. Aside from its being a natural law and therefore unavoidable, it also releases one from the people who surround one (ix. 3). You will be freed not merely from your similars, but also from men who are in opposition to you. Then you will see "what weariness there is in your discord with your associates, so that you may say, 'Come quickly, Death, lest some-

---

[24] The Emperor was probably unusually depressed when he jotted this down, for in another place (vi. 48) he says that when one is low in spirit one should think about one's fellows, their activity, their modesty, their generosity, and the like, and this will cheer one up. The *Meditations* were of course written on different occasions and in different moods, and it would be unfair to look for consistency of detail in them.

how I too lose control of myself.' " Civic occupations are vain (ix. 29) and one must be satisfied if only a little betterment is achieved. The best advice is to "live as if on a mountain top" (x. 15), and, if men cannot bear you, let them kill you (x. 15). For this would be better than to live the kind of life that they live. One might, remembering Zarathustra, conclude that a man is a solitary figure at best and that no hope is to be placed in the support of others. For "what sort of creatures are they, eating, sleeping, fornicating, evacuating, and so on?" (x. 19). But the most pessimistic note is struck when he writes (x. 36), "There is no one so fortunate that at his death there will not be someone to welcome the evil which is coming. He was an honest and wise man. At the last moment of his life someone will say to himself, 'We shall at last be able to breathe in peace in the absence of this teacher. He was not troublesome to any of us, but I perceived that secretly he condemned us.' " This, he says, will be true of us all, but in his own case even his associates, for whom he had toiled so hard and over whose welfare he had watched, long for his death, "hoping thereby for some chance relief from him." But since all this is in accordance with natural law, there is no point in resenting it.

There may indeed be no point in resenting the sharp tooth of benefits forgot, but to accept it as the general law of human nature is not to paint a rosy picture of human life. Yet if one has decided that the life of reason is the correct life, one is bound to find oneself in isolation from one's fellows, whether on a mountaintop or in the agora. Few if any philosophers have been in harmony with society, nor would they have much to do, so far as ethics is concerned, if they were. But we have already seen that from the days of Hesiod down, poets have agreed with philosophers in condemning the life of their fellows. This pessimistic streak was not peculiar to the pagans. Ecclesiastes, as we have intimated, is concordant with many of the views of Epictetus and Marcus Aurelius, in spite of the refrain that there is nothing new under the sun. What is stranger than the unhappiness of philosophers is their insistence upon living "in accordance with Nature," and thereupon excluding human nature from nature. When, like Diogenes, they turn to the animals as exemplars, they see in their instinctive routines something to be admired and copied. But the usual life of men, that which in Aristotle's phrase is that which happens on the whole and is therefore natural, is condemned as unnatural. The Roman Stoic is willing to accept universal law, the will of God, death, pain, and suffering, but he is not willing to accept men as they are and as they are by his own admission. This is one of the basic conflicts in the philosophic temper. Everything from the heavens to the depths of the earth is normal, natural, as it should be, with the outstanding exception of humanity. Man turns out to be essentially an unnatural animal, a glaring exception to the rule of law, a mixture of the bestial and the divine, a battleground between the forces of good and evil. In his case alone whatever is, is never right. What wonder then that the early Christians found this a mystery and gave up the search for a rational explanation of it as hopeless?

CHAPTER VIII

The Evidence
of Revelation

BETWEEN THE DEATH OF Aristotle and the composition of *De rerum natura* there was a space of three hundred years, more or less, from which we have but the most mutilated works of the philosophers who lived in it, works which consist only of quotations out of context and secondhand reports. It was during this period that the Macedonian conquest of Greece was completed and in its turn disintegrated. The freedom of the city-states disappeared into the Roman Empire when, in 146 B.C., Greece was conquered for a second time. It was the period of the growth of Alexandria as a metropolis, where Jews and other Asiatics, Egyptians, Greeks, and Romans began to associate in intellectual conversation. Provincialism was on the wane, as it was bound to be when men of different cultures met. The sciences, we know, began to take the form in which they have survived, in rational systems rather than merely as unconnected groups of data. The critical method of editing texts based on grammatical and rhetorical studies was developed. And whereas on the one hand there was a general fusion of the many gods into a few divinities, Cronus, Moloch, and Saturn for instance becoming one in spite of their profound differences, on the other there was a proliferation of gods. By the time of Cicero, as we have seen, there was a temple to Faith, another to Courage (*Virtus*), a third to Honor, and others dedicated to *Ops, Salus, Concordia, Libertas,* and *Victoria* in Rome.[1] This was not something which died out with Paganism. For only a short time later we find the Christians deifying the *Logos, Sophia, Providentia,* and possibly *Spiritus.* By the time when William Blake wrote that he saw Eternity the other night, such synonyms for God had become habitual.[2] In fact, the pagan practice in this regard as well as in doctrine, was so close to that of the Christians and Jews that it was possible for Philo to pronounce his famous sentence that Plato was Moses speaking Greek. This was repeated in various forms by others and no one seems to have been sure just who was its author. Eusebius attributes it to Numenius, but it could also be found, though much later, in Clement of Alexandria.[3] For our purposes we need only note that the truth was lodged in an individual and that this individual expressed the meaning of some sacred text. The contribution of the individual was not the discovery of a new truth or even of new evidence for old truths. It was simply exposition of a text which was eternally and irrefutably true.

In Philo Judaeus the sacred text was of course the Bible as translated by the Seventy. No pagan author, not even Cicero or Seneca, and certainly not such Stoics as Posidonius or Panaetius, hesitated to find fault with the founders of what they called schools of philosophy. They seem to have taken it for granted

---

[1] There was also a multiplication of philosophic sects. Varro counts 288 of them in his day. See Zeller, *History of Eclecticism,* p. 173, n. 1. Cf. Cicero *De legibus* ii. 11. 28 (Teubner ed., p. 415).

[2] Cf. L. Gordon Rylands, *The Beginnings of Gnostic Christianity* (London: Watts and Co., 1940), p. 144, and J. M. Robertson, *Christianity and Mythology* (London: Watts and Co., 1910), *passim.*

[3] See Clement *Stromata* i. 1, and Eusebius *Praeparatio evangelica* (Teubner ed., 1867) xi. 10. 14 (p. 25) and ix. 6. 9 (p. 477). In Jerome we find the phrase, "Either Philo Platonizes or Plato Philonizes" (*De viris illustribus* c. 11; Migne, *PL,* xxiii, p. 659).

that a man was free to criticize anyone, even when they believed in the authority of the *consensus gentium*. In fact the *consensus* eliminated the individual errors by its very nature. Edelstein, in his article on Posidonius to which we have already referred, points out how that writer differed in his doctrines from his Stoic predecessors, and in Panaetius we find similar points of originality.[4] But when we come to Philo we find his contribution only in his peculiar interpretation of the sacred text and, though there is certainly plenty of room for doubt about the accuracy of it, we need not doubt that for him philosophy was exegesis. It is no longer an autonomous science; it consists in drawing out of an authority what is concealed and therefore unrecognized in him. Philo, one can be confident in saying, believed that what we call his philosophy was "implicit" in the Bible. His task was simply to make it explicit.

We all have to use authorities for certain information. If we wish to find out how the Law of Gravitation was phrased, we go to Newton, but we do not believe that the business of a physicist is first to find out what Newton believed to be gravitation and then to expound it. We do not think that because Newton deduced and framed that law, it must be true and that any evidence to the contrary must be explained away. The use of a sacred text which we are discussing in this chapter is diametrically opposed to this. Whatever the sacred text says is absolutely true, and, if there is anything apparently true and yet inconsistent with the text, it must be false. If, moreover, there is anything in the text which for some reason or other seems to be untrue, then the exegete must show that in spite of appearances, it really is true. This technique has survived into our own times, not merely in Biblical exegesis, but also in the exegesis of philosophic authors. It is often assumed that if there appear to be inconsistencies in Plato, Aristotle, Plotinus, Thomas Aquinas, or Immanuel Kant, to take outstanding examples, one of the statements must be unauthentic, a corruption of the text, an interpolation, a scribe's error,

[4] Cf. Basile N. Tatakis, *Panétius de Rhodes* (Paris: Vrin, 1931), *passim*.

or the effect of traditional misinterpretations of the text. To take but one example, and that a famous one, if there are inconsistencies in Aristotle, they must be explained away as evidence of the growth of his thought; those ideas closest to Plato's being the earliest and the others later. In effect this is based on the assumption that no man ever contradicts himself and, if he changes his mind, this is anomalous. Fortunately for Philo, he was mainly interested in interpreting the Pentateuch where the inconsistencies, though they occur between the first and second chapters of Genesis, are not so great as those which are to be found, let us say, between Jeremiah and Amos, Ecclesiastes and Job. To reduce these inconsistencies, it was necessary that he have a method clearly defined and fortunately one had been prepared for him in the tradition of allegorical interpretation. Minucius Felix (*Octavius* xix. 10) attributes to Zeno the identification of Juno with air, Jupiter with the heavens, Neptune with the sea, Vulcan with fire, and the reinterpretation of the other gods of the populace as the elements. In Cornutus[5] we find Athena explained as God's sagacity and her identity with Providence; she was after all born from the head of Zeus and this could not be accepted literally. (It could of course be rejected.) Saint Augustine refers to Varro as maintaining that Minerva really means "the archetypes of things which Plato called ideas" (*De civitate Dei* vii. 28). Bréhier points out how Philo accepted several of the allegorical interpretations of Cornutus and how he does this without "trying to justify them by Biblical texts."[6]

In Plato those myths which related indecent or otherwise unworthy stories of the gods were not allegorized. In the *Republic* they are simply rejected as lies, however old they might be; gods just could not be thought to have committed the acts reported of them by the mythographers. Moreover, to Plato and Aristotle, as to their predecessors, Xenophanes and Heraclitus, no text was

[5] Lang, p. 35, 7.
[6] E. Bréhier, *Les idées philosophiques et religieuses de Philon d'Alexandrie* (Paris: Vrin, 1950), p. 38.

sacred. But in the post-Aristotelian period the myths were retained as if they were sacred and the literal meaning of the stories
was supplanted by allegory. It is hardly necessary to point out
that the Greeks had no Bible, for even Homer and Hesiod were
not supposed to be inspired recipients of divine revelation. On the
contrary, the standard myths, like the genealogies of the gods,
often existed in variant forms and a man was free either to accept
or to reject them, or to accept some versions and to reject others.[7]
But as time went on we find the descendants of these men under
a compulsion to accept them all, as if they were true because they
were part of the tradition of their culture. Moreover, men began
to feel that the truth was something to be concealed from the
populace which was either too ignorant or too untrustworthy to
be given such knowledge. This distrust of the people may have
been due to several causes, to the actual treatment meted out to
certain philosophers, the main of whom was Socrates, to the difficulty of making the man in the street understand the literal expression of scientific truths, and to the sheer pleasure of knowing
something which the great majority of men do not know. To
share in a secret is, I suppose, a great delight, but part of the delight comes from the small number of initiates with whom one
shares it. If need be, one invents secrets in order to keep the
majority in the dark. Thus in the Italian Renaissance we find the
opinion current among the intellectuals that an emblem has a
value measured by the difficulty of understanding it.[8] That a
parable might be clearer than that which it illustrates does not
seem to have occurred to these men. Some went so far as to say
that the reason why Christ spoke in parables was that He knew
that the people were not fit to be given the naked truth. The
Pinax of Cebes in ancient times was analogous to the *Faerie
Queene* to the extent that it represented something which anyone could understand on the surface, but which only a few could

[7] In Jewish and Christian circles the acceptance and rejection were done
for the individual by the establishment of canonical and apocryphal versions.
[8] See the introduction to my translation of *The Hieroglyphics of Horapollo* (New York: Pantheon Books, 1950).

interpret. To write obscurely and to do so deliberately is not a practice which died out with Lycophron. The invention of allegories, however, is the reverse of allegorical interpretation. In the one case a supposititious concealed meaning is read out of what purports to be a literal statement; in the other the literal meaning of an idea is deliberately concealed.

If then one assumes that a text is allegorical, its interpretation requires a code by means of which it can be translated into non-figurative language. If, for instance, one speaks of the sun as Helios and of the earth as Gaia and says that Gaia yearns for the embraces of Helios who repulses her advances, one can then turn this about and explain it as the attractive and repulsive forces of gravitation and even, if one wishes, measure the strength of the yearning and repulsion by the masses of the two divinities and their distance from each other. Many of the alchemical descriptions were not less fantastic than this and all had to be translated into terms of alembics and fire, distillations and precipitations. In my first example one takes the language of Newtonian physics as literal; in the second, the recipes of a chemical laboratory.

Philo could do no more than this. To his way of thinking the Bible had to contain not only the truth but all the truth. Hence whatever was said by Plato, Aristotle, and the early Stoics which was true, must be hidden in the Bible. And, in reverse, since there must be a literal version of Biblical wisdom, that version must be found also in those teachings of the philosophers which were true. When the Bible spoke of individual people, Abraham, Isaac, and Jacob, they must be seen to be incarnations of psychological characters, in their turn to be interpreted as moral qualities. For the significance of any human being at this time was his moral behavior. This may seem strange, but when one realizes that to Cicero the Academic and Peripatetic philosophies were the same, differing only in name,[9] one sees that it was not difficult to pick and choose one's thoughts wherever one wished.

---

[9] *Qui rebus congruentes nominibus differebant* (*Academica* i. 4. 17).

In harmony with this vagueness, this negligence of rationality, we find Philo translating his allegories into the language of Aristotle, Plato, and the Stoics at will. He goes even further on the road to complete confusion than this, for when he uses the number symbolism of the Pythagoreans to interpret any Biblical verse in which a number is mentioned, he translates an allegory into another allegory before reaching a literal version of its meaning. The one philosophical school which he disdains is naturally that of Epicurus, in which he agreed with Cicero. His eclectic method is obvious when one runs through his writings even hastily. In the *De congressu quaerendae eruditionis gratia*, for example, he says (79), "Now just as our general education tends towards the acquisition of philosophy, so philosophy too is for the possession of wisdom. For philosophy is a cultivation of wisdom, but wisdom is the science of divine and human affairs and of their causes." [10] If now we turn to Aëtius,[11] we find him saying, "The Stoics said that wisdom was the science of divine and human affairs, and philosophy the training in useful art." Philo also took over with modifications his doctrine of the *Logos* from the Stoics, that of his Intelligible World from Plato, his interpretation of the angels as powers from Aristotle. He makes the "first man" a cosmopolite (*De opificio mundi* xlix. 142; LCL, p. 112), and his *Life of Moses*, as is generally recognized, is an account of the life of a Stoic Sage. Yet it is also true that he corrects all such ideas when it is necessary to draw a conclusion which is in harmony with traditional Judaism, as he understands it, and when he sees that his philosophic information would be discordant with it. The Intelligible World hence is created by God and exists in God's mind (iv. 16; LCL, p. 14). The powers of Aristotle are far from being angels and are not even arranged hierarchically between heaven and earth. Though he accepts the Stoic notion of rigorous laws of

[10] I am using the text in the Loeb Classical Library (edited by Colson and Whitaker), since the Cohn-Wendland edition is not available to me. It is abbreviated as LCL.

[11] *Placita* i, *Proemium* 2 (Diels, *Doxographi graeci*, p. 273). Cf. Seneca *Epistles* xxxi. 8.

nature which are immanent in nature, he does not identify Fate
or the system of natural law with God.[12] Commenting on the
Twenty-Third Psalm (*De agricultura* xii. 51; LCL, p. 134), he
speaks of God, the shepherd and king, as ruling the elements and
the heavenly bodies, as if He were the Zeus of Cleanthes, but he
adds that God has appointed his "own right reason and first born
son" as his lieutenant, a phrase that is far from the theology of
Cleanthes. In the treatise on the giants (*De gigantibus* ii. 6; LCL,
p. 448), he identifies the angels with those beings "whom the
philosophers call *daimones*," but whereas the *daimon* of Socrates
dwelt within his soul and prevented his doing wrong, the angels
of Philo inhabit the air as other beings inhabit the sea, the land,
and even the fire, the last being "chiefly in Macedonia." And
finally, though the Sage is to model his life on that of the Stoic
Sage, nevertheless the first man to be created was the best man
who had ever been created and each successive generation is
weaker by the extent to which it is farther from the Creator
(*De opificio mundi* xlix. 140 f.; LCL, p. 110).[13] It therefore cannot be denied that both Bréhier and Wolfson are correct in insisting that, in spite of Philo's use of current philosophies to
translate his allegories, he also had a philosophic position of his
own.[14] It is not our purpose here to write a summary of his system in so far as it is a system, but to indicate the changes which
he introduced into the solution of the traditional problems which
previous chapters have dealt with.

I

1.   The division of things into the apparent and the real is not
based merely on the distinction between the world as perceived

[12] See esp. *De migratione Abrahami* xxxii. 179–81; LCL, p. 236.

[13] He uses Plato's symbol of the magnet and the iron rings which hang
from it as the appropriate emblem of the successive degrees of weakness.
Cf. Ion 533d, e.

[14] Bréhier, *op. cit.*, esp. chap. 1, on Philo's conception of God; H. A.
Wolfson, *Philo* (Cambridge: Harvard University Press, 1948), Vol. I, p. 45,
and esp. pp. 107 ff.

and the world as known to the reason, but also upon the Platonic distinction between the particulars and the universals. Philo takes over the ideas of Plato, but first he makes them archetypes existing in the mind of God. His God, it should be recalled, is neither the Demiurge of *Timaeus* nor the Unmoved Mover of Aristotle. He is the God of the Bible who, as history went on, was to share some of the characteristics of each. To begin with, He was a Creator, whereas the Demiurge had at hand unformed matter which it was His function to organize and fashion.[15] In the second place, though He is also transcendent, He is a person resembling a man all of whose powers and faculties have been magnified and purified. Neither the Demiurge nor the Unmoved Mover was a shepherd or king nor did he care for human beings as the Biblical and Philonic God did. The action of the Demiurge apparently ceased once He had fashioned the universe according to strictly rational procedures, and that of the Unmoved Mover, though very obscure, was called attraction and was probably directly felt by the first of the spheres.[16] The ideas, as archetypes, were not God's thoughts, nor did the Unmoved Mover effectuate his purposes by intermediaries such as angels. In neither Stoicism nor Epicureanism is there any mention of a *logos* which could be the first-born son of God, and any myths which might have mentioned the children of the gods would have been interpreted allegorically or rejected. In Philo the gap between God and the world is filled by the angels. And just as in the Pseudo-Aristotelian *De mundo* God rules from within His palace, like the Great King (*De mundo* 398a, b), so Philo's God (*De decalogo* xiii. 61, xxxiii. 178; LCL, pp. 36, 94) rules invisibly and remotely,[17] surrounded by bodyguards and minor officials. These are but a few evidences of Philo's independence of his philosophic predecessors. It is

[15] See F. M. Cornford, *Plato's Cosmology*, p. 35.

[16] For differences between the Unmoved Mover and God, cf. G. Boas, *Some Assumptions of Aristotle*, p. 25.

[17] For the reverse of this, viz., that the Emperor is a terrestrial replica of God, see V. Valdenberg, "*Discours politiques de Thémistius dans leur rapport avec l'antiquité*," *Byzantion*, I (1924), 557. Cf. Wolfson, *op. cit.*, Vol. I, p. 220.

measured by his ability to fit their doctrines into the truth which is expressed in the Bible. Where Biblical truth cannot be successfully interpreted as an anticipation of secular truth, it is the latter which was to be modified. Since Moses speaks of creation, Philo's God must be a creator, and since a created world must have had a beginning in time, the world of Aristotle, without beginning or end, must be rejected.[18]

If Philo had not been interpreting the Bible, it is likely that his work, like that of so many others would have perished. But in view of its usefulness to Christian exegetes, it was preserved. There can surely be no other reason. For in it are so many ideas that run counter to the prevailing philosophic theses, and its method is so different from that utilized by the pagan philosophers that they would have thought of it as simply another of those barbarian eccentricities which were hardly worthy of serious consideration. Its purpose was to make Judaism as a religion intelligible, to turn the Bible, especially the Pentateuch, into a philosophic treatise, and, though that might have made Judaism more palatable to Romans who were looking for novel religious doctrines, it had no influence on such philosophers as Marcus Aurelius and Seneca, both of whom used their philosophies as guides to life. It was the Christian Fathers who saved Philo for posterity.[19]

Of Philo's application of the allegorical method, little need be said, for at best his interpretations of Scriptural texts are simply literary curiosities. One or two examples will perhaps suffice. In

---

[18] *De aeternitate mundi* might seem evidence to the contrary, for the arguments in favor of an uncreated and indestructible world are presented with vigor, in keeping with Peripatetic doctrine. But at the same time the treatise ends with the words, "What then has been passed on to us about the indestructibility of the world has been said forcefully. But what is to be said against each of the arguments must be shown in what follows." This would seem to indicate that something was to follow and that in it Philo would present the other side of the case.

[19] See, e.g., Eusebius *Praeparatio evangelica* vii. 13 (ed. Dindorf, Leipzig, 1867, Vol. I, p. 373) and xi. 15 (Vol. II, p. 33). Philo is used by Eusebius as one who testified to the Second Person of the Trinity and who proved the antiquity of Jewish lore.

De opificio mundi (iii) he is speaking of the six-day creation. The question arises of why six rather than any other number of days. The answer is that six is the most productive of numbers, being twice three, three times two, and six times one, and since the odd is male and the even female, six is both. The reasoning may seem strange and would induce one to believe that every human being is a hermaphrodite in view of the undeniable fact that his parents were each of a different sex. For Philo points out that three is the first of the odd numbers—one is not a number—and two is the first even number, and six is their product. The perfection of six is thus established and the world which was made "in accordance with" the perfect number is therefore also perfect.[20] The numerical allegories are paralleled by others. One of the best known is Philo's interpretation of the story of man's fall and rehabilitation. Adam here becomes the Reason (*nous*) and Eve External Sensation (*aisthesis*).[21] If one ask why such identifications should be made, the answer is simply that man is active and woman passive according to an old tradition and that the reason and sensation are also active and passive, respectively. Since man for years had been characterized as a rational animal and the word *Adam* meant *man* and Philo was interpreting the story of the Fall, he argued that something must have happened to man's essential nature when the Apple was eaten. What happened was a weakening of the reason. But what was the temptation? The temptation was incarnated in the Serpent which was pleasure (*Legum Allegoria* ii. 18. 71; LCL, p. 268). The yielding to the enticements of pleasure corrupts the reason. "Pleasure is likened to a serpent for the following reason. Just as the motion of a serpent is twisting and various, so is that of pleasure" (ii. 18. 71). It attaches itself to the five senses and to sexual activity as well.

[20] If one's appetite for number symbolism is not satisfied with this sample, one might read *De opificio mundi* xiv. 45 ff. (LCL, pp. 34 ff.) on the wonderful number four or the long section beginning at xxx. 89 (LCL, pp. 72 ff.) on seven.

[21] *Legum Allegoria* i. 30. 92 (LCL, p. 208) and ii. 11. 38 (LCL, p. 248), respectively.

Philo proceeds to expatiate upon the sensual pleasures in detail, as if it were necessary to prove to his readers that each sense has its pleasures and that the sensual life is especially pleasant. These can be mastered only by self-control, temperance, which is also lodged in the reason. But if the reason has been corrupted by the pleasures of the senses, something more is required to rehabilitate it. The rehabilitation is told in the story of the three Patriarchs. Each of them typifies a way of searching for the good—"one through instruction," Abraham—"one from nature," Isaac—and "one from practice," Jacob (*De Abrahamo* xi. 52; LCL, p. 30). Thus three men, historical figures, stand for three ways of achieving virtue, not that the Pentateuch says so overtly, but that Philo so interprets their lives. That the Bible might be simply a historical narrative and nothing more does not seem to have occurred to him. That if he had wished to show that virtue was to be attained by instruction, nature, and practice, he might have done so without recourse to Revelation also does not occur to him. That, furthermore, if God had wished to show man the way to moral excellence, He need not have done it so obscurely, is not questioned. The Ten Commandments are after all as clear and simple and literal as the restrictions on food and the other laws in *Leviticus* and *Deuteronomy*. Why then is the way to rehabilitation so clouded in allegory? This is not explained by Philo. One wonders whether his problem did not really arise from his inability to believe the story of the Patriarchs as it stands in *Genesis* and for that reason alone he resorted to allegorical interpretation.

To return to our main theme, the first distinction in Philo is that between the world of things, men, historical events, and that world which is eternal and imperishable, consisting of what the former world signifies morally. One finds nothing of this sort in either Plato or Aristotle, Epicurus or the early Stoics. But after Philo it became customary to search for hidden—moral—meanings in physical events and such a book as, for instance, *The City of God*, is constructed about that search. It is to be sure a history of the Mediterranean peoples, but it is a history beyond which is the lesson of crime and punishment. This lesson was of course also taught in the Bible and it is possible that when the Bible was introduced into the pagan world through Philo, history made sense for the first time, if by "sense" one means something other than the literal meaning of the narrative. The Fall of Man and his subsequent degeneration did not make consistent sense in Hesiod, for no one reason is given by him to account for it. When the story was moralized by Aratus,[22] degradation was caused by man's loss progressively of his innate sense of justice, though why this sense should have been lost is not explained. Aristotle in his *Politics* also made sense out of certain political events in his theory of the three forms of government which are inevitably corrupted. Polybius in the second century A.D. did likewise. Many historians were willing and able to draw lessons from individual events of the past. But in Philo one sees a general pattern underlying the temporal series of events, the pattern determined by man's relation to God. His explanation of the Fall is based on a theory of knowledge, a theory which could be tested empirically, and his account of Adam and Eve as symbols of two of man's cognitive powers and their interrelations, though far from being accurate as Biblical exegesis, was nevertheless an account which could be accepted by men trained in the classical tradition of philosophy. The curious thing about its future is that instead of taking over this side of the story, philosophers took over the supernatural side instead, with the result that the lesson of history was a caution to obey divine commands instead of restoring the reason to its primordial position. One might have said that in every individual are to be found both Adam and Eve and the Serpent, and that is undoubtedly what Philo meant to convey to his readers. But that is not what either Saint Augustine or any other of the Fathers wished to convey to theirs. It was man's first disobedience which was important to them, a disobedience which

[22] *Phaenomena* 96–136. For the fortunes of Aratus, see *Primitivism in Antiquity*, pp. 34 ff.

could be redeemed only by the Vicarious Atonement of the Second Adam.

Another distinction was that between the sensible world and the intelligible world. According to Wolfson, the term Intelligible World or noetic cosmos "is not known to have been used before him [Philo]."[23] In any event, the term names the archetypal pattern of the world in which we live, the sensible world. Its inhabitants, like the ideas of Plato, can be apprehended only by the reason, never by perception. But unlike the Platonic ideas, they form an organic pattern in which each item is related to every other. Just what this relationship is is obscure, but since the pattern is created by the divine *Logos*, it is not unreasonable to conclude that it is rational, possibly that between genera and the species which they include, and those more general classes which include them. Another difference between Philo's world of ideas and the ideas of Plato is that in Philo they are first created by God and then have an existence of their own outside of their Creator. But since one can have nothing intellectual without an intellect to think it, they exist within an incorporeal mind, the *Logos*.[24] This *Logos* is not the mind of God but a distinct being, sometimes referred to as the Son of God, as in the Fourth Gospel.[25] Thus in the supernatural world there are also two beings, God and the *Logos*, whose mind is the world of ideas. But there is still a "lower" form of beings, powers immanent in the material world which are not the angels, though they too are called powers, and which account for the permanence of things.[26] God does not enter the material world, for that would be "unlawful." But these powers can enter into it and they conserve the shapes and qualities of corporeal things. The separation between the Creator and His creation is made a bit wider here than it would seem to have been in the Bible, where God speaks directly to Moses on Mount Sinai, as He did to Adam after the Fall or to

[23] H. A. Wolfson, *op. cit.,* Vol. I, p. 227.
[24] Cf. Wolfson, *op. cit.,* Vol. I, p. 232.
[25] See *De agricultura* xii. 51; LCL, p. 134.
[26] I follow Wolfson here, *op. cit.,* Vol. I, p. 278.

the young Samuel. Such speaking may not come under the heading of entering the material world, but at any rate the Creator's intimate relation to the creation in such passages seems to amount to direct contact with at least one item in it, the mind of man. On such occasions, then, the gulf is bridged, but normally it remains open.

We now come to a fourth group of beings between God and the sensible world, the angels. The angels are guardians of nations, cities, and sometimes individuals. They are at times called powers but their chief function is to carry out the commands of God, not to maintain the permanence of objects. They fall into choirs, but whether they are grouped into inferior and superior ranks, as in Pseudo-Dionysius, is not clear. There is an indication in *De Cherubim* (ix. 27; LCL, p. 24) that the Cherubim symbolize God's goodness and absolute power and are thus closest to Him. But nothing is said here of any hierarchy of angels running from the Cherubim down.[27] "The other philosophers," says Philo (*De somniis* i. 141; LCL, p. 372), "call them *daimones*, but Sacred Scripture prefers to call them angels, using a more suitable word. And this because they transmit the exhortations of the Father to His children and the needs of the children to their Father." In *De plantatione* (iv. 14; LCL, p. 218) he assigns them to the air and gives some of them a more elevated position than he gives to others. These, he says, the Greeks called Heroes. There is thus indicated, but vaguely, a difference in degrees of power or nobility of function among some of the angels. When he interprets Jacob's ladder, he makes it the symbol of the air with one end on earth and the other in heaven. Just as heaven is inhabited by the astral intelligences, the water by aquatic animals, and the earth by terrestrial, so the air is inhabited by these invisible beings. They are as a group better than the terrestrial beings (*De somniis* i. 22.

---

[27] In Ps-Dionysius *De Coelesti Hierarchia* c. 6 (Migne, *PG*, iii), the heavenly beings (*ousiai*) are grouped into three orders, the "most sacred Thrones," the Cherubim and Seraphim; the Powers, Dominations, and Virtues; the Angels, Archangels, and Archons (principalities). There is nothing so detailed in Philo.

137 f.; LCL, p. 370).[28] Moreover, the purest and best of them, the *daimones*, are the eyes and ears of God and watch over the cosmos as a whole. These would surely be superior to the others. Some angels descend to earth and inhabit human bodies. As a whole then the angels fill the space between heaven and earth and exercise a constant katabasis and anabasis. Hence we have here a definite, if vaguely phrased, conception of a cosmic hierarchy of beings. But whether it is original with Philo or derived by him from contemporary writers now lost, we do not know. Its importance to us here is its similarity to ideas to be developed by the Neoplatonists.[29]

The two worlds, then, of Philo are linked by the beings who exist between God and Matter. There is first the *Logos*, identified with the Intelligibles, then the highest and purest angels, then the lower angels, then in an indefinite position the powers who maintain and conserve the shapes of things, then men and of course the irrational animals and plants. Below them all is matter. The reason why God created the world is precisely the reason why Plato's Demiurge created as many things as were compossible, namely that, being good Himself, He wished everything to partake of goodness and could not begrudge spreading His goodness as far as possible. But since in the beginning there was nothing but God Himself to share His goodness, he had to create a world into which His bounty could spread. In doing this, He first created the Intelligible World as a perfect pattern for the world of material things (*De opificio mundi* iv. 16; LCL, p. 14). This act of creation was an act of thought and neither was there pre-existent matter for God to manipulate and fashion nor was there any command that matter appear. The corporeal world of the heavens was not created until the second day. Whether Philo believed that primary matter was itself created by God or not is

---

[28] This whole passage, by the way, anticipates Plotinus' account of the descent and return of the soul, as given in *Enneads* v. 1. 1 and iv. 3. 8.

[29] Bréhier moreover points out the parallel between this and *Epinomis* 981b, as well as certain parts of *Phaedrus* 248. See *op. cit.*, p. 128.

a moot point.[30] Since he clearly said that God alone is real (*Quod deterius* xliv. 160; LCL, p. 308), if he was to be consistent he must have thought that matter, unless it were identified with God, was unreal. At the same time when he thinks of the creation of material things, he thinks in terms of an idea being incorporated, as an architect's plan is put into material form. But in the case of that matter which is the human body, Philo maintains that it was created not by God's direct act but through the co-operation of assistants. Why He did this, Philo admits (*De opificio mundi* xxiv. 72; LCL, p. 56), is really known to God alone and one can only offer a guess as a solution to the problem. Philo's guess is that man is of a mixed nature, partly good and partly bad, and that it was unfitting for God to create anything evil. He is responsible for the good in man, the assistants for the evil. There is therefore a notion in the back of his mind that there runs throughout the universe of beings a principle of decreasing goodness corresponding to their priority and posteriority in the order of creation. In Plotinus, as in Porphyry and the later Neoplatonists, a similar principle is found to the effect that the maker is always superior to what he makes.[31] And we find here at least a dim premonition of that principle in Philo. In a fashion it was anticipated by both Plato and Aristotle, since they both believed that an idea when incorporated was always imperfect, but of course in neither of them was there any hierarchy of goodness running through the *scala naturae*, for except in certain scattered sentences of Aristotle there is no *scala naturae*. The vegetative soul does indeed exist as matter in relation to the sensitive soul and the sensitive soul as matter in relation to the rational. But the general tenor of Aristotelianism runs counter to the idea of a hierarchical universe.

2. In such passages of Philo as those which discuss the significance of numbers we find evidence of what has been called Neopythagoreanism. Cicero attributes the revival of Pythagoreanism to Nigidius Figulus, but what Nigidius actually taught is not

---

[30] See Wolfson, *op. cit.*, Vol. I, p. 300, for an analysis of the question.
[31] See for instance *Ennead* v. 2. 2.

known. Diogenes Laertius gives the teachings of the Pythagorean circle in an epitome of an account by Alexander Polyhistor, a contemporary of Philo. This epitome is therefore twice removed at least from its source. It runs as follows (Diogenes Laertius, viii. 25):

> The monad is the first principle. And from the monad comes the indefinite dyad, as it were, matter supporting the monad which is a cause. And from the monad and the indefinite dyad are the numbers. And from the numbers the points. And from these the lines, and from these plane surfaces, and from planes solids, and from these sensible bodies, of which moreover there are four elements, fire, water, earth, air. And there are interchange and intermingling throughout all things and there is born of these the animate cosmos, intellectual, in the likeness of a sphere, the earth holding the central position and being spherical and encompassing.

We have seen notions similar to this in the fragments of Speusippus, so that whether they go back to the semimythical Pythagoras or not, they are much older than the first century B.C. Whether their author had any clear idea of what he meant by the indefinite dyad's being, as it were, matter to the monad, I cannot say, but one guesses that he had in mind the picture of the *tetraktys* in which the first four integers were arranged as points under the One, and when they were added up, they made ten, the basis of the decimal system. The common-sense way of explaining the generation of numbers after two, is to point to the operation of addition. But Pythagoreans were interested in the generation of numbers not in operations which might presuppose the existence of that upon which the operation is made. And since one was not supposed to be a number, even by Aristotle, the existence of two could not be explained by addition. That lines, planes, and solids should be generated out of numbers became a generally accepted idea well into the Renaissance, and the words *square* and *cube* were taken literally, even when applied to the product of a number by itself and the product of a number by its square. To generate the elements out of the geometric simples could have been derived from *Timaeus*, in which various regular solids were associated with them. But a detail which I have not found in Philo or in his predecessors, but which was to reappear in Plotinus, is that of the constant interchange and intermingling of the elements, analogous to the collisions of the Epicurean atoms—a relative novelty in this period, though it too had been anticipated in a different form in the mixture of Anaxagoras' atoms. In Philo, God is also the One and the first principle of all things, but there is no indefinite dyad in him and no generation of the points, lines, planes, and solids, to say nothing of the elements, out of the numbers. The numbers in his writings have symbolic meaning, as we have seen, but creation is attributable to the ideas and the ideas were not numbers.

3. In Pseudo-Archytas,[32] the monad and the indefinite dyad are replaced by two primary principles, "one corresponding to the ordered and the definite, the other corresponding to the unordered and indefinite." These belong to two opposing classes, the definite being beneficent, the indefinite maleficent. "Wherefore when they have come into being in art and in nature, they share in these two primary things, both in form and in substance." The forms are causes of particularity; the substance is the underlying matter which receives the forms. But now there must be something to bring about this junction and that is the work of God. "So now we say that there are three first principles, God and substance and form. And God is the artificer and mover, substance is matter and the moved, and form the art and the source from which substance is moved by the mover." God then has the function not of creation but of bringing together into some sort of harmony matter and form, evil and goodness. Though the language here is Aristotelian, the underlying idea is not. There is no first principle in Aristotle which harmonizes good and evil, form and matter. Opposites are not harmonized in him; they remain what they are and replace each other in cases of change. That is, if a good thing changes in respect to its goodness, it can only be-

[32] From Stobaeus, Vol. I, p. 278.

come evil. And though forms become particularized when embedded in matter, (1) there is no external cause which brings this about, except in the case of art where the artist incorporates the form, and (2) it is inherent in the natural order that most forms be potentially present in their matter. Moreover, there is no identification of matter with maleficence and of form with beneficence; that which has perfected its form is always better than the unrealized potentialities of a thing, but the substratum has no power to do anything whatsoever, good or bad. It receives forms and that is all. One can see even in this small fragment, however, the beginnings of a pluralism which also appears in Philo and which later thinkers were to try to organize.

This comes out more clearly in some words of Syrianus commenting on Aristotle's *Metaphysics*[33] where he says that Archytas called the first cause (God) a "precausal cause." This removes God from the cosmos, while retaining Him as the ultimate cause of it. It foreshadows Philo's statement (if the author was earlier in date than Philo) commenting on Genesis 2:18, "It is not good for man to be alone," and "the only being which is alone and in itself is God and nothing is like God." (*Legum Allegoria* ii. 1. 1; LCL, p. 224).[34] Though the arguments by which the complete transcendence of God is proved are not given, one can see that if there is to be a cause of everything whatsoever, it cannot be found in the known cosmos, for everything in that cosmos is assumed to have been itself caused. But if it is outside the cosmos, then nothing can be said of it except that it is alone, unique, and, as later theologians were to see, unqualifiable and ineffable. Furthermore (*De opificio mundi* ii. 8; LCL, p. 8), anything which we can see has been caused, and if something has been caused, it is acted upon. Therefore there must have been an agent to cause it. When it is a question of the whole cosmos, its cause must be purely active and in no respect passive. But such a being is pre-

[33] Mullach, Vol. II, p. 117.

[34] Nothing is like God, one suspects, only in the matter of being alone, for Philo needless to say does not deny that man was made in the image and likeness of God.

causal in the sense that it is prior in nature to all observable causes. They are acted upon as well as acting.

4. Onatus, a figure so obscure that there is some doubt whether he ever existed, seems to take up the challenge. For he says,[35]

God knows the life of animate beings, but He is neither seen nor perceived, except to an extremely few men. For God is intelligence (*Nous*) and soul and the guiding principle of the whole cosmos.[36] Now God Himself is neither seen nor perceived, but is contemplated in thought only and in the mind. But his works and deeds are both visible and perceptible to all men. But it would seem to me that God is not one, but that there is one greatest and highest and the ruler of the whole, while there are also many others differing in degrees of power. But He rules as a king over them all. He who excells in might and greatness and virtue. And this God encompasses the entire cosmos, but the other gods traverse the heaven in concourse with the whole, accompanying according to the reason the first and noetic God. Now they who say that there is but one God and not many are mistaken. For they do not at the same time contemplate the most high honor of the divine supremacy. But I say that the rule and power over similar things belong to Him who is mightiest and superior to the others. And the other gods are so related to the first and intelligible God as the chorus to the chorus master, and soldiers to their general, their taxiarch and commander, it being their nature to follow and obey the orders of Him who is rightly their leader. It is the duty common to both the ruler and the ruled, nor can the ruled carry out their orders if they are abandoned by their guide, any more than singers can sing in unison without their leader or soldiers can win a victory without their general. Nature is such that it lacks nothing, either that which is innate or that which comes from without, wherefore it is not put together from two things, soul and body, for soul is throughout the whole, nor from some sort of opposites, for opposites are made to conquer and be conquered. In fact the mixture with the body weakens the purity of the soul, for it is pure and divine, whereas the body is mortal and mixed with dirt. . . . In every respect God has given the body to mortal animals because of eternal and inescapable necessity. For everything which shares in becoming is poor in nature and needy. The real God then, just as I have said in the beginning of my discourse, is Himself the first principle and the primary god. And divine is the

[35] Mullach, Vol. II, p. 113.
[36] The author uses the Stoic term (Doric), τὸ ἁγεμονικόν.

cosmos and all things revolving within it. So in the same way is the soul a *daimon* for it rules and moves the entire animal. One must make this distinction, between god and the divine, and *daimones* and the daimonie.

It becomes clearer than ever that the distinction between appearance and reality is that between the inert, passive, unordered, formless, chaotic, and that agent or those agents which are active and introduce the order and form into matter. This active power is suprasensible, since the sensible is always the material, but who the few men are who can know God is not told us. Moreover, in their case God is seen and perceived, and it is tempting to conclude that they have a mystic vision of Him. Such a vision is hinted at by Philo too, though he also says that God is indefinable (*De posteritate Caini* xlviii. 167; LCL, p. 426), incomprehensible (xlviii. 169; LCL, p. 427), unnamable and ineffable (*De somniis* i. 11. 67; LCL, p. 330).[37] The hint is given in *De migratione* (vii. 34; LCL, p. 150) when he is speaking about inspiration. It has happened to him "thousands of times" when he has sat down to write and found his mind barren. Suddenly, he says, he has found his mind "by the power of the living God" filled with ideas. He was as in a Corybantic seizure and unaware of all things, "the place where I was, the persons present, myself, the things being said and the things I was writing." He was given then, he says, "expressions, conceptions, enjoyment of light, keenest vision, the utmost brilliance of distinct objects, such as might be produced through the eyes from clearest demonstration." Here, to be sure, Philo is not face to face with God, as he might be were he having a beatific vision, but some of the details such as the lack of self-consciousness, the intense light, the clarity of what he contemplates, are so similar to some of the details of the mystic experience as usually reported that one may at least wonder whether his experience of inspiration is not that of the mystic. For if God is incomprehensible, He can be known only indirectly through His works, and the most important of His works for a philosopher

[37] On the problem of knowing God, see Wolfson, *op. cit.,* Vol. II, p. 110.

would be inspiration, as close a contact with the divine nature as would be possible. Unfortunately Onatus does not tell us just what the seeing and perception of God is like when they come to the happy few. And so we can draw only the vaguest conclusions from the resemblance between what he says about the knowledge of God and what Philo says about inspiration. But it is clear that the only knowledge which one could have of an ineffable, incomprehensible being would be through a vision.

Each of these writers, it will be observed, can give reasons for asserting the incomprehensibility of God. They may not know what He is, but they do know what He is not. And since He, the incomprehensible, is the one reality, known to exist through reasoning but not known through reasoning, we seem to have come to the point where even the reason is unable to reach what really is. Since, moreover, it arrives at the truth through inspiration, not through reasoning, man is left in the desperate condition of knowing what he wishes to know but incapable of finding it through his own efforts. It would be absurd to attribute such a conclusion to the philosophers whose works remain only in scraps and tatters, for we naturally can have little idea of what they said in the lost pieces. But at least in Philo's case we have plenty of evidence that the truth is before us in a book, that the underlying meaning of that book is to be discovered only through interpreting it as an allegory, and that the meaning of the allegory comes, or at least sometimes comes, through inspiration. There are of course dozens of passages where the exegesis relies on the commonplaces of Stoicism, Platonism, and Aristotelianism, and Philo does not tell us at what point his reliance on the philosophic tradition breaks down and he has to wait for revelation. One suspects that the point is reached when the tradition or its implications seem to be in conflict with the Bible, as Judaism interpreted the Bible. An example of this would be the matter of the eternity of the world. Hence one is forced to conclude that Zeno and Cleanthes, Plato and Aristotle, were all Moses speaking Greek when they agreed with Moses. At other times they were simply mistaken. And it was Philo himself who could distinguish between what they had borrowed from Moses and what they had imagined for themselves.

II

1. The two worlds of Philo are linked, as we have said, by the angels, some mounting upward and some descending, as in Jacob's ladder. But there is little, if any, evidence that he was thinking of them as symbolizing different "degrees of reality," though apparently they did possess different degrees of power in the sense that some had functions which were more important than others. Moreover, though Philo, as we have seen, makes plentiful use of Pythagorean number symbolism, there is no text which I have found in which the overflowing of the One into the other numbers is asserted. God is a creator, not a fountain from which all other beings flow. The gap between the real and the perceptual is not filled with beings of decreasing "reality" which emanate from the *ens realissimum.* Whatever exists between God and this world is created by God, and this includes the ideas as well as the material world.

There were, however, in the first century b.c. the following data which might induce men to believe in a hierarchical universe, a term whose meaning we hope will become clearer later, as well as in emanation as opposed to creation. First, there were the psychobiological theories of Aristotle, to the effect that in the soul the vegetative faculty, corresponding to plant life, was a matter to the sensitive faculty, corresponding to animal life, and the sensitive faculty was as matter to the rational faculty. Moreover, within the rational faculty there was a division between the passive reason and the active reason and the former was as matter to the latter. But between the human reason and the Unmoved Mover there existed no graduated scale of beings. Aristotle also believed in the existence of zoophytes which were partly vegetable and partly animal and this might have suggested that there were intermediate stages of being between any two stages. But if this suggestion were accepted as more than what it actually is, namely a belief in the existence of sponges and polyps, a serious error would be committed, for there is no mention in Aristotle of beast men, unless one thinks of natural slaves as such. Again, as far as Aristotle is concerned, there was always the possibility, realized by Porphyry in his *Introduction to the Categories*, that the relation between the species and the genus would be generalized so that each genus would be a species of a higher genus, until one reached the genus of all genera. But since Aristotle believed in the radical separation of the ten categories, it would have been strange for him also to have thought that they were all somehow or other directly "deducible" from the highest all-inclusive genus. They are actually ten ways of being, arrived at by observation, if not by an inspection of the parts of speech, and none of them is subordinate to any of the others. In fact some of them, such as action and passion, are antitheses. Finally, there might be a hint of a hierarchy in his theory about the spheres which were spatially arranged in order from the outermost to the innermost. It is true that the outermost was the best and presumably the sphere of earth was the worst, though Aristotle himself does not draw this conclusion. But the influence of the Unmoved Mover upon the spheres is left vague, nor do they proceed out of Him, nor are they created one after another from Him, nor does each of those below the crystalline sphere emanate from that immediately above it.[38] Furthermore, since his world was without beginning or end, there was no thought in Aristotle of any genetic relation between parts of the world. Genesis occurs on earth in the growth of living beings and in art.

Nevertheless these various hints have induced some later thinkers to attribute to Aristotle a belief in a hierarchical universe and what induced modern scholars to make this inference may very

[38] For further discussion of the hierarchy in Aristotle, see G. Boas, *Some Assumptions of Aristotle*, chap. 7.

well have induced the ancients to do as much. But more influential than Aristotle was Plato in the *Timaeus* which, as Lovejoy has shown, proclaimed the Principle of Plenitude (the term is Lovejoy's) according to which all possibilities must be realized. But in Plato there is no suggestion of how the ideas came into being for the simple reason that he believed them to be eternal. They were not the thoughts of the Demiurge who, as a matter of fact created nothing, nor were they arranged in any serial order from the most inclusive to the least, nor were the primary categories of Identity and Difference, Motion and Rest, further reducible. Whatever the Demiurge fashioned, He fashioned in accordance with rational principles.

There was also a suggestion of a hierarchy in the works of the Pythagoreans, especially in their theory of numerical relationships. The *tetraktys* is a pattern of numbers which might be said to flow out of the One, their source.[39] It was, however, only a pattern and there is no evidence that between every two numbers there was supposed to be a third, nor that three, for instance, was better than or inclusive of or the source of four. The numbers were discrete integers in the Pythagorean fragments; how they "flowed" out of the One remains a mystery. There is a Pythagorean fragment preserved by Stobaeus (Vol. I, p. 188) which says that there are three species of number, the even and the odd and a third which is mixed, called "even-odd." But this division is ultimate. Similarly Plutarch reports (*Placita* iii. 100. 11) that Philolaus believed in the existence of both the earth and the counterearth, as well as a central fire, an opinion attributed to the "so-called Pythagoreans," with no mention of Philolaus, by Aristotle (*De caelo* 293a). But a cosmos with a central fire and two earths in opposite position is scarcely a hierarchical cosmos. We have also a fragment from Stobaeus (Vol. I, p. 16) which says

[39] Hippolytus, who is of course much later than the men of whom we have been writing, attributes the following to Pythagoras himself: "The *tetraktys* is the source of everflowing nature, having roots"—of everything else?—"in itself, and from this number all numbers have their origin." I quote this from Diels, *Doxographi graeci*, l. 20, p. 556.

that the decade is the guiding principle and organizer of the cosmos and another which says that one is the first principle of all things. In view of the almost impossibility of making any sense out of such scraps, it is perhaps wiser to suspend judgment.

The work known as "On the Soul of the World and Nature," ascribed to Timaeus of Locrus, is not authentic, for it reads as if it were of Platonistic origin, though it seemed Pythagorean to Proclus who has preserved it for us in his commentary on Plato's *Timaeus*. We shall leave in abeyance the question of its date and authorship, for it is certainly anterior to the fifth century A.D., and is in all probability much earlier. It may well be this work to which Clement of Alexandria refers in his *Stromata* (v. 604a) which would put it before the late second or early third centuries. Our own guess is that it is the work of some Platonizing eclectic of the early Christian period. It makes the cosmos the product of the *Nous* and of Necessity, the former being responsible for rational beings, the ideas, and the latter for material changes. "Of these on the one hand is that which is of the nature of good things and is called God and is the source of whatever is best, but the others, which are co-operative causes, are classed with Necessity. And things as a whole are divided into the ideal and sensible matter, which is as if a child of the ideas. And the one is without birth and unmoved and stable and *sui generis*, being both intelligible and the paradigm of the things which come into being. . . . But matter is a receptacle, both a mother and a nurse, productive of the third substance. For it has received into itself and been imprinted with images and by them it generates things as its children." The passage then proceeds to describe matter as itself eternal, though not immutable; it has simply the capacity for receiving ideas. It thus resembles Aristotle's substratum, and indeed what we have so far is a combination of Aristotle's matter and Plato's intelligible world with the particulars in between as the children of both. But now what was the *Nous* becomes God, and we are told that "before the heaven was, there existed in the *Logos* the ideas, the matter, and God, the Demiurge of the better." The *Logos* was not in God, but God, as well as the other two kinds of being, was in the *Logos*. This is neither Plato nor Aristotle nor anyone else whom we have discussed so far in this book, nor is it Philo nor the author of the Fourth Gospel. "And since the elder is prior to the younger and the ordered to the unordered, God, being good and seeing that matter received the ideas and was altered in every way but in a disorderly fashion, felt constrained to put it in order and from indefiniteness to change it into definiteness, so that they would be made harmonious with their bodily differences and not take on fortuitous directions." He thereupon made this cosmos out of all sorts of matter so that it might be capable of everything. It was made one, of one kind, perfect, animate, and rational, "for such is better than the inanimate and the irrational." It has a spherical body, "for this is better than any other shape." Here there are obvious resemblances to *Timaeus*, but again there is no mention of a graded series of beings filling the universe from heaven to earth or from absolute Being to Nonbeing.

2. In Moderatus of Gades, presumably a figure dating from the middle of the first century A.D., there is a clearer suggestion of an ontological hierarchy in which the lower stages are derived from the higher. His views are found in Porphyry's *Life of Pythagoras* and the *Physics* of Simplicius (p. 230). It is the account of Simplicius which contains the passage illustrating the hierarchy. According to the Pythagoreans, we are told, there is a "first One" which is defined as above being and all substance—or essence—and a "second One" which "is really real and intelligible," the ideas, and a third "which is psychical and shares in the One and the ideas." Then come the sensible things which do not participate in the ideas but are a reflection of them, like the images seen in Plato's cave, the probable source of the figure. These are not real at all but a sort of "shadow" cast by the multiplicity in the intelligible world "or better something which has descended from it." At last we have a clear case of degrees of reality ordered in a hierarchy, with a genetic relation running down from the

upper levels to the lower. How does the genesis of the lower levels come about? "The unique *Logos* . . . having desired that genesis of things come from himself, displaced by privation the multiplicity of all things and took away from them the *logoi* and ideas of himself. And this multiplicity he called amorphous and undifferentiated and unordered, though form, order, and difference and quality had been admitted throughout the whole." The descent is caused by privation. Genesis occurs by depriving a level of being of some of its characteristics. This could be a purely dialectical procedure, for one could reason that, if there is form in the world of ideas, there could be a lack of form somewhere else, and so with the other characteristics mentioned. So he says later that the material world does not have multiplicity as ideal but by privation and a "loosening" and removal and tearing asunder and degradation from being. Wherefore, he adds, matter is an evil thing, since it has fled from the good. Presumably then the genesis of the lower orders could come about only through a loss of "reality," for since the ideas are perfect, their exemplifications would have to be less perfect. The principle that the creation is always worse than the creator was to become a cardinal principle of Neoplatonism and the explanation of the inferiority of the created is adumbrated in Moderatus' theory of creation through successive privations. Since no one can be sure of the date of this account, it cannot be labeled a source of any other ideas of whose dates we are certain and is inserted here mainly for the interest which it would have if written in the first century.

3. In Nichomachus of Gerasa, also probably of the first century A.D., we find once again the theory that the world can be understood only mathematically, with the additional thesis that the numbers pre-exist in the mind of God.[40] They are the paradigms in accordance with which all things are made, and through the "technical *Logos*" there come into being the universe as a

---

[40] I follow the fragments printed in C. J. De Vogel, *Greek Philosophy, a Collection of Texts*, Vol. III, 1288.

whole, time, motion, the heaven, the stars, and all their revolutions. But above them all stands the Monad, which is both male and female, and in it are mingled together God and matter in some way, and, as in a general receptacle (lit., an inn) are found chaos, confusion, mixture, darkness, blackness, emptiness, Tartarus. The astonishing detail in this passage is the compresence of matter and God in the first principle, as well as all the horrors of which the author is aware.[41] In Neoplatonism evil is a lack of reality, so that as the world proceeds out of the One, it loses something. But in Nichomachus it is found embedded in the universal source. There is a possibility that the reasoning behind this lies in the nature of the bisexual Monad, for it was generally believed that whereas the good was odd and male, evil was even and female. But there is also a suggestion in the famous Pythagorean Table of Opposites as given by Aristotle (*Metaphysics* 986a 22), where the side of the table which contains the even, the unlimited, the female, contains mainly, though not entirely, privations. But to make sense out of such passages is too great a strain upon the most benevolent imagination. At any rate one can say that it contains nothing resembling emanation of a hierarchical series.[42]

Our brief survey then shows us but one man who anticipated— if our conjectural dating is right—the idea of an ontological hierarchy, Moderatus. His hierarchy has the One at the apex and matter at the base, and is formed by successive privations.

III

Alongside of a genetic hierarchy and a logical hierarchy there exists a hierarchy of value indicated roughly in Moderatus also.

---

[41] Miss De Vogel sees here an echo of the Stoic principle that God is material, but it could just as well have been an inference based on the principle *ex nihilo nihil*. If everything comes from the Monad, everything must be in it.

[42] For a similar, though far from identical, theory, see the selection from Butherus, in Mullach, Vol. II, p. 50.

Though there is a sharp distinction in Plato between the ideas and their exemplifications, it is also true that the ideas were inherently better than their exemplifications and there are passages so well known as to require no listing here which state that the good is the goal of all things, that which they are striving to reach. But Plato does not say that there are levels of reality, each of which has its own good and that all these goods can be arranged in order of betterness, the lower ones somehow or other descending from the upper. In fact in *Phaedrus* (250d) it is made clear that Beauty is the one link between the two worlds. In the *Symposium* there is a hierarchy of value in Diotima's speech, where men are urged to proceed from the love of individual beautiful bodies to the love of general corporeal beauty, to beautiful forms, and laws, until one reaches absolute Beauty which is not attached to anything. But it would be in vain that one would look for a more definite hierarchical scheme of values corresponding to an analogous hierarchy of reality.[43]

It is possible that the first step toward fusing a hierarchy of reality with a hierarchy of goodness was taken when matter was said to be worse than the immaterial, and when the distinction was believed to hold good in the case of the human body and the human soul. When it was further believed that all action came from the immaterial soul and that the material body was always passive and inert, a further step was taken. But this radical distinction, though it later turned into two ends of a graduated series of beings, was not such in Plato and Aristotle, in both of whom the preliminary ideas appear occasionally, particularly in their ethical writings. Neither of them flatly says that the body and the material world are inherently evil, but Plato looks down on the purely sensual life given over to corporeal delights, and Aristotle has a program too by which the demands of our vegetative souls can be curbed. Neither teaches asceticism, but neither teaches debauchery. And, though the Stoics were materialists in their ontology, the matter which was the human body was sub-

[43] Cf. Windelband's *History of Philosophy*, Part I, chap. 3, sect. 11, par. 5.

mitted by them to the rigid control of the reason. Similarly, though the Epicureans were also materialists, they distinguished between those pleasures of the body which were to be avoided and those which might be gratified. But all this is common to the ethical teachings of the ancients and in itself neither invested all matter with the principle of evil, whether as a positive power inherent in it or as the privation of goodness. Nor, let us repeat once more, did any of these men maintain that between the material world and the ideal was a graded scale of beings which were less and less material and less and less evil.

1. The deontological opposition between the world of goodness and the world of evil comes out forcibly, as all Christians know, in the New Testament.[44] Though the world is the creation of God and though, when it was finished, "He saw everything that He had made, and, behold, it was very good," there is in Saint Paul an intimation that there is a fundamental opposition between God's work and Him who made it. We have received, he says (I Cor. 2:12), "not the spirit of the world, but the spirit which is of God," and again (12:32), "When we are judged, we are chastened of the Lord, that we should not be condemned with the world." Saint John (8:23) has Jesus saying to the Jews, "Ye are from beneath; I am from above: ye are of this world; I am not of this world." In the same Gospel later (15:18–19) we read the words, "If the world hate you, ye know that it hated me before it hated you. If ye were of this world, the world would love his own: but because ye are not of this world, but I have chosen you out of the world, therefore the world hateth you."[45] In his ethical teaching the author of the first epistle of John (I John 2:15 ff.) is found to apply the distinction to action: "Love not the world, neither the things that are in the world. If any man love the

---

[44] See Simone Pétrement, *Le Dualisme chez Platon, les Gnostiques, et les Manichéens* (Paris: Presses Universitaires, 1947), p. 209, where the opposition between God and the world and similar "Gnostic" theses are fully documented from the New Testament.

[45] Cf. John 17:4, 7, 14. See also Jesus' prayer in 17:9, "I pray not for the world, but for them that thou hast given me." The world here is the cosmos.

world, the love of the Father is not in him. For all that is in the world, the lust of the flesh, and the lust of the eyes, and the pride of life, is not of the Father, but is of the world. And the world passeth away." The important words here, as far as our purposes are concerned, are in the verse, "All that is in the world . . . is not of the Father." In Chapter 4 of the same epistle, the two realms are said to be the habitations of good and bad spirits, the evil being of the world, the good of God. And in Chapter 19 (19) we come to the conclusion that "the whole world lieth in wickedness." It would seem to follow that the world (cosmos) either has fallen into a lower rank after its creation or was not created good. But neither conjecture is substantiated in the New Testament and we have here echoes of a philosophy foreign to the Hebraic tradition.

The split between the world and God is paralleled in Saint Paul by the split between the flesh and the spirit. This requires no documentation, for it is common knowledge. The division is that between the evil and the good, as was the parallel split. In pagan philosophy this is best illustrated by those passages from Epictetus which have already been discussed. And, though Saint Paul speaks of the Law as having been given to the angels, he does not attribute to them degrees of power or goodness. One cannot step by step ascend to the Spirit; one must kill the "old man" and be reborn. "For if we have been planted together in the likeness of his death, we shall be also in the likeness of his resurrection. Knowing this, that our old man is crucified with him, that the body of sin might be destroyed, that henceforth we should not serve sin" (Rom. 6:5, 6). The emphasis upon the evil of both the world and the body is continued to be expressed throughout the Pauline Epistles and the fact that God created them both seems to be forgotten. Whether, as in Saint John (8:44), the world was submissive to the Devil as to a secondary deity in battle with the primary, I do not profess to know. But apparently what was later to become a Christian heresy, Manichaeism, was known in some form or other and its doctrines felt at the time the Fourth Gospel was written.[46] For in the Epistles of Paul we find also intimations that man was not made to live here below, being "strangers and pilgrims on this earth" (Heb. 11:13), a phrase repeated in I Pet. 2:11. The alienation of man from his true nature, his dwelling in a realm in which he is a stranger and a wanderer, his nostalgia for his true home, seem to be new elements introduced into Christianity if only in the form of metaphors. But it is easy to understand why some of the early Christians emphasized these metaphors and built them up into theological doctrines. This was not a period in which the new authority had been crystallized and heterodoxy annihilated. The dualism between God and the Devil, good and evil, spirit and matter, was as prevalent a belief in the communities which turned toward Christianity as it was in pagan circles.

2. The ideas which we see adumbrated in the New Testament passages referred to are usually called Gnostic.[47] Though the root meaning of the term is *knowledge,* the kind of knowledge which it denotes is entirely different from perceptual or rational knowledge. Though there is no organized body of doctrine which is peculiarly and outstandingly Gnostic, as the New Testament is Christian, there are certain general ideas which appear among all the various Gnostic groups. First, as Puech points out,[48] Gnosticism is less a Hellenizing of Christianity than an increasing orientalizing of it. He cites as his New Testament sources II Peter and the Deutero-Pauline Epistles. But most of our information comes from sources outside the New Testament, such as Ignatius of Antioch and the Pastor of Hermas. Since I have not had access

[46] This is reinforced by the Greek text which runs, καὶ ὁ πατὴρ αὐτοῦ, and which would normally be translated, "and so is his father." But the Authorized Version runs, "and the father of lies." The Greek would induce one to believe that the Devil has a father, as Jesus had a father, and that the two fathers were in primordial conflict as are their sons. But I am far from capable of adjudicating such matters and prefer to leave them in the air.

[47] For a definition of *gnosis* and related terms, see G. Kittel, *Theologisches Wörterbuch zum N. T.* (Stuttgart: Kohlhammer, 1933), Vol. I, pp. 688 ff. (article by R. Bultmann).

[48] In his monograph, *Où en est le Problème du Gnosticisme?* in *Revue de l'Université de Bruxelles,* Nos. 2 and 3 (1934), following Reitzenstein.

to the original sources of this cluster of doctrines, I shall follow
Puech's outline which is based admittedly on a fusion of several
strains of thought.[49]

Above the world, then, there stand two figures, the Father and
the Mother, who is the Thought of the Father. She falls into the
material world where she is held captive by two angels, sometimes called *archontes*, who are beings living in this inferior world.
In the earliest Gnostic systems the Father descends to rescue his
Thought, who is variously called Sophia, Barbelo, or even the
mother of the Seven Archons. Elsewhere the primordial couple
is completed by a Son, a Son of Man, the Archetypal Man,
Christos, and so on. The general tendency of this kind of fantasy
is anti-Jewish, the chief Archon being Ialdabaoth or Sabaoth, the
God of the Old Testament. There are thus two Gods, a good
God who is transcendent and unknown, revealed by His incarnation, called Simon or more generally Jesus, and an evil God
who is responsible for this material world. In the beginning then
there is a complete dualism and a removal of the Father, the good
God, high above the knowable world into absolute isolation,
logical and existential. But sometimes there is what Puech[50] calls,
a "cascade of emanations forming a world of *aeons* presided over
by the Father and punctuated by dramas beyond time, of which
the principal one is the fall of Sophia."[51] *Gnosis*, or the knowledge of this confusion of myths and symbols, obviously could be
neither perceptual nor rational. For what could be perceived
which would be direct evidence of the transcendent or furnish
data from which the unknowable could be deduced? It is scarcely
possible to frame an intelligible sentence expounding the beliefs
which were pronounced with such majesty and incantatory
power. Since the traits of the transcendent are beyond reason,
they can only be revealed from a supernatural source, even

[49] The curious might consult C. J. De Vogel, *op. cit.*, pp. 407 ff., for a
bibliography and outline of some of the principal Gnostic doctrines.
[50] *Op. cit.*, p. 11.
[51] Cf. Irenaeus *Adv. Haeres.* i. 1. 1–2.

though the very existence of such a source is a matter of doubt. Arguments such as that of the identity of Adam with Christ *vs*. Christ's assumption of Adam's body when He wished to visit the earth,[52] clearly could not be settled by natural evidence. The very meaning of the terms is dubious and the kind of proof which would be satisfactory to both parties concerned has never been stated. The partisans of such views would demand either the production of some sacred text whose authority would be accepted by both sides or proof of some special revelation given to the proponent of one side or the other. There were probably sacred texts galore but their sanctity was not admitted by any consensus. And since revelation had a way of varying from individual to individual with the result that there appear to be inconsistencies even in the canonical writings of the orthodox Jews and Christians, whose interpretation of the text was to become authoritative?

However reasonable such questions may seem to the men who put them, it can hardly be denied that revelation is a vital experience whose significance outsiders may doubt but which was never doubted by the men who lived it. Like the beatific vision it carries its own proof within it. The end of the pagan period was moreover a time during which miracles were accepted not merely as unusual occurrences, but as evidence of a divine presence, though the classic philosophers had insisted that the best evidence of a god was the uniformity of nature. This was a time again when texts with clear factual meanings could be safely interpreted as concealing a "deeper" meaning, when gods could appear in mortal form not merely as incidents in fictions, as in the *Iliad*, but in sober truth. Philo, indoctrinated as he was with rationalism, could maintain that verses which proclaimed the creation of the world in six days must be interpreted allegorically since, for instance (*Legum Allegoria* i. 2), there could not be any days until the heavenly bodies had been created, but he still was under the compulsion to maintain the truth of the verses in ques-

[52] Cf. L. Gordon Rylands, *The Beginnings of Gnostic Christianity*, p. 144.

tion in spite of the paradoxes they contained. If one ask how men could accept inconsistent sentences as all being true, the answer probably is that revelation, being given to individuals, is bound to vary with the individuals who receive it, and that consequently consistency is not so important as the strength of one's faith.[53] The history of New Testament exegesis suffices to demonstrate what men will sacrifice for the sake of faith. Hence one should not be too astonished to find that emanation of aeons, the fall of Sophia, angels and *archontes* flying about between heaven and earth, supernatural evil and good, the imprisonment of the soul in the body, incarnation of gods in men, the deifying of moral qualities, were all accepted as intelligible ideas. It is understandable that teachers and prophets should have called upon their pupils to have faith, since reason could give them nothing by way of answering their questions. But what is incomprehensible to a philosopher is that the pupils never seemed to ask for a clear statement of what they were asked to have faith in. Saint Paul, for instance, could speak of the crucifixion as a stumbling block to the Jews and foolishness to the Greeks and proudly declare that he was a fool in God. But nowhere does he explain in rational language just how God in the person of His Son could be crucified, die, rise from the dead after three days and still remain at the helm of the universe. Was the world without God after the crucifixion and before the resurrection? Was God entirely present in His Son and also the *ens realissimum* above the heavens? The consequences of either an affirmative or a negative answer to such questions would have been disastrous. A Plato, an Aristotle, a Zeno, an Epicurus, would indeed have found belief in such doctrines simple foolishness. But it seems to have been possible then as now for good Christians to label them mysteries and cling to them as essential to one's salvation. Tertullian's famous remark on the incarnation might be taken to mean that anyone could believe

---

[53] I have myself heard a reputable geologist maintain that the six days of creation were six geological epochs and that the years of Methuselah's life were lunar months.

in rational demonstrations, but only a saint could believe in the logically absurd.

The breakdown in rationalism is best illustrated by citing a text or two from Gnostic literature. One of the simplest is in what is left of Valentinus, a second-century figure living in Egypt, as quoted by Irenaeus (i. 1. 1–2) in his book against the heretics. His series of supernatural beings is as follows:

> In the invisible and unnamable heights is the perfect Aeon, pre-existing. And this they call the ultimate *Proarche* (Source) and the *Propater* (Pre-father) and *Bythos* (Depths). And He is spaceless and invisible and timeless and without beginning, and was born in silence and great solitude in infinite aeons of time. Together with Him is *Nous*, whom they also call Grace and Silence. And it is also believed that from Him is emitted *Bythos* (the Depths), this, source of all things and their seed, so to speak, the emission itself which they think to be ejaculated. And it settles down as in a mother in *Sige* (Silence) which exists beside Him. And when She has accepted this seed and becomes pregnant, She brings forth *Nous*, both like and equal to the emission, and She alone possesses the greatness of the Father. And this *Nous* they also call the Only Begotten[54] and the Father and Source of all. And together with Him is emitted *Aletheia* (Truth). And this is the primordial and original Pythagorean *Tetraktys*, which they call the root of all. Now there exists *Bythos* and *Sige* and then *Nous* and *Aletheia*. But Perception and the Only Begotten alike are emitted from these and the Only Begotten emits *Logos* and *Zoe* (Life), father of all things which are to come after Him and source and form of all the Plenum. Then from *Logos* and *Zoe* are emitted in syzygy *Anthropos* (man) and *Ecclesia*. And the same is the primally born Ogdoad, root and hypostasis of all things, called by four names among them, *Bythos* and *Nous* and *Logos* and *Anthropos*, for each of these is both male and female.

The emission of the various beings is clearly described as begetting. The *Propater* of all things is beyond all affirmative description and is qualified exclusively in the negative: He is without space or time or beginning. But though He is spoken of as ultimate and alone, yet *Nous* also seems to be there at His side,

---

[54] Strictly speaking, the Unique. But I follow John 3:16, as Irenaeus undoubtedly did.

possibly simply as the female nature joined with the male, for at the end of the passage we read that all the beings mentioned are bisexual. But the production of *Nous*, however, seems to be posterior to the existence of the progenitor of all things. And its birth is followed by that of Perception and the Only Begotten, followed again by *Logos* and Life, Man and *Ecclesia*. Since each pair of these beings is both male and female and has several names, one might arrange the series as follows:

The *Propater*——*Nous*
  Bythos——Silence
    Nous (the Only Begotten)——Truth (the *Tetraktys*)
      Perception——the Only Begotten[55]
        Logos——Life
          Man——*Ecclesia*

The process by which the levels are created is described as pro-creation, not emanation. We can, in spite of the obscurity of the passage, see that the primordial source of all things is a transcendent being and consequently ineffable. To this extent it resembles the God of Philo as well as the One of Plotinus. Whether the hierarchy is one of decreasing "reality," goodness, and logical extension is not apparent, nor does there seem to be any way of reading a logical hierarchy of classes into it. One might say that the *Logos* and Life were more inclusive than Man and *Ecclesia*, but then we should have to infer that Perception (the Sensible World?) was superior to and inclusive of *Logos*, which seems unlikely.

There is, moreover, another hierarchical arrangement, this time of three kinds of beings, and this one does correlate them with levels of goodness. These (Irenaeus, i. 6. 1) are the spiritual, the psychic, and the material. The material is sinister and destructible; the psychical, which is of good omen, is between the spiritual and the material; the spiritual, which is in syzygy with the psychic, is "the salt and the light of the cosmos." The spiritual beings are

[55] The Only Begotten thus seems to be on two levels. But Irenaeus may be as confused as his source here.

never destroyed, for just as gold fallen into the mire does not lose its beauty, so the spiritual fallen into the material world remains spiritual. There are many material beings and many psychical, but few spiritual.[56] This passage, however, does not explain the generation of the three kinds of being nor can it be correlated with the generation of the various levels of reality out of the primordial Father.

3. In Numenius, a second-century writer whose opinions are preserved for us mainly in the *Praeparatio evangelica* of Eusebius, we find that the primary source of all things is a God who is "self-existent, simple, self-caused, and without any division."[57] Below Him are a second and a third God who are one. This dual God is torn between wishing to remain stable and to move (lit., "to flow"). He comes into being by taking charge of matter and is in contact with the sensible world, into which He apparently brings order. Numenius is clear in saying that the primary God is not the Demiurge. The first God is free from all works and is king of all, "whereas the demiurgic God rules over everything as He proceeds through the heavens." How the material world is made, whether out of pre-existing matter as in *Timaeus*, or out of the substance of the second God, what the role of the third God is in all this, since He seems to be a part or a name for one aspect of the second, are not clear. "When the God looks down upon us and considers us in His mind, He confers upon each of us the power both to live and to remain alive, as well as bodies, since the God attends to the control of things from afar." In other words He passes on to us the immediate control of ourselves. "And when the God returns to His own heights the same [life] is extinguished, but the *Nous* enjoys the power of living a happy life."[58] Here the second God acts the role of a guardian angel rather than that of a Demiurge. It is Numenius' account of the differences between the two Gods which interests Eusebius and not the creation

---

[56] This is from Clement of Alexandria. See De Vogel, *op. cit.*, 1335c.

[57] *Praeparatio evangelica* xi. 18; ed. Dindorf, Vol. II, p. 38.

[58] *Praeparatio evangelica* xi. 18. 10.

or genesis of the world below the first God. The first God, he is quoted as saying,[59] remains essentially Himself, whereas the second, on the contrary, is moved, that is, changes. Accordingly the first dwells in the Intelligible World, the second in both the Intelligible and the Sensible. "Do not wonder if I say such things, for you will hear much more wonderful things. For opposed to the productive movement of the second God, I say that the productive immobility of the first is inherent movement, from which both the order of the cosmos, alone eternal, and its preservation are conferred upon the whole." Moreover, this second God is not the *Nous*. Referring to Plato, Numenius says, the first God is utterly unknown, being self-existent, "as if someone should say, 'Men, He whom you conjecture to be *Nous* is not the first, but there is another *Nous*, older and more divine than this one.' " We are still left in the dark about the function of the third God and His relation to the second. Proclus interprets the doctrine somewhat differently. "Numenius," he says,[60] "celebrating the three gods, calls the first Father, and the second Creator, and the third Creation. For the cosmos, according to him, is the third God, so that the Demiurge in his opinion is twofold, being both the first and the second Gods, but that which the Demiurge has made is the third. For it is better to speak thus than, as he says exaggerating, grandfather, grandson, descendant." This is all very obscure and it may well be that Proclus misinterpreted Numenius,[61] living as he did some four hundred years later. But at any rate it gives a role to the third God. Even if the third God is the thought of the Demiurge, rather than the actual world created by Him, He remains an object, a substance, rather than an activity. So that we can, after making allowances for probable error, say that in Numenius we have, first, an unknowable, self-existent God, second a Demiurge, third an object of the Demi-

---

[59] *Praeparatio evangelica* xi. 18. 20.

[60] Proclus *in Tim.* i; ed. Diehl, Vol. I, p. 303.

[61] See De Vogel, *op. cit.*, Vol. III, p. 427, **1352a**, n. May I express my obligations to this work which reproduces many of the passages which have not been available to me at the time of writing this.

urge's thinking or making, and all three are divine. There can be little doubt that these three are ranked in descending levels of goodness and possibly of "reality." But there is no indication that they correspond to logical levels of abstraction, except possibly in the case of the first God who is the *ens realissimum*, though the pitiful fragments which remain of Numenius do not permit us to say that He is an all-inclusive class of beings.

Such then are what we have of philosophy based upon the uncritical acceptance of sacred texts and legends. By their very nature such ideas could not be made rational. At most they might stimulate visions and by the intensity of their emotional associations replace the results of hard thinking. It is interesting that they all result in some dimly envisioned cosmic hierarchy, a fusion of polytheistic and monotheistic religious beliefs. We shall now turn to the first clear and extended account of a hierarchical universe and to a philosopher from whom the early Christian thinkers drew most of their philosophic sustenance, Plotinus.

CHAPTER IX

The Final Capitulation

═══

ONE WOULD BE TEMPTED to end this study with Philo
Judaeus, for in him are the seeds of medieval philosophy and the
withering of classical rationalism. When philosophers accept
sacred texts as final authority, their task is at most exegesis and
the reason as an explorer of possibilities has laid down its arms.
There was no way of justifying the fantasies of the Gnostics and
Hermetists except by dogmatic assertion, or, if one prefers a
nobler name, by faith. But chronologically ancient philosophy did
not die out with the coming of oriental cults. Both Epictetus and
Marcus Aurelius, to say nothing of Seneca, survived the advent
of Christianity, and it goes without saying that the encyclopedic
work of the Alexandrine scholars continued until persecution
killed them. But no one of major importance appeared after Philo
until the third century when the so-called father of Neoplatonism,
Plotinus, opened his school in Rome.

Though Plotinus had no sacred text corresponding to the Bible,
which was directly inspired by God, he did have the works of the
ancients, and particularly those of Plato and Aristotle, whose in-

terpreter he was proud to be.[1] But I find no passage in which he disagrees, as he believes, with Plato, although modern scholars would, I think, find his interpretation sometimes questionable. He is more inclined to disagree with Aristotle, though here too one might question his interpretations. He lived after all about six hundred years, more or less, after the time of Plato and in that time philosophic method had changed, as we have seen, for the very accumulation of philosophic literature had made it difficult, if possible, for any man to start afresh. Moreover Plotinus grew up in Alexandria, not in Athens, and came in contact with Orientals, Egyptians, as well as with Greeks. His contemporary, Origen, was a Christian and both are said to have studied under the same master, Ammonius Saccas, of whom next to nothing is known.[2] But, be that as it may, no one studying in Alexandria at the end of the second century or the beginning of the third could fail to be influenced by the existence of doctrinal diversity and methodological confusion. No one studying philosophy in the United States today can avoid the influence of Kant, though he may never have read a line of Kant. He will inevitably start with epistemological questions as if they were the primary questions. So a philosopher living in Alexandria at that time would have begun with an intellectual stock of metaphysical ideas, including the distinction between the world of ideas and the sensible world, the existence of a supreme god in some form or other, and intimations that between the two worlds was a graduated scale of beings. They might differ on their interpretation of these terms and on the proper solution to the problems which they believed to be implicated in them. But whether one is reading Clement of Alexandria or Origen, one sees the same topics appearing in each.

[1] *Ennead* v. 1. 8, 10. I use the text of Henry and Schwyzer as far as possible, that is, through *Ennead* v. For *Ennead* vi, I use that of Bréhier. Only the first line of each reference is given, and in the body of the text I shall omit the title *Ennead*. Thus, v. 1. 8, 10 means *Ennead* v, tractate 1, section 8, line 10. On the wisdom of antiquity, see also ii. 9. 6, 35.

[2] There is some question whether the professor with whom Origen studied was really Ammonius Saccas. The datum comes from Porphyry. See Charles Bigg, *The Christian Platonists of Alexandria* (Oxford: Clarendon Press, 1913), p. 156.

I

To fill the gap between the two worlds seems to have been one of the most important of their problems. Philo filled it with angels and powers, the Gnostics, whatever their individual differences, filled it with other supernatural creatures begotten by their chief god. Origen filled it with Intelligences, created and corporeal spirits, who rose or fell according to their sinfulness. But no one before Plotinus developed a complete hierarchy which would be at one and the same time a hierarchy of reality, value, and logical concreteness. Since his metaphysics survived well into the Middle Ages, was fortified in the Italian Renaissance, and gained a certain vogue in post-Renaissance England, one would do well first to expound the meaning of the terms before proceeding to develop the ideas which it names.

Though the word "hierarchy" is Greek, it is not found in classical literature and first occurs in Pseudo-Dionysius, that is, in the fifth century A.D.[3] There it appears in the titles of two of his works, *The Celestial Hierarchy* and *The Ecclesiastical Hierarchy*. Both of these books, as far as our immediate interests are concerned, expound a system of power or governance running from the most powerful to the least. The ecclesiastical hierarchy is modeled on the celestial. As the latter runs from God down to man through the various choirs of angels, so the former runs from the head of the Church down to the catechumens. We are familiar with this idea in secular life in our armed services. A general commands armies, army corps, divisions, brigades, and so on, down to privates, and as one descends the hierarchy of rule each rank has more ranks above and fewer below it, and naturally official or legal power grows weaker the lower one goes. Hierarchical rule obtains in the Church today as it did in the beginning.

[3] In Boeck's *Corpus Inscriptionum*, Vol. I, p. 749, we find it in a Boeotian inscription. But it there means simply a man who presides at sacred ceremonies and has no metaphysical implications. The date of Ps-Dionysius can be determined by the date of Proclus whom he must have used. His definition of hierarchy is given in *De Coelesti Hierarchia* iii. 1 (Migne, *PG*, iii).

At the session, July 15, 1563, of the Council of Trent, in the canons on the sacrament of ordination, we find the words, "If anyone should say that in the Catholic Church there is not a hierarchy instituted by divine command, which consists of bishops, presbyters, and ministrants, let him be anathematized."[4] It is essential to this type of hierarchy that the individuals on each rank be fewer and fewer as one moves toward its apex until at the summit there is only one. But that does not prevent there being several hierarchies in existence at the same time. For instance, according to the *Catholic Encyclopedia* (art., "Hierarchy"), we have two hierarchies within the Church, the *hierarchia ordinis*, running from bishops, through priests, to deacons, and the *hierarchia jurisdictionis*, running from cardinals down through nuncios, delegates, patriarchs, primates, metropolitans, archbishops, vicars-general, archdeacons, deans, parish priests, to curates. So we have three hierarchies in the army, navy, and air force, but they are all under the command of the President of the United States according to the Constitution, just as both ecclesiastical hierarchies are submissive to the Pope. The Greeks had no ecclesiastical hierarchy. They had no single church as we have churches. They had temples dedicated to the service of their various divinities, but they were not organized into a single cult with various branches. The priest of Zeus or of Athena had no jurisdiction over the priest of Dionysus and similar conditions obtained in Rome. The individualism which the Greeks practiced in their civil and social affairs was duplicated in that of the gods. Indeed the gods as early as Homer squabble among themselves, and though Zeus is their Father, his parenthood seems to give him little power to settle their squabbles. The two goddesses who were affronted by the judgment of Paris are not made to sit down with

---

[4] Denziger's *Enchiridion* 966. See also the *Index systematicus* IIa. But as early as the third century, in the Epistle of Cornelius I, ἵνα δὲ γνῷς, to Fabius, Bishop of Antioch, it is stated that there is one supreme bishop, the Bishop of Rome, with presbyters, deacons, subdeacons, acolytes, exorcists, and so on, beneath him. For suggestions leading to the tradition of the ecclesiastical hierarchy, see the *Enchiridion* 42, 45, 272.

Aphrodite and talk things over, nor are they ever commanded by the Father of Gods and Men to cease interfering on the battlefield before Troy. Each goes his own way, as the Greeks themselves did, and it probably never occurred to any pagan that he ought to organize the priesthood into a hierarchy. But the Jews did have a hierarchy with the High Priest at the summit, and the Egyptian priesthood was also hierarchical. The Egyptian King was also the high priest, as Queen Elizabeth II is head of the Church of England. He was a manifestation of the god Horus. Local priests, who were the King's deputies, and lower priests filled out the Tables of Organization.[5] One can only guess at why there should have been this difference between Greek, Jewish, and Egyptian religious institutions. But it is to be noticed that the Old Testament records a parallel political organization as early as Judges and the history of Egypt shows that the Nile Valley came under the sway of a single absolute monarch very early. The Greeks on the other hand, living on a stretch of country almost unbelievably small as compared with the countries of Asia Minor and Egypt, retained their city-states up to the time of the Macedonian Conquest. The economy of Heaven often is modeled on that of Earth and that may be the reason why no Greek before the Macedonian Conquest shrank from theological pluralism.

Since the first clear intimation of a supernatural hierarchy comes from Alexandria and survives largely through the writings of Philo, it is likely that the metaphor of a cosmic hierarchy was suggested by the organization of the priesthood and of the state in Judea and Egypt. If the representatives of the divine power were organized hierarchically, it was easy to transfer the scheme to that which was governed by the powers which they represented. This connection cannot be proved, for how can one prove the origin of a figure of speech? Such things come into the mind without reflection and usually centuries before they enter philosophy. Did anyone calculate the chances of our God being a

[5] For details of the Egyptian hierarchy, see Hastings' *Encyclopedia of Religion and Ethics*, art. "Priests, Priesthood (Egyptian)," p. 293.

Father rather than a Mother? Of Heaven being above rather than beneath? The power of both the High Priests and Kings is transmitted orally of course, but how the power of the Supreme Being is transmitted is usually left vague. In the *De mundo*, which we have already cited, "God has the highest place in the cosmos," and "the body closest to him most enjoys his power, and then the one after that one, and so in succession down to the regions where we are." For this reason, says the author (397b), "earth and the things upon the earth, being farthest away from the benefits of God, seem to be weak and confused and full of disorder." God's power in this work extends through space and grows weaker the farther it extends, as the force of a magnet grows weaker the farther one gets from it.

In Aristotle the power of the first and outermost sphere is not transmitted to the next sphere by contact nor is the Unmoved Mover a God who gives commands. But there was one thing which moved through space and did grow weaker as it moved and that was light. As the beams of light spread, they reach out on all sides in spheres of decreasing luminosity. Professor Goodenough has traced the symbol of the sun as the source of light from Plato's Cave down through the Gnostics and also finds that though "the figure of royalty was certainly a source of the hierarchy of Power," "The light mysticism of the mystery religions" was another source "equally apparent."[6] Plotinus, as is well known, seized upon this metaphor and made it central to his system. The sun became a symbol both of the instantaneous spread of the divine power, and of its weakening as it penetrated into darkness (v. 3. 12, 39). The whole intelligible nature is compared to light emanating from its source, the Sun, a symbol for the One which is at the summit of the Intelligible World. The stream

---

[6] Erwin R. Goodenough, *By Light, Light* (New Haven: Yale University Press, 1935), p. 41. Cf. p. 11: "The sun was taken as a figure, that orb which burns, to all appearances, eternally, yet without need of fuel from outside itself. Independent of the world, a self-sufficient existence, it sends out its great stream of light and heat which makes life possible upon this earth. This stream may be called a stream of light, or of heat, or of life, or of creation."

of light, he says (v. 3. 12, 44), is not cut off from its source nor is it less real in spite of its not being identical with it, "nor is it a blind thing, but it sees and knows and is the primary knower" (v. 3. 12, 46). The congruence between seeing and knowing, even etymologically, seems to have been striking to those ancients to whom the problem of divine power was puzzling. Light is used by Plotinus as a symbol of intelligence (ii. 4. 5, 7), of the hierarchy of reality (iv. 3. 17, 12), of the vitality of seeds (v. 9. 6, 20), of the beatific vision (v. 3. 17, 28).[7] It is absolutely immaterial (iv. 5. 4, 6, iv. 5. 4, 41, vi. 4. 8); it travels in straight lines (iv. 5. 2, 10); it is indivisible (vi. 4. 7, 23); and it travels instantaneously (iv. 5. 4, 31). If one adds to this its radiation from the Sun which is in the heavens, one can understand why Plotinus, and others, argued as often from the symbol as they symbolized their logical conclusions.

In the *De mundo*, as I have suggested, the transmission of divine power was spatial and God was thought of as inhabiting a point in space. This point was literally, not figuratively, higher than any other point. The outer heaven was His home and therefore, though there may have been other reasons as well, that region of the cosmos was the best region, and as one moved downward to the center, one moved from better to worse.[8] To us it may seem strange that heights should be any better than depths, for though we locate God in Heaven, we also prefer profound thoughts to superficial ones. But even in Aristotle one finds that some directions are inherently better than others, up being better than down, to the right being better than to the left, forward being better than backward.[9] How much folklore remains in this and how much inference was in it I cannot pretend to say, but that the fusion of literal spatial position and deontological "superiority" exists is undeniable.

[7] See also i. 8. 14, 38; ii. 4. 5, 35; iii. 3. 4, 8; iv. 4. 29, *passim;* v. 3. 8, on self-knowledge; vi. 4. 3, 3. But these are only a few samples.

[8] For a discussion of the relation between height and goodness, see E. R. Bevan, *Symbolism and Belief* (Boston: Beacon Press).

[9] See *De caelo* iv. 4 and *De incessu* 705a 26.

The metaphor which inspired the fusion of height and better-ness was developed in several ways, but one of the most influential was the famous Tree of Porphyry. The series of logical classes, as given by him in his *Introduction to the Categories of Aristotle* runs "upward" from the least inclusive class to the most inclusive. Porphyry had the advantage of being a pupil of Plotinus and it is probable that he failed to see how unfaithful he was to the book to which he was introducing his readers. The Tree of Porphyry resembles the *tetraktys* in that in both a single idea generates a multiplicity of other ideas and in both cases the generated have properties which their sources do not have. In Aristotle there is, to be sure, material out of which the Tree could have been con-structed, but it was not constructed by the author of the *Cate-gories*. If it had been, what would have happened to the ultimate distinctions between the ten categories? The Unmoved Mover might be called God and the Form of the World, though the lat-ter is a non-Aristotelian term, but he was not an all-inclusive class and only in a figurative sense a logical being. It is also true, as we have said above, that there are passages in Plato in which the idea of the good is said to be that toward which all things are striving, but that does not prevent each class of things from having its own good. But the moment when the Good, with an initial capital, is identified with God and God identified furthermore with the Un-moved Mover and the three of them are fused together into an unknowable, ineffable being to which only the arithmetical name, *The One*, could be given, then the hierarchy which began as a hierarchy of power could become also a hierarchy of logical classes and of goodness and beauty. For when one reached the apex of the figurative pyramid in one's thoughts, one had a being from whom all beings flowed as light from the sun, but also a being with a logical name so that logical classes could be grouped under it, and also a being whose attributes of stability, *autarky*, unity, and the like, were precisely the marks generally agreed upon as the marks of supreme goodness.[10]

---

[10] It is amusing to observe the residues of this kind of thinking in the

The identification of value with metaphysical status was fortified by certain precedents, as I have tried to point out in preceding chapters. From the early days of pre-Socratic philosophy the belief in two worlds was not merely the belief in a real and an apparent world, but also a belief in a good and less good world, respectively. The real world was not only more real than the apparent; it was better. The world seen by the senses was worse than that grasped by the reason; the flux was worse than the world of law, the unnatural worse than the natural, the particulars as a collection were worse than the universals. In a time of great change, one imagines, men who do not profit from the change seek that which is permanent. Moreover the very character of science demands that one try to understand and organize the chaos of perceptions which flow by one's sense organs. Whether the early philosophers had more to lose than to gain by the revolutions of the sixth century B.C., we cannot say for we have nothing but legends to go on. But in any event most of them seemed to prefer a world of stability to one of impermanence and they found it in their science. But the pre-Socratics gave us two worlds which were in sharp opposition, not a graded series of levels of being. There was nothing between the two worlds and the only thing that held them together was human understanding. The discovery of a general law explaining the generation of multiplicity is not a denial of multiplicity. To discover that both molecular oxygen and ozone are composed of atomic oxygen does not deny their difference in anything except their substantial composition. Again, though the *Logos* of Heraclitus is a law which describes the flux, it is not a denial of the flux. It seems at least probable that if these

prestige which attaches to the Nobility, even when their power is no longer exercised, to the privileges which accrue to the several ranks in the armed services, and to our inveterate habit of arranging our values in hierarchies from "low" to "high." In old Japan, in the days of the Shoguns, one had a hierarchy of power in the Shogunate and a hierarchy of prestige in the Court. Is it farfetched to see a resemblance to this in American culture where political power is far from being in the hands of the social hierarchy? The governor of a state, to say nothing of the political boss of a party, does not have the same kind of prestige as the Social Leaders.

men had felt the need for intermediaries between appearance and reality, the men whose quotations from them are our only source of information about their ideas would have pointed it out. For aside from the special interests of Aristotle in reporting the ideas of his predecessors,[11] men like Hippolytus and Eusebius would surely have been glad to find anticipations of Christian theological theses in these early thinkers. The Fathers had no hesitation in profiting from Plato, Aristotle, Philo, and later, Plotinus. Why would they have shrunk from using the works of the pre-Socratics if they could have done so?

As far as the hierarchy of power is concerned, there is also a possible causal relation between astrology and the cosmic hierarchy. We have already spoken of the influence of solar theology. But also if the planets spread their influence downward, how was it carried? Through their light? As Seneca said, it is easier to doubt whether the stars have any power than to know what power they have.[12] Cicero, in the *De divinatione* (ii. 14. 33), explains mantics on the basis of cosmic "sympathy," a union and, as it were, a consensus of all the parts of nature. And this may indeed be the theory behind the use of astrological predictions. But in spite of this, the sympathy must be propagated somehow or other, for, as many ancient critics of astrology saw, the thousands of people who are born at the same moment do not all have the same fate, and one might well wonder why a given planet should select one individual for its benefactions or maleficence rather than another, if the cosmos as a whole behaves as a unit. One might also ask the question why the astral influences determine temperaments only at the moment of a person's birth, if sympathy be the explanation of their power. These are questions to which we have no answer, but the possibility remains that belief in astrology may well have suggested the cosmic hierarchy of power since it too

---

[11] For a full discussion of Aristotle's handling of the pre-Socratics, see Harold Cherniss, *Aristotle's Criticism of Pre-Socratic Philosophy.*

[12] *Non magis autem facile est scire quid possint, quam dubitare an possint, Quaestiones naturales* ii. 32. 8.

was based on the transmission of power from the heights of the universe to the center.

Such then are the main characteristics of the cosmic hierarchy in all its threefold aspects.

II

The first full-fledged hierarchy of being is found in Plotinus. At the summit of his hierarchy is the One. The One is absolutely unknowable in the sense of describable. "How then can we speak of it? We do indeed say something about it, but we do not express it itself, for we have neither direct knowledge (*gnosis*) of it nor conceptual knowledge (*noesis*). . . . We speak about what it is not. But what it is, we do not say" (v. 3. 14, 1). The One then is above all things, like the *Propater* of Valentinus, though differing from Him in almost all other respects. But since to know something directly is to be like it, we must make ourselves like the One in order to know Him. We must consequently divest ourselves of all particularity, of all sensation, of all self-directed thoughts, pay no attention to the demands of our body,[13] and in a beatific vision we shall come face to face with Him, or better, unite with Him. This can occur only infrequently—in his case it occurred four times—and, when it does occur, one is not necessarily aware of what has happened. "But just as those who are inspired and have become possessed would know that they have something better within themselves, even if they do not know what it is, something by which they have been moved, and they talk of it, from these things they derive some perception of the moving power, though the things themselves are different from the moving power. And so we are in danger, in relation to that power, when we have a pure *Nous*, of declaring that this is the inner *Nous* which has produced substance and the rest such as are of this rank, but it itself is such that it is not at all the same,

---

[13] For an account of Plotinus' asceticism and mystic visions, see Porphyry's *Life* ii, viii, and xxiii, in Henry-Schwyzer, Vol. I.

but something mightier than this which we call Being, but also greater and better than has been said, because He is superior to the *Logos* and the *Nous* and Perception, since He produced these things but is not any of them" (v. 3. 14). This gives rise immediately to the question of how the One produces (v. 3. 15).

It is laid down as a general principle in the tractate on the descent of the soul (iv. 8) that everything has to administer and govern something which is lower than itself. Since everything engendered is worse than its progenitor, the soul administers and governs a body. Hence the One, like everything else, has to produce. That much is clear. But now how does He produce? The first possibility is that He possesses all things within Him; but in that case how could He be simple? But if He does not possess them, how does multiplicity come from Him? Could it come about from His very simplicity? Plotinus sees this problem clearly (v. 3. 15) and sees also that the metaphor of stream of light may solve the problem of the One's productivity but does not solve that of the multiplicity of what He produces. What comes from the One cannot be identical with the One (v. 3. 15, 7) and must furthermore be inferior to Him. But the only thing that is inferior to the One is the Many. Thus, once one admits that the One does produce, the multiplicity of the product is proved in a purely dialectical manner. But in arguing thus, Plotinus abandons the principle *ex nihilo* in the literal sense of that phrase—which would signify that what comes out of the cause must have preexisted in the cause—and reverts to the ancient dialectical principle that there are always antitheses in change, of which one is the source of the change, the other its consequence. As in Aristotle all change is from affirmative to negative, from one opposite to another, so here, meditating on the unity of the One, Plotinus concludes that anything which emanates from it must be its antithesis, the Many. Yet he modifies the multiplicity of what is produced by asserting another of his cardinal theses, that though all things produce, they also strive to return to their source. This permits him to say that (vi. 4), considered as really existent beings, all things are one, or inversely, that the One is omnipresent. He would have to be omnipresent, for, as Plotinus also points out (vi. 8. 18), there was no time when the One was not emanating His influences; He is both Himself and the emanations. In short this is an attempt to deny the distinctness of that which is a subject's activity from the subject itself. One can in words distinguish between the sun and its rays, but in reality they form one whole. The distinction exists in thought and Plotinus does not deny that if one thinks exclusively of the nature of the One, one does not include in His nature all the beings which flow from it.

The reduction of all to the One and the encompassing of all by the One is a logical matter. In all probability Plotinus reached unity by arguing that all things are individually units, and that for that reason alone unity must be the most inclusive of all classes, or, if the phrase be preferred, the universal predicate. As far then as His unity is concerned, He is indeed in all things, just as red, the color itself, is both a separate color and also found in many objects. Unfortunately he also says (vi. 2. 11) that the unity of objects, such as a chorus, a ship, a house, or a military camp, is not the same in all cases and that moreover (vi. 2. 11, 11) the unity of the continuous is not the same as that of discrete objects. This of course destroys his former argument for unity has to be self-identical if it is to be both the most general idea and the most universally present in things. Plotinus here switches his point of view and relies now on the tendency of all beings to fuse together and form units (vi. 2. 11, 26). And this tendency, since it is a movement toward the One and since it is the goal of existence and since the goal is the good, also permits him to assert that the One is the Good in a transcendent sense. But the unity which is sought is not that of a collection; it is that of the absolutely homogeneous, the simple (v. 4. 1). "Everything born of another is either in that which made it or in another, even if it be in something which comes after that which made it" (v. 5. 9, 1). In other words things are not really cut off from their origins; there are no ontological gaps. So while the One produces the *Nous* and the Soul of the

World, they participate in His unity and reality and goodness. Just as the light streams forth from the sun, while the sun itself remains stationary, so the *Nous* emanates from the One, is inferior to the One, but "looks back" at the One and "has need of Him alone, though He has no need of the *Nous*" (v. 1. 6, 42).[14]

It is perhaps obvious that Plotinian emanation is very different from Gnostic generation. The Gnostic passages which we have cited all cut off the inferior beings from their progenitors and their inferiority gives evidence of the evil which characterizes this world. But Plotinus will have none of this. We need not point out that he wrote a whole tractate against the Gnostics (ii. 9), but it may be worth pointing out that his objections against Gnosticism were first the multiplicity of first principles which they set up, second the inherent evil of creation, and third the senselessness of the Fall which they posit. Throughout his attack upon them, one sees his impatience with their anthropomorphism which leads them to assert creation in time (ii. 9. 8).[15] There are only vestiges of anthropomorphism in Plotinus and they consist largely, though not entirely, in his accounts of the Soul of the World. He is very anxious to demonstrate the effortlessness of emanation: the One gives rise to the *Nous*, for instance, without an act of will (v. 3. 12, 28).[16] Turning to another of Plotinus' basic metaphors, we

[14] Where Plotinus uses demonstrative pronouns, I have substituted their antecedents.

[15] He is also outraged by their discourtesy toward their opponents. See especially ii. 9. 6, 43, where he admits that they do well to borrow ideas from Plato, but should not be insolent to their Greek predecessors. They should establish their doctrines "graciously and philosophically" and not by abuse. The passage is worth reading to see the effect which Christian propaganda had upon a sophisticated Pagan, though apparently he was not hostile to all Christians for, says Porphyry (*Vita* 16), there were many Christians who attended his discourses.

[16] See the English translation (by Geoffrey Lewis) of the Arabic *Epistola de scientia divina*, in Henry-Schwyzer, Vol. II, p. 321: "It is not that He wished to originate mind and then mind came into being, after the volition, nor that He wished anything else to come into being and then it came into being. Were it so, and were His acts preceded by volition, He would be defective, if volition came between Him and His act. He does not proceed from doing one thing to doing another. He makes and originates things all at one go. . . ."

see that the generation of the lower orders is as the generation of inferences out of theorems. He has a notion that there is a kind of cognition which contains in one theorem all the others *in potentia* (iv. 3. 2, 50).[17] The actualization of potentialities may of course take place in time and those of which we are aware do so. But the generation of theorems out of a given theorem does not take place in time if one encloses oneself within the system. So the multiplicity of ideas could be thought of as resident in a single idea and that seems to have been Plotinus' way of envisioning the situation.

This way too gave him a clue to another essential and novel aspect of his metaphysics. The stream of light could be used as a symbol of generation, but once it had reached the frontiers of darkness and its power had faded, what was to happen to the cosmos? Was one to think of an eternally enduring radiation which would have made man's life simply unending activity without a goal? All things flow from higher levels to lower, but Plotinus wanted a cosmos in which perfection as a process would be as important as emanation. For on the way down things got progressively worse, the creator being always better than the creature, and Plotinus wanted also a way up, moving along which things would get better. Everything aspires to return to its source, he says. "By a natural necessity all start from unity and return to unity" (iii. 3. 1, 9). The suggestion of an anabasis to balance the katabasis could not in all probability have been involved in the metaphor of radiation unless Plotinus had thought of the light as being reflected from a plane surface in the realm of matter. There is, however, no intimation of that as far as I know. On the contrary the anabasis is suggested by the aspiration of men toward the good and by extension that of all things. It is through the anabasis that men liberate their souls from their bodies. There is, says his pupil Porphyry (*Sententiae* 9), a double death, the corporeal death and philosophic death. In the latter the soul through contemplating the intelligibles is liberated from the body

---

[17] See also iii. 9. 2 and iv. 9. 5, both of which are earlier, according to Porphyry, than iv. 3.

while still alive. Plotinus gives us a description in his second tractate on *Forethought* (iii. 3) of how individuals, regardless of their diversity and antagonism, form a single and unique genus which constitutes their unity and of how this must be reproduced in our thinking. "One must combine all species into one species, that of animal; then again those which are not animals into one species; then once more the [animal] and the nonanimal; and then similarly, if desired, reduce them both to being; and then into that which possesses being" (iii. 3. 1). This is the logical anabasis. After it has been accomplished, one should begin the descent "by division." Here one sees unity dividing itself, analogously to the outpouring of the fullness of the One. But by what principle of division the descent is made is not told us, though from the example given in the text it would seem to be that of dichotomy.[18] So far so good, yet why anything should divide itself into two antithetical parts, instead of three or more parts, remains obscure, though there may be an echo here of the use of the Monad and the Indefinite Dyad as the two *archai*.

The One itself gives rise to two other hypostases which if, as some writers believe, they are "aspects" of the One and not effluences from it, would be evidence of a triple logical division within the nature of the One.[19] I am not sure of the meaning of an aspect as contrasted with a hypostasis, but I gather that the distinction rests on answering the question of the relation of the hypostases to the One. It is true that the One is omnipresent (iii. 8. 10) and yet the hypostases are posterior to it. It is all things and no particular thing (v. 2. 1, 1). It is self-sufficient (v. 3. 13, 17) and yet the potentiality of all things (iii. 8. 10) like "the life of a great plant permeating the whole while its vital principle remains stationary and not scattered through the whole but, as it were, established in the root" (iii. 8. 10, 10). At the same time Plotinus has no doubt of the distinction between the first three hypostases.

---

[18] This passage could be used as the literary source of the Tree of Porphyry, if any such source is needed.

[19] See Philippus Villiers Pistorius, *Plotinus and Neoplatonism* (Cambridge: Bowes and Bowes, 1952).

This comes out clearly in his tractate against the Gnostics. After the One "comes the *Nous* and thinking first of all; then the Psyche after *Nous*, for this order is in accordance with nature" (ii. 9. 1, 14). There follows a passage (ii. 9. 1, 15) which states flatly that there can be neither more nor less than these hypostases.

Neither more than these are located in the Intelligible World nor less. For if there were less, either the Psyche and the *Nous* would be the same or the *Nous* and the One. But that they differ from one another has been frequently shown. It remains then to see whether there are more than these three. Might there then be some natures besides these? Should the source of all things be said to exist in that fashion [that is, as a multiplicity of hypostases] no one could find anything simpler or higher. For after all they [the Gnostics] do not say that this exists potentially, but in actuality. For it would be absurd that in beings which are in actuality and are immaterial there be made more different natures both potentially and actually. Nor would this be true of things inferior to these. Nor must it be thought that some *Nous* is somehow or other at rest while some is as if moved. For what would rest and what motion and utterance of the one *Nous* or idleness or work of the other? The truth is that *Nous* is always remaining self-identical in actuality. But motion toward it and in it is in fact the world of Psyche, and the *Logos* put by it [*Nous*] into the soul causes the soul to think, not some nature between *Nous* and Psyche. There is absolutely no possibility of making several *Nous*[20] on this account, namely that one thinks and the other thinks that it thinks. For if one thing is thinking and another is thinking that one is thinking, then in that case a single sensory experience would not be unconscious of its own operations. For it would be absurd to burden the true *Nous* with this, but on the contrary it must remain entirely itself, whatsoever thinks when thinking that it thinks. If this were not so, then it would exist only while thinking; when it thinks that it is thinking it would be different, and furthermore it would not be the same that has thought in the past.

In short, there is no need for a separate subject for every act of a given type. All noetic acts are performed by *Nous*, all psychic operations by Psyche. The proliferation of Aeons which is found in Gnosticism is superfluous.

[20] Purists may substitute *Noi*.

But there is a further implication of this doctrine. The *Nous* is the source of all intelligence that exists, the Soul of all souls and hence of all things done by souls. A distinction therefore is made between the ideas, which are the property of *Nous* and the sensations, feelings, and aspirations which are those of the Psyche. But below the three hypostases there is the world in which we live, the world in a word of bodies and matter. That world contains the three animate kingdoms and the minerals as well, the distinction between animation and inanimation being one of degree, for even the stones grow (iv. 4. 27, 9). Hence Psyche, as one of the three hypostases, gives rise to a series of lesser souls beginning with the Soul of the World, the souls of men, and descending gradually to the purely material world. This diversity is explained (iv. 8. 3, 6) as follows.

Since all *Nous* as an entirety is in the place of thinking which we call the Intelligible World, and since also all the intelligible powers included in it there and the intelligences individually as well—for there is not only one intelligence but many, and there must be also many souls and one too, and from the one proceed the many differences, just as from genus there are species both better and worse, on the one hand and the more intellectual, on the other such as are less so in actuality. For yonder in the Intelligible World the *Nous* encompasses all the rest potentially like a great animal, but every other in actuality which it encompasses in potentiality. So if a city were animate and included other animate beings, it would be more perfect and more powerful, but nothing would prevent both its own nature and that of the others from existing. Similarly from all fire there would be great fires and small. And the whole being—or essence—of fire as a whole exists or rather both the being of that fire and the being of the whole. But the task of the more logical soul is to think, to be sure, but not merely to think. For in that case how would it differ from *Nous*? For when it has come into contact with the *Nous*, it is both intellectual and otherwise, to the degree that *Nous* has not remained inactive.

Difficult as this and similar passages are, the most plausible conclusion they permit us to draw is that the logically possible divisions within a genus or species are equivalent to existential divisions. The class is cut at the joints by nature, as in *Phaedrus*. Hence if any being is logically divisible into two parts, that division will be exemplified. And its exemplifications will be emanations from the ideas which are its source. Since time is the moving image of eternity, generation is the moving image of logical inclusion. And since (iv. 8. 6) the thing created is always worse than its creator, the temporal katabasis will always be degeneration. But the process stops when the absence of all reality is reached. And that is the world of matter, evil, and ugliness.[21] At that point the anabasis begins, each type of being longing for perfection in the type above it with the ultimate purpose of being absorbed in the One. And since Plotinus believed that there were ideas of individuals, and not merely of classes (v. 7), the individuals can aspire to higher, better, and realer levels. Concretely this means that the purpose of a human being is to realize his humanity, not simply his individuality, just as it is the problem of an artist to imitate not the peculiar characteristics of that which he is depicting, but the essence of that class to which it naturally belongs.

In the tractate on the *Descent of the Soul into Bodies* (iv. 8. 6) the Principle of Plenitude is stated in so many terms:

The One must not remain alone. For if He did, all things would be buried in Him without form, nor would there exist any of the beings which are within Him, nor would the multitude of those beings which are generated by the One exist if they did not take their path downward from Him, those beings which have the rank of souls. Similarly the souls must not remain alone with the beings whom they might generate hidden within them, for it is inherent in each nature to produce something lower than itself and to unfold as from a seed out of some indivisible source, proceeding finally to the Sensible World, the prior meanwhile always remaining in its own place, but the posterior coming into being from a nameless power. However great it was in the Intelligible World, it must not stand still as if enclosed in jealousy, but must always proceed until all has come to the ultimate limits of the

---

[21] For an excellent and neglected account of this, see B. A. G. Fuller, *The Problem of Evil in Plotinus* (Cambridge: Cambridge University Press, 1912).

possible, because of the boundless power extending into all things from itself, and it knows nothing without a share in its power.[22]

Plotinus, as if he saw the problem of making the possible real, of deducing existence from possibility, lays it down as an axiom that all possibilities must be realized. This, moreover, probably lies behind his strange doctrine that there are ideas of individuals, though he does not state it overtly in the tractate which takes up the problem. There the argument is that there are so many differences between individual souls that one archetypal soul would not account for them (v. 7. 1). The differences between two men are so great that they must be traced back to the source of all souls, even though in the strictly ethical treatises the good, which is of course the end of all action, is the same for all. It will be observed that in Plotinus' hierarchy there is a loss of individuality as one goes down toward matter, matter being a complete loss of all characteristics. In that respect it has a curious similarity to the One who is its antithesis. The One is absolutely prior to everything, to *Nous* and to ideas and to being (vi. 9. 2). It has neither quality nor quantity nor intelligence nor soul, is neither in space nor in time, but is absolutely *sui generis*, "or rather without genus since it is prior to all genera" (vi. 9. 2, 3), to change (motion) and to rest. Consequently on the principle that only similars can sustain the cognitive relation, we must become like the One in order to know it, but when we succeed, we shall have lost all specificity, all individuality. To become like the unique is impossible unless one becomes merged with the unique, for how can one become like something which is like nothing else and yet remain outside it?

---

[22] It was this principle which differentiated Aristotle's thought from Plato's in the sharpest manner. See *Metaphysics* 1050b 8: "That which is capable of being may either be or not be. . . . And that which is capable of not being may possibly not be." See also 1071b 13: "That which has a potency need not exercise it."

III

So far we have tried to expound the philosophy of Plotinus as a sample of rationalism with axioms and inferences, with dialectical distinctions, with the Law of Contradiction utilized to produce consistency. But there is another side to the man which should not be obscured. We have already pointed out how he relies on Plato and some of the pre-Socratics as if their writings were sacred texts.[23]

But he also accepted the traditional myths and gave them the same kind of allegorical interpretation which Philo gave to the Biblical stories. Since this became an integral part of the Neoplatonic tradition, lasting into our own times *via* Ficino, Leone Ebreo, and the English Platonists, not to mention scores of others, it may be well to cite a few examples. The Theogony is mentioned in the tractate on Intellectual Beauty (v. 7. 12) with Zeus as a symbol of the visible world, Zeus the youngest child of Cronus. This is followed (v. 7. 12, 13) by what later became typical Neoplatonic allegory:

> The god who had been bound so as to remain as he was and who had conceded to his son the rule of this universe—for it was not in his character to abandon the rule over yonder and to seek a younger and later sphere of sovereignty as if he had a surfeit of beauty— leaving such things he both established his own father in his place and over his province extending upward. But he also established what lay in the downward direction to be ruled over by his son after him, so that between them both there would be constituted a difference between that which was severed from above and that which linked him to the region below him, between both his better father and his worse son.

It is with some surprise that one learns the meaning of the successive castrations of divine fathers by their sons. Uranus turns into the One, beyond the highest realm of being, Cronus the realm

---

[23] There are also curious parallels to Philo which Bréhier has pointed out. See, for instance, iii. 6. 6, 65; iii. 3. 7, 10; v. 4. 1, 30; and the argument against the destruction of the cosmos in ii. 1. 1, 12.

of the *Nous*, and Zeus the god of the visible world. But sometimes the interpretation depends on what Plotinus believes to be the etymology of the divine names. Thus (v. i. 7) Rhea becomes the flux, though in most mythographers she was the wife of Cronus; Cronus is the father of Zeus because, by a play upon words, *Nous* has such a fullness of being that he overflows into Psyche.[24]

In the tractate on the *Impassivity of the Incorporeals* (iii. 6. 19) we find Plotinus taking over Plato's phrase from *Timaeus* (50d) that matter, "the recipient," is similar to the Mother, the source of things to the Father, and what comes from the two, to the Offspring. But he cannot bring himself to leave this figure of speech as it stands. Mothers in Greek science were passive receptacles. Hence the priests of the Great Mother were castrated to show that Matter was incapable of generation.

If the Mother should give anything to her offspring, it would not be in her status as matter, but that she also is somehow a form. For only the form is generative, but the other nature is sterile. Wherefore, I think, the ancient sages, speaking darkly in mystic symbols and rites, made the archaic Hermes with his organ of generation always erect for generation to show that the things in the Sensible World are the offspring of the Noetic *Logos*, but the sterility of Matter, always remaining itself, they showed by the eunuchs surrounding it.

We have seen that Zeus stands for the cosmic Psyche. But in the second tractate on problems concerning the soul (iv. 4. 10), he acquires an additional meaning. Here he is said to stand both for the Demiurge and also for the guiding principle of the cosmos. But in the tractate on Love (iii. 5. 8), he becomes the *Nous* and his daughter Aphrodite becomes his soul. "And this is understandable for if we make the male gods symbols of the *Nous* and the female their souls, so that to each *Nous* there will be an accompanying Psyche, then again Aphrodite would be the soul of Zeus to which account the priests and theologians bear witness when

---

[24] Henry-Schwyzer in a note on this passage refers to Saint Augustine's *De consensu Evang.* i. 33. 35 (PL XXXIV, 1058) for a Latin interpretation of the etymological pun.

they identify Hera and Aphrodite and call the star of Aphrodite in the heavens Hera." It would seem, as a matter of fact, that the priests and theologians did not bear witness to this, since Hera, though the wife of Zeus and his sister, was never said to be also his daughter. But one must not be too critical of such interpretations. Moreover, earlier in the same tractate (iii. 5. 2, 15), Plotinus had made Plato's distinction between the two Aphrodites, the Earthly and the Heavenly, and Zeus was the father only of the former.

The habit of allegorical interpretation began early in his career, if we may trust Porphyry's chronological order of the tractates, for in the first of them all, *On Beauty* (i. 6. 8, 16), he interprets Odysseus' flight from Circe and Calypso as the return of the soul to its celestial home.

'Let us flee to our beloved fatherland,' someone would order more wisely. What then is this flight? How shall we escape? This is what Odysseus means by the flight from Circe or Calypso, not satisfied to linger even though he enjoys the pleasures of eye and great sensual beauty. Our fatherland then, whence we have come, and our Father are yonder. What then is the journey and the flight? It is not a journey on foot, for feet can do no more than bear one from one land to another. Nor need you prepare a horse-drawn carriage or a little ship, but rather must you abandon these things as a whole and refuse to look, but close your eyes and seek another kind of vision and wake up to its sights, which all men possess but few make use of.

The story of Pandora (iv. 3. 14) is said to mean that Epimetheus' rejection of her is the wisdom of remaining in the Intelligible World and that Prometheus' enchainment means that the creator is bound by what he creates. The River of Lethe (iv. 3. 14, 26 and 55) is the body which is fleeting and therefore cannot remember, whereas the soul, which is stable, alone has memory. Heracles (i. 1. 12) leads a twofold existence: he was as a shade in the lower world, but as himself among the gods; by his services he was worthy of divinity, but since his merit was earned in action rather than contemplation, something of him remained here below the

Intelligible World.[25] These will suffice as samples of Plotinus' use of ancient myths.

The reversion to mythology, anticipated by Philo and exaggerated by the Gnostics, was obviously a rejection of rationalism. For the best that one can do is to absorb the old stories into what one has already constructed as a philosophy. It is in essence an expression of the belief that the ancients had a kind of wisdom which they either could not or would not express in literal speech. That the ancients had greater wisdom than one's contemporaries has been frequently maintained in the intellectual history of Europe. It is a species of epistemological primitivism analogous to that suggested by the myth of recollection in Plato's *Meno*. Just as the newborn child comes into this world with a stock of ideas untarnished by sensory experience, so our earliest forefathers were created wise and had no need of science or reasoning to discover the truth. Why they expressed their wisdom in myths was perhaps more difficult to explain, for if they were wise there seems to have been no reason for them to conceal their wisdom. One could not say that they resorted to myth because they were unable to express themselves literally. For that would imply that they lacked one of their descendants' most prominent traits. On the contrary, one usually said that there was a kind of superior wisdom in myth, perhaps because of its concreteness, perhaps because of its emotional efficacy. In *Ennead* v. 8. 6, Plotinus praises the Egyptians for expressing their wisdom, "whether by accurate knowledge or innate insight, not in letters which express words and propositions nor by imitating sounds and the pronunciation of sentences, but drawing pictures and carving an image of each thing for each thing in their temples as a declaration that [the ideas] do not leave the world over yonder, and these images are a sort of understanding and wisdom and underlying substance and undivided unity and not discursive reasoning and willing."[26] In short, the image is a kind of compact visual presentation of an

[25] Cf. iv. 3. 27, 7.

[26] For a sketch of the subsequent fortunes of this idea, see G. Boas, *The Hieroglyphics of Horapollo*, Introduction.

idea which spares the image maker the use of language. Similarly the dream has a meaning which is not limited to the appearances which one sees but requires interpretation.

The knowledge which is conveyed in a myth or a vision or a hieroglyph is analogous to what one experiences in the mystic vision. There too there is nothing discursive and indeed every attempt to translate it into words is to fail. It is of course impossible to do more than name what one sees or hears or feels and the name suffices to communicate colors and sounds and textures. And, it goes without saying, nothing will be communicated to the person whose eyes are blind, whose ears are deaf, and whose feelings are anesthetized. If then one values direct experience above scientific thought, and Plotinus did so, one will ask for direct experience of the Platonic ideas as well as of normal sensory objects. But the closest one can come to a face-to-face encounter with such ideas as Justice, Goodness, and Beauty, is through myth. For myths, like parables, present one with concrete cases illuminating that of which one is trying to give a description. Even so abstract a document as Newton's *Principia* gave examples to clarify, if not to prove, its deductions.

One could then say that Plotinus' reversion to myth and allegory was an attempt to render the abstract concrete, though in practice he was rendering the concrete abstract. It would be better, he seems to be saying, to see the truth, rather than to hear it. And he turns to the ancients as people who did see it. We, he seems to continue arguing, have lost that power and the Sage will strive to revive it in his discourses. But he had no proof that the ancients were any wiser than we, had minds any the more penetrating, or had any ulterior motive in writing their stories beyond the telling of them. The attribution of such a capacity to his forebears was simply that nostalgia for a happier past which affects men in troubled times. And no proof is needed that the third century A.D. was troubled. When one thinks of the Roman Empire under Gallienus, one understands a man's re-echoing the cry of Odysseus, "Let us flee to our beloved fatherland."

IV

1. Though the idea of a cosmic hierarchy is complete in Plotinus, it is worth indicating, no matter how roughly, the subsequent history of the idea. In Neoplatonism we first find his pupil, Porphyry, carrying on his master's main tenets, as well as writing elaborate allegorical interpretations of mythology and quasi-biographical studies. One of his best-known surviving works is the *Sententiae*, a series of apothegms on philosophical subjects. He is, as might be expected, closest to Plotinus of all the school, although he also wrote an introduction to the categories of Aristotle, a work which became a textbook in the Middle Ages. Plotinus had maintained that Aristotle's categories held good only of the Sensible World; the four categories of Plato alone pertained to the Intelligible. Porphyry, however, re-established the Aristotelian categories as generally applicable. Though the work in which he expounded his position is superficial and of no inherent importance, it was translated into Latin by Boethius and that translation carried on the tradition for the Christian philosophers.

In the *Sententiae* we find certain passages which are relevant to the cosmic hierarchy. For instance, we find (*Sent.* 10) that the kinds of cognitive objects are four in number and that there are four manners consequently of knowing them. We know intellectually whatever is in the *Nous;* logically, whatever is psychical; "spermatically," whatever is vegetative; by images, whatever is in bodies; but when it is a question of knowing the things that are over Yonder, these we know without thought and, magic word, superessentially. It is probably futile to try to reduce this to anything intelligible, though one can understand why we use images to know material things and why we must have a mystic vision to know the superessential. But what is meant by the distinction between noetic and logical knowledge, I leave to men more skilled in mysteries than I can hope to be. To know vegetative life spermatically might easily mean that since we too have a vegetative soul (*vide* Aristotle), so by a kind of sympathy we understand growth and vitality. But it is by no means sure that this suggestion is right.

There are other principles enunciated in this work which were carried over almost without alteration into medieval philosophy. As the incorporeals descend from on high, they are divided and multiplied until they reach the individuals, but going upward they unite and coalesce (*Sent.* 11). Now, as was pointed out above, one cannot deduce by any logical means the existence of individual exemplifications of any idea, or class concept, whatsoever. But in his *Introduction to the Categories* Porphyry places individual men immediately after rational animality as if their existence could be deduced from their essence. This may be attributable to his acceptance of the Principle of Plenitude, in that, since there is no inner contradiction in the idea of rational animality, and since all possibilities must be realized, exemplifications of rational animality must exist. Again, he carries on the Plotinian theory that the product is always worse than the producer, being lower in the scale of beings, and that everything turns back toward its source. Matter, moreover, as in Plotinus, is nonbeing (*Sent.* 21), and the cosmos is produced through emanation (*Sent.* 25). Knowledge is achieved by becoming like one's object of knowledge (*Sent.* 26) and consequently not only virtue, but also knowledge itself, depends on our becoming like God (34).

The process of becoming like God, or of uniting with the Cosmos, as he puts it in one place (*Sent.* 41), is not available to everyone. Seeking this union you may be distracted into contemplating something else. But if you seek for nothing, standing firmly in yourself and your essential nature, you will become like the whole and will not descend into anything lower than yourself. "Say not then, 'I am such and such.' If you leave out 'such and such,' you become all. For before this [before birth?] you indeed were all." The argument here seems to be based on the alternative of specificity or generality. If specificity is asserted, generality is denied; if generality is asserted, specificity is denied. But precisely in what does the assertion consist? Porphyry seems elsewhere to suggest that it consists in practicing asceticism, as in his treatise on abstinence from flesh. This would resemble a withdrawal from the body. But as a matter of fact, the body is not his principle of individuation; the soul was an individual before birth and may continue to be one after death. But since he previously had said (*Sent.* 31) that God is both everywhere and nowhere, that Intelligence is in God and the Soul in both Intelligence and God and nowhere in the body, its existence is already predicated upon its being distinct from and detached from the body. Hence its *apostasis*, or withdrawal from the body, can be brought about exclusively by something which is only metaphorically spatial withdrawal. There are, he says (*Sent.* 32), four kinds of virtue, the theoretical which leads to apathy, the end of which is likeness to God; the purgative, which is in *gnosis;* the intellectual, which is wisdom and prudence; and the "paradigmatic" which is in the Intelligence and apparently consists in contemplating eternal ideas. All of these vaguely defined kinds of virtue assist in elevating the soul, while still this side of the grave, beyond the body or, what amounts to the same thing, in giving it a vision of "true being." Since true being is neither quantitative (*Sent.* 36), nor spatial nor material nor multiple nor made up of parts (38), the problem, if virtue is to lead to knowledge of true being, is clearly to find a discipline which will lead one to thinking in independence of the usual categories. Moreover, true being is both one and many, being unity in variety (*Sent.* 38). It is clear then that the human mind must be purged of its feelings, in so far as feelings make it conscious of its difference from other souls, and it must also be purged of anything which will cause it to assert multiplicity in its objects. But this is a discipline which runs counter to the use of the laws of logic, for nothing in true being can be asserted to be identical, in so far as identity is based on difference from other things; to be in contradiction with others, for true being is continuous harmony; to exclude alternatives, for it has no alternative. But such a being can be only seen, intuited, contemplated, not talked about (*Sent.* 44). In intelligence, as Aristotle had said, the intelligence and its objects are one. In Porphyry, as in Plotinus, the union is expressed as follows: "If the *Nous* is what is known to the *Nous*, then the *Nous* would be that which is known to itself. . . . It is itself both the knower and the known, the whole of the whole."[27] The paradox that self-knowledge is also knowledge of true being runs parallel to the other paradox that true being is everywhere and nowhere.

2. One might imagine that we had by now reached the end of the road and that mystery could gain no further ground. But the successors to Plotinus and Porphyry won more victories over the claims of evidence and logic. For just as the Christians defeated every attempt to produce a system of theology in which the Law of Contradiction would be the thinker's guide, so the Neoplatonists juggled with concepts, allegories, intuitions, revelations, and Pythagorean number symbolism in order to construct a system in which piety might take the place of truth and religion that of science. The old words, *logos*, *nous*, sensation, might be used, but they were given meanings foreign to their origin and requiring reinterpretation. To call the *Logos* the son of God, as in Philo, might have been a figure of speech indicating Philo's high regard for rationality, but it did not take very long for the metaphor to become literal truth in the Fourth Gospel. Similarly if the *nous* in Aristotle was the power which we had of systematizing logically the data of sense and of contemplating the results of the system, in Plotinus it was something so far removed from sense that it was useless to appeal to it if one was engaged in natural science. The *nous* in Aristotle had been active as well as passive, and the active reason had a genealogy which went back to Anaxagoras. But where Socrates could say that it did nothing whatsoever to enlighten men who wanted enlightenment, in Plotinus it was the only faculty which we had, for enlightenment. Its detachment from all sensory knowledge was the sign of its importance. Again, where the Stoics and Epicureans as well could base their philosophies on their observation of the elements, the plants, animals, and

[27] This whole section (44) contains an excellent account of nondiscursive thought.

human beings, and construct "reality" out of the conclusions of natural science, by the time of Epictetus natural science was at best only a lower form of knowledge and the great poem of Lucretius was a futile gesture which few cared to follow. If one wished to depict the intellectual situation in dramatic terms, one could imagine Lucretius and the later Stoics engaged in a battle in which magic got the upper hand over scientific reason. There is no indication in the first Christian centuries of anyone's dreaming of the possibility of a scientific philosophy. Marvels, mysteries, miracles, and magic—the alliteration is inevitable, if regrettable— were accepted not as something to be explained away, but as something which refuted science. Philosophy was no longer the love of wisdom, but a guide to life. Its fruits were to be ethical, not intellectual. Apparently no one saw that one human problem was to accept the truth, however bitter, and to adjust one's life to it. For the truth was now revealed by insight, not painfully acquired by observation and logical discipline. Ironically the attacks of the Skeptics led not to a rejection of mystery but to a rejection of the reason.

A fair sample of the kind of thinking which was to reign in the early centuries of the Christian period is seen in such Neoplatonists as Iamblichus and Proclus. Seven centuries, roughly speaking, separate Euclid, the geometer, from Iamblichus. In spite of twentieth-century criticism of the logic of Euclid's *Elements*, no one, as far as I know, has ever maintained that they were full of mystical symbols. But when one comes to Iamblichus, one sees that mathematics was to serve as a religious initiation. Take the following from his *Protrepticus*.[28] The divine doctrine of Pythagoras "instructs us to mistrust nothing said about the gods. . . . For the fact that the same things are proved to be true both by mathematics and by contemplative insight and to be alone lacking in deceit, proves decisively that they stand fast in all their applications and as a complex whole. And these same studies can direct one to the knowledge of the gods. They lead to the possession of such un-

[28] Ed. H. Pistelli (Leipzig: Teubner, 1888), p. 110, l. 21.

derstanding that we mistrust nothing of the theories about the gods or of the divine doctrines." Again, the study of mathematics will transmit to us a knowledge of the "great mysteries" instead of the minor ones and of philosophy instead of elementary education (p. 10, l. 4). Nor must one think that one can learn the significance of mathematics by ordinary rational means. Quite the contrary. Insight into it is transmitted to us by the gods. But when one asks what these mysteries are and how one learns them, one finds the answer in allegory.

Thus, if the *Theologoumena arithmeticae* is an authentic work, we find each of the numbers from one to ten described as symbols of various theological attributes.[29] The Monad is the *arche* of number and "has no local position," that is, is not really a number at all, a belief which was common to the ancients. It gets it name, *Monad*, from the fact that it remains [unchanged], a pun on the Greek verb μένειν. "For the Monad, from which number is generated, keeps the same form, just as every three remains three, every four remains four" (i. 4, p. 1). So far so good. But soon (vi. 6, p. 6) we learn that it is called "essence [or substance], the cause of truth, simple, paradigm, order, unison, the equal in matters of quantity, the mean between increase and diminution, the measure in magnitude, the present moment in time, and again a ship, a chariot, a friend, life, and happiness." It lies between the two upper elements and the two lower as a fiery cube, at the middle point of the cosmic order, "as Homer is known to say, 'So deep is Hades, as great a distance below as Heaven is from Earth.'" It is also called, we find (x. 19, p. 81), Mnemosyne, who it will be recalled, was the mother of the Muses. But it would be folly to continue, not only because little sense can be made out of such a jumble of attributes and symbols, but also because they are easily found in de Falco's Index. In spite of the absurdity of it all, such symbols were constantly used throughout the Middle Ages, transmitted by writers like Martianus Capella and Isidore of Se-

---

[29] I use the edition of V. de Falco (Leipzig: Teubner, 1922). Whether the work is really by Iamblichus or not, it is typical of his kind of thinking.

ville. Each of the first ten numbers was treated similarly and historians of numerical symbolism will find the little compilation of the greatest utility. When one remembers the awe in which numbers like three and seven were held, one realizes that men given to Pythagoreanism were not without influence. Much of what is in this work is also to be found in Philo, and Philo undoubtedly derived it from earlier writers. But after all the emotional aura which surrounds Unity even today is no less irrational.

Iamblichus also began to fill in the cosmic hierarchy with additional levels. Whereas Plotinus was satisfied with three hypostases, Iamblichus located an "ineffable *arche*" before the One, for if one calls the beginning of things "the One," something has been said about it.[30] After this *Arche* come the three hypostases. In the *De mysteriis* (viii. 2; Berlin, Nichoaus, 1857) we discover that "before the really real and the universal *archai* is one god, prior both to the primary god and king, remaining immutable in the unity of his oneness. For neither thoughts nor anything else must be associated with him. For he is established as the paradigm of the self-begotten, self-generated, and solely paternal god of the really good. For something is best and first and a source of all things and root of the primary intellectual ideas. And from this one the autarkic God radiates Himself, wherefore He is His own father and is independent [of all else]. For He is the *arche* and God of gods, a monad out of the One, superessential and the source of being. For from him come substantiality and being [or essence], wherefore he is called the father of being. For he is pre-essential being, *arche* of the intelligibles, wherefore he is also addressed as the source of intelligence. Accordingly these *archai* are the oldest of all things, which Hermes [Trismegistus] placed before the gods of the ethereal regions and the empyrean and the upper heaven." This is the result of a struggle to find an absolute beginning for all things, a beginning which will be only a beginning and nothing

---

[30] This comes from the *Dubitationes et solutiones* of Damascius, a sixth-century figure of the Athenian school. As his text is unavailable to me, I use the quotations as given in De Vogel.

else. The scientific principles of an earlier period had maintained that nothing could come from nothing, and this would push back the *arche* into infinite recesses. Iamblichus does not want a temporal beginning for things; he wants a logical beginning, for emanation does not go on in time. But if one takes the Plotinian triad as the summit of one's hierarchy, each member must share in some common property to be there. This common property must be the most general of all characteristics, a characteristic such as "pure being." But as soon as anything is asserted of being, it falls from its supreme position. It is probably for this reason that Iamblichus insists on its ineffability. The monstrous terms by which he names it, self-father, self-begotten, and so on, are inventions whose monstrosity does not bother him, for he would admit the impossibility of finding a suitable vocabulary to name that which is unnamable. But perhaps enough has been said to illustrate the intellectual technique of Iamblichus and to show how philosophy was turning into religion.

3. The last Neoplatonist whom we shall mention is Proclus, for he too in his metaphysical writings was more occupied with constructing a continuous series of beings than in anything else. His commentaries on Plato's *Timaeus* and some of the other dialogues are still extant and contain material which is invaluable to anyone who would see how such works could become by the fifth century A.D. works of esotericism. But we are more interested here in his *Elements of Theology*, for it supplies us with a sample of a cosmic hierarchy which is fuller than any upon which we have touched so far.[31]

Dodds has pointed out that the importance of Iamblichus in the development of Neoplatonism lay in his triads, since they all involved a mean term between extremes, and in the triadic scheme of that which is alone, that which proceeds out of the alone, and of the notion of a return to the alone. Thus he preserved from Plotinus the ideas of the katabasis and the anabasis. There was also in

---

[31] I use the edition of E. R. Dodds, *The Elements of Theology* (Oxford: Clarendon Press, 1933).

him a mirroring at successive levels of identical structures, so that each level of the hierarchy reproduced the level above it. But, as we see from the *Elements* themselves (Prop. 25), that which is most remote from the *arche* of all things is sterile and consequently there is a terminus to the emanations. There is also in Proclus (Prop. 55) a hint of a distinction between eternal, or logical, and temporal duration, and this is important. For the eternal has logical duration in the sense that its inner relations are timeless and the priority and posteriority of its beings are logical. The conclusions of a logical deduction come *after* the premises only in a special sense, since they are implicit in the premises and it is only when human beings draw them out that they take on temporal posteriority. Temporal duration is seen in "things which are becoming." The world of time is a world of process. The child is not implicit in the father but is born later than the father.[32] Moreover, there is clear evidence in Proclus that he was thinking of his hierarchy as a series of logical classes, for (Prop. 62) "every manifold which is nearer to the One has fewer members than those more remote, but is greater in power," or it may be that he means in potencies. There are more "somatic natures" than souls, more souls than intelligences, more intelligences than "divine units." This agrees not only with observation but also with the old rule of the inverse ratio between connotation and denotation. The more inclusive class contains more members than the less inclusive: there are more animals than men. But the more inclusive class has fewer qualifications than the less inclusive: one can say more things which will be true of men than will be true of animals as a whole. But this rule in itself does not entail any conclusions about power. If the power of the upper levels is greater than that of the lower, then we have at last found the principle of the original hierarchy

[32] If geneticists were interested in such problems, they might raise the question of the pre-existence of the genes, for, though we get them from both of our parents, each gene appears to go back in time to the beginning of the human race, though radioactive matter may have caused changes in them, as it may also do in the future. Furthermore, if a gene is simply a chemical substance, the elements in it are also everlasting. But none of this is relevant perhaps to Proclus.

of priests embedded in the cosmic hierarchy. If the upper levels are the source of the lower, and plurality increases as one descends, then clearly the range of the superior powers is greater than that of the inferior. In Christian terms, God has power over everything; the Pope, His vicar on earth, has power over the entire Church; the bishops over their dioceses, the parish priests over their parishes. And since the word for power was also the word for potentiality, and one never knows in just which sense it is being used, for both senses will appear whenever the word appears, one can see that by playing upon power as potentiality the generation of the hierarchy could be clarified. When one finds Proclus saying (Prop. 86) that the infinitude of the really real resides not in quantitative terms but in power, one can understand somewhat why the really real could be the source of all else.

It may also be true that such statements, found in Plotinus as well as in Proclus and other Neoplatonists, as "everything is in everything" (Prop. 103), ultimately rest upon the principle *ex nihilo nihil*. For since the hierarchy is a logical hierarchy, the specific traits must have been implicit in the generic traits, though not exemplified there. The rationality of man, for instance, could not have come from his animality, for some animals are not rational. Yet there must be a potency of rationality in animality, if it was to be explained, and the principle of *omnia in omnibus*, if interpreted as potentiality, would serve as an explanation.[33] In Being, says Proclus (Prop. 103), are both Life and Intelligence; in Intelligence both Being and Life; and in Life both Being and Intelligence. But "each of these exists upon one level intellectually, on another vitally, and on a third ontologically." The levels here would appear to mean what we should call contexts, but in a hierarchical scheme the contexts are also graded in relation to their proximity to the "really real," and it is not a matter of indifference whether we think of a person as an animal, a soul, or an intelligence.

---

[33] But of course some principle would have to be introduced to explain why so many of these potentialities are not realized. For, as Aristotle had pointed out, everything does not come out of everything indiscriminately, but oak comes from acorns, not from wheat seeds.

It is hard to see how Proclus' hierarchy could be extended any further. If the Principle of Plenitude had not been accepted, then it would not have been plausible to infer that every possibility must be exemplified. Consequently there might have been some ranks which would have existed in the logical hierarchy but not in the ontological. If the idea of a king and ruler, governing in secret, had not seemed the proper way to imagine a government, exemplified not only in the governance of the Great King but also in that of the Roman Emperors, one of the fundamental metaphors of the system would have been missing and the Lord of Creation might have been more anthropomorphic. But as Professor Goodenough has said,[34] the figure of royalty while certainly the source of the hierarchy of powers, in Philo "another source is equally apparent, the light mysticism of the mystery religions." The use of the Sun as a symbol for the One, or for God, and the radiation of light from it, gave the Neoplatonists, as it gave Philo, a figure of speech which could easily lose its figurative character. To quote Professor Goodenough (p. 11) again, the sun was "that orb which burns, to all appearances, eternally, yet without need of fuel from outside itself. Independent of the world, a self-sufficient existence, it sends out its great stream of light, or of heat, or of life, or of creation." Here then was a perfect symbol for the kind of creation which was needed and it seems only natural that when Julian the Apostate wanted to restore the polytheism of his ancestors, he should have placed Helios at the apex of his divine hierarchy.[35]

[34] *By Light, Light,* p. 41.

[35] Cf. A. H. Armstrong, *The Architecture of the Intelligible Universe in the Philosophy of Plotinus* (Cambridge: Classical Studies, 1940), p. 54. For the use of light as a metaphor in Ps-Dionysius, see the *Celestial Hierarchy* i, following Jas. 1:17, where God is called the Father of Lights, and *On the Divine Names* i. 6, ii. 4, and iv *passim.* It is curious, in the face of this and similar evidence, that E. Zeller, in his *Philosophie der Griechen* (5th ed.; Leipzig, 1923), pt. 2, sect. 1, Vol. VI, pp. 560 f., should deny that Plotinus believed in emanationism. He prefers to call the system "dynamic pantheism." He distinguishes between emanationism *welche die Emanation als Mittheilung des Wesens* [*ist*] and one *welche sie nur als Mittheilung der Kraft fassen.* And he concludes that *nur in letzteren Sinn kann Plotins Lehre emanatisch genannt werden.* But it would seem as if the distinction in Plotinus himself was not existential but purely verbal.

V

There is still one more peculiarity about philosophy from Philo which deserves a word or two. In our earlier chapters we wrote sections on the appraisal of life, in which it appeared that few if any philosophers thought that human life could be justified without examination or criticism. But all nevertheless up to the time of Philo thought that the saving grace could come from man himself. One lived the rational life; one avoided excess and was temperate; one sought simple pleasures and avoided pain; one gave up everything that was not strictly necessary; one recognized one's place in the Cosmopolis and lived as a citizen of the world. But as soon as the Bible became a sacred text, agreement with which was the ultimate test of truth, then salvation could come only through supernatural aid. Philo's interpretation of man's redemption through divine instruction, endurance, and grace, was, if not the first, at least the first on record of successive essays on the need for salvation through God's intervention. Now it is true that as early as Homer the records show Greeks being aided as well as hindered by the gods, initiations into the various mystery cults, metamorphoses, the nonrational working of fate, and, as in the case of Socrates, a genuine distrust of pure rationality. Dodds's book on *The Greeks and the Irrational* is eloquent proof that not all Greeks followed the way of the geometer. But no one has as yet exhibited a philosopher following any other path and, as we have tried to show early in this book, even the gods could be asked to prove their point on certain occasions. Aeschylus' *Eumenides* is not post-Aristotelian. It was addressed after all to the Athenian people, not to a small élite. The debate between the Furies and Apollo is the presentation of a genuine conflict of ideas. And something similar appeared in Sophocles' *Antigone*. A purely rational philosophy is to be sure impossible, since the premises of the most rational systems have to be taken for granted and certain metaphors will be used as a mold for the whole system. But at the same time, once the basic metaphors were accepted and the premises laid down, the rest proceeded as if it were rational discourse.

Moreover the earlier philosophers were interested in the whole range of the sciences. Aristotle was not the first to write on physics and biology, government, ethics, and art. Everything goes to make it probable that this sort of thing was typical of philosophy before his time. Indeed it was one of the peculiarities of Socrates that he had no interest in cosmic questions. The early Stoics and certainly Epicurus were as occupied with what we would call science as with metaphysics. But when once Philo began his interpretation of a sacred text, interest was oriented toward the supernatural. What goes for science in Seneca and Pliny is pitiful. Their scientific writings are an uncriticized mass of legend and myth. It is only in Lucretius that one finds a philosopher who is also a scientist, not one to be sure in his own right, but a man who felt the need of basing his philosophic conclusions on science. And the very fact of his ineffectuality is proof enough of the decline of reason at the end of the Pagan period.

One of the nonlogical causes of the differences in temper between the classical and the postclassical philosophers may well be that the former lived in small communities and the latter in amorphous empires. When a city of 50,000 is the world, the philosopher does not feel the invasions of large crowds with their strange ideas as a menace. But when the center of civilization shifted from Athens to Alexandria to Rome, too much was known of conflicting methods of thinking and conflicting aspirations to give a philosopher who lived "in the world" any peace of mind. At the present time we are in a similar situation, for our consciousness of Indian and Chinese philosophies shakes our confidence in both the logical and the scientific methods of thought. We have been made aware of the nonlogical sources of the reason, be they economic, psychodynamic, or religious. But the fact that we articulate our ideas in symbols which are prompted by the Unconscious does not compel us to refuse to submit them to the test of fact, to the Law of Contradiction, to experimentation. The fact that we talk of square and cubic numbers does not force us to think of four as a plane figure bounded by four equal sides, nor of eight as a solid each of whose edges is two units long. The stimuli to our systems may be as unconscious as one please; the system itself may be conscious and constantly submitted to rational criticism. If we speak of a melancholy person, we are not committed to the theory of the four humors, temperaments, and elements. But we seem to feel that if Indians or Chinese or Japanese or North American Redskins think in ways which are fundamentally different from ours, either we must be wrong and they right, or, what is worse, that an amalgam of all the ways of thinking must be melted together and accepted by us. There is little doubt that as long as a people lives in a small enclosed community, it will look on outsiders as inferiors, and that is of course stupid provincialism. But the fact that two people disagree does not in itself prove that either of them is right or wrong, that they can and should be "reconciled"—for both may be wrong—and, if the words which they use only seem but are not ambiguous, both may be right. But there simply is no way of reconciling inconsistent ideas. One can explain the cause of the inconsistency historically. It may reside in the choice of different premises determined by cultural traditions. But that is no more reconciliation, if I understand the term, than showing that the difference between molecular oxygen and ozone lies in the latter's possessing an extra atom of oxygen destroys the difference between them. Their differences remain real, but they are now understood.

If I speak of a decline of the rational spirit in Pagan philosophy, I mean by "decline" the submission of reason to dreams, allegory, mysteries, and mythology. To say that Neptune "means" water and Pluto earth is not submitting science to mythology; it is rather giving a scientific meaning to mythology. The two gods in question did not mean anything of the sort, it goes without saying, and as an explanation of mythology, it is incorrect to say that they did. But it is not quite the same thing as identifying the creation of the world as the overflowing of the One. For one can at least prove that the names of the gods were not names of the elements whereas there is no way of verifying or disproving the theory of emanation. One cannot verify metaphors, though one can distinguish between those which are apt and those which are inapt. But to do even this requires a knowledge of some literality which is expressed figuratively in the metaphor under examination. If one were to compare the earth to a running brook, or fire to a stolid rock, most of us would think the comparison inept for the simple reason that we have a pretty good idea of what the two elements look like and they do not look like brooks and rocks respectively. But we have no way of knowing what emanation would be and when it is compared to streams of light coming from the sun, we still do not know how streams of light could turn into people, beasts, and minerals. When a rationalistic philosopher wishes to explain the origin of the universe, he is expected first to ask on what grounds it is believed to have had an origin. If to avoid an infinite regress of causation, he posits a first cause, he will then be expected to endow the first cause with only those traits which are needed to explain its effectiveness as a cause. If he proceeds by abstraction to reach a concept such as pure being, then he can reasonably be asked to explain its assumption of traits which are not inherent in its nature, such as materiality, sensory qualities, multiplicity, temporality. For since he is sticking to dialectical devices, he must show that the gap between a concept and that which is subsumed under it can be bridged by the same devices. If it cannot be bridged, then his technique is faulty at that point and he must either accept at least a duality of beings or try another technique.

But one has only to turn to Plotinus to see how little he cared for such enterprises. The emanation of the three hypostases may be a beautiful vision and many later philosophers have thought it to be one. But why should the One not remain the One forever? Plotinus evokes the principle of the necessity of production and he certainly has a right to introduce such a postulate. But why should the second hypostasis be the *Nous* rather than something else? His tractate against the Gnostics does indeed try to prove that there can be neither more nor less than three hypostases (ii. 9.

1) but it does not tell us how one deduces *Nous* from the One. He knows somehow or other that Unity, Intelligence, and Soul are "over Yonder," and that they exist there in actuality, not in potentiality, but one can only conclude that he knows this because the ancients have said so. Once that much is granted, the inference becomes plausible that no more than these three are needed. But just to meditate upon the nature of Unity or Being would provide no evidence whatsoever that it implies either Intelligence or Soul. Even if one make the further assumption of the inevitability of emanation to lower levels of reality, that in itself would not prove that the level below the One would be Intelligence, rather than anything else. Here what the modern mathematician calls intuition enters. And the business of the Reason is organizing what one intuits into systematic order.

The intuitions of Plotinus come in the main from Plato as he understood him. It is because of his reading of Plato that he identifies the One with the Good. Having then accepted the supremacy of the One, he attempts to organize Intelligence in relation to it. And since he had also taken over the theory of ideas and inferred that all ideas must be the objects of an Intelligence, he situates a collective Intelligence in the Intelligible World. He may have argued that since all beings participate in some idea, and since all ideas must be the objects of an intelligence, the *Nous* must rank highest in the hierarchy after the One. But the reverse process, of drawing the cosmic Intelligence out of the One with no other evidence of its existence is quite a different matter. By the process of abstracting common properties one can of course mount the Tree of Porphyry, but to climb down the Tree before one has climbed up is bound to be frustrating, since one has no way of knowing *a priori* that it is a tree, to say nothing of the location of its branches. The procedure permits one to imagine all sorts of possibilities and on the basis of the Principle of Plenitude to infer that all which are not inconsistent must be realized.

The use of reason, it may not be amiss to point out, is at least twofold. First, it is a technique of drawing inferences out of premises, as in the syllogism, or in geometry, usually by substitutions of terms which are equivalents. The premises are taken for granted, either because they are supposed to be self-evident or because they give one the conclusions which one needs or which seem to be true according to observed facts or which have been accepted by men working in the field whose authority is unquestioned. The only premises which are self-evident in the strict sense are tautologies, though they may not look like tautologies. For instance, definitions do not look like tautologies, but since by agreement the predicate means the same thing as the subject, they are nevertheless tautological. One sometimes works backward from beliefs which for one reason or another are accepted as true to fact by means of accepted laws of causality or statements of natural rhythms and cycles. Thus if the cause of a disease is known and the symptoms are present and are uniquely the symptoms of a statable disease, then one can infer that the disease's cause must have been present to cause the symptoms or is still present. If one knows the cause of typhoid fever and a patient shows the symptoms of typhoid fever, then one can argue backward from the symptoms to the cause. (In this case to that which transmitted the bacilli in question.) But there are also certain beliefs which at a given time in the history of a science have been checked by observation and experiment. These when properly phrased can and do become premises from which inferences are legitimately drawn. By the time of Plotinus, it is true, it was generally believed that the human soul had the two faculties of intelligence *(nous)* and the "lower" faculties of sensation, imagination, desire, memory, and volition. The lower faculties, with the possible exception of volition, were shared by the higher animals. If then everything in an effect could be, indeed must be, traced back to its cause and the lower faculties were all grouped as psychic rather than as intellectual (or noetic), one could infer that they must come from a source of psychic faculties to which one could give the name of Soul with an initial capital. And if one has already assumed the hierarchical arrangement of all beings, it was reasonable to infer that the source in question must be present close to the summit of the hierarchy. The main question remaining was how the effects emerged from the cause and the metaphor of emanation took care of that. In this way the logical hierarchy gave one the taxonomy of beings, and the Principle of Plenitude took care of their origin. As Lovejoy has pointed out, the temporalizing of the principle was based on a logical surd: one simply could not deduce from any taxonomical order a temporal order. T. H. Morgan, for instance, showed how in spite of the possibility of arranging the mutations of the fruit fly in easily recognizable orders, from, for instance, vestigial wings to full-sized wings or the reverse, they did not occur in time in any such order.[36] We do have a tendency, it seems, to believe that events must occur in orders which are easily named, the order of simple to complex or complex to simple, good to bad or bad to good, little to big, ignorant to intelligent, and so on. What induces us to think in this way is unknown, but it may be that the observation of the growth of plants and animals had some influence here, for seeds and eggs look to the naïve eye simpler and actually are smaller, and most people would agree "worse" than the adult creatures. But this is merely a guess on my part. Whatever the reason, philosophers who believed in a cosmic hierarchy also believed in both the absolute simplicity and the infinite potentiality of the source of all things and both terms were terms of praise. But the gap between eternity and time was never bridged by such men except in symbols.

The attribution of goodness and beauty to the hierarchy was another logical surd. But from the time of Plato on the immutable and the unified were believed to be better than the changing and multiple. This could only be an assumption. But once the assumption was made, one could assert that as one went up the hierarchy one proceeded toward the better. This was the logical source of the notion that the return to the Intelligible World was progress toward the good. And though the One was both producing and

---

[36] See his *Critique of the Theory of Evolution* (Princeton: Princeton University Press, 1916).

also unchanging, in spite of the apparent contradiction in terms, human beings were urged, as we have seen, to pursue the anabasis in place of the katabasis. I say that this was the logical source of the notion. But I do not maintain that men looked upward because of any logical motives whatsoever. Otherworldliness, the desire to flee to one's beloved fatherland, renunciation of terrestrial life, may come about as the result of the weariness of living. And one suspects that the most metaphysical arguments can do in relation to this problem is what theology can do in relation to religion.

The coincidence in history between Neoplatonism, Gnosticism, and Christianity, their success in conquering the souls of Western Europeans, regardless of their differences, prevents anyone from denying the satisfaction which they conferred upon people. Men seemed to be capable of sacrificing the Law of Contradiction for the sake of comfort. When one reads such a work as the *De mysteriis* of Iamblichus, a work which is written soberly and carefully, and realizes that it defends everything which modern man would call superstition, divination, sacrifices, revelations from supernatural powers of various degrees of sanctity, auguries from dreams, and so on, one can only wonder why it should have been preserved intact, if it is intact, and so many tough-minded scientific works should have been lost. I find it hard to believe that Cicero, Epictetus, and Seneca were as intelligent as Theophrastus, not to speak of his teacher, and yet they were preserved almost *in toto* and used by later Christians as authorities. But then Vergil was used as a prophet and Pliny and Aelian as zoologists.

The second role of the reason is that of the critic. And here we find that the postclassical writers were as sharp as their predecessors when it was not a question of their own beliefs. Their beliefs, as early as Philo, were fixed and it was sinful to modify them. When it became a sin to scrutinize one's ideas for logical flaws, philosophy had made the final capitulation. The Skeptic might criticize the operations of the reason, but he did it not in the interest of faith or revelation; he did it in the interest of consistency.

Nevertheless there was also that element of peace of mind which skepticism was to bring about, as noxious an element as the desire for fame or good repute. When faith, hope, and charity took the place of wisdom and prudence, what are called spiritual values took the place of epistemological values. The ancients took it for granted that disagreement would exist among men, though each philosopher undoubtedly did his best to make disciples and form a school. And we do have the case of Socrates' fate to confute the idolater of everything Greek. Whether the attitude of the ancients be called indifference or tolerance, they did not succeed in imposing any body of philosophic doctrine on the population as a whole. To do that was the work of the Church aided of course by the State.

Index

A

Action at a distance, denied by Aristotle, 212
Active reason, in Aristotle, 228
Aenesidemus, 333, 335, 339, 341
Aeschylus, 43, n. 20, 47, 318
Aetius, 25, 242, 262, 399
Alcuin, 168, n. 19, 277
Alexander of Aphrodisias, 262, 293
Allegorical interpretation, 396; in Philo, 399; in Stoicism, 270; in Plotinus, 456
Anaxagoras, 59; and Empedocles, *ibid.* and 61; his method, 86; Aristotle's criticism of, 208
Anaximander, 5; method of, 24
Anaximenes, 6; method of, 25
Angels, in Philo, 407
Anonymous Iamblichi, 66
Antiintellectualism, of Epicurus, 288
Antiprimitivism, in Epicurus, 288
Antisthenes, appraisal of life, 106; and contradiction, 125
Aphrodite, the two, 174
Apollonius of Tyana, 376
Appraisal of life, Xenophanes, 49; Heraclitus, 50; Empedocles, 52; Sophists, 98; Critias, 100; Cynics, 105; Plato, 159; Aristotle, 215; Crantor, 277; Epicureans, 281; Stoics, *ibid;* Epicurus, 287; Epictetus, 387, Marcus Aurelius, 389
Aratus, 405
Arcesilaus, 325
Archytas, pseudo, 411
Aristophanes, on Socrates, 76; 283, 315
Aristotle, as source of our knowledge of Presocratics, 4, 47; Contrasted with Plato, 188, 202; on Anaxagoras, 62; on Antisthenes, 125; on Socrates, 91; 104; references to in Sextus Empiricus, 352; 17, 24, 29, 33, 34, 43, 86, n. 16, 120, 145, 263, 267, n. 28, 276, 288, 292, 326, 333, 401, 417, 418, 423, 440, 441, 446
Arius Didymus, 250, n. 14, 251, n. 15
Armstrong, A. H., 470, n. 35
Arnim, 268, n. 30
Artistry, as source of metaphor in Aristotle, 190

Asceticism, not taught by Plato, 174
Athenaeus, 260
Atomic lines, in Xenocrates, 263
Atomism, of Democritus, 36; of Epicurus, 255, 273
Augustine, St., 4, 286, 381, 396
Autarky, in Cynicism, 108, 119; of the good, in Plato, 184; in Aristotle, 217, 229; in New Testament, 217; in Stoics and Epicureans, 283; of God, 302; in Epictetus, 378
Authority, appeal to, 316; reliance on in Epictetus and Marcus Aurelius, 376; use of common, 395; appeal to in Plotinus, 455

B

Bacon, 88
Bailey, C., 256, n. 20; 272, 304
Bastian, 33
Bautain, Abbé, 63, n. 2, 316
Bayle, 110, n. 35
Beare, J. I., 37, n. 17
Being, meanings of, 123, 148; in Xenocrates, 263
Belief in gods, in Cleanthes, 269, in Chrysippus, *ibid.*
Bergson, 15, n. 7
Bernardin de Saint-Pierre, 362
Bevan, E. R., 441, n. 8
Bible, as sacred text, 394
Biography and philosophy, 377, 384
Biological metaphor in Aristotle, 190
Blake, William, 394
Body, soul's independence of, 379; in Plato, 171, 176; in Epictetus, 362; in Marcus Aurelius, 368
Book of Common Prayer, 379
Brehier, E., 343, 396, 400, 408, n. 29
Bruno, 367
Burnet, J., 18, n. 8, 25, 172, n. 24
Bury, R. G., 331, n. 12, 347, n. 22
Butcher, S. H., 44, n. 21

C

Calvin, 286
Cataleptic impressions, 267; in Stoicism, 310; combatted by Arcesilus, 327

Categories, of Aristotle, 197, 236; Stoic, 310
Causation, and necessity, 34; in early Stoicism, 247, 266; criticized by Aenesidemus, 341; skepticism on, 350
Cebes, 397
Change, in Heraclitus, 29
Characters of Theophrastus, and *personae dramatis* of Platonic dialogues, 279; and character sketches of Aristotle, 280
Cherniss, H. A., 4, 131, n. 2, 157, n. 10, 182, n. 27, 444, n. 11
Choice, in tragedies, 42; in Greek philosophy, 227
Chrysippus, 375, 380; story of his dog, 338
Cicero, confuses Plato and Aristotle, 194, n. 2; 247, 250, 251, n. 15, 253, n. 16, 268, 269, 270, n. 31, 281, n. 42, 319, 325, 326, 333, n. 14, 359, 364, 394, 398, 409, 444
City of God, in Stoicism, 285
Clark, Sir Kenneth, 344, n. 19
Classification, 157; class concepts as standards, 179; determined by Nature in Aristotle, 235; scientific classification in Plato, 178
Cleanthes, *Hymn to Zeus*, 251; on the *tonos*, 265
Clement of Alexandria, 52, 108, 394, 419, 432, n. 56
Common sense, as test of truth, 316
Consensus gentium, 268
Consistency and truth, 34
Contradiction, in Antisthenes, 125
Copernicus, 209
Copleston, Rev. F. C., 130
Cornford, F. M., 215, n. 9, 401
Cornutus, 396
Cosmic hierarchy, in Iamblichus, 466; in Proclus, 468
Cosmic unity, in Stoicism, 294
Cosmological argument, in Stoicism, 270
Cosmopolis, 366, 369, 382
Council of Trent, 438
Crates, 287

Cratylus, 91, 127
Critias, his appraisal of life, 100
Custom and Nature, 66
Cycles, in Empedocles, 20; in Stoicism, 296
Cynicism, appraisal of life, 105; autarky in, 119; compared with Stoicism, 284

D

Daimon, of Socrates, 94, 118
Daimones, 247, 407
Dalton, not anticipated by Democritus, 20
Darwin, 24
Davids, Rhys, 282, n. 43
Death, appraisal of, Socrates, 80; Prodicus, 99; fear of in Epicureanism, 300; in Marcus Aurelius and Epictetus, 386
Definition, example of Platonic, 139
Demetrius, 109, n. 33
Demetrius Poliorcetes, 318, n. 3
Democritus, his rationalism, 39; and Empedocles, 36; method of, 36; ethics of, 53; two worlds in, 20; theory of effluences, 31; mentioned in passing, 209, 273, 249
Demosthenes, 187
Descartes, 43, 297, n. 68, 329
Determinism, and free will, 295
De Vogel, C. J., 328, n. 10
Dewey, John, 76, n. 12, 307
Dialectic, in Eleatics, 15; in Parmenides, 30; in Zeno, *ibid.*, in Gorgias, 71
Dialogues, as form of philosophic discourse, 155; early classification of Platonic, 95, n. 20
Dichotomy, in Plato, 185
Diels, H., 4
Dio Chrysostome, 110, n. 34
Diogenes Laertius, 4, 248, 298, 307, 323, 333, 361, 410
Diogenes of Sinope, our knowledge of, 109; as ideal of Epictetus, 380; mentioned in passing, 105, 284, 287, 363
Dionysius, pseudo, 407, n. 27, 437, 470, n. 35

Dissoi logoi, 66, 113
Division, logical, in Plato, 182
Dodds, E. R., 301, n. 70, 314, n. 1, 318, n. 3, 362, n. 8, 467, 471
Dog of Chrysippus, 338
Dualism of good and evil in New Testament, 424
Duns Scotus, 167

E

Ecclesiastes, 379, n. 18
Eclecticism, of Philo, 399
Edelstein, Ludwig, 157, n. 10, 358, n. 2, 395
Education, in Plato, 167; of the philosopher in Plato's *Symposium*, 175
Effluences, theory of, 31; in Democritus, 36
Egocentric predicament, 339
Eidola, 274
Einstein, 264
Ekpyrosis, 254
Eleatics, 9; dialectical method of, 30
Eliot, T. S., 283
Emanation, 448
Emblems, 397
Emerson, 384
Emotions, in Stoicism, 298
Empedocles, and Parmenides, 17, 31; and Democritus, 36; and Anaxagoras, 59, 61; two worlds in, 17; cycles, 20; knowledge, 30; fall of man, 46; appraisal of life, 52
Empiricism, 143
Epictetus, 110, 287, 361
Epicureanism, and Christianity, 301
Epicurus, 255, 364; and Parmenides, 306
Epiphanius, 359
Ethics, in Plato, 171; Aristotle, 221; Speusippus, 291; Xenocrates, 292; Stoic, 294; of Epicurus, 300
Eudemus, 258
Eusebius, 4, 75, 215, 324, 402, n. 10
Evil, its origin, in Marcus Aurelius, 383
Excluded middle, law of, 10

Ex nihilo nihil, 13, 21; in Leucippus, 32; in Anaxagoras, 60; in Aristotle, 207; in Epicurus, 272, 304

Experience, problem of its congruence with reason, 156

Explanation, in Plato, 183; in early Stoicism, 265; causal, criticized by Aenesidemus, 341

F

Fall of Man, 45; in Paganism in general, 112; in Philo, 403

Fallacy of third man, 145

Falsity, criterion of in Arcesilaus, 326

Faraday, 24

Form, meaning of term in Aristotle, 191

Freedom, in Epictetus, 378

Free will and determinism, 295

Freud, 355

Fuller, B. A. G., 453, n. 21

G

Galileo, 256

Gautama Buddha, 282

Generalization, problem of, 121

Genesis, problem of in Speusippus, 243

Geometrical universe, 42

Gnosticism, 426, 448

God, in early Stoicism, 249; in Epictetus, 364; in Marcus Aurelius, 367; in Philo, 401, 409; in Ps-Archytas, 411; in Onatus, 413; in Numenius, 432; His incomprehensibility, 415; man's relation to, in Porphyry, 461; the gods, how identified by Xenocrates, 246; fear of in Epicureanism, 300

Goodenough, E., 440

Gorgias, 70; and Socrates, 85; method of, 89; opposition in, 124

Great Animal, 251

Great Year, 254

Greece, religious organization of, 54

Gruenbaum, A., 64, n. 5

H

Happiness, in Aristotle, 226

Hecataeus, 27

Hegel, 90, 258

Heinze, R., 244, n. 2

Helm, on Cynicism, 112

Heracles, Choice of, 99

Heraclitus, two worlds in, 7; method of, 26; appraisal of life, 50

Herillus, 297

Hermodorus, 51

Herodotus, 65

Hesiod, appraisal of life in, 45; mentioned in passing, 6, 27, 46, 405

Hicks, R. D., 285

Hierarchy, the word, 437; cosmic, its source, 439; hints of before 1st century A.D., 416; in Moderatus, 420; Valentinus, 430; Plotinus, 445; Porphyry, 460; Iamblichus, 466; Proclus, 467

Hippolytus, 4, 249, 418

Hirzel, Th., 101, n. 27

Hitler, 280

Hobbes, 257, 267, 330

Homer, appraisal of life, 44; 318

Hope, Richard, 4

Horace, 162

Hoyle, Fred, 32, n. 15

Human nature, Plato's theory of, 161

Hume, 34, 267, 329, 341

Hunsaker, J. C., 342, n. 17

Hypostases, of Plotinus, 451

I

Iamblichus, 464

Ideas, Platonic, 131; four interpretations of, 146; as standards, 177; of the Godd, 138; in Philo, 401

Idols of the Tribe, 88

Impressions, never isolated according to Carneades, 331

Individuals, in Aristotle, 194; no knowledge of, 197

Inductive method and problem of universals, 92

Innate ideas, 373

Intelligible world, in Philo, 399
Irenaeus, 430
"Is", meaning of, 18

J

James, William, 315
Jebb, R. C., 279, n. 40
Jerome, St., 394, n. 3
Job, 365
Joel, Karl, 76, n. 12
John, St., logos in, 28
Judgment, suspension of, in Arcesilaus, 326
Jung, 271
Justinian Code, 168

K

Kant, 39, 341
To know, two meanigs of, 122
Knowledge, in Plato, 142; scientific vs. observation in Aristotle, 206; its origin in Stoicism, 267; theory of in Epicurus, 272; skeptical attacks on, 322; two kinds of in Presocratics, 23; of first principles, 149; and revelation, 428; in myth and allegory, 459

L

Lang, P., 242, n. 2
La Rochefoucauld, 101
Law, in Socrates, 81; human and divine, in Plato, 186; of Excluded Middle, 10; of Natural Development, in Aristotle, 189; of Contradiction, its implications, 327; Laws of Thought, in Plato, 185
Learning, in Plato, 145
Leibniz, 254
Lewis, Geoffrey, 448, n. 16
Leucippus, 20, 32
Life, appraisal of, 44; in poets, *ibid.*; in the tragedies, 47; in Xenophanes, 49; Heraclitus, 50; Empedocles, 52; Democritus, 53; Sophists, 98; Critias, 100; Thrasymachus, 101; Socrates, 102; Cynics, 105; Plato, 159; Aristotle, 215; Crantor, 277;

Theophrastus, 279; Chrysippus, 281; Epicurus, 287; Epictetus, 377; Marcus Aurelius, 383
Light mysticism, 440
Locke, 35
Loewenberg, J., 155, n. 8
Logic, and the Sophists, 122; logical classes in Plato, 163; Logical analysis in Aristotle, 210; system of logic in Aristotle, 231; in Epicurus, 303; in Stoicism, 308; in Epictetus, 374
Logos, in Heraclitus, 28; in Philo, 406; in Moderatus, 421; in Ps-Timaeus, 420; of an essence, 259
Love, in Plato, 141, 174
Lovejoy, A. O., 45, 68, n. 8, 112, n. 36, 139, 187, n. 29, 418, 477
Lucian, 112, 281
Lucretius, 32, 213, 275, 272, n. 33, 288, 298, 357

M

Machiavelli, 168
Malebranche, 341
Manual work, in Aristotle, 216
Marcus Aurelius, 365
Materialism, Stoic, 248; Epicurean, 256
Mates, Benson, 311, n. 74
Maximus of Tyre, 67
Mean, the mean as standard, 220
Meaning in Stoicism, 309
Melancholy of the Greeks, 44
Melissus, 30
Meno, problem of, 144
Metaphysics and mythology, 245
Method, of Presocratics, 24; of Empedocles, 30; of Anaxagoras, 86; of Sophists, 88; of Gorgias, 89; of Socrates, 91; of Aristotle, 203; of Speusippus, 258; of Xenocrates, 261; of Epicureans, 271; of Epictetus and Marcus Aurelius, 371
Meyerson, E., 207, n. 6
Mill, J. S., 147, 346, 349
Minucius Felix, 396
Moderatus of Gades, 420

Montague, W. P., 122, n. 40
Moore, George, 254, n. 18
Moral life as self-criticism, 171
Morgan, T. H., 477
Motion, concept criticized by skeptics, 352
Myth, 355; in Plato, 144, 156; and metaphysics, 245

N

Natorp, P., 147
Nature, permanence of, 19; and custom, 64; why variations in, 65; ambiguities of the term, 68; order of in Aristotle, 195; its supposed simplicity, 213; as norm, 111, 181, 283; how discovered, 182, 219; its goodness in Aristotle, 219; and the rational, 285
Necessity, causal and formal, 34
Newton, Isaac, 156, 210, n. 8
Nichomachus of Gerasa, 421
Nietzsche, 254, 297, n. 67
Nigidius Figulus, 409
Nous, in Anaxagoras, 61, 87; in Speusippus, 242. See also Chapter IX
Number symbolism, in Philo, 403; in Iamblichus, 465
Numbers, generation of, 410
Numenius, 394, 432

O

Observation, how controlled in Aristotle, 205
Oldfather, W. A., 365
Omnis determinatio est negatio, 259
Onatus, 413
The One, in Speusippus, 242; in Xenocrates, 262. See also Chapter IX
Opinion, in Parmenides, 10; in Plato, 142
Opposition, in Presocratics, 14; in Heraclitus, 29; Table of Opposites, 42; in Gorgias, 89, 124; in Aristotle, 208
Order of Nature in Aristotle, 195
Orestes, his meeting with Electra, 330

P

Panaetius, 319, 359, 360
Panofsky, E., 99, n. 23
Parian Chronicle, 76, n. 11
Parmenides, truth and opinion, 9; two worlds in, 10; dialectical method, 30
Pasteur, 33
Paul, St., 130, 282, 286, 425, 429
Peace of mind, in Stoicism, 297; in skepticism, 321, 348
Peale, Norman Vincent, 283
Periclean Age, 57
Peripatetics, lack of development, 258
Perry, R. B., 339
Personifications in Roman religion, 246
Pétrement, Simone, 424, n. 44
Philo, 138, 271, 428; logos in, 28
Philoponos, 259, 264
Pindar, appraisal of life in, 44
Pistorius, P. V., 450, n. 19
Planets, influence of, 444
Plato, 5, 69, 91, 115, 261, 319, 323, 362, 364, 423; Pseudo-Plato, 98, 278; on Socrates, 78; theory of knowledge, 142, 150; two worlds in, 131; appraisal of life in, 159
Platypus, sophistic proof of its nonexistence, 90
Plautus, 281
Plotinus, 408, n. 28; see also Chapter IX
Plutarch, 18, n. 8, 26, 267, n. 29, 277, 364, 418
Pneuma, in Anaximenes, 25; as universal agent, 265; in early Stoicism, 249
Polybius, 405
Popper, K. R., 154
Porphyry, 51, 263, 417, 449, 460
Posidonius, 359
Presocratics, sources of information about, 4; how colonial, 56
Primitivism, in poets, 45
Principle of parsimony in Aristotle, 208
Principle of plenitude, 139, 418, 453

Priority, natural, in Aristotle, 204
Problem of genesis, in Speusippus, 243
Problem of *Meno*, 144
Proclus, 433, 467
Prodicus, on death, 99
Prolepses, 274, 307
Protagoras, 68, 152; ethical views of, 116
Prout, 20
Purpose, in Aristotle, 191, 192
Pyrrho, 340
Pythagoreans, 27, 40

R

Ramayana, contrasted with *Iliad*, 180
Rational, how discovered, 286
Rationalism, breakdown of, 430
Reality, 2; rational in Aristotle, 197
Reason, how term is used, 107, 475; and experience, 156; its function in Plato, 166
Recollection, myth of, 144
Regularity, a matter of degree in Aristotle, 204
Rehabilitation of man, in Philo, 404
Relations, problem of in Plato, 151, 172; in Aristotle, 233
Revelation, as source of knowledge, 428
Roberts, W. R., 109, n. 33
Robertson, J. M., 394, n. 2
Roosevelt, F. D., 76, n. 12; 388, n. 21
Rules for attaining happiness in Aristotle, 226
Russell, Bertrand, 376
Rylands, L. G., 394, n. 2, 428, n. 52

S

Santayana, G., 123, n. 42, 327
Sayre, Farrand, 109, n. 32
Scientific knowledge, in Aristotle, 206
Schopenhauer, 9
Self-sufficiency, in Aristotle, 217
Seneca, 248, 268, 271, 281, 444
Sensory perception, vs. reason, 27; always of particulars in Aristotle, 206; sensory qualities not pre-existent in their causes, 32

Serial order, in Aristotle, 203
Sextus Empiricus, 5, 28, 50, 70, 107, 260, 273, 278, 285, 292, 309, 320, 325, 328, 333, 335, 337, 341, 345
Sheen, Rev. Fulton, 283
Shelley, 254, n. 18
Shorey, P., 164, n. 15, 181, n. 26
Simple life, in Antisthenes, 108
Simples, indestructible, 173
Simplicius, 30, 263, 247, n. 9
Skepticism, of Sextus, 321; of Carneades, 329; of Pyrrho, 319; in Middle Academy, 325; its roots in Greek tradition, 318; purpose of, 321
Socrates, our knowledge of, 76; his *Daimon*, 79; two worlds in, 80; his method, 91; the midwife, 93; appraisal of life, 102; vs. the Sophists, 113; ethical views, 116; on Anaxagoras, 62; mentioned, 316
Sophists, method of, 88; interest in logic, 120, 122; vs. Socrates, 113; Plato's attacks on, 160; began overthrow of rationalism, 128
Soul, descent of, in Plotinus, 446
Speusippus, 242, 410
Spinoza, 167, 229, 297, 323, 367
Standards of value, in Aristotle, 217
Starkie, W. J. M., 77, n. 13
States, kinds of, in Plato, 162
Stobaeus, 53, 110, 245, 418
Stoicism, and Christianity, 299. See also Chapter V
Superiority of the end, in Aristotle, 217; of the whole, 218
Syllogism, 231; note on Aristotle's failure to use, 238; skeptical attacks on, 346
Syrianus, 412

T

Table of Opposites, 42, 208
Tatakis, B. N., 395, n. 4
Taylor, A. E., 144, n. 5
Teaching, futility of, according to Epictetus, 389
Tennessee, Legislature of, 317
Terence, 246, n. 6

Tertullian, 255, n. 19, 316
Themistius, 250, n. 13
Theognis, 46
Theophrastus, his *Characters*, 279; and individual character, 162; mentioned in passing, 4, 24, 31, 37, n. 18, 39, 87, 258, 352
Third Man, fallacy of, 145
Thomas Aquinas, St., 224
Thomson, G., 22, n. 10
Thrasymachus, appraisal of life, 101
Timaeus of Locrus, 419
Timon, 319; on Pyrrho, 322
Tod, M. N., 76, n. 11
Touch, primary sense in Democritus, 37
Tragedy, appraisal of life in, 47; debates in, 97
Traitors, Greek, 55, n. 27
Tree of Porphyry, 442; source in Plotinus, 450
Tropes, of Aenesidemus, 333
Truth, in Parmenides, 10; in Heraclitus, 27; in Socrates, 84; in Plato, 142; and consistency, 34, 145; criterion of, 372; in Timon, 324; in Carneades, 329; of perceptions, its implications, 275; and common sense, 316
Two worlds, problem of, 1; in Anaximander, 5; in Anaximenes, 7; in Heraclitus, *ibid.*; in Parmenides, 17; in Democritus, 20; in Anaxagoras, 59; in Socrates, 80; in Plato, 131; in Aristotle, 188; in early Stoicism, 247; in Epicureanism, 255; in Posidonius, 360; in Epictetus, 361; in Marcus Aurelius, 366; in Philo, 401, 408; in New Testament, 424; how Plotinus bridged them, 437

U

Unmoved Mover, not God of the Bible, 236; and *Nous* of Anaxagoras, 210
Untersteiner, M., 101, n. 27

V

Valdenberg, V., 401, n. 17
Valentinus, 430
Values, standards of, in Aristotle, 217; and facts, in Plato, 169; metaphysical status, 443; in Timon, 323; in Epictetus, 377; in Marcus Aurelius, 382
Varro, 394, n. 1
Vergil, 254, n. 18
Vox populi, vox Dei, 168, n. 19

W

Whitehead, A. N., 15, n. 7
Whole, superior to its parts, in Aristotle, 218
Will and reason, 64
Windelband, W., 95, 423, n. 43
Wolfson, H. A., 400, 406, 414, n. 37
World of observation, in Aristotle, 201

X

Xenocrates, 244
Xenophanes, 27, 49, 315, 349
Xenophon, on Socrates, 77, 118

Z

Zeller, E., 64, n. 4, 242, n. 1, 282, n. 44, 308, 357, 394, n. 1, 470, n. 35
Zeno, the Eleatic, 16, 352; his dialectical method, 30
Zeno, of Citium, 247, 323